THE AMERICAN IDEOLOGY

"In *The American Ideology*, Brian Vanyo pinpoints the fundamental values that made the United States the greatest nation in the history of the world. Anyone who cares about the future of America must read this book."
— **Rick Santorum**

"We all have a moral obligation as citizens to know and understand the fundamentals of government that our Fore Fathers meant for this country – without bias. *The American Ideology* is a brilliant, insightful, and informative means to that end." — **Dr. Laura Schlessinger**

"Brian Vanyo's *The American Ideology* is without a doubt one of the most authoritative books yet written on the greatness of America and the internal risks to sustained self-government. I commend this book to every lover of liberty." — **U.S. Senator Mike Lee**

"Brian comes from a family committed to service and to America. His affection for this great country is clear." — **U.S. Senator John Hoeven**

*Only by knowing the basis of our rights
can we act with boldness to restore them.*

THE
AMERICAN
IDEOLOGY

Taking Back our Country with the
Philosophy of our Founding Fathers

☆ BRIAN VANYO ☆

Manufactured in the United States of America

10 9 8 7 6 5 4 3 2 1

First Edition

Library of Congress Cataloging-in-Publication Data

Vanyo, Brian C.

The American Ideology: Taking Back our Country with the
Philosophy of our Founding Fathers / Brian Vanyo

Includes bibliographical references

1. Political Science: Government—U.S. Government
2. Law: Constitutional
3. Philosophy: Political

Library of Congress Control Number: 2012913080

ISBN 978-0-9831933-0-2 (hc.)
ISBN 978-0-9831933-1-9 (pb.)
ISBN 978-0-9831933-2-6 (ebk.)

Published by
Liberty Publishing LLC
www.libertypublishingllc.com

For information about special discounts for bulk purchases, please contact
Liberty Publishing LLC at info@libertypublishingllc.com.

To my wife,
for your enduring love, patience, and support

THE FOUNDING FATHERS

Signers of the Continental Association

John Adams
Samuel Adams
John Alsop
Edward Biddle
Richard Bland
Simon Boerum
Richard Caswell
Samuel Chase
Stephen Crane
Thomas Cushing
Silas Deane
John De Hart
John Dickinson
James Duane
Eliphalet Dyer
William Floyd
Nathaniel Folsom
Christopher Gadsden
Joseph Galloway
Benjamin Harrison
Patrick Henry, Jr.
Joseph Hewes
William Hooper
Stephen Hopkins
Charles Humphreys
John Jay
Thomas Johnson, Jr.
James Kinsey
Richard Henry Lee
Philip Livingston
William Livingston
Isaac Low
Thomas Lynch
Thomas McKean
Henry Middleton
Thomas Mifflin
John Morton
William Paca
Robert Treat Paine
Edmund Pendleton
Peyton Randolph
George Read
Caesar Rodney
George Ross
Edward Rutledge
John Rutledge
Roger Sherman
Richard Smith
John Sullivan
Matthew Tilghman
Samuel Ward
George Washington
Henry Wisner

Signers of the Declaration of Independence

John Adams
Samuel Adams
Josiah Bartlett
Carter Braxton
Charles Carroll
Samuel Chase
Abraham Clark
George Clymer
William Ellery
William Floyd
Benjamin Franklin
Elbridge Gerry
Button Gwinnett
Lyman Hall
John Hancock
Benjamin Harrison
John Hart
Joseph Hewes
Thomas Heyward, Jr.
William Hooper
Stephen Hopkins
Francis Hopkinson
Samuel Huntington
Thomas Jefferson
Francis Lightfoot Lee
Richard Henry Lee
Francis Lewis
Philip Livingston
Thomas Lynch, Jr.
Thomas McKean
Arthur Middleton
Lewis Morris
Robert Morris
John Morton
Thomas Nelson, Jr.
William Paca
Robert Treat Paine
John Penn
George Read
Caesar Rodney
George Ross
Benjamin Rush
Edward Rutledge
Roger Sherman
James Smith
Richard Stockton
Thomas Stone
George Taylor
Charles Thomson
Matthew Thornton
George Walton
William Whipple
William Williams
James Wilson
John Witherspoon
Oliver Wolcott
George Wythe

Signers of the United States Constitution

Abraham Baldwin
Richard Bassett
Gunning Bedford, Jr.
John Blair
William Blount
David Brearly
Jacob Broom
Pierce Butler
Daniel Carroll
George Clymer
Jonathan Dayton
John Dickinson
William Few
Thomas Fitzsimons
Benjamin Franklin
Nicholas Gilman
Nathaniel Gorham
Alexander Hamilton
Jared Ingersoll
William Jackson
Daniel of St. Thomas Jenifer
William Samuel Johnson
Rufus King
John Langdon
William Livingston
James Madison
James McHenry
Thomas Mifflin
Gouverneur Morris
Robert Morris
William Paterson
Charles Pinckney
Charles Cotesworth Pinckney
George Read
John Rutledge
Roger Sherman
Richard Dobbs Spaight
George Washington
Hugh Williamson
James Wilson

Other Notable Founders

Thomas Paine
(author, *Common Sense*)

Mercy Otis Warren
(political writer)

Noah Webster
(writer, educator)

CONTENTS

Introduction

It is easy to be frustrated by politics today.

Our federal government is constitutionally limited in power, yet it exerts an unbounded regulatory authority over all.

We are taxed on every sort of productive activity while government spends money on so many wasteful, illegitimate programs.

The national debt continues to rise, and there is no plan to pay it off.

We live in a representative republic, but politicians today submit to the dictates of an unelected judicial body. The Supreme Court can validate or strike down any law in the land by its command over the Constitution, which it can construe to mean anything or nothing at all.

Politicians themselves have become experts at pretense, so much so that the deliberate distortion of fact (commonly known as "spin") is now regarded as inherent in the political process. We must regularly discern truth from deceit in the words of pandering politicians, whose integrity and ethics are sometimes questionable at best.

In a nation founded on the ideals of popular sovereignty and individual responsibility, it is dispiriting to think that our hopes for political change so often depend on the righteousness of corrupted politicians. Every election cycle, we hear different candidates make the same political promises. They will bring change to government. They will make government more efficient, more accountable, more transparent, and more responsive to the people. But nothing about government ever seems to change. No matter who is president or which political party is in control, our large federal government continues to grow. Reckless spending persists. Regulations increase. And we remain subject to a distant and domineering administrative power. As time passes, hope gives way to cynicism, and we grow ever more exasperated by our insensible political reality.

Sadly, such political frustration is nothing new. Political thinker and historian Alexis de Tocqueville once wrote:

> Has every other century been like this one? Has man always confronted, as he does today, a world in which nothing makes sense? In which virtue is without genius and genius without honor? In which the love of order is indistinguishable from the lust of tyrants? In which the sacred cult of liberty is confounded with contempt for the law? In which conscience casts but an ambiguous light on the actions of men? In which nothing any longer seems forbidden or allowed, honest or shameful, true or false?[1]

Though germane to the United States today, Tocqueville's commentary was written in another era with another nation in mind. Tocqueville was directing his irritation at the political scene in France in the 1830s, for a new constitutional monarch was proclaimed king on the promise of greater empowerment to the people, but nothing changed. The strong central government that had arisen in France years before was still in place, and the common man remained without political power. Frustrated by the illusory nature of governmental reform in France, Tocqueville soon called for genuine political change.

Similar cries for reform are echoing across the American political landscape today. The unprecedented scope of federal regulations and the immense size of the federal debt have provoked many of us to action. No longer will we quietly acquiesce to an ever expanding federal government; no longer will we stand by as it spends us into bankruptcy; and no longer will we accept the political charade that has sustained this assault on our liberty. This is our government. We may have lost control of it, but we are determined to take it back.

But how? What will it take to renew our claim to power and truly restore liberty in America?

Tocqueville asked a similar question in his day. He wondered what was necessary for liberty to take hold at all, in any land. And he found his answer in America.

During a 9-month trip to the United States in 1831, Tocqueville became so fascinated by American freedom that he endeavored to discover its source. And he believed that his unique perspective in that time enabled him to do just that. In his renowned book on American society, *Democracy in America*, Tocqueville explained why he was perfectly situated to illuminate the "first causes," or fundamental sources, of American liberty. He wrote:

> Close enough to the time when the societies of America were founded to be acquainted in detail with their elements, yet far enough away to form a judgment of what those seeds have produced, we seem destined to see further into human events than our predecessors did. Providence has placed within our reach a torch our fathers lacked, a torch that allows us, when examining the destiny of nations, to make out first causes that the obscurity of the past hid from our forebears.[2]

As Tocqueville traveled the United States to study its society, he grew confident that he had discovered the true source of its freedom.

American liberty was the product of its unique political ideology. More than a theory about the proper design of government, it was a philosophy that directed how individuals should govern themselves. Liberty prevailed in America because the people respected certain canons of morality in addition to the rule of law. Tocqueville found that these ideals were necessary for liberty to take hold and endure in any land. He emphasized in *Democracy in America* that "laws and above all mores [fundamental values] could allow a democratic people to remain free."[3] Without proper mores, no nation could sustain liberty for long.

Consequently, when Tocqueville called for political change in France, his focus extended beyond its government. He of course called for the introduction of republican institutions, the decentralization of power, and other legal reforms. But he was clear that freedom would never come to France if the people did not accept the fundamental values that made liberty possible. He wrote, "[I]f we forsake the idea of instilling in all our citizens ideas and feelings that will first prepare them for liberty and then enable them to make use of it, then there will be no independence for anyone . . . but only equal tyranny for all."[4]

Tocqueville's admonition is just as applicable to America today. If we do not restore the values that enabled liberty to take hold here centuries ago, then our current course toward despotism and ruin will never change. In our efforts to reclaim power over government, we certainly must assert popular control over our Constitution, we must enforce the limits of federal power, and we must rein in federal spending. But above all, we must renew our faith in our founding philosophy.

Like Tocqueville, we can acquaint ourselves with the first causes of American liberty. The common ideals that made the United States so exceptional in the world are not hard to find—they exist in the many writings, speeches, and letters of our Founding Fathers. We can learn from history what it was that facilitated liberty in America at a time when tyranny reigned everywhere else.

But our perspective today offers us something more. We can also identify the points of departure from those founding principles. The federal government's aggressive plays against our liberty of late have awakened us to the reality that it has long been encroaching on our power. We now see that, throughout the last century, progressive forces have persistently labored to fundamentally change American government by political and judicial means. By recognizing when and how those insidious transformations of our government were made, we can pinpoint the reforms that must be enacted and the kind of policies that must be rejected going forward if we are to regain our liberty at last.

We owe it not just to ourselves to change our nation's course. Countless Americans before us have sacrificed dearly to establish and preserve for us a free constitutional republic. Generation after generation has handed down the fundamental blessing of liberty, but that liberty has since diminished over time. And it will continue to fade away if we fail to act. Our continued acquiescence to the government's growing power inevitably consigns our children to a more repressive authority tomorrow. We are forcing upon them the great responsibility and challenge to mend our ways.

So to honor the legacy of generations past, to establish justice for ourselves, and to fulfill our duty to generations to come, let us finally change our course. Let us reclaim our authority over government by renewing our faith in the ideals that make liberty possible. Let us take back our country with the philosophy of our Founding Fathers.

To that end, let our rediscovery of the American Ideology begin.

1

On Natural Law

Natural Law theory is based on the idea that God grants to each individual certain rights that no other person or government may arbitrarily take away. These natural rights specifically include the rights to life, liberty, and property. The influential British legal scholar Sir William Blackstone wrote in the 1760s that the natural rights of all mankind "may be reduced to three principal or primary articles; the right of personal security, the right of personal liberty, and the right of private property."[1]

These were the ideals that inspired the American Revolution. When the Founding Fathers signed the Declaration of Independence in 1776, they were not just cataloging their grievances against the King of Great Britain. They were not just announcing American independence to the world. Above all, the Founding Fathers were accentuating the principles that justified their separation and would forever guide them in freedom. The Declaration of Independence set forth the American creed "that all men are created equal, that they are endowed by their Creator with certain unalienable rights, that among these are life, liberty and the pursuit of happiness."[2] These natural rights comprised the core of the founding philosophy. And they were truths that applied not just to the American people, but to all mankind. As Thomas Jefferson later wrote, the Declaration of Independence became the "Declaratory Charter of our rights and the rights of man."[3]

The American experiment in liberty on the basis of natural rights was so significant at the time because Natural Law theory had previously existed only as an idea. First articulated by Greek and Roman philosophers of antiquity, Natural Law theory was further developed by Western philosophers of the Enlightenment Era. And its popularity grew significantly as enlightenment spread because Natural Law is based on developed logic and reason—British philosopher John Locke stated in 1698 that "the Law of Nature . . . is the Law of Reason."[4] As education increased in society, more and more people increasingly viewed their tyrannical governments as illegitimate on the basis of Natural Law. And many political thinkers soon began to speak out for change.

Natural Law theory remained radical, however, because it challenged the longstanding, deep-seated belief that kings possessed an unlimited authority over the people. Defenders of such absolute power commonly argued that kings held a divine and hereditary authority over their subjects—that anyone born in the kingdom owed his faithful allegiance to the king and his heirs. For example, Sir Robert Filmer, a British political theorist and ardent supporter of monarchical power, wrote in *Patriarcha* in 1680:

> Men are not born free, and therefore could never have the liberty to choose either governors, or forms of government. Princes have their power absolute, and by Divine Right, for slaves could never have a right to compact or consent. Adam was an absolute monarch, and so are all princes ever since.[5]

In essence, Filmer argued that a king's inherited power first originated from the patriarchal authority that was divinely bestowed upon Adam, the first man on earth. That power was then passed on through his heirs. This justification of course was impossible to prove, given the obscurity of hereditary succession over such a long history. For the same reason, hereditary succession was also impossible to disprove, and few individuals anyway dared to challenge the veracity of the royal bloodline.

Philosopher John Locke instead used Natural Law theory to directly challenge the legitimacy of the divine right itself. In his *Two Treatises of Government*, which was mostly written in exile and first published anonymously, Locke made an extensive attack on *Patriarcha* by undermining the Scriptural support that Filmer used to substantiate patriarchal power. Locke argued that the Bible does not at all support

Filmer's assertion that God granted Adam complete dominion over all other men that followed. The only power that God gave to Adam was a dominion over the animals on earth, and this power belonged not just to Adam but also to "to the whole species."[6] Locke also showed that there was no basis for a patriarchal power when the Bible in fact granted women a shared parental authority over their children—women held the same power on earth as men.[7] And Locke challenged the idea of hereditary power by arguing that God bestowed upon every individual of every generation the same freedom and fundamental rights. He wrote, "Man has a natural freedom . . . [and] since all that share in the same common nature, faculties, and powers, are in nature equal, [each] ought to partake in the same common rights and privileges."[8]

Locke's argument against divine hereditary power predominated throughout the Enlightenment Era and greatly influenced American political thought. Thomas Paine, for example, expressed a similar argument against hereditary succession in *Rights of Man*, his published guide to Enlightenment ideas. Paine wrote:

> If any generation of men ever possessed the right of dictating the mode by which the world should be governed forever, it was the first generation that existed; and if that generation did it not, no succeeding generation can show any authority for doing it, nor can set any up. The illuminating and divine principle of the equal rights of man (for it has its origin from the Maker of man) relates, not only to the living individuals, but to generations of men succeeding each other. Every generation is equal in rights to the generations which preceded it, by the same rule that every individual is born equal in rights with his contemporary.
>
> . . . [A]ll men are born equal, and with equal natural rights, in the same manner as if posterity had been continued by *creation* instead of *generation*, the latter being only the mode by which the former is carried forward; and consequently every child born into the world must be considered as deriving its existence from God. The world is as new to him as it was to the first man that existed, and his natural right in it is of the same kind.[9]

Paine regarded the idea of hereditary succession to be completely absurd and illogical. He explained that a person cannot make a will to take the property of another and give it to a third party, yet this was how hereditary succession operated by law:

> A certain former generation [those who instituted hereditary kingly power] made a will to take away the rights of the commencing generation, and all future ones, and convey those rights to a third person [the king's heir], who afterwards comes forward, and tells them . . . that they have *no rights*, that their rights are already bequeathed to him and that he will govern in *contempt* of them. From such principles, and such ignorance, Good Lord deliver the world![10]

Paine believed that common ignorance enabled such tyrannical ideas. He observed that monarchs actually preferred an ignorant society because "[i]gnorance submits to whatever is dictated to it. . . . [T]he more ignorant any country is, the better it is fitted for this species of government."[11]

On the other hand, the more enlightened the people are, the more suited they are for republican government, which Paine described as "government by election and representation."[12] Where reason prevails in society, individuals understand that they hold equal rights with others and are subordinate in power only to God. Paine wrote that each enlightened individual in society "sees the *rationale* of the whole [republican] system, its origin and its operation; and, as it is best supported when best understood, the human faculties act with boldness, and acquire under this form of government a gigantic manliness."[13] With confidence in their natural rights and authority over government, the people can boldly assert their claim to liberty and challenge anyone who usurps it.

The Founding Fathers did just that. Enlightened by the ideas of John Locke, William Blackstone, and French political thinker Charles de Montesquieu—whose written works together have been described as "the political Bibles of the constitutional fathers"[14]—the Founding Fathers proclaimed their right to be free from the tyrannical British government as it grew intolerably repressive toward the American colonies. They repeatedly asserted the primacy of Natural Law and declared that no government in America could ever arbitrarily infringe upon the people's natural rights to life, liberty, and property.

John Adams wrote in 1763, "Resistance to sudden violence, for the preservation not only of my person, my limbs, and life, but of my property, is an indisputable right of nature which I have never surrendered to the public by the compact of society, and which perhaps, I could not surrender if I would."[15]

In 1769, Samuel Adams quoted Blackstone to assert that individuals were always free to take up arms "'to protect and maintain inviolate the three great and primary rights of personal security, personal liberty, and private property.'"[16]

Samuel Adams and Benjamin Franklin together wrote in 1772, "Among the natural rights of the colonists are these: first, a right to life; secondly, to liberty; thirdly, to property; together with the right to support and defend them in the best manner they can."[17]

George Washington declared in 1774 that the first American settlers have always been, "by the Laws of Nature and Nations, entitled to all its privileges, immunities and advantages; [and those Laws] have descended to us, their posterity, and ought of right to be as fully enjoyed."[18]

Thomas Jefferson asserted in 1774 that Americans were "a free people, claiming their rights as derived from the Laws of Nature, and not as the gift of their chief magistrate."[19]

The First Continental Congress in 1774 declared that the American people, "by the immutable Laws of Nature . . . have the following rights: . . . that they are entitled to life, liberty and property."[20]

Alexander Hamilton wrote of the supremacy of Natural Law in 1775, citing Blackstone:

> Good and wise men, in all ages . . . have supposed that the Deity . . . has constituted an eternal and immutable law, which is, indispensably, obligatory upon all mankind, prior to any human institution whatever.
>
> This is what is called the Law of Nature, "which, being coeval with mankind and dictated by God Himself, is, of course, superior in obligation to any other. It is binding over all the globe, in all countries, and at all times. No human laws are of any validity, if contrary to this; and such of them as are valid, derive all their authority, mediately, or immediately, from this original." *Blackstone.*
>
> Upon this law, depend the natural rights of mankind.[21]

And the Founding Fathers famously declared in 1776 "that all men are created equal, that they are endowed by their Creator with certain unalienable rights, that among these are life, liberty and the pursuit of happiness."[22]

Although Natural Law theory had long existed as a political idea in the minds of the world's greatest philosophers throughout history, the Founding Fathers at last placed it into practice in America by declaring their independence on the basis of its guarantees. They broke their political connection with Great Britain to "assume among the powers of the earth, the separate and equal station to which the Laws of Nature and nature's God entitle them."[23] They declared independence to secure and preserve their natural rights to life, liberty, and property.

The State of Nature

Upon declaring their independence from Great Britain, the American people temporarily had no national government. (The Articles of Confederation were not drafted until 1777 and were not officially ratified by the states until 1781.) In many ways, this freedom from government—this "separate and equal station" that the Founders referenced in the Declaration of Independence—resembled the State of Nature.[24]

In the State of Nature, the people live in their most basic existence without any political order. But even without government, lawlessness does not prevail. Locke wrote, "The State of Nature has a Law of Nature to govern it, which obliges everyone: and Reason, which is that Law, teaches all mankind, who will but consult it, that being all equal and independent, no one ought to harm another in his life, health, liberty, or possessions."[25] Order can be maintained in the State of Nature as long as individuals respect the fundamental principles of Natural Law—principles that apply at all times, in any setting.

These principles—the natural guarantees of equality, life, liberty, and property that underlie the founding philosophy—are perhaps best understood when considered in the context of the State of Nature, where an individual's relationship with others is stripped of all societal laws and norms.

The fundamental principle of equality is a guarantee under Natural Law because every person in any land is granted the same rights by God. In the State of Nature, where government does not exist, no one holds a special power or privilege over any other. For this reason, Locke regarded the State of Nature as a "state of perfect equality."[26] He wrote that "nothing [is] more evident, than that creatures of the same species and rank, promiscuously born to all the same advantages of Nature and the use of the same faculties, should also be equal one amongst another without subordination or subjection."[27]

The fundamental right to life is absolute because life is a possession of God. Locke wrote that "men . . . [are] the workmanship of one omnipotent and infinitely wise Maker; [and because men are] all the servants of one Sovereign Master, sent into the world by His order and about His business, they are His property, . . . made to last during His, not one another's, pleasure."[28] Locke reasoned that, unless justice so requires, life at all times must be preserved because the power over life is the province of God. Therefore, man has no authority to take another man's life, to commit suicide, or to enslave himself to another. Locke wrote that "nobody can give more power than he has himself; and he that cannot take away his own life cannot give another power over it."[29] Blackstone referred to life as "the immediate gift of God, a right inherent by nature in every individual."[30] And like Locke, Blackstone believed that man holds no supreme power over life, whether his own or another's. He wrote, "The natural life, being . . . the immediate donation of the Great Creator, cannot legally be disposed of or destroyed by any individual, neither by the person himself, nor by any other of his fellow-creatures, merely upon their own authority."[31] Life, therefore, is a natural right that must be always respected and protected, for no man may seize the power of his maker, God.

The fundamental right to property is derived from the fundamental right to life. As man is bound to protect life, he is also bound to preserve it. Just as man cannot arbitrarily kill another, he also cannot steal his property, which sustains his life. In the State of Nature, the efforts of man to nourish life by growing, gathering, and hunting food create property rights in the products of that labor. What man removes from or improves in the State of Nature becomes his property—all other things and creatures are common to all men, at least as they first existed. Blackstone reasoned that the "earth . . . and all the things therein, are the general property of all mankind, exclusive of other beings, from the immediate gift of the Creator."[32] He explained that "a vine or other tree might be said to be in common, as all men were equally entitled to its produce; and yet any private individual might gain the sole property of the fruit, which he had gathered for his own repast."[33] Locke similarly wrote:

> God, when he gave the world in common to all mankind, commanded men also to labor, and the penury of his condition required it of him. God and his Reason commended him to subdue to the earth, *i.e.* improve it for the benefit of life, and therein lay out something upon it that was his own, his labor. He that in obedience to this command of God, subdued, tilled and sowed any part of it, thereby annexed to it something that was his property, which another had no title to, nor could without injury take from him.[34]

Through man's labor and creativity, a common good can thus become personal property. And property, being essential for the preservation and sustenance of life, must be protected as a fundamental natural right.

The fundamental right to liberty is manifest in the State of Nature because man is free from governmental restraint. But that freedom is not unlimited. Man is still bound by Natural Law. For if one may arbitrarily take the lives or possessions of others, then man truly has no freedom except by the mercy and grace of others stronger than he. Liberty is thus a freedom that is moderated by Natural Law. Locke explained:

> Liberty is to be free from restraint and violence from others, which cannot be where there is no law: But freedom is not . . . a liberty for every man to do what he lists: (For who could be free, when every other man's humor might domineer over him?) but a liberty to dispose and order, as he lists, his person, actions, possessions, and his whole property, within the allowance of those Laws under which he is; and therein not to be subject to the arbitrary will of another, but freely follow his own.[35]

Locke further described the State of Nature as "a state of perfect freedom [for individuals] to order their actions and dispose of their possessions and persons as they think fit, within the bounds of the Law of Nature, without asking leave or depending upon the will of any other man."[36] Blackstone also reasoned that man's natural liberty—"a right inherent in us by birth and one of the gifts of God to man at his creation"[37]—is not unrestrained. He wrote that "natural liberty consists properly in a power of acting as one thinks fit, without any restraint or control, *unless by the Law of Nature*."[38] Benjamin Franklin and Samuel Adams similarly wrote, "The natural liberty of man is to be free from any superior power on earth, and not to be under the will or legislative authority of man, *but only to have the Law of Nature for his rule*."[39] The fundamental right to liberty, therefore, is always constrained by the Natural Law. As Locke simply wrote, "[W]here there is no Law, there is no freedom."[40]

In the State of Nature, then, all men are free and equal, and all men must respect the fundamental rights to life, liberty, and property. In an ideal world, men would abide by Natural Law without coercion, but the world is not so ideal. Conflict and disagreements are common in most all human relationships. As a consequence, there must be some authority to enforce Natural Law for it to have any effect. Locke wrote, "[T]he Law of Nature would, as all other Laws that concern men in this world, be in vain, if there were nobody that, in the State of Nature, had a power to execute that Law, and thereby preserve the innocent and restrain offenders."[41] But who is naturally entrusted with this supervisory role if all men are equal in the State of Nature and no governing authority exists?

Reason directs that executive power in the State of Nature is held by every individual. Locke explained, "[So] that all men may be restrained from invading others' rights and from doing hurt to one another, and [so that] the Law of Nature be observed, . . . the execution of the Law of Nature is, in that State, put into every man's hands."[42] Because all men are equal in this "state of perfect equality," Locke wrote, "where naturally there is no superiority or jurisdiction of one over another, what any may do in prosecution of that Law," it follows that all may do.[43]

Every individual in the State of Nature thus possesses a combined executive and judicial power—each enforces Natural Law and sits in judgment of those who violate it. Locke stated:

[Man has] by nature a power not only to preserve his . . . life, liberty, and estate, against the injuries and attempts of other men; but [also] to judge of and punish the breaches of that Law in others as he [believes] the offence deserves, even with death itself, in crimes where the heinousness of the fact, in his opinion, requires it.[44]

Individuals may seek retribution from offenders of Natural Law in proportion to their misconduct and only so much as may serve to compensate and deter—the two goals of punishment, according to Locke.[45] An enforcer has an independent "power to punish the crime to prevent its being committed again by the right he has of preserving all mankind and doing all reasonable things he can in order to that end."[46]

In cases of extreme violence, such as murder, death is authorized as a punishment to preserve innocent life. Although capital punishment can never compensate the victims of murder, it serves to prevent the criminal from killing again. Locke justified this extreme form of punishment by writing that a violent criminal, "having renounced reason. . . [effectively declares] war against all mankind, and therefore may be destroyed as a lion or tiger, one of those wild savage beasts with whom men can have no society nor security."[47]

Although equal enforcement of Natural Law is reasonable in the State of Nature, it is problematic in practice. When everyone in the State of Nature holds this kind of autonomous executive power, abuse and other difficulties inevitably arise. The strong may flaunt their power to disadvantage the weak. Others might lack the means to impose justice on the Law's offenders. And many other disputing parties may never reach a settlement when each has an innate authority to adjudicate the matter himself. Locke wrote that "inconveniences of the State of Nature . . . necessarily follow from every man's being judge in his own case."[48] He added that man's property is "constantly exposed to the invasion of others. For all being kings as much as he, every man his equal, and the greater part no strict observers of equity and justice, the enjoyment of the property he has in this state is very unsafe, very unsecure."[49] In the end, man's natural rights to life, liberty, and property in the State of Nature are left vulnerable to arbitrary enforcement or judgment. No matter how free the

State of Nature may be, Locke concluded, it is always "full of fears and continual dangers."[50]

From the State of Nature into Society

These problems and dangers in the State of Nature ultimately motivate individuals to enter into society. Government is thus formed out of necessity, for no rational individual, having complete sovereignty in the State of Nature, would surrender his autonomy to government if he could independently maintain his natural rights without it. Echoing this truth, James Madison wrote, "If men were angels; no government would be necessary."[51] Thomas Paine similarly believed that "government, even in its best state, is but a necessary evil; in its worst state an intolerable one."[52]

Individuals ultimately join society to better protect their natural rights. Locke wrote that people unite in society "for the mutual preservation of their lives, liberties and estates, which [are referred to] by the general name, property."[53] He emphasized that the "great and chief end" of men organizing under government institutions "is the preservation of their property."[54] If government did not aim to safeguard these natural rights, Locke wrote, then no one would ever enter society, "[f]or no rational creature can be supposed to change his condition with an intention to be worse."[55]

Man's interest in preserving his natural rights is what drives him into political union with others, and thus government is formed by consent. Locke wrote that "all peaceful beginnings of government have been laid in the consent of the people."[56] St. George Tucker, a legal scholar of the founding era, elaborated on the necessity of consent to establish legitimate government. Known as the "American Blackstone," Tucker wrote in his 1803 *Blackstone's Commentaries*:

> All men being by nature equal, in respect to their rights, no man nor set of men, can have any natural, or inherent right, to rule over the rest.
> This right cannot be acquired by conquest, for the few, are, in a state of nature, unable to subdue the many.
> . . .

The right of governing can, therefore, be acquired only by consent, originally; and this consent must be that of at least a majority of the people.[57]

The Founding Fathers embraced this majority consent requirement. Benjamin Franklin and Samuel Adams wrote in 1772, "When men enter into society, it is by voluntary consent; and they have a right to demand and insist upon the performance of such conditions and previous limitations as form an equitable original compact."[58] The Founding Fathers wrote in the Declaration of Independence that "to secure these [natural] rights, governments are instituted among men, deriving their just powers from the consent of the governed."[59] The Founding Fathers imposed a unanimous consent requirement on the Articles of Confederation before the national government became effective. And they later required a supermajority of states to ratify the Constitution.

Under Natural Law theory, a consent requirement remains for every generation. When a child comes of age in society, he may of course leave society to join another. Otherwise, he may consent to the existing government by directly participating in society and showing express support for government institutions. He may also give his implied consent to government by enjoying the protections and benefits that government provides. Locke explained:

> [E]very man, that hath any possession, or enjoyment, of any part of the dominions of any government, doth thereby give his *tacit consent*, and is as far forth obliged to obedience to the laws of that government, during such enjoyment, as anyone under it; whether this his possession be of land, to him and his heirs forever, or a lodging only for a week; or whether it be barely travelling freely on the highway; and in effect, it reaches as far as the very being of any one within the territories of that government.[60]

Just as a child who inherits property must abide by the same covenants to which his parents consented, he must also abide by the law of the government under whose jurisdiction the inheritance, purchase, or privilege originated. Although tacit consent grants an individual certain privileges and protections—and imposes on him certain obligations—Locke asserted that he does not become a full member of society until he "actually enter[s] into it by positive engagement, and express promise and compact."[61] Requiring such affirmative action is consistent with Natural Law and acknowledges that man's natural executive power can only be willingly surrendered by consent or wrongfully usurped by force.

When an individual consents to government, he must always submit to the will of the majority, for if the majority does not control, then the original compact by those who gave their consent would signify nothing.[62] Individuals do not enter society to become subjects to the arbitrary rule of the minority. If one minority can exert its will, then any minority can, and lawlessness emerges—the majority of individuals would then be no better off than they were in the State of Nature. Locke wrote that the original compact would cease to exist if man "be left free, and under no other ties, than he was in before in the State of Nature."[63] Those who consent to government, therefore, must always respect the majority, assuming that it operates within the boundaries of Natural Law.

Importantly, an individual does not surrender his natural rights by consenting to government. He merely surrenders the sovereign executive and adjudicative power that he held in the State of Nature. He authorizes the representative legislative body to make laws as required for the public good and consistent with the chief end of society: the preservation of life, liberty, and property. He authorizes the instituted executive body to enforce those laws. And where controversies arise, he authorizes an impartial judicial authority to resolve them. Benjamin Franklin and Samuel Adams explained:

> In the State of Nature every man is, under God, judge and sole judge of his own rights and of the injuries done him. By entering into society he agrees to an arbiter or indifferent judge between him and his neighbors; but he no more renounces his original right than by taking a cause out of the ordinary course of law, and leaving the decision to referees or indifferent arbitrators.[64]

Franklin and Adams unequivocally stated that no individual could ever surrender his natural rights to government:

> In short, it is the greatest absurdity to suppose it in the power of one, or any number of men, at the entering into society, to renounce their essential natural rights, or the means of preserving those rights; when the grand end of civil government, from the

very nature of its institution, is for the support, protection, and defense of those very rights; the principle of which, as is before observed, are life liberty, and property. If men, through fear, fraud, or mistake, should in terms renounce or give up any essential natural right, the eternal law of reason and the grand end of society would absolutely vacate such renunciation. The right to freedom being the gift of God Almighty, it is not in the power of man to alienate this gift and voluntarily become a slave.[65]

God: the Source of all Natural Rights

Natural Law theory is nothing without God. Because the theory is predicated on the supremacy of a Higher Power, it is essential for all to recognize the existence of that Power. John Quincy Adams once commented that the American creed is based on "the Laws of Nature and of Nature's God and of course presupposes the existence of a God, the moral ruler of the universe."[66] Without God, an individual has no guarantee to the preservation of his life, liberty, or property, all of which then become subject to the arbitrary will of those in power.

The Founding Fathers well understood that a government is truly without limit if it does not recognize the supreme power of God or the fundamental rights that He bestows on all people. Thomas Jefferson argued that American liberty could never be preserved if the people denied His existence. He asked, "Can the liberties of a nation be thought secure when we have removed their only firm basis, a conviction in the minds of the people that these liberties are the gift of God? That they are not to be violated but with his wrath?"[67] John Dickinson explained that American rights to life, liberty, and property were unlike the ephemeral promises made by governments of men; American rights were inalienable rights endowed by God. He wrote:

> Kings or parliaments could not give the rights essential to happiness. . . . We claim them from a higher source—from the King of kings and Lord of all the earth. They are not annexed to us by parchments and seals. They are created in us by the decrees of Providence, which establish the laws of our nature. They are born with us, exist with us, and cannot be taken from us by any human power without taking our lives.[68]

Alexander Hamilton similarly said, "The sacred rights of mankind are not to be rummaged for, among old parchments, or musty records. They are written, as with a sun beam, in the whole volume of human nature, by the hand of the divinity itself; and can never be erased or obscured by mortal power."[69] Given the importance of God to American society, John Adams wrote into the Massachusetts Constitution, "It is the duty of all men in society, publicly, and at stated seasons, to worship the Supreme Being, the great Creator and Preserver of the universe."[70] Other states wrote similar provisions into their state constitutions.

Although Natural Law presupposes the existence of God, the Founding Fathers and other Natural Law philosophers did not take for granted that God existed. They did not base their strong conviction in God on religious dogma. Rather, they deduced that God must exist because any alternative conclusion was irrational. It was absurd to them to think that man's existence was nothing more than chance and circumstance—that man was nothing more than a collection of matter without purpose. Montesquieu wrote, "They who assert that a blind fatality produced the various effects we behold in this world talk very absurdly; for can anything be more unreasonable than to pretend that a blind fatality could be the productive of intelligent beings?"[71] Thomas Paine acknowledged the existence of God because of the "tenfold difficulty of disbelieving" in Him.[72] He explained:

> It is difficult beyond description to conceive that space can have no end. It is difficult beyond the power of man to conceive an eternal duration of what we call time; but it is more impossible to conceive a time when there shall be no time. In like manner of reasoning, everything we behold carries in itself the internal evidence that it did not make itself. Every man is an evidence to himself, that he did not make himself; neither could his father make himself, nor his grandfather, nor any of his race; neither could any tree, plant, or animal make itself; and it is the conviction arising from this evidence, that carries us on, as it were, by necessity, to the belief of a first cause eternally existing, of a nature totally different to any material existence we know of, and by the power of which all things exist; and this first cause, man calls God.[73]

Thomas Jefferson wrote that it is impossible for a reasoning human mind to believe that God does not exist, given the order and wonder of all things in the universe:

> [W]hen we take a view of the universe in its parts, general or particular, it is impossible for the human mind not to perceive and feel a conviction of design, consummate skill, and indefinite power in every atom of its composition. The movements of the heavenly bodies, so exactly held in their course by the balance of centrifugal and centripetal forces; the structure of our earth itself, with its distribution of lands, waters, and atmosphere; animal and vegetable bodies, examined in all their minutest particles; insects, mere atoms of life, yet as perfectly organized as man or mammoth; the mineral substances, their generation and uses; it is impossible, I say, for the human mind not to believe that there is, in all this, design, cause, and effect, up to an ultimate cause, a Fabricator of all things from matter and motion, their Preserver and Regulator while permitted to exist in their present forms, and their regeneration into new and other forms. We see, too, evident proofs of the necessity of a Superintending Power, to maintain the universe in its course and order.[74]

James Wilson also wrote that God must exist because it is impossible to reason otherwise:

> When we view the inanimate and irrational creation around and above us, and contemplate the beautiful order observed in all its motions and appearances, is not the supposition unnatural and improbable that the rational and moral world should be abandoned to the frolics of chance or to the ravage of disorder?[75]

Belief in God was so common among the founding generation that further validation of God's existence was often unnecessary and unwelcome. For example, when Benjamin Franklin presented "A Lecture on the Providence of God in the Government of the World," he skipped over his analysis of God's existence to avoid insulting his audience. He said to them:

> It might be judged an affront to your understandings should I go about to prove this first principle: the existence of a Deity and that He is the Creator of the universe; for that would suppose you ignorant of what all mankind in all ages have agreed in. I shall

therefore proceed to observe that He must be a being of infinite wisdom.[76]

Contemporary atheists often assert that Charles Darwin's influential theory of natural selection—introduced in his 1859 book *On the Origin of Species*—has since diminished God's importance in our understanding of our origin. But this theory actually predated the founding generation. Countless scientists and philosophers throughout history have considered God's existence in light of the longstanding theory of evolution—which may have originated in 495-455 B.C.—and have maintained that God must exist.[77] Some of these individuals, such as Aristotle, St. Augustine, St. Thomas Aquinas, Emanuel Swedenborg, and Charles Bonnet, believed that evolution might be the means by which God chose to make man.[78] Others, like Descartes, Newton, Kant, Mendel, and Cuvier, were less accepting of the theory of evolution and maintained that the specifics of creation were unsettled and debatable.[79] Significantly, even Charles Darwin embraced the latter theistic approach. Darwin's description of his conviction in God in his autobiography closely resembles the reasoning of Paine, Jefferson, and Wilson. He wrote:

> Another source of conviction in the existence of God, connected with the reason and not with the feelings, impresses me as having much more weight. This follows from the extreme difficulty, or rather impossibility, of conceiving this immense and wonderful universe, including man with his capacity of looking far backwards and far into futurity, as the result of blind chance or necessity. When thus reflecting I feel compelled to look to a First Cause having an intelligent mind in some degree analogous to that of man; and I deserve to be called a Theist. This conclusion was strong in my mind about the time, as far as I can remember, when I wrote the *Origin of Species*.[80]

Contrary to contemporary misperceptions, evolutionary theory does not supersede belief in God, and it is not even mutually exclusive with creationism. The greatest minds throughout history—and even the scientist who developed the modern theory of natural selection—have reasoned that God must exist as the Creator of all living things and all Laws of Nature.

The Founding Fathers themselves reasoned that God exists as the Supreme Authority in the world and that each individual derives his natural rights from that Authority. With conviction, they declared "that all men are created equal, that they are endowed by their Creator with certain unalienable rights, that among these are life, liberty and the pursuit of happiness."[81] The Founding Fathers understood that God's existence could never be denied without undermining the very basis of American liberty. They respected Natural Law principles, and they ultimately based the American political philosophy on a foundational belief in God.

The State of War

Under Natural Law, God grants to each individual life, liberty, and property—rights that each individual has a duty to preserve. When these rights are threatened by others, a State of War is commenced, and any action in defense of these natural rights is permitted. Locke wrote that it is "reasonable and just [that] I should have a right to destroy that which threatens me with destruction."[82]

In a State of War, life may be destroyed in defense of it. Although life should always "be preserved as much as possible," Locke wrote, if one's life is in jeopardy, then "the safety of the innocent is to be preferred."[83] He explained:

> [O]ne may destroy a man who makes war upon him, or has discovered an enmity to his being, for the same reason that he may kill a wolf or a lion; because such men are not under the ties of the common Law of Reason [and] have no other rule but that of force and violence, and so may be treated as beasts of prey, those dangerous and noxious creatures, that will be sure to destroy him whenever he falls into their power.[84]

Lethal force is authorized under Natural Law not only to defend one's life, but also to defend one's liberty or personal property. In either case, the aggressor is using unlawful force to hold the victim under his power and therefore cannot be trusted to exercise further restraint. Locke wrote:

> I have no reason to suppose that he, who would take away my liberty, would not, when he had me in his power, take away everything else. And therefore it is lawful for me to treat him as one who has put himself into a State of War with me, i.e., kill him if I can; for to that hazard does he justly expose himself, whoever introduces a State of War and is the aggressor in it.[85]

In this State of War, where force rules over reason, an individual's natural rights may be defended by any means as justice so requires.

The Founding Fathers fully embraced this idea of self-preservation. Samuel Adams believed that individuals permanently hold a right of self-preservation under Natural Law—a right that must be used "'to protect and maintain inviolate the three great and primary rights of personal security, personal liberty and private property.'"[86] He and Benjamin Franklin together wrote:

> Among the natural rights of the colonists are these: first, a right to life; secondly, to liberty; thirdly, to property; together with the right to support and defend them in the best manner they can. These are evident branches of, rather than deductions from, the duty of self-preservation, commonly called the first Law of Nature.[87]

James Wilson likewise stated:

> The defense of one's self, justly called the primary Law of Nature, . . . is not confined merely to the person; it extends to the liberty and the property of a man: it is not confined merely to his own person; it extends to the persons of all those, to whom he bears a peculiar relation—of his wife, of his parent, of his child . . . ; nay, it extends to the person of everyone, who is in danger; perhaps to the liberty of everyone, whose liberty is unjustly and forcibly attacked. It becomes humanity as well as justice.[88]

Alexander Hamilton wrote, "Self-preservation is the first principle of our nature. When our lives and properties are at stake, it would be foolish and unnatural to refrain from such measures as might preserve them because they would be detrimental to others."[89] John Adams described self-preservation as an eternal right that could never be given away. He wrote, "Resistance to sudden violence, for the preservation not only of my person, my limbs, and life, but of my property, is an indisputable right of nature which I have never surrendered to the public by the compact of society, and which perhaps, I could not surrender if I would."[90]

Although self-defense is always permitted under Natural Law, the State of War ends in society once an act of aggression ceases, for society's laws then control how relief or punishment is provided. Locke explained that a thief in society may be killed when he is in the act of stealing, because the "law, which was made for [man's] preservation, cannot interpose [in time] to secure [the victim's] life from present force, which, if lost, is capable of no reparation."[91] But after the theft has occurred and force has passed, the victim can only "appeal to the law," which is the common authority that governs criminal and civil justice in society.[92]

By contrast, the State of War continues in the State of Nature even after the unlawful force has ended because there is no common authority in the State of Nature to which the victim may appeal for relief. Locke explained:

> [I]n the State of Nature, for want of positive laws and judges with authority to appeal to, the State of War once begun, continues, with a right to the innocent party to destroy the other whenever he can, until the aggressor offers peace and desires reconciliation on such terms as may repair any wrongs he has already done and secure the innocent for the future.[93]

This is exactly what happens between nations at war. Because they have no common superior between them, independent nations in the world are no different than individuals in the State of Nature. When one nation comes under assault by another, a State of War commences and continues until the nations reconcile on agreeable terms. International law essentially operates under Natural Law. Montesquieu wrote, "The life of governments is like that of man. The latter has a right to kill in case of natural defense: the former have a right to wage war for their own preservation."[94] Montesquieu expanded on this point:

> With individuals [in society] the right of natural defense does not imply a necessity of attacking. Instead of attacking they need only have recourse to proper tribunals. They cannot, therefore, exercise this right of defense but in sudden cases, when immediate death would be the consequence of waiting for the assistance of the law. But with states the right of natural defense carries along with it sometimes the necessity of attacking; as for instance, when one nation sees that a continuance of peace will enable another to destroy her, and that to attack that nation instantly is the only way to prevent her own destruction.[95]

Blackstone similarly wrote that, because independent nations do not recognize "superiority" in other nations, no single nation "can dictate or prescribe the rules of [international] law to the rest."[96] He explained:

> [S]uch rules must necessarily result from those principles of natural justice, in which all the learned of every nation agree; or they depend upon mutual compacts or treaties between the respective communities; in the construction of which there is also no judge to resort to, but the Law of Nature and Reason, being the only one in which all the contracting parties are equally conversant, and to which they are equally subject.[97]

Blackstone further detailed how Natural Law operates in different cases where a nation comes under attack. Where war is commenced by another sovereign nation, Blackstone wrote that "recourse can only be had to war; which is an appeal to the God of hosts, to punish such infractions of public faith, as are committed by one independent people against another: neither state having any superior jurisdiction to resort upon earth for justice."[98] Where select individuals of a nation violate international law, however, Blackstone argued that it is incumbent on the individual's home nation to punish those individuals to maintain peace. He explained, "For in vain would nations in their collective capacity observe these universal rules, if private subjects were at liberty to break them at their own direction and involve the two states in a war."[99] Blackstone suggested that the injured nation must first demand justice from the subject's resident nation, "and if that be refused or neglected, the sovereign then avows himself an accomplice or abettor of his subject's crime, and draws upon his community the calamities of foreign war."[100] Finally, Blackstone addressed piracy, which is akin to terrorism for its penchant for force and complete disregard of law and reason. He wrote:

> [T]he crime of piracy, or robbery and depredation upon the high seas, is an offense against the universal law of society . . . . [Because the pirate] has renounced all the benefits of society and government, and has reduced himself afresh to the savage State of Nature by declaring war against all mankind, all mankind must declare war against him: so that every community hath a right by the rule of self-defense to inflict that punishment upon him, which every individual would in a State of Nature have

been otherwise entitled to do for any invasion of his person or personal property.[101]

In the end, no matter what kind of response is warranted for a given offense against a nation, each response is directed by Natural Law ideals.

The Founding Fathers likewise articulated the extension of Natural Law principles to international law, which is also known as the Law of Nations. For example, John Witherspoon wrote:

> [T]he Law of Nature and Nations is nothing else but the law of general reason, or those obligations of duty from reason and conscience, on one individual to another, antecedent to any particular law derived from the social compact, or even actual consent. On this account, it is called the Law of Nature; and because there are very rarely to be found any parties in such a free state with regard to each other, except independent nations, therefore it is also called the Law of Nations. One nation to another is just as man to man in a State of Nature.[102]

Thomas Jefferson similarly wrote:

> The Moral duties which exist between individual and individual in the State of Nature accompany them into a state of society, and the aggregate of the duties of all the individuals composing the society constitutes the duties of that society towards any other; so that between society and society the same moral duties exist as did between the individuals composing them while in an unassociated state, their Maker not having released them from those duties on their forming themselves into a nation.[103]

Jefferson also explained how international treaties supplement the Law of Nations. Just as two individuals in the State of Nature may enter into contract with one another, two nations may form agreements that direct their relationship. Such treaties, Jefferson wrote, "are obligatory on [nations] by the same moral law which obliges individuals to observe their compacts."[104] Moreover, because the Law of Nations preserves a nation's right to self-defense, international agreements are not eternally binding. Jefferson wrote that if the "performance [of a treaty] becomes self-destructive to the party, [then] the law of self-preservation overrules the laws of obligation to others."[105] Each nation ultimately decides for itself whether to honor its obligations under a treaty. As Jefferson explained, "no one nation has a right to sit in judgment over another" on the international stage, because each nation is equal and autonomous under the Law of Nations.[106]

Despite the moral underpinning of international law, the Founding Fathers recognized that most other nations did not live by Natural Law ideals. Most nations in their day ruled by force rather than reason, and so a State of War could be forced upon any nation at any time. As a consequence, the Founding Fathers believed that liberty was best preserved from external threats by deterring foreign aggression with military might—they advocated lasting peace through strength. For instance, George Washington advised, "To be prepared for war is one of the most effectual means of preserving peace."[107] Benjamin Franklin wrote, "[T]here is much truth in the Italian saying, 'Make yourselves sheep, and the wolves will eat you.'"[108] Thus, Franklin instructed, "The way to secure peace is to be prepared for war."[109] And Thomas Jefferson echoed this guidance, writing, "Whatever enables us to go to war, secures our peace."[110]

The Founding Fathers were so committed to securing peace in liberty because what they had achieved in the American Revolution was so unprecedented in history. Gaining independence from British rule was unquestionably a great feat in that day, but it was relatively insignificant compared to the purpose for which that war was fought and won. Thomas Paine wrote:

> The independence of America, considered merely as a separation from England, would have been a matter of but little importance had it not been accompanied by a revolution in the principles and practice of governments. She made a stand, not for herself only, but for the world, and looked beyond the advantages herself could receive.[111]

What was so remarkable about the American Revolution was that, for the first time in history, Natural Law theory was applied in the foundation of popular government. St. George Tucker wrote that "the American Revolution [] formed a new epoch in the history of civil institutions by reducing to practice what before had been supposed to exist only in the visionary speculations of theoretical writers."[112] The American people, by their independence, had at last reduced to practice the enlightened idea "that all men are created equal, that they are endowed by their Creator with certain unalienable rights, that among these are life, liberty and the pursuit of happiness."[113] A free and independent people came together in society to form a government by consent, based in reason, and dedicated to the precepts of Natural Law.

2

ON AMERICAN GOVERNMENT

On a Natural Law foundation, the Founding Fathers raised the American government, structured as a republican confederacy to preserve individual liberty and provide for national security. They learned from history that a balanced, confederate government is essential to maintain a free and strong nation. Montesquieu had earlier warned, "If a republic be small, it is destroyed by a foreign force; if it be large, it is ruined by an internal imperfection."[1] To avoid either fate, Montesquieu advanced the idea that small republics join in a confederate, or federal, republic.[2] A government so constituted would combine its strength to withstand foreign aggression while preserving smaller governing bodies that better safeguard individual liberty. It would also enhance internal stability, as James Madison instructed in The Federalist No. 43. He wrote, "Among the advantages of a confederate republic enumerated by Montesquieu, an important one is, 'that should a popular insurrection happen in one of the states, that others are able to quell it. Should abuses creep into one part, they are reformed by those that remain sound.'"[3] The Founding Fathers determined, therefore, that a republican confederacy would provide the best opportunity for the new American nation to grow in liberty and peace.

But not any republican confederacy would do. The Founding Fathers soon discovered that the nation's first government under the Articles of Confederation was manifestly weak. The Articles, which were established in haste to unite the colonies during the Revolutionary War, created a national government that consisted solely of a legislative body. Each state, no matter how large or small, had a single vote, and a two-thirds majority in Congress was needed to pass all laws. Although Congress could enact legislation, it could do no more. It could not implement or enforce the law, and it could not even collect taxes needed to sustain the government. Due to the feeble nature of the national government, the states often acted in their self-interests, commercial protectionism arose at home, and weakness was projected abroad. In short order, the union was at risk of dissolution.

Determined to preserve the union, the Founding Fathers met again at the Philadelphia Convention in the summer of 1787 to address the shortcomings of the Articles. They had learned by experience that the benefits of a confederate republic could not be realized while the national government was so impotent. They needed to strengthen federal power and bring it into balance with that of the states. Choosing to abandon the Articles altogether rather than amend them, the Founding Fathers formed a new Constitution that aimed to achieve that balance. They sought to empower the national government without compromising individual liberty.

Despite the necessity to augment federal powers, the Founding Fathers were very careful to avoid tipping the balance of power toward the federal government. They had no intention to create an overbearing consolidated government. Although the states had to cede some power to the federal government, they retained their sovereignty in all functions not enumerated in the Constitution. James Madison, who is regarded as the "Father of the Constitution" for his integral role in its drafting, emphasized in The Federalist No. 14 that "the general government is not to be charged with the whole power of making and administering laws. Its jurisdiction is limited to certain enumerated objects, which concern all the members of the republic."[4] He reiterated the limited scope of federal power in The Federalist No. 45:

> The powers delegated by the proposed Constitution to the federal government are few and defined. Those which are to remain in the state governments are numerous and indefinite. The former will be exercised principally on external objects, as war, peace, negotiation, and foreign commerce; with which last the power of taxation will for the most part be connected. The powers reserved to the several states will extend to all the

objects, which, in the ordinary course of affairs, concern the lives, liberties and properties of the people; and the internal order, improvement, and prosperity of the state.[5]

Alexander Hamilton also wrote in The Federalist No. 32 that the Constitution did not create a consolidated national government. He assured, "[T]he state governments would clearly retain all the rights of sovereignty which they before had and which were not by that act [the Constitution] *exclusively* delegated to the United States."[6] And Thomas Jefferson explained at length why the limited design of federal power in the Constitution was so essential to lasting liberty:

> The way to have good and safe government is not to trust it all to one, but to divide it among the many, distributing to everyone exactly the functions he is competent to [perform best]. Let the national government be entrusted with the defense of the nation, and its foreign and federal relations; the state governments with the civil rights, laws, police and administration of what concerns the state generally; the counties with the local concerns of the counties, and each [township] direct the interests within itself. It is by dividing and subdividing these republics, from the great national one down through all its subordinations, until it ends in the administration of every man's farm by himself; by placing under everyone what his own eye may superintend, that all will be done for the best. What has destroyed liberty and the rights of man in every government which has ever existed under the sun? The generalizing and concentrating all cares and powers into one body, no matter whether of the autocrats of Russia or of France, or of the aristocrats of a Venetian Senate.[7]

The Founding Fathers thus increased the power of the federal government only where necessary to enable it to perform its limited national functions. The federal government would administrate matters such as foreign affairs, interstate commerce, immigration, and war. And the American people would retain power over all other matters in their state and local governments—particularly for those issues pertaining to the health, safety, welfare, and morals of the people. Power would remain decentralized so that liberty would be preserved.

As an added restraint on the federal government, the Founding Fathers made its elected representatives largely dependent upon the exercise of state power. For instance, the election of the president would require the intervention of the state legislatures to appoint electors.[8] In addition, senators would be elected exclusively by state legislatures (until this was changed by amendment in 1913).[9] And even the elections of members of the House of Representatives might be influenced by state legislatures, as Madison explained:

> Representatives, though drawn immediately from the people, will be chosen very much under the influence of that class of men, whose influence over the people obtains for themselves an election into the state legislatures. Thus each of the principal branches of the federal government will owe its existence more or less to the favor of the state governments, and must consequently feel a dependence, which is much more likely to beget a disposition too obsequious, than too overbearing towards them.[10]

By tying state functions to the federal government's organization, Madison envisioned that state governments would become "constituent and essential parts of the federal government."[11] Hamilton likewise wrote:

> The proposed Constitution, so far from implying an abolition of the state governments, makes them constituent parts of the national sovereignty by allowing them a direct representation in the Senate, and leaves in their possession certain exclusive and very important portions of sovereign power. This fully corresponds, in every rational import of the terms, with the idea of a federal government.[12]

This level of integration was meant to ensure that the augmented power of the federal government in the Constitution would never surpass the power of the states.

Incidentally, the Founding Fathers believed that federal power would never trump state power if the Constitution's limits were maintained. They predicted that any potential power imbalance would more likely result from the national government's inherent weakness, not from its usurpation of state power. This weakness stemmed in part from the people's greater loyalty to their state governments. Hamilton explained that individuals naturally favor their local institutions over more distant governing bodies:

It is a known fact in human nature that its affections are commonly weak in proportion to the distance or diffusiveness of the object. Upon the same principle that a man is more attached to his family than to his neighborhood, to his neighborhood than to the community at large, the people of each state would be apt to feel a stronger bias towards their local governments than towards the government of the Union.[13]

Such a bias was clear under the Articles of Confederation when state loyalties trumped national allegiance. With that experience in mind, Hamilton concluded that "there is an inherent and intrinsic weakness in all federal constitutions; and that too much pains cannot be taken in their organization to give them all the force which is compatible with the principles of liberty."[14] Madison agreed. Writing in The Federalist No. 45, he referenced some historical examples to show that dissolution in past confederacies had resulted from the federal government's inability to hold the union together:

In the Achaean league, it is probable that the federal head had a degree and species of power, which gave it a considerable likeness to the government framed by the [American Constitutional] Convention. The Lycian confederacy, as far as its principles and form are transmitted, must have borne a still greater analogy to it. Yet history does not inform us that either of them ever degenerated or tended to degenerate into one consolidated government. On the contrary, we know that the ruin of one of them proceeded from the incapacity of the federal authority to prevent the dissentions, and finally the disunion of the subordinate authorities.[15]

Given the historical tendency of confederacies to dissolve due to federal weaknesses, Madison reasoned that "the balance [of power in America] is much more likely to be disturbed by the preponderancy" of the state governments.[16]

No matter what impact the Constitution would have on the actual distribution of power in America, the Founding Fathers were clear that the goal behind its design was simply to achieve balance. They believed that a balanced government would best protect the people's liberty, and they believed that the Constitution's design would help achieve that end. In a speech to the New York ratifying convention, Hamilton stated that the "balance between the national and state governments . . . forms a double security to the people. If one encroaches on their rights, they will find a powerful protection in the other. Indeed, they will both be prevented from over-passing their constitutional limits by certain rivalry which will ever subsist between them."[17] Hamilton also wrote in The Federalist No. 28, "Power being almost always the rival of power, the general government will at all times stand ready to check the usurpations of the state governments, and these will have the same disposition towards the general government."[18]

Even if the institutional checks on power failed to maintain relative parity between the national and state governments, the people could always exercise their elective power to restore it. Hamilton trusted that the people, who "will hold the scales [of power] in their own hands, . . . will always take care to preserve the constitutional equilibrium between the general and the state governments."[19] When necessary, the people could augment the power of either government "by throwing themselves into either scale . . . . If their rights are invaded by either, they can make use of the other as the instrument of redress."[20] Madison made the same argument in The Federalist No. 46, in which he addressed critics of the Constitution's distribution of power:

> The adversaries of the Constitution seem to have lost sight of the people altogether in their reasonings on this subject; and to have viewed [state governments and the federal government], not only as mutual rivals and enemies, but as uncontrolled by any common superior in their efforts to usurp the authorities of each other. These gentlemen must here be reminded of their error. They must be told that the ultimate authority, wherever the derivative may be found, resides in the people alone; and that it will not depend merely on the comparative ambition or address of the different governments, whether either, or which of them will be able to enlarge its sphere of jurisdiction at the expense of the other.[21]

The Founding Fathers assured that there was no reason for anyone to fear the augmented national power under the Constitution because the people controlled the scope of that power. They could at any time readjust the nation's balance of power in a manner that would best preserve liberty in America.

The Founding Fathers did not just divide power between the states and the federal government. They further divided power at the federal level to guard against corruption that too often surfaces as a failing of human nature. Montesquieu once wrote that "constant experience shows us that every man invested with power is apt to abuse it, and to carry his authority as far as it will go."[22] Madison similarly stated, "The essence of government is power; and power, lodged as it must be in human hands, will ever be liable to abuse."[23] The Founding Fathers therefore sought to prevent such abuse in the federal government by dividing its constitutionally limited powers among three separate and coequal branches. Madison wrote in The Federalist No. 51, "In the compound republic of America, the power surrendered by the people is first divided between two distinct governments [state and national], and then the portion allotted to each, subdivided among distinct and separate departments."[24]

The Founding Fathers organized the federal government under the legislative, executive, and judicial branches—each branch being independent to prevent abuse that can arise by the consolidation of power. According to Montesquieu, if the legislative and executive powers were united, then that combined authority could "enact tyrannical laws, to execute them in a tyrannical manner."[25] If the judiciary power were joined with the legislative, then "the life and liberty of the subject would be exposed to arbitrary control; for the judge would be then the legislator."[26] And if the judiciary power were united with the executive, then "the judge might behave with violence and oppression."[27] The Founding Fathers heeded this caution by giving to each branch of government independent constitutional authority to perform its delegated responsibilities and to check the power of the other branches.

As the general principles that govern the three federal branches of government are introduced below, it is important to keep in mind the context in which they were formed. The American people had recently declared their independence from the British monarchy, announcing to the world the Natural Law foundation upon which their sovereignty was based. The Founding Fathers soon after constructed a makeshift confederate government to unite the colonies amid war. And after victory had been achieved, they realized that a new compact was needed to sustain the new nation in liberty. The Constitution of the United States was the product of the Founding Father's best efforts to create a lasting government that was committed to the basic principles of their political ideology. The Constitution created a federal republic that aimed to preserve the people's natural rights to life, liberty, and property.

The Legislative Power

Establishing the legislative power is generally the first act of a people who join together in society. John Locke explained:

> The great end of [people] entering into society [is] the enjoyment of their properties in peace and safety, and the great instrument and means of [achieving that end are] the laws established in that society; the first and fundamental positive law of all [governments therefore] is the establishing of the legislative power.[28]

The Founding Fathers established the federal government's legislative power in the first Article of the Constitution. They designed the bicameral legislature to reflect the dual nature of the federal government—it is both a national government and an organization of states. The Senate is composed of two Senators from each state to give small states representative parity with large states. And the seats in the House of Representatives are apportioned by population to honor the equal representation principle of popular government.

The Founding Fathers enumerated in Article I, section 8, of the Constitution the specific legislative powers that the people delegated to the national government. And to underscore the limited scope of federal power, they clearly stated that Congress could only exercise those "legislative powers *herein granted.*"[29] Congress was given no legislative power other than those powers explicitly found or implied in the Constitution. All powers not delegated to Congress in the Constitution were reserved to the states or the people, as the Founding Fathers made abundantly clear by amendment soon after ratification.

In addition to the Constitution's express limitations on Congress' power, the Founding Fathers also believed that the legislative power included an inherent limitation: it could not be wielded in contravention of Natural Law. Congress could not abridge an individual's natural right to life, liberty, or property. Alexander Hamilton wrote, quoting Blackstone, "[T]he Law of Nature, 'which, being coeval with mankind and dictated by God Himself, is, of course, superior in obligation to any other. It is binding over all the globe, in all countries, and at all times. No human laws are of any validity if contrary to this.'"[30] James Wilson similarly explained that human law is always restrained by Natural Law, which "is the law of God. . . . Human law must rest its authority ultimately upon the authority of that law, which is Divine."[31] Rufus King agreed that the "law established by the Creator, which has existed from the beginning, extends over the whole globe, is everywhere and at all times binding upon mankind."[32] Thomas Jefferson wrote, "It is not only vain, but wicked, in a legislator to frame laws in opposition to the Laws of Nature."[33] George Mason asserted, "The Laws of Nature are the laws of God, whose authority can be superseded by no power on earth."[34] Samuel Adams and Benjamin Franklin advised, "All positive and civil laws should conform, as far as possible, to the law of natural reason and equity."[35] Theophilus Parsons wrote that "no power was given to Congress to infringe on any one of the natural rights of the people by this Constitution; and, should they attempt it without constitutional authority, the act would be a nullity, and could not be enforced."[36] The Founding Fathers ultimately expected that Congress, when legislating, would respect the Natural Law foundation upon which its constitutional government was built—that it would enact only those laws that were designed to sharpen the government's aim at preserving man's fundamental rights to life, liberty, and property.

Legislative power under Natural Law principles also contains the inherent limitation that it cannot be wielded arbitrarily over the people. Just as an individual may not arbitrarily take from another in the State of Nature, he cannot also take in society through the arm of the legislative body. Furthermore, the legislature cannot contravene the principle of equality by passing laws that favor or target certain individuals or groups. Locke considered it "too gross an absurdity" that an individual would ever join a society governed by arbitrary legislative power.[37] He stressed that legislatures must "govern by promulgated established laws, not to be varied in particular cases, but to have one rule for rich and poor, for the favorite at court, and the country man at plow."[38]

The Founding Fathers were strong proponents of uniformity in all legislation. Benjamin Franklin declared, "The ordaining of laws in favor of *one* part of the nation, to the prejudice and oppression of *another*, is certainly the most erroneous and mistaken policy. An *equal* dispensation of protection, rights, privileges, and advantages, is what every part is entitled to, and ought to enjoy."[39] Benjamin Rush also asserted that "nothing deserves the name of law but that which is certain and universal in its operation upon all the members of the community."[40] James Madison wrote in The Federalist No. 57:

> [T]he House of Representatives . . . can make no law which will not have its full operation on themselves and their friends, as well as the great mass of society. This has always been deemed one of the strongest bonds by which human policy can connect the rulers and the people together. It creates between them that communion of interest and sympathy of sentiments of which few governments have furnished examples; but without which every government degenerates into tyranny.[41]

The Founding Fathers naturally mandated uniformity in the Constitution. It imposes a uniformity standard on all direct taxes, which must to be "apportioned among the several states . . . according to their respective numbers."[42] It requires that "all duties, imposts and excises shall be uniform throughout the United States."[43] And it also prohibits Congress from passing bills of attainder or ex post facto laws, both of which are designed to target select individuals or groups.[44] By these constitutional conditions of uniformity, the Founding Fathers sought to protect the natural rights of the people from arbitrary legislative power. Yet the people themselves would remain the most important check against that form of abuse, as Madison explained in The Federalist No. 57:

> If it be asked, what is to restrain the House of Representatives from making legal discriminations in favor of themselves and a particular class of the society? I answer: the genius of the whole system; the nature of just and constitutional laws; and above all,

the vigilant and manly spirit which actuates the people of America, a spirit which nourishes freedom, and in return is nourished by it.

If this spirit shall ever be so far debased as to tolerate a law not obligatory on the Legislature as well on the people, the people will be prepared to tolerate anything but liberty.[45]

That spirit served as the underpinning of the federal government's legislative authority. The scope of congressional power was limited not just by the Constitution, but also by Natural Law. Congress had no power to expand its jurisdiction. It had no power to arbitrarily favor certain individuals or groups under the law. And it had no power to deprive the people of their natural rights to life, liberty, and property. As long as the American people continued to respect these Natural Law principles, then the legislative power would forever remain within its proper bounds.

The Executive Power

While lawmaking is a relatively short and periodic process, law enforcement is a constant obligation that necessitates an ever-present executive power. Locke wrote that the laws "have a constant and lasting force, and need a perpetual execution, or an attendance thereunto: therefore it is necessary [that] there should be a power always in being, which should see to the execution of the laws that are made, and remain in force."[46] The Founding Fathers placed the perpetual executive power of the federal government in the President of the United States.

Even though the president is the chief law enforcement officer in the nation, the Founding Fathers gave him an added constitutional duty to recommend legislation to Congress. Article II of the Constitution reads, "He shall from time to time . . . recommend to [Congress'] consideration such measures as he shall judge necessary and expedient."[47] The Founding Fathers imposed this requirement on the president because they determined that the president might often have the most information pertaining to national matters. While members of Congress are largely familiar with the conditions of their state and local constituents, the president is the one person who truly represents the nation as a whole. And because he is always on duty, the president can more readily discern whether new laws are needed to govern national concerns.

The Constitution also mandates in Article II that the president "shall take care that the laws be faithfully executed."[48] Although this duty to execute congressional law seemingly subordinates the president to Congress, he is not an automaton that blindly enforces the law. The executive branch is a separate and coequal branch of government, and the president has independent constitutional authority to "preserve, protect, and defend the Constitution of the United States," which is always superior to congressional law.[49] Consequently, if the president believes that an act of Congress is unconstitutional, then he may use his discretion to either veto the bill before it becomes law, if able, or refuse the law's enforcement.

This kind of executive discretion derives from Natural Law theory. Locke believed that all executives should have the "power to act according to discretion for the public good, without the prescription of the law, and sometimes even against it."[50] He reasoned that as long as the executive power acts pursuant to the end of society—to protect the people, their liberty, and their property—then executive discretion, or prerogative, should not be feared. He wrote:

> [S]ince a rational creature cannot be supposed when free to put himself into subjection to another for his own harm, . . . prerogative can be nothing but the people permitting their rulers to do several things of their own free choice where the law was silent, and sometimes too against the direct letter of the law for the public good; and their acquiescing in it when so done.[51]

Although the Founding Fathers disdained royal prerogative for its arbitrariness, they generally accepted Locke's reasoning on executive discretion in exceptional circumstances. Such discretion would be more tolerable under the Constitution because the people would always retain a political check on executive power directly through the ballot box or indirectly through the impeachment process. So any excessive or unpopular use of executive discretion could be reversed politically. Furthermore, where urgency is required, it may be that the president is the only elected representative ready to act, for Congress might not be in session to respond. (The Constitution requires Congress to meet only once a year.) Lastly, because the Constitution limits federal power, the president's ability to exercise executive prerogative would also be limited to matters of national concern.

President Jefferson's Louisiana Purchase in 1803 was an early example of executive discretion in action under the Constitution. Jefferson believed that he had no constitutional authority to complete the land purchase from France without an act of Congress, but he also believed that the opportunity to buy the vast western territory might pass if he were to wait for congressional action. So Jefferson decided to make the purchase on behalf of the people without congressional approval. Despite his admitted unconstitutional act, the American people ultimately ratified his exercise of executive discretion by overwhelmingly reelecting him to a second term in office.

While the Founding Fathers were likely to question the use of executive discretion on domestic concerns since it preempted congressional action, they were generally more permissive of its application in foreign affairs. In fact, they gave the president broad constitutional powers to manage foreign relations. Under the Constitution, the president commands the armed forces as Commander-in-Chief, he makes treaties with foreign powers, and he appoints and receives Ambassadors to and from foreign countries. These powers cannot be limited by Congress or the Supreme Court, for they were written into the Constitution as exclusive powers of the president. An early Senate Report from the Committee on Foreign Relations underscored this point. The Committee declared in 1816:

> The President is the constitutional representative of the United States with regard to foreign nations. He manages our concerns with foreign nations and must necessarily be most competent to determine when, how, and upon what subjects negotiation may be urged with the greatest prospect of success. For his conduct he is responsible to the Constitution.[52]

Especially in national security matters, the president is responsible to the Constitution, for Article II imparts upon him a sworn obligation "to preserve, protect, and defend the Constitution of the United States."[53] To discharge this duty, the president has broad war powers as Commander-in-Chief. Although Congress has the sole constitutional power to declare war—to initiate hostilities in a time of peace—its authority goes no further. Hamilton emphasized in The Federalist No. 69 that congressional war powers extend only "to the *declaring* of war and to the *raising* and *regulating* of fleets and armies."[54] It is the president who leads the armed forces as Commander-in-Chief. And it incumbent upon the president, who is always on duty, to decide when military force is necessary to preserve, protect, and defend the Constitution.

Altogether, the Founding Fathers designed the new executive power to give force to the national government that the Articles of Confederation lacked. They empowered the chief executive to implement the will of the people within the federal government's limited authority. They tasked him to advance the people's interests at home and abroad. And, most importantly, they charged him with the duty to provide for the nation's defense. These primary responsibilities, when fulfilled, would allow the young American nation to grow and prosper in freedom.

The Judicial Power

The Founding Fathers vested the judicial power of the federal government in the Supreme Court of the United States. In this Court, and in lower courts established by Congress, judicial power operates to resolve all controversies that arise under the law. But because the Constitution limits the scope of Congress's lawmaking power, the scope of the Court's judicial power is limited just the same. The Court is permitted settle cases between diverse parties—for example, between citizens of different states, between a state and a citizen of another state, or in any case in which the United States is a party. But if diversity jurisdiction does not apply, then the Supreme Court can only exercise judicial power over matters arising under federal law—under the narrow body of law that the Constitution authorizes Congress to enact.

In addition to that jurisdictional limitation, federal courts are prohibited by design from encroaching upon legislative power. In any republic, it is the legislative body that controls the content of the law; the judicial branch merely applies it. Judges may not make law from the bench. Blackstone argued that judges would bring instability to society if they were to disregard the letter of the law and instead rule according to their own notions of fairness. He wrote:

> [L]aw, without equity, though hard and disagreeable, is much more desirable for the public good, than equity without law: which would make every judge a legislator, and introduce most infinite confusion; as there would then be almost as many different rules of action laid down in our courts as there are differences of capacity and sentiment in the human mind.[55]

Montesquieu similarly wrote, "In republics, the very nature of the constitution requires the judges to follow the letter of the law; otherwise the law might be explained to the prejudice of every citizen, in cases where their honor, property, or life is concerned."[56] The Founding Fathers naturally expected the same judicial discipline in America. Alexander Hamilton strongly emphasized that judges were not at liberty to rule according to their own predilections, for doing so would usurp the power of Congress. He wrote in The Federalist No. 78, "The courts must declare the sense of the law; and if they should be disposed to exercise *will* instead of *judgment*, the consequence would equally be the substitution of their pleasure to that of the legislative body."[57]

Expecting that the courts would stay true to the law, the Founding Fathers considered judicial power to be the weakest and least threatening to liberty of all federal powers. Hamilton explained:

> Whoever attentively considers the different departments of power must perceive, that, in a government in which they are separated from each other, the judiciary, from the nature of its functions, will always be the least dangerous to the political rights of the Constitution; because it will be least in a capacity to annoy or injure them. The executive not only dispenses the honors, but holds the sword of the community. The legislature not only commands the purse, but prescribes the rules by which the duties and rights of every citizen are to be regulated. The judiciary on the contrary has no influence over either the sword or the purse, no direction either of the strength or of the wealth of the society, and can take no active resolution whatever. It may truly be said to have neither force nor will, but merely judgment; and must ultimately depend upon the aid of the executive arm even for the efficacy of its judgments.[58]

The Founding Fathers actually sought to counterbalance the inherent weakness of judicial power by giving federal judges the longest terms in office. Madison wrote in The Federalist No. 52, "It is a received and well founded maxim, that, where no other circumstances affect the case, the greater the power is, the shorter ought to be its duration; and, conversely, the smaller the power, the more safely may its duration be protracted."[59] While members of the House of Representatives received short, two-year terms in office, federal judges were given life terms.

Hamilton believed that life terms would insulate federal judges from political influence and assist them in upholding the Constitution. He argued that judges with life terms would likely possess more fortitude to strike down unconstitutional laws passed by the political majority, thereby preserving the limited nature of federal power. Hamilton wrote:

> If then the courts of justice are to be considered as the bulwarks of a limited constitution against legislative encroachments, this consideration will afford a strong argument for the permanent tenure of judicial offices, since nothing will contribute so much as this to that independent spirit in the judges, which must be essential to the faithful performance of so arduous a duty.[60]

That independent spirit, Hamilton continued, would bring vigor to the judicial branch and help federal judges become the "faithful guardians of the Constitution."[61] They would more boldly "declare all acts contrary to the manifest tenor of the Constitution void" because the Constitution, which is the supreme law of the land, must always "be preferred to the statute, [and] the intention of the people to the intention of their agents."[62]

The Founding Fathers ultimately expected that the Supreme Court's judicial power would be wielded in earnest to uphold the Constitution's original design. Although the Court was limited by its function and jurisdiction, it was free from political influence and bound only to the Constitution. It would serve as an independent advocate of the people, supporting their will so that liberty might endure.

The Bill of Rights

Any discussion of the key principles underlying the Constitution's design would be incomplete without mentioning the Bill of Rights—the first ten amendments to the Constitution. Although adopted after ratification, the Bill of Rights was vital to that effort, for many Americans were unwilling to support the Constitution without some assurance that federal power would remain limited. To allay their concerns, some proponents of the Constitution promised to add a Bill of Rights by amendment after ratification. The Bill was ultimately added, but some of the Founding Fathers questioned whether it was even necessary at all.

James Madison, who was one of the most influential figures at the Constitutional Convention, saw no need for a Bill of Rights.[63] He generally considered Bills of Rights to be unnecessary since they often "do no more than state the perfect equality of mankind. This, to be sure, is an absolute truth, yet it is not absolutely necessary to be inserted at the head of a constitution."[64] Madison understood the desire to enumerate added protections in the Constitution, but he found such wants to be contrived, since the Articles of Confederation lacked the same guarantees. Opponents of the Constitution seemed to be grasping for any basis to thwart ratification. He wrote in The Federalist No. 38, "Is a Bill of Rights essential to liberty? The Confederation has no Bill of Rights."[65] Madison found it curious that those who opposed the Constitution for this trivial reason "never call[ed] to mind the defects of that which it is to be exchanged for it."[66]

Alexander Hamilton objected to a Bill of Rights even more. He first reasoned that the popular nature of the new American government rendered a Bill unnecessary. He explained that past Bills of Rights in other countries had originated to restrain the otherwise unlimited power of government—they were "stipulations between kings and their subjects, abridgments of prerogative in favor of privilege, reservations of rights not surrendered to the prince."[67] The Magna Charta, for example, was "obtained by the Barons, sword in hand, from King John. . . . [T]he petition of right [was] assented to by Charles the First, in the beginning of his reign."[68] The English Bill of Rights was similarly acquiesced by the Prince of Orange in 1688.[69] These and other Bills of Rights were concessions by the ruling monarch to the people. In America, however, the people ruled. And when all rights naturally reside in the people, there was no need to enumerate in the Constitution specific rights of the people.

Hamilton wrote that the Constitution was "founded upon the power of the people, and executed by their immediate representatives and servants. Here, in strictness, the people surrender nothing, and as they retain everything, they have no need of particular reservations."[70]

Hamilton also argued that a Bill of Rights was inappropriate based on the limited design of the Constitution. He acknowledged that specific declarations of rights of the people might be applicable "to a constitution which has the regulation of every species of personal and private concerns."[71] But this was not the Constitution that the Founding Fathers had designed. The American Constitution "merely intended to regulate the general political interest of the nation."[72] It identified the governing powers that the people delegated to the federal government and organized those limited powers in the government's three departments. Hamilton believed that the enumeration of specific rights of the people in a document that merely set forth the limited powers of government was inconsistent and wholly unnecessary.

Hamilton further warned that a Bill of Rights would be "not only unnecessary in the proposed Constitution, but would even be dangerous."[73] He reasoned that the inclusion of a Bill of Rights might be taken to imply that the people had transferred to the federal government a regulatory power over these rights. Consequently, ambitious individuals in government might use this implication as their basis to claim an expansive federal authority. Hamilton wrote:

> [W]hy declare that things shall not be done which there is no power to do? Why for instance, should it be said, that the liberty of the press shall not be restrained, when no power is given by which restrictions may be imposed? I will not contend that such a provision would confer a regulating power; but it is evident that it would furnish, to men disposed to usurp, a plausible pretence for claiming that power. They might urge with a semblance of reason, that the Constitution ought not to be charged with the absurdity of providing against the abuse of an authority, which was not given, and that the provision against restraining the liberty of the press afforded a clear implication, that a power to prescribe proper regulations concerning it was intended to be vested in the national government. This may serve as a specimen of the numerous handles which would be given to

the doctrine of constructive powers, by the indulgence of an injudicious zeal for bills of rights.[74]

Hamilton was clearly concerned that a Bill of Rights might be twisted by cunning politicians to be read as a grant of positive authority to the federal government to regulate those enumerated rights on behalf of the people. Under this radical interpretation, for example, the constitutional guarantee that the federal government shall not abridge the people's freedom of the press could be construed to sanction a federal regulatory power over the press to oversee the fair exercise of that right. Such reasoning would effectively enable an administrative state to emerge. This was not the intent of those who advocated a Bill of Rights, and Hamilton tried to warn them of this potential danger to American liberty.

Despite the many objections to a Bill of Rights, the Founding Fathers ultimately decided that the promise of a Bill was necessary to garner enough support for the Constitution's ratification. So with the assurance that a Bill of Rights was forthcoming, the American people ratified the Constitution. Many states even sent lists of recommended amendments with their ratification documents to speed the First Congress along in passing a Bill of Rights.

James Madison—a newly elected representative of Virginia in 1789—assumed leadership of this amendment process in the First Congress of the United States. By directing the process, Madison was able to steer the phrasing of the amendments in a way that restricted federal power as much as possible. He intentionally avoided language that suggested government was the source of all rights. For example, he did not write that "the people are granted the freedom of speech" or "the people may bear arms." Rather, Madison used prohibitive language to make abundantly clear that these rights naturally belonged to the people, and that the federal government could not interfere with them in any way. For example, in the First Amendment, he wrote, "Congress shall make no law . . . abridging the freedom of speech."[75] The Second Amendment states that "the right of the people to keep and bear arms shall not be infringed."[76] And the Fourth Amendment reads, "The right of the people to be secure . . . against unreasonable searches and seizures shall not be violated."[77] By wording these amendments this way, Madison was able to reinforce the principle that all power and rights in America naturally reside in "We the People"—not in government.

Madison also authored two special amendments in the Bill of Rights to make certain that the enumeration of these rights would never "be so construed as to diminish the just importance of other rights retained by the people, or as to enlarge the powers delegated by the Constitution" to the federal government.[78] The Ninth Amendment specifically reinforces the principle that the people, as the source of all governmental power, hold many more rights than those stated in the Constitution. It reads, "The enumeration in the Constitution, of certain rights, shall not be construed to deny or disparage others retained by the people."[79] And the Tenth Amendment places a clear boundary on federal power. It states, "The powers not delegated to the United States by the Constitution, nor prohibited by it to the states, are reserved to the states respectively, or to the people."[80]

To remove all doubt about the source of power in America, Madison proposed yet another amendment that further reinforced popular sovereignty. He recommended that the people attach the following declaration to the Preamble of the Constitution:

> That all power is originally vested in, and consequently derived from the people. That government is instituted, and ought to be exercised for the benefit of the people; which consists in the enjoyment of life and liberty, with the right of acquiring and using property, and generally of pursuing and obtaining happiness and safety. That the people have an indubitable, unalienable, and indefeasible right to reform or change their government, whenever it be found adverse or inadequate to the purposes of its institution.[81]

Madison essentially restated the Natural Law philosophy of the Declaration of Independence. He aimed to reassure the American people that they would always retain the right to alter or abolish government should it become destructive of its primary end—to secure man's natural rights to life, liberty, and property.

Madison's proposed prefix to the Constitution never made it out of committee in Congress, but not because the ideas that inspired the Revolution had suddenly become outdated—all representatives

unquestionably agreed with the substance of the amendment.[82] The
proposal was abandoned in large part because Congress decided to add
amendments to the end of the Constitution rather than interweave them
into the original text.[83] Moreover, the ideas behind Madison's prefix were
already incorporated throughout the Constitution. Article V permits the
people to amend the Constitution should the federal government ever fail
to secure their natural rights. The same authority exists in the First
Amendment's guarantee against any federal restriction of people's right
"to peaceably assemble."[84] This guarantee is not just a license for groups
to meet in leisure or protest. It was meant to encompass the natural and
collective right of the American people to gather in a future convention
and exercise their sovereign right to alter or abolish government that no
longer serves its purpose.[85] Furthermore, the Ninth and Tenth
Amendments effectively restate the founding principle that all power
delegated to government is derived from the people. Consequently, many
representatives considered Madison's proposed prefix to be superfluous
when Natural Law ideals were already well integrated in the Constitution.
So they passed and the people ratified the first ten amendments to the
Constitution as their Bill of Rights.

In the end, Natural Law philosophy manifested itself throughout the
design of the American government. The Constitution's limitations on
federal authority, its division of power among three branches of
government, and its various checks on that power all were instituted with
an aim to preserve the people's natural rights. The Founding Fathers did
not establish the Constitution to create rights for the American people.
Rather, as James Wilson wrote in 1790, they created the Constitution to
secure for the American people their God-given natural rights:

> What was the primary and principal object in the institution
> of government? Was it . . . to acquire new rights by a human
> establishment? Or was it, by human establishment, to acquire
> new security for the possession or the recovery of those rights, to
> the enjoyment or acquisition of which we were previously
> entitled by the immediate gift, or by the unerring law, of our all-
> wise and all-beneficent Creator?
> The latter, I presume, was the case.[86]

Given the failure of the hastily-constructed Articles of Confederation to adequately secure the people's natural rights, the Constitution of the United States, which was the product of great deliberation and debate at the Philadelphia Convention, presented the American people with a new opportunity. James Madison wrote in The Federalist No. 1 that the American people at last had the chance "to decide the important question, whether societies of men are really capable or not, of establishing good government from reflection and choice, or whether they are forever destined to depend, for their political constitutions, on accident and force."[87] By ratifying the Constitution of the United States, the choice of the American people was clear. They raised their government upon a foundation based in reason to be forever guided by the principles of Natural Law.

3

ON AMERICAN MORES

The Founding Fathers invested much time and effort to construct a government in harmony with Natural Law, but they recognized that the people's natural rights could not be preserved by the form of government alone. Lasting liberty in America would also depend on the knowledge and character of the people. It would depend on the preservation of certain fundamental values and practices that shaped American culture during the founding era. It would depend on the people maintaining their mores.

The Founding Fathers deemed education to be indispensable to enduring liberty in America. For example, James Madison believed that education would remain "essential to the preservation and the enjoyment of the blessing [of liberty]."[1] In any republic where the people rule, they must naturally be educated to direct their government. Madison wrote, "A popular government, without popular information or the means of acquiring it, is but a prologue to a farce or a tragedy, or perhaps both. Knowledge will forever govern ignorance; and a people who mean to be their own governors must arm themselves with the power which knowledge gives."[2] John Adams likewise wrote, "Wisdom and knowledge, as well as virtue, . . . [are] necessary for the preservation of [American] rights and liberties."[3] Benjamin Franklin noted, "The good education of youth has been esteemed by wise men in all ages as the surest foundation of the happiness both of private families and of commonwealths."[4] Thomas Jefferson wrote, "No one more sincerely wishes the spread of information among mankind than I do, and none has greater confidence in its effect towards supporting free and good government."[5] And James Wilson stated, "Law and liberty cannot rationally become the objects of our love, unless they first become the objects of our knowledge."[6]

At the core of any education in liberty is the acknowledgment of God as the source of all natural rights. The Founding Fathers consequently proposed that every American be raised with an appreciation of God so that liberty would long endure. James Madison in fact regarded the recognition of God's supreme authority as a precondition to citizenship in any free society. He stated:

> It is the duty of every man to render to the Creator such homage, and such only, as he believes to be acceptable to him. This duty is precedent both in order of time and degree of obligation, to the claims of civil society. Before any man can be considered as a member of civil society, he must be considered as a subject of the Governor of the Universe.[7]

Thomas Jefferson openly accepted God as the grantor of all rights, for he wrote, "The God who gave us life, gave us liberty at the same time."[8] And he cautioned that American liberty would be in peril if the people ever rejected God's authority. He asked, "Can the liberties of a nation be thought secure when we have removed their only firm basis, a conviction in the minds of the people that these liberties are the gift of God?"[9] Benjamin Franklin also questioned whether the new American nation could grow in liberty without acknowledging God. He wrote:

> I have lived, sir, a long time; and the longer I live, the more convincing proofs I see of this truth, that God governs in the affairs of men. And if a sparrow cannot fall to the ground without His notice, is it probable that an empire can rise without His aid?[10]

To sustain liberty in America, the Founding Fathers believed that younger generations must be taught to respect God and His authority in nature. They must grow enlightened in the principles of Natural Law.

Thomas Paine was one of the most ardent proponents of theological teaching in schools in support of Natural Law instruction. He believed that education would be grossly inadequate if students were not taught that God is the source of all life and laws. Paine argued:

It has been the error of schools to teach astronomy, and all the other sciences and subjects of natural philosophy, as accomplishments only; whereas they should be taught theologically, or with reference to the Being who is the Author of them: for all the principles of science are of divine origin. Man cannot make, or invent, or contrive principles; he can only discover them, and he ought to look through the discovery to the Author.

When we examine an extraordinary piece of machinery, an astonishing pile of architecture, a well-executed statue, or a highly-finished painting . . . our ideas are naturally led to think of the extensive genius and talent of the artist. When we study the elements of geometry, we think of Euclid. When we speak of gravitation, we think of Newton. How, then, is it that when we study the works of God in creation, we stop short and do not think of God? It is from the error of the schools in having taught those subjects as accomplishments only and thereby separated the study of them from the Being who is the Author of them.[11]

Just as the study of law entails "looking through human laws up to the power that ordained them," Paine insisted that science must similarly "look[] through nature up to nature's God."[12] He believed that bringing God into the classroom would offer students a complete education based in reason. Paine wrote:

The mechanic of every profession will there [in school] be taught the mathematical principles necessary to render him a proficient in his art. The cultivator will there see developed the principles of vegetation; while, at the same time, they will be led to see the hand of God in all these things.[13]

Paine believed that the intentional omission of God in education would only spawn atheism, which he considered "evil" for its incessant ignorance of truth. He wrote:

The evil that has resulted from the error of the schools in teaching natural philosophy as an accomplishment only has been that of generating in the pupils a species of atheism. Instead of looking through the works of Creation to the Creator Himself, they stop short and employ the knowledge they acquire to create doubts of His existence. They labor with studied ingenuity to ascribe everything they behold to innate properties of matter; and jump over all the rest by saying that matter is eternal.[14]

Paine further explained, "God is the power of first cause, nature is the law, and matter is the subject acted upon. But [atheism], by ascribing every phenomenon to properties of matter, conceives a system for which it cannot account and yet it pretends to demonstrate."[15] By ignoring God in education, Paine wrote, the atheist "perverts the sublime and enlightening study of natural philosophy into a deformity of absurdities by not reasoning to the end."[16]

If taught about God, then new generations of Americans could develop their ability to "reason to the end." They could discover the boundaries of Natural Law within which they must live for liberty to prevail. Locke wrote that man's claim to liberty "is grounded on his having reason, which is able to instruct him in that Law he is to govern himself by, and make him know how far he is left to the freedom of his own will."[17]

If children are not taught to reason—if they are not taught about God as the source of all things—then their prospect for liberty cannot be assured by even the best system of laws. Locke wrote that children are born "ignorant and without the use of reason."[18] And if their reason is never developed by education, then they "cannot be said to be under this [Natural] Law."[19] Those who are uninhibited by Natural Law constraints live not in liberty, but in an unrestrained freedom in which force and faction dominate. Locke warned parents that a dismal fate awaits any child who is released into the world with no ability to reason. He wrote:

> To turn him loose to an unrestrained liberty, before he has reason to guide him, is not the allowing him the privilege of his nature to be free; but to thrust him out amongst brutes and abandon him to a state as wretched, and as much beneath that of a man, as theirs.[20]

John Adams later echoed, "If we suffer [our children's] minds to grovel and creep in infancy, they will grovel all their lives."[21] Jefferson also asserted that no nation could long endure in liberty if reason deteriorated and ceased to guide government. He said, "If a nation expects to be ignorant and free in a state of civilization, it expects what never was and never will be."[22]

For liberty to last in America, the people must not only learn about the source of their natural rights. They must also learn to appreciate their government, which was designed to preserve those rights. Noah Webster, who is regarded as the "Father of American Scholarship and Education" for his great impact on early American education, wrote that a proper education should "inspire [Americans] with just and liberal ideas of government and with an inviolable attachment to their own country."[23] He emphasized that knowledge of American history would be an essential component of that education. He advised, "Every child in America should be acquainted with his own country. . . . As soon as he opens his lips, he should rehearse the history of his own country."[24] George Washington was adamant that young Americans must be imbued with a sense of appreciation for their constitutional government before their minds might potentially become corrupted by the allure of other inferior systems. He wrote, "[W]e ought to deprecate the hazard attending ardent and susceptible minds, from being too strongly and too early prepossessed in favor of other political systems, before they are capable of appreciating their own."[25] Legal scholar St. George Tucker likewise advised that Americans must understand the design of their political system if they hope to preserve their liberty. He cautioned that "to be ignorant of the law and the Constitution is to be ignorant of the rights of the citizen. Ignorance is invariably the parent of error: where it is blended with a turbulent and unquiet temper, it infallibly produces licentiousness, the most terrible enemy to liberty, except despotism."[26]

The Founding Fathers plainly believed that establishing a common knowledge of history, law, and government is paramount for the nation to remain free. But this understanding need not be, and should not be, solely academic. By actively participating in government, individuals are able to gain a practical education in self-rule that fosters an even greater appreciation for liberty—a phenomenon that Alexis de Tocqueville observed when he visited the United States in 1831. He wrote in admiration:

[An American can] tell you what his rights are and how they may be exercised. He understands the customs of the political world. You will find that he is aware of administrative rules and familiar with the workings of the law. Americans do not take their practical knowledge and concrete notions from books. Their literary education may prepare them for such learning, but it does not supply them with it.

The American learns about the law by participating in the making of it. He teaches himself about the forms of government by governing. He watches the great work of society being done every day before his eyes and, in a sense, by his hand.[27]

Tocqueville became convinced that strong local governments provide the most people with the best opportunity to obtain a practical education in liberty. He wrote that local governments "foster a taste for liberty among the people and teach them the art of being free."[28] Participation in local institutions allows the people to learn firsthand that freedom in society must be accompanied by restraint and responsibility, and it gives the people a sense of ownership and pride in their governments. Tocqueville grew certain that "the most powerful way of persuading men that they have a stake in their country's fate . . . is to see to it that they participate in its government."[29] Without such experience, the people only learn dependence on more distant powers, and tyranny can more easily emerge. Tocqueville explained:

Local institutions are to liberty what elementary schools are to knowledge; they bring it within reach of the people, allow them to savor its peaceful use, and accustom them to rely on it. Without local institutions, a nation may give itself a free government, but it will not have a free spirit. Fleeting passions, momentary interests, or chance circumstances may give it the outward forms of independence, but despotism repressed within the body of society will eventually resurface.[30]

Tocqueville discovered that the American people learned about law and liberty not just in elected office, but also in the courtroom by participating in the legal process. Jury trials were designed to protect the rights of the accused, but they also served to educate citizens who sat on the jury. Tocqueville wrote of this practical education in law and equity:

> The jury vests each citizen with a kind of magistracy. It teaches everyone that they have duties toward society and a role in its government. By forcing men to be concerned with affairs other than their own, it combats individual egoism, which is to societies what rust is to metal.
>
> The jury is incredibly useful in shaping the people's judgment and augmenting their natural enlightenment. This, in my view, is its greatest advantage. It should be seen as a free school, and one that is always open, to which each juror comes to learn about his rights, and where he enters into daily contact with the best educated, most enlightened members of the upper classes and receives practical instruction in the law in a form accessible to his intelligence, thanks to the efforts of the lawyers, the counsel of the judge, and the very passions of the litigants. I think that the primary reason for the practical intelligence and political good sense of Americans is their long experience with juries in civil matters.
>
> I do not know if juries are useful to civil litigants, but I do know that they are very useful to the people who judge them. I see the jury as one of the most effective means available to society for educating the people.[31]

The prevalence of these practical educational opportunities helped produce a society that was very knowledgeable in liberty—something that Tocqueville marveled at. Everywhere he went in America, he found people with a high level of interest in law and politics. Such concerns were not limited to particular social circles in large cities. Even in the outer reaches of the states, Tocqueville met pioneers who were as refined in culture as those he met in the city. He described an adventurer he met as follows:

> Everything around him is primitive and wild, but he is the product, so to speak, of eighteen centuries of effort and experience. He wears the clothes and speaks the language of the city. He knows the past, is curious about the future, and argues about the present. He is a highly civilized man who, having plunged into the wilds of the New World with his Bible, ax, and newspapers, has chosen to live for a time in the forest.
>
> It is difficult to imagine how rapidly thought propagates through this wilderness.
>
> I do not think that there is as much intellectual activity in the most enlightened and populous cantons of France.[32]

Tocqueville attributed this stark intellectual difference between Americans and Europeans to the divergent aims of their education. In Europe at that time, education was not designed to enlighten. Rather, Tocqueville wrote, "its principal purpose is to prepare people for private life. Citizens take part in public affairs too seldom to prepare them for it in advance."[33] Living under government with no share in its operation, Europeans had little use for political education. In America, on the other hand, the people had to learn civics, for they governed themselves. Tocqueville observed, "In the United States, all of education is directed toward politics."[34] The American people were not being trained to submit to government; they instead were being raised to lead it.

To preserve their liberty, the American people had to be educated in Natural Law and familiar with the operation of their constitutional republic, but that was not all. Learning about the natural boundaries of freedom and the function of government is pointless if the people disregard those limits or disobey the law. So the people also had to be educated in virtue, for a nation's capacity for liberty is a function of its moral character. When virtue prevails in a republic, the law retains its force by the people's self-control. Liberty thrives because the people responsibly govern themselves. As virtue erodes and lawlessness spreads, however, then government must increasingly regulate and control in order to maintain order and compliance with the law. The coercive force of government then supplants individual discipline and responsibility, and liberty soon diminishes.

The Founding Fathers well understood that virtue is a necessary component of lasting liberty. The 1776 Virginia Declaration of Rights proclaimed, "That no free government, or the blessings of liberty, can be preserved to any people but by . . . virtue, and by frequent recurrence to fundamental principles."[35] Richard Henry Lee said that "a popular government cannot flourish without virtue in the people."[36] Samuel Adams declared that "neither the wisest constitution nor the wisest laws will secure the liberty and happiness of a people whose manners are universally corrupt."[37] He believed that a republic's truest friend to liberty is one "who tries most to promote its virtue, and who, so far as his power and influence extend, will not suffer a man to be chosen into any office of power and trust who is not a wise and virtuous man."[38] James Madison similarly said:

> If there be not [virtue among us], we are in a wretched situation. No theoretical checks, no form of government can render us secure. To suppose that any form of government will secure liberty or happiness without any virtue in the people is a chimerical idea. If there be sufficient virtue and intelligence in the community, it will be exercised in the selection of these men; so that we do not depend on their virtue, or put confidence in our rules, but in the people who are to choose them.[39]

Benjamin Franklin also emphasized "that nothing is of more importance for the public weal, than to form and train up youth in wisdom and virtue. Wise and good men are in my opinion, the strength of the state; more so than riches or arms."[40] Noah Webster added, "The virtues of men are of more consequence to society than their abilities; and for this reason, the heart should be cultivated with more assiduity than the head."[41] George Washington wrote that "a good moral character is the first essential in a man . . . . It is therefore highly important that [man] should endeavor not only to be learned but [also] virtuous."[42] He also declared that "the foundations of our national policy will be laid in the pure and immutable principles of private morality."[43] And John Adams wrote:

> Public virtue cannot exist in a nation without private, and public virtue is the only foundation of republics. There must be a positive passion for the public good, the public interest, honor, power and glory, established in the minds of the people, or there can be no republican government, nor any real liberty.[44]

It was clear to the Founding Fathers that the erosion of virtue in America marks the decline of liberty. The longer that government dominates to maintain order in society, the more the people become accustomed to the heavy hand of government managing the details of their everyday lives. The government's power soon appears to be more natural and absolute. Those in government begin to identify themselves as protectors, rather than servants, of the people. Instead of following the people's will, politicians begin to act according to their own notions of what is best for all. And by that point, popular sovereignty matters little, for liberty is lost. Samuel Adams warned that "when people are universally ignorant and debauched in their manners, they will sink under their own weight without the aid of foreign invaders."[45] Benjamin Franklin wrote that "only a virtuous people are capable of freedom. As nations become corrupt and vicious, they have more need of masters."[46] John Witherspoon likewise said that servitude follows the decay of virtue, "Nothing is more certain than that a general profligacy and corruption of manners make a people ripe for destruction. A good form of government may hold the rotten materials together for some time, but beyond a certain pitch, even the best constitution will be ineffectual, and slavery must ensue."[47] Thomas Jefferson also asserted, "It is the manners and spirit of a people which preserve a republic in vigor. A degeneracy in these is a canker which soon eats to the heart of its laws and constitution."[48] And James Madison wrote that if "there is not sufficient virtue among men for self-government," then "nothing less than the chains of despotism can restrain them from destroying and devouring one another."[49]

A nation could avoid this despotic end by imbuing virtue in the people. Samuel Adams wrote, "If virtue and knowledge are diffused among the people, they will never be enslaved. This will be their great security."[50] George Washington also advised that "government . . . can never be in danger of degenerating into a monarchy, an oligarchy, an aristocracy, or any other despotic or oppressive form so long as there shall remain any virtue in the body of the people."[51] To protect against the collapse of the republic, therefore, new generations of Americans had to be educated in virtue.

The Founding Fathers believed that virtue is best cultivated in religion. Benjamin Rush wrote that "the only foundation for a useful education in a republic is to be laid in religion. Without this there can be no virtue, and without virtue there can be no liberty, and liberty is the object and life of all republican governments."[52] Gouveneur Morris also advised, "Religion is the only solid basis of good morals; therefore education should teach the precepts of religion and the duties of man toward God."[53]

The Founding Fathers so valued religion because they recognized that scripture could guide man's morality where his reason alone might falter in comprehension of Natural Law. The relationship between religion and Natural Law was explained by Blackstone as follows:

> The doctrines thus delivered we call the revealed or divine law, and they are to be found only in the Holy Scriptures. These precepts, when revealed, are found upon comparison to be really a part of the original Law of Nature, as they tend in all their consequences to man's felicity. But we are not from thence to conclude that the knowledge of these truths was attainable by reason in its present corrupted state; since we find that, until they were revealed, they were hid from the wisdom of ages. As then the moral precepts of this law are indeed of the same original with those of the Law of Nature, so their intrinsic obligation is of equal strength and perpetuity. Yet undoubtedly the revealed law is of infinitely more authenticity than that moral system, which is framed by ethical writers, and denominated the Natural Law. Because one is the Law of Nature, expressly declared so to be by God himself; the other is only what, by the assistance of human reason, we imagine to be that law. If we could be as certain of the latter as we are of the former, both would have an equal authority; but, till then, they can never be put in any competition together.[54]

In essence, the moral system revealed by divine law in scripture is a more reliable source of virtue than any system devised by man—even one devised by the collective genius of the Founding Fathers, who demonstrated their humility by trusting religion to supply virtue in society.

The only vocal exception was Thomas Paine, who believed that virtue could be taught independently of religion—a position for which he was widely criticized at the time. As mentioned before, Paine was an ardent proponent of Natural Law theory and believed that schools must teach about God's supreme authority, but he also stood against religious institutions in his book *Age of Reason*. Benjamin Franklin, who often advised Paine on his political writings, urged him on this occasion to "burn this piece" before publishing it to avoid suffering widespread condemnation and personal regret.[55] In a personal letter to him, Franklin suggested that Paine might be discounting the influence that religion had in shaping his character. He wrote, "You yourself may find it easy to live a virtuous life without the assistance afforded by religion . . . . [But] perhaps you are indebted . . . to your religious education for the habits of virtue upon which you now justly value yourself."[56] Franklin thought it was disingenuous for Paine to attack religion as being irrelevant to the development of virtue when it had surely nurtured that quality in him. It was just as absurd, Franklin wrote, "that a youth, to be raised into the company of men, should prove his manhood by beating his mother."[57]

The other Founding Fathers believed that religion, as the best source of virtue in society, was important to sustained liberty in America. John Adams declared that the "foundation of a free constitution is pure virtue" and that "it is religion and morality alone which can establish the principles upon which freedom can securely stand."[58] In his Farewell Address to the nation, George Washington said:

> Of all the dispositions and habits which lead to political prosperity, religion and morality are indispensable supports. . . . And let us with caution indulge the supposition that morality can be maintained without religion. . . . [for] reason and experience both forbid us to expect that national morality can prevail to the exclusion of religious principle.[59]

Samuel Adams wrote of the close relationship between religion and liberty:

> The religion and public liberty of a people are intimately connected; their interests are interwoven, they cannot subsist separately; and therefore they rise and fall together. For this reason, it is always observable, that those who are combined to destroy the people's liberties practice every art to poison their morals.[60]

Gouverneur Morris stressed, "There must be religion. When that ligament is torn, society is disjointed and its members perish . . . . [T]he most important of all lessons is the denunciation of ruin to every state that rejects the precepts of religion."[61]

The Founding Fathers understood that religion enables self-government by imbuing moral discipline in the people. Religion restrains individual behavior in a way that lessens the need for an overbearing government to maintain order in society. Robert Winthrop said that the people are controlled either by the Word of God or by the coercive power of government—"either by the Bible or by the bayonet."[62] James McHenry similarly said:

> [P]ublic utility pleads most forcibly for the general distribution of the Holy Scriptures. The doctrine they preach, the obligations they impose, the punishment they threaten, the rewards they promise, the stamp and image of divinity they bear, which produces a conviction of their truths, can alone secure to society, order and peace, and to our courts of justice and constitutions of government, purity, stability and usefulness. In vain, without the Bible, we increase penal laws and draw entrenchments around our institutions. Bibles are strong entrenchments. Where they abound, men cannot pursue wicked courses, and at the same time enjoy quiet conscience.[63]

John Adams noted that religion and liberty intersected in a more practical sense in that religion most effectively spreads the teachings of Natural Law throughout the nation. He explained:

> One great advantage of the Christian religion is that it brings the great principle of the Law of Nature and Nations—Love your neighbor as yourself, and do to others as you would that others should do to you—to the knowledge, belief, and veneration of the whole people. Children, servants, women, and men, are all professors in the science of public and private morality. No other institution for education, no kind of political discipline, could diffuse this kind of necessary information, so universally among all ranks and descriptions of citizens. The duties and rights of the man and the citizen are thus taught from early infancy to every creature.[64]

James Wilson observed that religion naturally complements Natural Law by imposing limitations on individual behavior. He wrote, "Far from being rivals or enemies, religion and law are twin sisters, friends, and mutual assistants. Indeed, these two sciences run into each other. The divine law, as discovered by reason and the moral sense, forms an essential part of both."[65]

Given the importance of religion to sustained liberty, the Founding Fathers naturally encouraged its continued practice in America. John Jay believed that it is "the duty of all wise, free, and virtuous governments to countenance and encourage virtue and religion."[66] Abraham Baldwin said that "a free government . . . can only be happy when the public principles and opinions are properly directed . . . by religion and education. It should therefore be among the first objects of those who wish well to the national prosperity to encourage and support the principles of religion and morality."[67] Charles Carroll asserted, "Without morals, a republic cannot subsist any length of time; they therefore who are decrying the Christian religion, whose morality is so sublime and pure, . . . are undermining the solid foundation of morals, the best security for the duration of free governments."[68] Jedidiah Morse similarly wrote:

> To the kindly influence of Christianity we owe that degree of civil freedom and political and social happiness which mankind now enjoys. All efforts made to destroy the foundations of our Holy Religion ultimately tend to the subversion also of our political freedom and happiness. In proportion as the genuine effects of Christianity are diminished in any nation . . . in the same proportion will the people of that nation recede from the blessings of genuine freedom . . . . Whenever the pillars of Christianity shall be overthrown, our present republican forms of government, and all the blessings which flow from them, must fall with them.[69]

Fisher Ames stated, "Our liberty depends on our education, our laws, and habits . . . ; it is founded on morals and religion, whose authority reigns in the heart, and on the influence all these produce on public opinion before that opinion governs rulers."[70] Henry Laurens wrote, "I had the honor of being one among many who framed that Constitution. . . . In order effectually to accomplish [its] great ends, it is incumbent upon us to begin wisely and to proceed in the fear of God; . . . and it is especially the duty of those who bear rule to promote and encourage piety."[71] John Hancock stated, "Sensible of the importance of Christian piety and virtue to the order and happiness of a state, I cannot but earnestly commend to you every measure for their support and encouragement. . . . [T]he very existence of the republics . . . depend much upon the public institutions of religion."[72] John Adams wrote that "we have no government armed with power capable of contending with human passions unbridled by morality and religion. . . . Our Constitution was made only for a moral and religious people. It is wholly inadequate to the government of any other."[73]

A moral and religious society existed at the time of the nation's founding, and the American people were intent upon maintaining it for generations to come. In their early state constitutions that were drafted amid the Revolutionary War, the people demonstrated their understanding that liberty relied on religion to flourish. For example, the Massachusetts Constitution declared:

> As the happiness of a people, and the good order and preservation of civil government, essentially depend on piety, religion, and morality; and as these cannot be generally diffused through the community but by the institution of a public worship of God, and of public institutions (instructions) in piety, religion and morality: therefore, to promote their happiness, and to secure the good order and preservation of their government, the people of this commonwealth have a right to invest their Legislature with power to authorize and require . . . the several towns, parishes, precincts, and other bodies politic, or religious societies, to make suitable provision, at their own expense, for the institution of the public worship of God, and for the support and maintenance of public Protestant teachers of piety, religion, and morality, in all cases where such provision shall not be made voluntarily. . . . And every denomination of Christians, demeaning themselves peaceably, and as good subjects of the commonwealth, shall be equally under the protection of the law; and no subordination of any sect or denomination to another, shall ever be established by law.[74]

The Delaware Constitution asserted that "it is the duty of all men frequently to assemble together for the public worship of the Author of the universe; and piety and morality, on which the prosperity of communities depends, are thereby promoted."[75] The New Hampshire Constitution stated:

> Every individual has a natural and unalienable right to worship God according to the dictates of his own conscience, and reason . . . . As morality and piety, rightly grounded on high principles, will give the best and greatest security to government, and will lay, in the hearts of men, the strongest obligations to due subjection, and as the knowledge of these is most likely to be propagated through a society, therefore, the several parishes, bodies, corporate, or religious societies shall at all times have the

right of electing their own teachers, and of contracting with them for their support or maintenance, or both. . . . And every person, denomination or sect shall be equally under the protection of the law; and no subordination of any one sect, denomination or persuasion to another shall ever be established.[76]

The Connecticut Constitution said:

It being the duty of all men to worship the Supreme Being, the great Creator and Preserver of the universe, and their right to render that worship in the mode most consistent with the dictates of their consciences; no person shall, by law, be compelled to join or support, nor be classed with or associated to any congregation, church, or religious association. . . . And each and every society or denomination of Christians in this State shall have and enjoy the same and equal powers, rights, and privileges; and shall have power and authority to support and maintain the ministers or teachers of their respective denominations, and to build and repair houses for public worship.[77]

The Vermont Constitution declared the freedom of religious worship, and advised that "every sect or denomination of Christians ought to observe the Sabbath or Lord's day, and keep up some sort of religious worship, which to them shall seem most agreeable to the revealed will of God."[78] The Virginia Constitution said:

That religion or the duty which we owe to our Creator, and the manner of discharging it, can be directed only by reason and conviction, not by force or violence; and, therefore, all men are equally entitled to the free exercise of religion, according to the dictates of conscience; and that it is the mutual duty of all to practice Christian forbearance, love, and charity towards each other.[79]

The New Jersey Constitution included similar provisions granting the free exercise of religion, but added a religious eligibility requirement for public service:

[A]ll persons professing a belief in the faith of any Protestant sect, who shall demean themselves peaceably under the government, as hereby established, shall be capable of being elected into any office of profit or trust, or being a member of either branch of the Legislature, and shall fully and freely enjoy every privilege and immunity enjoyed by others their fellow-subjects.[80]

The South Carolina Constitution said that "all persons and religious societies who acknowledge that there is one God, and a future state of rewards and punishments, and that God is publicly to be worshipped, shall be freely tolerated."[81] The Maryland Constitution stated that "it is the duty of every man to worship God in such manner as he thinks most acceptable to him, all persons professing the Christian religion are equally entitled to protection in their religious liberty."[82] Maryland also decreed that to qualify for state office, a person must express "a declaration of belief in the Christian religion."[83] The North Carolina Constitution also declared that "no person who shall deny the being of a God, or the truth of the Protestant religion, or the Divine authority of either the Old or New Testament, or shall hold religious principles incompatible with the freedom and safety of the State, shall be capable of holding any office, or place of trust or profit, in the civil department within this State."[84]

Religion clearly was integral to American culture and education in the revolutionary era, and the Founding Fathers had no intention to disturb that institution in any way under the new United States Constitution. By omitting any reference to religion in that document, they rendered the federal government powerless over religious concerns—the federal government's authority extends only to those powers enumerated in the Constitution. Richard Dobbs Spaight explained, "As to the subject of religion, . . . no power is given to the general government to interfere with it at all. Any act of Congress on this subject would be a usurpation."[85] James Madison similarly assured Virginians at their ratifying convention that "there is not a shadow of right in the general government to intermeddle with religion. Its least interference with it would be a most flagrant usurpation."[86]

To remove all doubt about this constraint on federal power, the Founding Fathers also wrote into the First Amendment of the Constitution that "Congress shall make no law respecting an establishment of religion, or prohibiting the free exercise thereof."[87] The amendment effectively precluded the federal government from wielding any power over religion.

As Thomas Jefferson later wrote, it erected a "wall of separation between church and state" that blocked the federal government from encroaching on religious freedom in America.[88]

Incidentally, the Founding Fathers never intended to segregate religion from public life by the First Amendment. The "wall of separation" that Jefferson spoke of operated only on the federal government. The people in their states, on the other hand, retained all authority to regulate such matters. As the aforementioned state constitutions indicate, the people in many states required their citizens to observe the Sabbath; they encouraged them to publicly worship God; they provided for religious education; and in some states they even denied public office to atheists. Citizens were guaranteed the right to exercise the faith of their choosing, but a number of states promoted particular denominations by establishing state religions, some of which continued well into the nineteenth century. Whether some of these legal provisions and preferences are appropriate is debatable. But it is undeniable that the U.S. Constitution reserved to the people in their states complete control over religious matters. Jefferson himself explained this distinction as follows:

> I consider the government of the United States as interdicted by the Constitution from intermeddling with religious institutions, their doctrines, discipline, or exercises. This results not only from the provision that no law shall be made respecting the establishment or free exercise of religion, but from that also which reserves to the states the powers not delegated to the United States. Certainly, no power to prescribe any religious exercise or to assume authority in any religious discipline has been delegated to the general government. It must then rest with the states.[89]

Jefferson actually took pride in the fact that an institution of local government—his hometown courthouse—was used for church services. He wrote in 1822:

> In our village of Charlottesville, there is a good degree of religion, with a small spice only of fanaticism. We have four sects, but without either church or meeting-house. The courthouse is the common temple, one Sunday in the month to each. Here, Episcopalian and Presbyterian, Methodist and Baptist, meet together, join in hymning their Maker, listen with

attention and devotion to each others' preachers, and all mix in society with perfect harmony.[90]

The First Amendment did nothing to restrict the states from supporting religion. It merely prohibited the national government from interfering with religious liberty. Religion was left alone to flourish in the states. And so it did.

The pervasive nature of religion in America fascinated Tocqueville during his visit in 1831. He wrote, "When I first arrived in the United States, it was the country's religious aspect that first captured my attention."[91] He was so surprised by the strength of religious belief in America because many European thinkers had theorized that a nation's religious enthusiasm would fade away as its people became more enlightened and free. As Tocqueville observed, however, "the facts do not bear this theory out. In Europe the unbelief of certain segments of the population is rivaled only by their brutishness and ignorance, whereas in America we find one of the freest and most enlightened peoples in the world zealously observing all of religion's outward requirements."[92] Captivated by his discovery, Tocqueville wrote extensively about the positive force of religion in America.

Tocqueville noticed that Americans were free to practice the religions of their choosing, independent of any direction by the federal government. Although religion in America was less controlling than in nations that endorsed an official religion, its impact on the people was actually more enduring. Tocqueville observed:

> Religion in America is perhaps less powerful than it has been at certain times in certain other countries, but its influence is more durable. It has been reduced to its own forces, which no one can take away. Its influence is limited to a particular sphere, but there it is pervasive and dominates effortlessly.[93]

Tocqueville theorized that religion grows stronger and more lasting when it is detached from centralized government—when its force is drawn from within the individual.[94] But when religion is propped up by government, "it becomes almost as fragile as any temporal power."[95] He explained:

Alone, [religion] can hope for immortality; linked to ephemeral powers, it shares their fortune and often falls with the fleeting passions that sustain them.

Thus whenever a religion joins forces with political powers of any kind, the alliance is bound to be onerous for religion. It has no need of their help to live, and in serving them it may die.[96]

Religious freedom had existed in America since its founding, and Tocqueville determined that the nation's capacity for self-government actually developed as a byproduct of religious faith. He wrote, "[I]n America, it was religion that showed the way to enlightenment; it was respect for divine law that showed man the way to freedom."[97] Religion imbued in the American people certain moral restraints on conduct that inspired confidence in their ability to govern in liberty. Tocqueville observed that, "most of all, mores enabled them to establish and maintain the sovereignty of the people,"[98] and "the great severity of American mores is due primarily to religious beliefs."[99]

Religious values also served as an inherent check against the legislative majority in America. Tocqueville observed, "[E]ven as the law allows the American people to do anything and everything, there are some things that religion prevents them from imagining or forbids them to attempt."[100] He expounded upon these divine limitations on the majority, writing:

[Americans] in the United States value mores, respect beliefs, and recognize rights. They profess the opinion that insofar as a people is free, it must be moral, religious, and moderate. The name 'republic' is applied in the United States to the tranquil reign of the majority. Once the majority has had time to identify itself and confirm its existence, it becomes the common source of power. But the majority itself is not all-powerful. Standing above it in the moral realm are humanity, justice, and reason, and in the political realm, established rights.[101]

By imposing natural restraints on the majority, religion enabled liberty in accordance with Natural Law. Tocqueville decided that, "even if religion does not give Americans their taste for liberty, it does notably facilitate their use of that liberty."[102]

Tocqueville ultimately discovered a clear link between religion and liberty in America. He found that religion and liberty actually "advance in harmony and seem to support each other."[103] He explained:

> Religion looks upon civil liberty as a noble exercise of man's faculties, and on the world of politics as a realm intended by the Creator for the application of man's intelligence. Free and powerful in its own sphere and satisfied with the place ascribed to it, religion knows that its empire is more secure when it reigns through its own intrinsic strength and dominates the hearts of men without assistance.
>
> Liberty looks upon religion as its comrade in battle and victory, as the cradle of its infancy and divine source of its rights. It regards religion as the safeguard of mores, and mores as the guarantee of law and surety for its own duration.[104]

Recognizing the great importance of religion to American liberty, Tocqueville added, "Although religion in the United States never intervenes directly in government, it must be considered as the first of America's political institutions."[105]

The importance of this institution was well understood by the American people in that day. They regarded religion as a fundamental component of lasting liberty in America, just as the Founding Fathers had articulated in their time. Tocqueville wrote:

> I do not know whether all [Americans] have faith in their religion—for who can read the bottom of men's hearts?—but I am certain that they believe it to be necessary for the preservation of republican institutions. This opinion is not peculiar to a class of citizens or to a party, but it belongs to the whole nation and to every rank of society.[106]

To illustrate the depth of religious faith in America, Tocqueville discussed a case in which a New York county judge refused to accept the testimony of an atheist in court. The judge explained that, because of his expressed disbelief in God, "the witness had destroyed in advance any credibility that his testimony might possess."[107] Tocqueville cited the *New York Spectator* of August 23, 1831, which reported:

> The presiding judge remarked that he had not before been aware that there was a man living who did not believe in the existence

of God, that this belief constituted the sanction of all testimony in a court of justice, and that he knew of no case in a Christian country where a witness had been permitted to testify without such a belief.[108]

Tocqueville pointed out that "[t]he newspapers reported the incident without commentary," indicating that the judge's action was completely acceptable and ordinary in that day.[109]

Disbelief in God was the rare exception in America, and most people recognized that religious belief was vital to liberty. Given its importance, many Americans endeavored to spread the teachings of God throughout the land. Tocqueville recounted:

> I saw Americans form organizations to send ministers to the new states of the West to found schools and churches there. They were afraid that religion might be forgotten in the backwoods and that the people who settled there might not be as free as their forebears. I met wealthy New Englanders who left the places where they were born to lay the groundwork for Christianity and liberty on the banks of the Missouri or in the prairies of Illinois. In the United States, religious zeal never ceases to warm itself at patriotism's hearth. You might imagine that these people act as they do solely out of concern for the other life, but you would be wrong: eternity is only one of their concerns. If you were to question these missionaries of Christian civilization, you would be quite surprised to hear how frequently they speak of the goods of this world, and you would find politicians where you had thought there were only men of religion. "All the American republics are intimately associated," they would tell you. "If the republics of the West lapse into anarchy or succumb to despotism, the republican institutions now flourishing along the Atlantic seaboard would be in great danger. It is therefore in our interest that the new states should be religious, so that we may remain free."[110]

It was clear to Tocqueville that the American people did not practice their faith simply for individual salvation. They understood that religious practice actually sustained American liberty. Tocqueville wrote that "Americans so completely confound Christianity with liberty that it is almost impossible to induce them to think of one without the other."[111] He added that this was "by no means a sterile belief, a legacy of the past that lies moldering in the depths of the soul"—it was instead "a vital article of faith."[112]

Because Americans recognized the great value of religion to lasting liberty, they naturally treated it as a primary component of education. In fact, religious teaching was so fundamental in America, Tocqueville reported, that "[m]uch of education [was] entrusted to the clergy."[113] Religious instruction was just as important in the classroom as were lessons in history or American government. Tocqueville wrote:

> In New England, every citizen receives instruction in the elementary notions of human knowledge. He also learns the doctrines and proofs of his religion. He is made familiar with the history of his country and the principal features of the Constitution that governs it. In Connecticut and Massachusetts, one seldom encounters any man whose knowledge of these things is merely superficial, and anyone absolutely ignorant of them would be something of a phenomenon.[114]

Tocqueville became convinced that the unique blend of civics and morality in the classroom provided new generations of Americans with the tools necessary to extend their liberty into the future. He wrote, "There can be no doubt that the education of the people in the United States contributes powerfully to the perpetuation of the democratic republic. This will be so, I think, wherever the education that enlightens the mind is not divorced from the upbringing that regulates mores."[115] By developing both reason and virtue in the people, self-government becomes more lasting.

While Tocqueville lauded religions for nurturing people to be virtuous, he also cautioned them to refrain from venturing into the political realm of society. Religions, he wrote, should educate the people in the "ideas pertaining to God and human nature" without dictating political rules to society.[116] Religions "must carefully circumscribe the limits within which they claim to mold the human mind, and beyond those limits they should leave the mind entirely free to set its own course."[117] Tocqueville opined that religions which enter into the political arena—religions which do not confine themselves to man's spiritual duties to his fellow man— were more compatible with tyranny than liberty. He wrote:

> Mohammed professed to derive from heaven, and placed in the Koran, not only religious doctrines but also political maxims,

civil and criminal laws, and scientific theories. By contrast, the Gospels deal only in a general way with man's relation to God and men's relations with one another. Beyond that, they teach nothing and oblige one to believe in nothing. Among countless other reasons, that alone is enough to show why the first of these two religions cannot rule for long in ages of enlightenment and democracy, whereas the second is destined to reign in such times as in all others.[118]

In essence, if religion is to support liberty in society, then its force must be spiritual and not political.

Tocqueville observed that religion facilitated liberty in America because its force was exclusively spiritual—because the "American clergymen stay[ed] out of public affairs."[119] The American people practiced a number of faiths in their communities, yet each denomination limited itself to the spiritual realm. Tocqueville wrote of the various religious sects in America, "Each reveres the Creator in a different fashion, but all agree about man's duties to his fellow man. Each worships God in his own way, but all preach the same morality in God's name."[120]

To further illustrate the restraint of American religious teachings, Tocqueville described how the Catholic Church encouraged its members to independently discover political truth:

> The Catholic priests of America have divided the intellectual world into two parts: in one they have left revealed dogmas, to which they submit without discussion; in the other they have placed political truth, and this they believe God has left for man to investigate freely. Thus American Catholics are at once the most docile believers and the most independent citizens.[121]

As long as religion produced individuals like these, Tocqueville believed, liberty could have no better companion.

Tocqueville in fact singled out Catholics in *Democracy in America* as "constitut[ing] the most republican and democratic class in the United States," notwithstanding the similarities between the various religious sects in America.[122] He reasoned that Catholicism is "among those [Christian doctrines] most favorable to equality of conditions" because its "religious society consists of just two elements: the priest and the people. Only the priest stands above the faithful: below him, everyone is equal."[123]

And because the priest lacks any political power in America, the people "are left with conditions more equal than in any republic."[124] Tocqueville further observed that Catholics were not content with their equality in the church—they sought to extend this principle throughout society. He wrote that "no faith does more than the Catholic faith to encourage adepts to take the idea of equality of conditions and carry it over into the world of politics."[125] Given their inherent sense of equality and their inspired commitment to it, Tocqueville reasoned that Catholics were natural supporters of republican government and best embodied the republican spirit in America.

Despite his focus on the value of Catholicism, Tocqueville emphasized that liberty in America was not dependent upon the triumph of any one religion over others. Liberty in America was, and would always be, dependent upon the presence of any apolitical religion in society. Tocqueville wrote:

> Though it matters a great deal to each individual that his religion be true, this is not the case for society. Society has nothing to fear from the other life, and nothing to hope for, and what matters most to it is not so much that all citizens profess the true religion as that each citizen profess some religion.[126]

Society benefits from religion not only because it sustains liberty, but also because it conditions individuals to be mindful of the future in everything they do. Religion teaches the people that their actions today have consequences for the afterlife. It teaches them that the promise of eternal salvation cannot be attained easily, quickly, or by chance—individuals must make an enduring commitment to God to achieve that final aim. The great social benefit of this religious inspiration is that it carries over to other individual challenges in life. Tocqueville wrote that individuals who are so inspired understand "that wealth, fame, and power are the rewards for work; that great success comes to those who sustain the desire for it over a long period of time; and that nothing durable is acquired without effort."[127] Ultimately, religion produces a focused and industrious individual who has the capacity to positively contribute to society.

As religion weakens in individuals, however, their reasoned consideration about the future diminishes, much to the detriment of society. Tocqueville wrote, "As the light of faith dims . . . man's vision becomes more constricted and with each passing day the objectives of human action come to seem nearer."[128] Less concerned about the afterlife, individuals become more interested in momentary pleasures. They begin to seek instant gratification and comfort. Tocqueville continued:

> Once men stop worrying about what is to come when their lives are over, they lapse easily into that state of complete and brutish indifference to the future that is only too consistent with certain instincts of the human species. As soon as they lose the habit of situating their principal hopes in the long run, their natural inclination is to seek to satisfy their slightest desires without delay. The moment they despair of living for an eternity, they are inclined, it seems, to act as though they had but a single day's existence allotted to them.[129]

In a free society where faith and virtue decline, lawlessness grows, and so government naturally asserts itself. Yet the vision of republican government narrows just the same, for it mirrors the cares of society. James Madison wrote, "[W]hat is government itself but the greatest of all reflections on human nature?"[130] Aiming to satisfy the fleeting demands of the people, the government loses sight of its way into the future. Looming challenges go unnoticed, and productive opportunities are left untaken. Tocqueville wrote that such a myopic society can establish "nothing great or peaceful or durable."[131] While it may sustain itself for some time, a society with weakened religious faith signals its pending decline.

And when a free society has completely lost its religious faith, it will cease to be free. From a philosophical perspective, individuals who reject God as the source of life no longer hold a claim to natural rights of life, liberty, and property. In a Godless world, man is an accident of nature entitled to nothing and subject to earthly power. Tocqueville also argued that those who cannot reason—and determine that God exists—are mentally unprepared for liberty and consequently find solace in servitude. He wrote of such individuals, "[D]oubt takes hold of the highest regions of the intellect and half paralyzes all the others. Individuals become accustomed to making do with confused and fluctuating notions about the matters of greatest interest to themselves and their fellow men."[132] Unable to reason with confidence concerning important matters such as the existence and purpose of man, such individuals "defend their opinions badly or give them up altogether, and because they despair of resolving on their own the greatest problems with which human destiny confronts them, they cravenly cease to think about such things at all."[133] Tocqueville wrote that this kind of cowardly mentality "inevitably enervates the soul; it weakens the springs of the will and prepares citizens for servitude. Not only will citizens then allow their liberty to be taken from them; in many cases they surrender it voluntarily."[134] Ultimately, when individuals lose their faith, they lose their confidence in their being and they lose all direction in their lives. To compensate for such uncertainty and disarray, individuals naturally seek stability and order in servitude. Tocqueville wrote:

> When no authority exists in matters of religion, any more than in political matters, men soon become frightened in the face of unlimited independence. With everything in a perpetual state of agitation, they become anxious and fatigued. With the world of the intellect in universal flux, they want everything in the material realm, at least, to be firm and stable, and, unable to resume their former beliefs, they subject themselves to a master.[135]

Tocqueville was certain that man could never live in liberty without religion. He concluded, "I am inclined to think that if he has no faith, he must serve, and if he is free, he must believe."[136]

When Tocqueville first arrived in the United States, he never expected to find religion to be as influential as it was. Yet he soon discovered what the Founding Fathers well understood: that religion was central to lasting liberty in America. He learned that the vitality of religion in America served to fortify its republican institutions by cultivating reason and virtue in the people. Tocqueville wrote, "There is no better illustration of the usefulness and naturalness of religion, since the country where its influence is greatest today is also the country that is freest and most enlightened."[137]

The American people were religious, and they were also educated in the fundamental principles and practices of a government aimed to preserve their natural rights. Altogether, these teachings and practices sustained their liberty, and Tocqueville emphasized their importance in *Democracy in America*. He wrote:

> If, in the course of this work, I have failed to make the reader aware of the importance that I attach to the practical experience, habits, and opinions—in a word, to the mores—of the Americans in maintaining their laws, then I have failed to achieve the principal goal I set myself in writing it.[138]

It was not the greatness of government that made liberty possible in America, for government was merely an extension of the people. The United States became a beacon of liberty in the world in that day because its mores created a culture of independence, enlightenment, and charity. Liberty persisted in America because its people were educated, self-disciplined, and good.

American liberty was, and will always remain, a function of the wisdom and character of its people. It will forever depend on the people maintaining their mores.

4

ON POPULAR CONSTITUTIONALISM

In the United States, the people rule. All governing power is derived from them. When the American people in the founding era elected to institute a new government under the Constitution, they underscored their sovereign authority by declaring in the Preamble, "*We the People* . . . do ordain and establish this Constitution for the United States of America."[1] By the consent of the people, the federal government came into being—not to rule over the people, but to serve their will within the boundaries of the Constitution.

The Founding Fathers were well aware that the exact boundaries of the Constitution would be subject to dispute. They understood that interpretive questions over constitutional meaning might arise on occasion. James Madison explained that language itself—no matter how specific it may be—is inherently ineffective as a medium to convey true meaning. He wrote:

> The use of words is to express ideas. Perspicuity therefore requires not only that the ideas should be distinctly formed, but that they should be expressed by words distinctly and exclusively appropriate to them. But no language is so copious as to supply words and phrases for every complex idea, or so correct as not to include many equivocally denoting different ideas. Hence, it must happen, that however accurately objects may be discriminated in themselves, and however accurately the discrimination may be considered, the definition of them may be rendered inaccurate by the inaccuracy of the terms in which it is

delivered. And this unavoidable inaccuracy must be greater or less, according to the complexity and novelty of the objects defined.[2]

Because words are so imprecise and often carry multiple meanings, they may be misinterpreted. This is true for any document, including the Constitution. Thomas Jefferson said:

If [the Constitution] has bounds, they can be no others than the definitions of powers which that instrument gives. It specifies and delineates the operations permitted to the federal government, and gives all the powers necessary to carry these into execution. . . . Nothing is more likely than that their enumeration of powers is defective. This is the ordinary case of human works.[3]

To protect against interpretive error or abuse, the Founding Fathers stressed that the Constitution should always be construed with its original intent in mind, for the meaning of any law is best ascertained by its purpose. They drew from Blackstone, who explained that "the most universal and effectual way of discovering the true meaning of a law, when the words are dubious, is by considering the *reason* and *spirit* of it; or the cause which moved the legislator to enact it."[4] In a similar fashion, James Wilson declared, "The first and governing maxim in the interpretation of a statute is to discover the meaning of those who made it."[5] Thomas Jefferson also wrote, "The true key for the construction of everything doubtful in a law is the intention of the lawmakers. This is most safely gathered from the words, but may be sought also in extraneous circumstances provided they do not contradict the express words of the law."[6] Jefferson further emphasized the importance of original intent when construing the Constitution. He said that the Constitution ought to be interpreted "according to the safe and honest meaning contemplated by the plain understanding of the people of the United States *at the time of its adoption.*"[7] Jefferson later wrote:

On every question of construction, [let us] carry ourselves back to the time when the Constitution was adopted, recollect the spirit manifested in the debates, and instead of trying what meaning may be squeezed out of the text or invented against it, conform to the probable one in which it was passed. . . . Laws are made for men of ordinary understanding, and should, therefore, be construed by the ordinary rules of common sense. Their meaning is not to be sought for in metaphysical subtleties, which may make anything mean anything or nothing at pleasure.[8]

Madison similarly endorsed the use of original intent as the best way to construe constitutional meaning. He explained:

I entirely concur in the propriety of resorting to the sense in which the Constitution was accepted and ratified by the nation. In that sense alone it is the legitimate Constitution. And if that be not the guide in expounding it, there can be no security for a consistent and stable, more than for a faithful exercise of its powers. If the meaning of the text be sought in the changeable meaning of the words composing it, it is evident that the shapes and attributes of the government must partake of the changes to which the words and phrases of all living languages are constantly subject. What a metamorphosis would be produced in the code of law if all its ancient phraseology were to be taken in its modern sense.[9]

A faithful reading of the Constitution requires that its terms be interpreted not only according to their original intent, but also against the structural backdrop of the Constitution's foundation. The Constitution's limited design necessitates a narrow reading of federal power—a reading that is always biased against the enlargement of federal power. As previously discussed, the American people gave to the federal government only those powers that are expressly enumerated or implied in the Constitution, and they added the Ninth and Tenth Amendments to underscore those limitations on federal power—all power not delegated to the federal government is reserved to the people in their states. St. George Tucker explained that the intent behind these amendments was "to guard against [federal] encroachments on the powers of the several states . . . and of the people."[10] Given these manifest constraints, the Constitution must always be interpreted narrowly to protect against federal usurpation. Tucker wrote, "[T]he powers delegated to the federal government, are, in all cases, to receive the most strict construction that the instrument will bear, where the rights of a state or of the people, either collectively or individually, may be drawn in question."[11] Jefferson followed this rule as president. He explained in 1803:

> When an instrument admits two constructions, the one safe, the other dangerous, the one precise, the other indefinite, I prefer that which is safe and precise. I had rather ask an enlargement of power from the nation, where it found necessary, than to assume it by a construction which would make our powers boundless. Our peculiar security is in the possession of a written Constitution. Let us not make it a blank paper by construction.[12]

Notwithstanding this obligation to strictly construe federal powers according to the Constitution's original intent, many judges throughout American history have failed to do so—they have instead brazenly declared that constitutional law should not be anchored to such ancient intentions. As times and people change, their argument goes, so too should constitutional law. For example, Justice Felix Frankfurter in 1949 asserted that the Constitution's provisions were "purposefully left [imprecise] to gather meaning from experience."[13] Justice John Marshall Harlan also argued in 1961 that Supreme Court decisions should build on traditions that continue or have emerged since the Constitution was founded because "tradition is a living thing."[14]

Unrestrained by original intent, activist courts are free to twist constitutional meaning to achieve desired outcomes. Activist judges can effectively make new law by reading it into broad provisions of the Constitution.

By the Constitution's design, federal courts have no power to modify constitutional meaning—only the people themselves can act to change it. The Constitution's demanding amendment process supports its strict, original interpretation. Under Article V of the Constitution, amendments become valid only when ratified by three-fourths of the states, and they may be considered only when proposed by two-thirds of the states or both Houses of Congress.[15] When the American people who ratified the Constitution placed such a high burden on their own ability to change the Constitution, it defies reason to suggest that they would permit an unelected body of judges to more easily do the same by varying their interpretation over time. George Washington said in his Farewell Address that the Constitution "is sacredly obligatory upon all" until "changed by an explicit and authentic act of the whole people."[16] The Constitution's onerous amendment process exists because its original design and meaning was meant to be preserved.

Although judicial decrees made by activist courts are illegitimate, they are not altogether problematic, for the judicial power in any republic is so inherently weak. In fact, the judicial branch is ineffective without the assistance of the political branches of government. Judges must base their decisions on laws crafted by the legislature, and they must depend on executive power to enforce those judgments. Alexander Hamilton stressed the relative weakness of judicial power compared to the other branches when he wrote in The Federalist No. 78 that "the judiciary is beyond comparison the weakest of the three departments of power."[17] He further emphasized, quoting Montesquieu, that "'of the three powers [of government] above mentioned, the judiciary is next to nothing.'"[18]

Given the Court's inherent weakness, the Founding Fathers believed that any activist rulings would present an insignificant threat to popular sovereignty. As Hamilton explained, if judicial abuse were ever to occur in America, its impact would be limited:

> Particular misconstructions and contraventions of the will of the legislature [by the courts] may now and then happen; but they can never be so extensive as to amount to an inconvenience, or in any sensible degree to affect the order of the political system. This may be inferred with certainty, from the general nature of the judicial power, from the objects to which it relates, from the manner in which it is exercised, from its comparative weakness, and from its total incapacity to support its usurpations by force.[19]

The threat of judicial usurpation of power was such a phantom risk because the legislative and executive branches each could stand against excessive judicial power. Hamilton believed the Congress' impeachment power—which applies to judges and presidents alike—would deter activist judges from usurping legislative power. He wrote, "There never can be danger that the judges, by a series of deliberate usurpations on the authority of the legislature, would hazard the united resentment of the body entrusted with it, while this body was possessed of the means of punishing their presumption, by degrading them from their stations."[20] The president may also check judicial power by withholding his enforcement of unlawful judicial decrees or by exercising his pardon power to grant reprieves, amnesty, or commutation of sentences. Altogether, the Founding Fathers determined that these checks on the Court's limited power would adequately deter or cure any occasion of judicial abuse.

While judicial activism alone is relatively harmless, it can imperil liberty when the Court's overreaching rulings are not challenged—when even its most illegitimate decisions are accepted as the supreme law of the land. Judicial supremacy is the idea that the Court's constitutional interpretation is final and binding on all—on the other branches of government, on the states, and on the people. If judicial decisions are so obligatory, then the Constitution can mean whatever the Court says it means, and American liberty is subject to the mercy of the court. Judicial supremacy thus removes all checks on judicial power. It completely undermines popular sovereignty. It forces the nation to operate less like a republic and more like a judicial oligarchy.

The Founding Fathers never expected that judicial power would ever threaten American liberty in this way, but they soon discovered the great danger that it posed. In 1821, Thomas Jefferson described the federal judiciary as "an irresponsible body . . . working like gravity by night and by day, gaining a little today and a little tomorrow, and advancing its noiseless step like a thief over the field of jurisdiction, until all shall be usurped from the state, and the government of all be consolidated into one."[21] Jefferson further wrote in 1823:

> At the establishment of our constitutions, the judiciary bodies were supposed to be the most helpless and harmless members of the government. Experience, however, soon showed in what way they were to become the most dangerous: that the insufficiency of the means provided for their removal gave them a freehold and irresponsibility in office; that their decisions, seeming to concern individual suitors only, pass silent and unheeded by the public at large; that these decisions, nevertheless, become law by precedent, sapping, by little and little, the foundations of the Constitution, and working its change by construction, before anyone has perceived that the invisible and helpless worm has been busily employed in consuming its substance.[22]

This busy worm has since swallowed the Constitution whole. And it has done so without challenge, for the nation has long acquiesced to judicial supremacy. Few Americans today even dare to challenge the Court's presumed authority over constitutional meaning, and so every judicial decision is accepted without question as the law of the land. Consequently, the only unelected body of government is now free to impose its distinct constitutional interpretation on all—on the political branches of the federal government, on the states, and on the people. Constitutional meaning no longer reflects the sovereign will of the people; it is instead the illegitimate construct of the Court.

This was never meant to be. The American people did not fight for their freedom from one unelected and unrepresentative body just to let another rise in its place. They fought for independence to govern themselves in liberty for all time. They emphasized their sovereignty over government in the Constitution by identifying themselves as its origin, stating, "We the People of the United States . . . do ordain and establish this Constitution of the United States."[23]

As the supreme source of all governing authority in the nation, it is not the Court, but the people who must ultimately decide whether their representatives in office are faithfully serving the Constitution. In many cases, the Court's ruling on constitutionality may comport with their own, but if it does not, then the people are free to follow their own interpretation of the Constitution. The people, not unelected judges, are the final arbiters of constitutional meaning. It is their understanding of constitutionality that must always prevail, for popular sovereignty would mean nothing if their public servants in government can set the scope of federal authority— particularly those who are appointed to the Court.

The American people maintain their sovereignty over government— and they express their constitutional understanding on divisive issues—by their elective power over their representatives. Whenever the federal government exceeds its constitutional limits as determined by the people, they can elect new representatives who will more faithfully serve the Constitution according to their sense of constitutionality, not the Court's. Thomas Jefferson wrote, "When the legislative or executive functionaries act unconstitutionally, they are responsible to the people in their elective capacity."[24] Alexander Hamilton similarly stated in The Federalist No. 33:

> If the federal government should overpass the just bounds of its authority and make a tyrannical use of its powers, the people, whose creature it is, must appeal to the standard they have formed, and take such measures to redress the injury done to the Constitution as the exigency may suggest and prudence justify.[25]

James Madison also wrote in The Federalist No. 44:

> If it be asked, what is to be the consequence, in case the Congress shall misconstrue . . . the Constitution and exercise powers not warranted by its true meaning? In answer the same as if they should misconstrue or enlarge any other power vested in them . . . . In the first instance, the success of the usurpation will depend on the executive and judiciary departments, which are to expound and give effect to the legislative acts; and in a last resort a remedy must be obtained from the people, who can by the elections of more faithful representatives, annul the acts of the usurpers.[26]

Constitutional meaning is ultimately for the people to decide through their political representatives. The Supreme Court is obligated to provide its opinion when cases come before it, but its determination of constitutionality is only final as long as the people accept that it is. For in the United States, the people are sovereign, and the Constitution is theirs.

As the following examples illustrate, there have been a number of constitutional controversies throughout American history in which the Founding Fathers and subsequent generations renounced judicial supremacy. They are cases in which the people asserted their power over government by enforcing their constitutional interpretation through their political representatives. They are cases in which the people saved their republican government and its founding ideals from the forces of tyranny seeking to subvert it.

This journey through American history also reveals how modern judicial supremacy has since formed upon a fraudulent foundation. It shows how the Court has usurped the people's sovereignty by stealing their rightful place as the final arbiter of constitutional meaning.

While the present state of political subservience to the Court is undoubtedly discouraging, this historical survey in the end shows that the people have always been, and still are, the supreme authority over constitutional meaning; that the people still possess the power to reclaim their control of government; and that popular constitutionalism can prevail once again.

The Sedition Act of 1798

The Sedition Act of 1798 generated the first popular uprising against excessive federal power for an unmistakable violation of the Constitution. By passing the Sedition Act, Congress made it a federal crime to publish "false, scandalous, and malicious writing" against the government or its officials.[27] Congress, however, has no power whatsoever to regulate speech or the press. Under the Constitution's limited design, federal power extends only to those functions enumerated in the Constitution, and there is no mention of speech or press anywhere in Article I's list of legislative powers. Moreover, the First Amendment explicitly prohibits the federal government from restricting these freedoms, stating that "Congress shall make no law . . . abridging the freedom of speech, or of the press."[28] The people reserve all power over speech and the press for themselves to exercise in their state governments.

It may seem incredible that Congress would so brazenly usurp state power over speech and the press just seven years after the First Amendment was ratified. Yet defenders of the Sedition Act maintained that the Act did not impair any rights protected by the states. As long as the people did not falsely smear government officials, they claimed, their speech would remain unrestrained—truth would remain a valid defense to a seditious libel charge. Furthermore, proponents of the Sedition Act believed that the federal government had an inherent right to preserve itself by prosecuting those who undermined its legitimacy in the press. If the government were left open to frivolous attack, they asserted, then its reputation would diminish and its utility would decline.

Although these arguments in support of the Sedition Act were not entirely insensible, they failed to address the law's blatant disregard of the text of the Constitution—the American people had expressly restricted federal power in this arena. To those who supported and passed the Sedition Act, however, the Constitution was not so limiting. The first political party in the United States was actually organized around principles that were fundamentally opposed the spirit of the Constitution. Members of the new Federalist Party[*] advanced their governing philosophy of centralized power in spite of express constitutional restraints.

The Federalist Party was formed in 1792 by Alexander Hamilton, who was then serving as Secretary of the Treasury under President George Washington. Hamilton built the party out of a broad coalition of urban bankers and businessmen who supported his ambitious national economic policies. He later expanded that coalition, hoping to ensure that like-minded individuals would retain control over the national government. As the Federalist Party matured under his leadership, it ultimately came to embody his true political philosophy.

Hamilton in truth was a strong nationalist who had always favored centralized power in America. Thomas Jefferson described Hamilton as a "monarchist" who was "so bewitched and perverted by the British example" that he favored "a hereditary king with a House of Lords and Commons, corrupted to his will, and standing between him and the people."[29] Hamilton in fact viewed the Philadelphia Convention in 1787 as an opportunity to form a new government in America under aristocratic rule. Consistent with that aim, he proposed that senators and the chief executive rule for life under the Constitution.[30] Hamilton's proposals of course were soundly rejected.

Despite the new government's republican design, Hamilton remained a staunch advocate of the Constitution during the ratification debates for its increased power compared to the Articles of Confederation. In his view, even a limited national government was better than an impotent one. Hamilton's advocacy of the Constitution remained guarded, however.

---

[*] The Federalist Party is not to be confused with the group known as the Federalists, which existed only during the Constitution's ratification process between 1787 and 1788. These Federalists, which included the Founding Fathers, supported ratification while Anti-Federalists opposed the new Constitution. Both groups disbanded after ratification.

Many Americans at the time were fearful of national dominance under the new government, and so to avoid stoking those fears, Hamilton was forced to conceal his radical views about centralized power. Historian Bruce Miroff wrote that Hamilton "would go to great lengths to deny to the public what he had advocated in the Convention: the resemblance of the president to the British monarch."[31] So while Hamilton publicly assured that the Constitution created a limited and representative federal government in *The Federalist Papers*, he privately believed that a select group of social elites could best govern the nation.

Such aristocratic thinking prevailed in the new Federalist Party. The writings of prominent Federalist Nathanael Emmons particularly exemplified the kind of monarchical mindset that was fashionable among Federalists. He characterized citizens of republican government not as rulers over government, but instead as "subjects" who "promise submission to the powers that be."[32] The actual "rulers" of government, Emmons wrote, were those in political office.[33] He explained, "Every person is born the subject of some government and has no right . . . to refuse obedience to those who are in the peaceable possession of civil power."[34] Emmons continued:

> All subjects ought to obey their rulers for the sake of the public good. It is the duty of civil magistrates to seek the general welfare of the people; and so long as they diligently and faithfully attend upon this very thing, they justly merit the obedience and concurrence of every one of their subjects.[35]

Essentially, Federalists believed that government was without limit as long as it served the public interest. No law or constitutional restraint could impede any government that acted on behalf of the people. It is not surprising, then, that Federalists took an expansive view of the Constitution and their authority in power.

Many Americans had already become distrustful of the Federalists' apparent monarchical aims, and the Sedition Act further amplified their concerns. Aside from unconstitutionally expanding federal power over speech and the press, the Sedition Act also served as an incumbent protection plan—it effectively shielded incumbents, but not challengers, from political attack in the press. Because Federalists controlled the legislative and executive branches at the time the Sedition Act was passed, they were the clear beneficiaries of the law. Critics of the Act pointed to its sunset provision as proof that the Sedition Act was an example of pure self-dealing by the people's agents in government. The sunset provision stated that the Act would expire in early 1801—after the next elections were held. Thus, even if the Sedition Act failed to entrench Federalists in office, Federalists would never face the same obstacle in later attempts to regain power.

Aggravated by the Federalists' clear abuse of power under the Sedition Act, many Americans soon joined the political party that was formed to oppose them. Members of the new Republican Party—founded by Thomas Jefferson and James Madison—demanded that the federal government honor its limitations in the Constitution. They criticized legislative overreach under the Sedition Act, they criticized executive sanction of excessive federal power, and they also criticized judicial inaction for acquiescing to the Act's constitutionality.

Republican attacks on the judicial branch soon triggered an extended debate between the parties over the supremacy of judicial decisions.

Federalists argued that all federal laws are valid until declared unconstitutional by the Supreme Court, and once the Court decides a constitutional question, its decision is final and binding on the other branches of government, on the states, and on the people. Federalists generally believed that federal judges were more capable of preserving constitutional values than the political branches, because elected representatives were always subject to the fleeting passions of the people. Federalists also feared that popular assertions of constitutionality would create instability and uncertainty in constitutional law. And they pointed out that the people could always amend the Constitution if they disagreed with the Court's judgment on an issue, so the power to change the law would always remain in their hands.

Republicans, on the other hand, vehemently opposed the idea of judicial supremacy—they found irrational the Federalist belief that the Supreme Court was somehow more qualified to interpret the will of the people than the people themselves. William Cocke of Tennessee mocked the Federalist idea that "the nation [must] look up to these immaculate judges to protect their liberties; to protect the people against themselves."[36] As Republican Congressman John Randolph pointed out, the courts could not be regarded as protectors of liberty when they had so quickly condoned the diminution of individual liberty under the Sedition Act. He said, "[F]ar from protecting the liberties of the citizen, or the letter of the Constitution, you find [the courts] outdoing the legislature in zeal; pressing the common law of England to their service where the sedition law did not apply."[37]

Republicans certainly did not oppose judicial review, which is the courts' obligation to validate acts of the legislature. They recognized that the judicial branch, as an independent and coequal branch of government, must examine federal law and determine for itself whether a law conforms to the Constitution. James Madison acknowledged that the people might grow confident in the Court's opinions as a result of its natural function to decide cases. They might even regard the Court as the most qualified interpreter of the Constitution. Madison wrote:

> It is the judicial department in which questions of constitutionality, as well as of legality, generally find their ultimate discussion and operative decision: and the public deference to and confidence in the judgment of the body are peculiarly inspired by the qualities implied in its members; by the gravity and deliberations of their proceedings; and by the advantage their plurality gives them over the unity of the executive department, and their fewness over the multitudinous composition of the legislative department.
>
> Without losing sight, therefore, of the co-ordinate relations of the three departments to each other, it may always be expected that the judicial bench, when happily filled, will, for the reasons suggested, most engage the respect and reliance of the public as the surest expositor of the Constitution, as well as in questions within its cognizance concerning the boundaries between the several departments of the government as in those between the Union and its members.[38]

Although the purpose and practice of the Supreme Court might inspire greater public confidence in its *ability* to interpret the Constitution, the Court has no more *authority* to interpret the Constitution than the other two branches of government. Judicial opinions on constitutional questions are not supreme. The Founding Fathers created three separate and coequal branches of government, each possessing independent authority to fulfill its duties according to its own notion of constitutionality. This independence is lost if the political branches must obediently follow the constitutional interpretations of the judicial branch. Madison wrote:

> I beg to know, upon what principle it can be contended that any one department draws from the Constitution greater powers than another, in marking out the limits of the powers of the several departments. The Constitution is the charter of the people to the government; it specifies certain great powers as absolutely granted, and marks out the departments to exercise them. If the constitutional boundary of either be brought into question, I do not see that any one of these independent departments has more right than another to declare their sentiments on that point.[39]

Madison more explicitly proclaimed that the Supreme Court is not the final authority over constitutional meaning. He wrote:

> However true, therefore, it may be that the judicial department is, in all questions submitted to it by the forms of the Constitution, to decide in the last resort, this resort must necessarily be deemed the last in relation to the authorities of the other departments of the government; not in relation to the rights of the parties to the constitutional compact, from which the judicial as well as the other departments hold their delegated trusts. On any other hypothesis, the delegation of judicial power would annul the authority delegating it; and the concurrence of this department with the others in usurped powers might subvert forever, and beyond the possible reach of any rightful remedy, the very Constitution which all were instituted to preserve.[40]

Republican Congressman John Bacon of Massachusetts similarly rejected judicial supremacy by emphasizing the independence of each branch of government. He said:

> The judiciary are so far independent of the legislative and executive departments of the government, that these, neither jointly or separately, have a right to prescribe, direct, or control its decisions. It must judge for itself, otherwise the decisions made in that department would not be the decisions of that, but of some other department or body of men. The Constitution, and the laws made pursuant thereto, are the only rule by which the judiciary, in their official capacity, are to regulate their conduct.

The same is the case with other departments. The judiciary have no more right to prescribe, direct or control the acts of the other departments of the government, than the other departments of the government have to prescribe or direct those of the judiciary.[41]

Thomas Jefferson also believed that the authority to interpret the Constitution was not exclusive to the judicial branch. In a letter to Abigail Adams, he stressed the independence of each federal branch and warned that judicial supremacy left unchallenged would result in judicial tyranny. He wrote:

You seem to think it devolved on the judges to decide on the validity of the sedition law. But nothing in the Constitution has given them a right to decide for the executive, more than to the executive to decide for them. Both magastracies are equally independent in the sphere of action assigned to them. The judges, believing the law constitutional, had a right to pass a sentence of fine and imprisonment; because that power was placed in their hands by the Constitution. But the executive, believing the law to be unconstitutional, was bound to remit the execution of it; because that power has been confided to him by the Constitution. That instrument meant that its co-ordinate branches should be checks on each other. But the opinion which gives to the judges the right to decide what laws are constitutional, and what not, not only for themselves in their own sphere of action, but for the legislature and executive also, in their spheres, would make the judiciary a despotic branch.[42]

To guard against judicial tyranny, the people must be able to make use of their other agents in government to act on their behalf. There is no reason to fear the political branches—even if they give force to unconstitutional interpretations—because the people can always vote their members out of office. Jefferson wrote, "When the legislative or executive functionaries act unconstitutionally, they are responsible to the people in their elective capacity."[43] No similar check exists over judges, however, and Jefferson considered "their power the more dangerous as they are in office for life and not responsible, as the other functionaries are, to elective control."[44] Whenever disputes arise over the meaning of the Constitution, therefore, each branch of government has an independent obligation to the people to advance its faithful interpretation. Judges may give their opinions, and the political branches may act on theirs. In the end, the people decide the matter by expressing their will at the ballot box. Jefferson was certain that, for liberty to endure, the people—not judges— must always control constitutional questions. He said:

> I know of no safe depository of the ultimate powers of the society but the people themselves; and if we think them not enlightened enough to exercise their control with a wholesome discretion, the remedy is not to take it from them, but to inform their discretion by education. This is the true corrective of abuses of constitutional power.[45]

Republicans pursued this educational avenue of change in response to the Federalist Party's abuse of constitutional power under the Sedition Act. They rallied the people to formally denounce the Act by articulating its unconstitutionality in two state resolutions.

The Kentucky and Virginia Resolutions of 1798 and 1799 were passed in their respective state legislatures to inspire others to stand firm against the ensuing expansion of federal power. Thomas Jefferson, then serving as Vice President under John Adams, secretly drafted the Kentucky Resolutions, and James Madison drafted the Virginia Resolutions. The resolutions declared the Sedition Act unconstitutional for encroaching upon a power that belonged to the people in their states. Jefferson's Third Kentucky Resolution reads:

> [Because] no power over the freedom of religion, freedom of speech, or freedom of the press [was] delegated to the United States by the Constitution, nor prohibited by it to the states, all lawful powers respecting the same did of right remain, and were reserved to the states, or to the people; . . . [I]n addition to this general principle and express declaration, another and more special provision has been made by one of the amendments to the Constitution, which expressly declares, that "Congress shall make no law respecting an establishment of religion, or prohibiting the free exercise thereof, or abridging the freedom of speech, or of the press," . . . [L]ibels, falsehoods, and defamations, equally with heresy and false religion, are withheld from the cognizance of federal tribunals. . . . [T]herefore the [Sedition Act] . . . , which does abridge the freedom of the press, is not law, but is altogether void and of no effect.[46]

Madison's Fifth Virginia Resolution similarly states:

> [The Sedition Act is an] alarming infraction[] of the Constitution
> . . . [and] exercises . . . a power not delegated by the Constitution
> but on the contrary expressly and positively forbidden by one of
> the amendments thereto; a power which more than any other
> ought to produce universal alarm, because it is leveled against
> that right of freely examining public characters and measures,
> and of free communication among the people thereon, which has
> ever been justly deemed the only effectual guardian of every
> other right.[47]

Madison believed that the American republic would be in peril if the
Constitution's language could be as easily distorted or ignored as it was by
the Federalists in justifying the Sedition Act. If the Constitution could be
construed to grant legislative powers that are explicitly forbidden by its
text, he reasoned, then the text would be rendered meaningless and any
other usurpation of power could be similarly justified. Power may then
accrue in the federal government at the expense of individual liberty.
Madison wrote in the Fourth Virginia Resolution:

> [T]he [Virginia] General Assembly doth also express its deep
> regret that a sprit has in sundry instances been manifested by the
> federal   government,   to   enlarge   its   powers   by   forced
> constructions of the constitutional charter which defines them;
> and that indications have appeared of a design to expound certain
> general phrases . . . so as to destroy the meaning and effect of the
> particular enumeration, which necessarily explains and limits the
> general phrases, and so as to consolidate the states by degrees
> into one sovereignty, the obvious tendency and inevitable result
> of which would be to transform the present republican system of
> the   United   States   into   an   absolute,   or   at   best,   a   mixed
> monarchy.[48]

Madison, Jefferson, and other Republicans feared that the Sedition
Act, if tolerated, would pave the way toward tyranny in America. They
believed that the Federalists' casual disregard of the Constitution was
destructive to the republic, and so they called on the people to join them in
opposition to Federalists in power. Republicans united around the nation's
founding principles of federalism, limited government, and popular
sovereignty, and they trounced the Federalists in the elections of 1800.

Republicans took control of both Houses of Congress even though the Federalists previously had strong majorities in each. And Thomas Jefferson won the popular vote for president by nearly a 2-to-1 margin.

Once in office, President Jefferson quickly exercised his departmental independence—he governed according to his own interpretation of the Constitution. Believing that the Sedition Act was unconstitutional, he immediately pardoned all who were convicted under that law, and he ordered the federal government to remit all fines resulting from convictions. In the end, the Act that had aroused so many Americans against the expansion of federal power soon became a dead letter.

The change in governing philosophy that came to the federal government with the Republican Party was so great that the elections of 1800 soon became known as the "Revolution of 1800." Years later, Jefferson compared the significance of this election to the American Revolution. He wrote, "The Revolution of 1800 was as real a revolution in the principles of our government as that of 1776 was in its form; not effected, indeed, by the sword, as that, but by the rational and peaceable instrument of reform, the suffrage of the people."[49]

The Revolution of 1800 serves as an early example of how the American people reasserted their dominance over an invasive federal government. Limitations on federal power were restored in this case without resort to the Supreme Court. The people rejected the Sedition Act as unconstitutional on their own authoritative judgment—they did not wait for the Court to decide the matter for them. They elected a new body of representatives to forestall the Act's extension, and they chose a new president as their executive agent to carry out their will.

Republicans showed throughout this controversy that there was nothing to fear from popular constitutionalism. The people were not an unruly mob that was eager to revolt whenever they dissented from government action, as many Federalists had asserted. The new Republican Speaker of the House, Nathanial Macon, pointed to the Republicans' peaceful resistance to the plainly unconstitutional Sedition Act as proof that the people were more than capable of restraining themselves in the face of a controversial law. He said:

> Whenever we supposed the Constitution violated, did we talk of
> civil war? No, sir; we depended on elections as the main corner-
> stone of our safety; and supposed, whatever injury the state
> machine might receive from a violation of the Constitution, that
> at the next election the people would elect those that would
> repair the injury and set it right again; and this in my opinion
> ought to be the doctrine of us all; and when we differ about
> constitutional points, and the question shall be decided against
> us, we ought to consider it a temporary evil, remembering that
> the people possess the means of rectifying any error that may be
> committed by us.[50]

Republicans believed that the people, through the election process, could reasonably resolve any constitutional crisis. They argued that elected representatives must be able to execute the people's understanding of constitutionality for popular sovereignty to hold its meaning. They argued the popular constitutionalism must prevail in the United States. Madison wrote, "The authority of constitutions over governments, and of the sovereignty of the people over constitutions, are truths which are at all times necessary to be kept in mind."[51] Federalists abandoned these truths and consequently paid a heavy political price in the elections of 1800— they were forced out of political power and never got it back.

The Federalist Party ultimately withered away in time, but its aristocratic philosophy would live on, particularly in the judicial branch. One of the most influential Federalists in that day, John Marshall, became the Chief Justice of the Supreme Court in 1801, and he served until 1835. By his long tenure as Chief Justice, Marshall was able to incorporate his political philosophy into legal precedents that would shape judicial doctrine going forward. As evidence of Marshall's lasting influence, his opinion in *Marbury v. Madison*, which was decided in 1803, is still cited today by the Supreme Court as the case that laid the foundation for judicial supremacy in the law.

Marbury v. Madison

Before the Republicans took office after the Revolution of 1800, Federalists devised a plan to retain their influence over government. Unable to maintain control of the political branches, they sought to dominate to the judicial branch by enlarging its size and quickly filling its newly-created positions. So in their final lame-duck session of Congress, the Federalists passed the 1801 Judiciary Act, which created 16 new circuit court judgeships and 42 justices of the peace.[52] President Adams immediately nominated loyal Federalists to these posts, and the Senate quickly confirmed them. The Act earned the nickname "Midnight Judges Act" because it was rumored that Adams signed some of the appointments well into the night of his last day in office.

In addition to populating the judicial branch with Federalists, the Midnight Judges Act was designed to thwart President-elect Jefferson's ability to influence the Supreme Court. The Federalists included a provision in the Act that reduced the number of Supreme Court Justices from six to five. At the time, only five of the six seats on the Court were filled because Chief Justice Oliver Ellsworth had resigned in 1800, so a reduction in the Court's size should have been easy to achieve and uncontroversial. But the Act stated that the Court's reduction would take effect "after the *next* vacancy that shall happen" in the Court.[53] Adams was thus allowed to fill the sixth seat on the Court, and if a *subsequent* vacancy occurred, then Jefferson would be denied the same privilege of filling it. Adams ultimately nominated John Marshall, who was then serving as his Secretary of State, to assume the sixth seat on the Court as its Chief Justice. Marshall would serve as Chief Justice for 34 years.

The lawsuit *Marbury v. Madison* arose as a consequence of the Midnight Judges Act. William Marbury, a Federalist, was one of the newly-appointed justices of the peace for the District of Columbia. His commission was signed by President Adams and affixed with the seal of the United States, yet it was never delivered to him by the outgoing Secretary of State and new Chief Justice, John Marshall. When the incoming Secretary of State James Madison took office, he found the commission undelivered. Newly-elected President Thomas Jefferson ordered Madison to withhold the commission from Marbury, who then filed suit in the Supreme Court.

In the case, Marbury requested the Court to issue a writ of mandamus—an order compelling an officer to perform a ministerial duty. The writ of mandamus, if issued, would have compelled Madison to carry out his ministerial duty of delivering Marbury his commission so that he could assume his position as justice of the peace.

Marbury actually had little interest in serving as justice of the peace, but he followed through with his lawsuit because of the competing political interests at stake.[54] Federalists charged that President Jefferson was denying Marbury his private right to the position for political purposes. They believed that the new president had no discretion to withhold the commission when it was already signed by former President Adams. They argued that the Supreme Court would not be encroaching upon executive power by forcing Madison to deliver the commission. Republicans on the other hand complained that Federalists on the Court were attempting to subordinate executive power. They argued that the appointments did not vest until delivered by the Secretary of State, and no court could disturb the independent power of the executive branch to withhold final appointments. Republicans were so steadfast in their support of executive independence in this case because they so deeply despised the Midnight Judges Act for the tainted purpose for which it was passed—to entrench Federalists in the federal government. Jefferson characterized many of the midnight appointments as an "outrage on decency" and was determined to oppose such a partisan maneuver.[55] The lawsuit thus set up a heated confrontation between Federalists asserting judicial power and Republicans claiming executive independence.

Chief Justice Marshall was keenly aware that the Supreme Court's legitimacy was also at stake in *Marbury v. Madison*. Jefferson had already expressed his intention to treat many of the midnight appointments by Adams as illegal.[56] This announcement put the Court on notice that any decision in favor of Marbury might be ignored by the President. No matter how strong Marbury's legal position might have been, Marshall knew that a judgment in his favor would be meaningless without the cooperation of the executive branch. And if a president were to ignore a Supreme Court decision, then the Court's legitimacy would be greatly diminished.

Yet Marshall was unwilling to yield to political pressure. Republicans had attacked the federal courts for their role in enforcing the Sedition Act, and their assault intensified after they took office in 1801 and debated the repeal of the Midnight Judges Act.[57] Republicans repeatedly questioned and condemned the Supreme Court's authority, and the Federalist Chief Justice certainly took exception to these attacks.[58]

When Marshall finally spoke for the Court in his ruling, he ultimately avoided the controversy altogether—he declared that the Court lacked jurisdiction to even decide the matter. Marbury's remedy was still available, but he would have to seek it in a lower court, not the Supreme Court.

The outcome of the case pleased Jefferson, but the opinion did not. Although the Court did not compel Jefferson to deliver Marbury's commission, Marshall opined about the merits of the case in a manner that undermined Jefferson's executive authority. (Generally, when a court determines that it lacks jurisdiction over the parties or subject matter, it typically dismisses the case without reaching the substance of the dispute. A court without jurisdiction not only wastes its time by discussing the dispute at hand, but it also disserves the parties by passing judgment on the case when that judgment is not binding.) In his opinion, Marshall needlessly declared that Marbury's rights were violated and that mandamus would have been a proper remedy, if only the Court had the power to give it in this case.[59] He essentially indicated that Marbury would have prevailed had he filed his suit in the proper court.

Much of Marshall's opinion was not controversial. For instance, he wrote at length about the Court's power to review federal laws for their constitutionality—a power that few challenged at the time and is undisputed today.[60] Marshall also suggested that the political branches had the same duty to honor the Constitution instead of laws that contravene it. He wrote that "a law repugnant to the Constitution is void; and that courts, *as well as other departments*, are bound by that instrument."[61]

Marshall's opinion was so troublesome, however, because he insisted that the judicial branch had the power to compel other branches of government to act according to its interpretation of the Constitution. Marshall suggested that the Supreme Court is the only authoritative interpreter of the Constitution. He wrote, "It is emphatically the province and duty of the judicial department to say what the law is."[62] By itself, this statement lacks force if the other branches adhere to their independent interpretations of the Constitution. Yet Marshall hinted that courts could issue writs of mandamus to force the other branches to comply with its reading of the law—as a lower court could do for Marbury. Thus, if the political branches were to yield to such commands, then the courts would ultimately control the Constitution's meaning, and unelected judges could then reshape the supreme law of the land.

Jefferson believed that the people's liberty would be in great danger if they turned to the courts to resolve their constitutional controversies. He said, "To consider the judges as the ultimate arbiters of all constitutional questions [is] a very dangerous doctrine indeed, and one which would place us under the despotism of an oligarchy."[63] He wrote that the Constitution was not designed to be controlled by the judicial branch:

> [The Constitution] has more wisely made all the departments coequal and co–sovereign within themselves. If the legislature fails to pass laws for a census, for paying the judges and other officers of government, for establishing a militia, for naturalization as prescribed by the Constitution, or if they fail to meet in Congress, the judges cannot issue their mandamus to them; if the President fails to provide the place of a judge, to appoint other civil and military officers, to issue requisite commissions, the judges cannot force him.[64]

Jefferson understood that the people, and not judges, must hold their elected representatives accountable under the Constitution. In the case at hand, if the people disagreed with Jefferson's decision to withhold Marbury's commission, then they had the power to impeach him or oppose his reelection. By relying on judges to decide every constitutional question, the people ultimately surrender their liberty to the mercy of the unelected judicial branch, which can never be fully apolitical. Jefferson wrote:

> Our judges are as honest as other men and not more so. They have with others the same passions for party, for power, and the privilege of their corps. . . . [T]heir power [is] the more dangerous as they are in office for life and not responsible, as other functionaries are, to the elective control.[65]

If judges can wield complete control over constitutional meaning, Jefferson warned, then the Constitution "is a mere thing of wax in the hands of the judiciary, which they may twist and shape into any form they please."[66]

Despite his annoyance by *Marbury v. Madison*, Jefferson never had his executive independence tested by the Court—Marbury ended his legal challenge and never became a justice of the peace. Such a challenge to executive independence would have been a wasted effort anyway. Jefferson had the support of the people after the Revolution of 1800, and the people were not about to cede popular control over government to the judicial branch. Marshall's opinion that endorsed judicial supremacy was completely irrelevant to the people in that day, and it should have withered away with the Federalist Party. Yet it did not.

Marshall's opinion lived on as it became ensconced in a judicially-created body of constitutional law based on precedential development. Indeed, the Founding Fathers never intended the Constitution to be subject to common law reasoning, as if it were a legal code that could be refined by the courts. But courts by habit turned to precedent and ordinary legal interpretation to guide their decisions involving constitutional questions. What emerged, according to historian G. Edward White, was "a fusion in early-nineteenth-century American jurisprudence of a methodology by which common law rules were promulgated by courts and a methodology by which the text of the Constitution was interpreted."[67] Essentially, the Supreme Court treated decisions concerning constitutional questions the same as ordinary law—past rulings and judicial doctrine would direct future judicial reasoning. The significance of this development is that popularly-rejected Supreme Court opinions could reemerge in future cases as authoritative law.

Marshall's decision in *Marbury v. Madison* was such an opinion, and it soon reemerged in the 1807 treason case against Aaron Burr, much to the dismay of President Jefferson. In a letter to the U.S. prosecuting attorney, the president expressed his contempt for courts that referred to the *Marbury* decision as authoritative in any way. He wrote:

> I observe that the case of *Marbury v. Madison* has been cited, and I think it material to stop at the threshold the citing that case as authority and to have it denied to be law. 1. Because the judges, in the outset, disclaimed all [jurisdiction over] the case; although they then went on to say what would have been their

opinion had they had [jurisdiction over] it. This, then, was confessedly an extra-judicial opinion, and, as such, of no authority. . . . I have long wished for a proper occasion to have the gratuitous opinion in *Marbury v. Madison* brought before the public and denounced as not law; and I think the present a fortunate one, because it occupies such a place in the public attention. I should be glad, therefore, if, in noticing that case, you could take occasion to express the determination of the executive, that the doctrines of that case were given extra-judicially and against law, and that their reverse will be the rule of action within the executive.[68]

Jefferson rejected the *Marbury* decision because much of the opinion had no bearing on the Court's ultimate holding. He also discredited it because the decision ignored the political climate in which it was made. It ignored the widespread support for popular constitutionalism in the aftermath of the Revolution of 1800. It ignored the people's desire to limit federal power and protect individual liberty—not just from an aggressive legislature, but also from an unrestrained judiciary. If any future Court were to neglect that history when determining the opinion's precedential value, then the *Marbury* decision would come to stand for something that the people so fervently opposed: the idea that the Court's judgment reigned supreme over all.

The *Marbury* opinion carried little force at the time it was decided, but it has since had a lasting effect on the Supreme Court's role in constitutional controversies. Although Chief Justice Marshall avoided a direct confrontation with the president over the Court's control over constitutional meaning, he planted the argument for judicial supremacy in constitutional law that subsequent Courts exploited to their advantage.

Through the development of constitutional law, the Supreme Court institutionalized the law of precedents and other judicially-created doctrines of interpretation that elevated prior holdings as decisive readings of the Constitution. By wielding these judicial tools, the Court gradually transformed the Constitution from a laymen's document into a legal code. Constitutional law soon became so complex that only those individuals trained in the Court's doctrines could truly make sense of its reasoning. As Tocqueville pointed out in 1831, "there is nothing more obscure to the uninitiated, nothing less within their grasp, than a body of law based on precedent."[69]

So as the Supreme Court continued to "say what the law is" in its convoluted way, constitutional law became a teaching unto itself. Tocqueville observed that the "American man of law in some ways resembles an Egyptian priest. Like the priest, he is the sole interpreter of an occult body of knowledge."[70] And that body of knowledge, under judicial supremacy, is passed down from the Court. Thus, while the Federalists and their elitist governing philosophy were politically rejected by the people when *Marbury* was decided, a new kind of elitism later emerged in constitutional law: the Supreme Court would issue orders according to its reading of the Constitution and expect the people to obey.

It is important to keep in mind that constitutional law is merely a body of case law that the judicial branch relies on to guide *its* analysis of constitutional meaning. It is not to be confused with the Constitution itself. As the Founding Fathers asserted, each branch of government is independently bound by the Constitution, and no branch is supreme over the others. The Supreme Court is free to judge constitutionality by any method it desires, but that process and its decisions do not bind Congress or the president in deciding constitutionality on their own—they are not bound by judicially-crafted constitutional law.

Because each political branch may act on its own reading of the Constitution, it is ultimately the people who decide all constitutional questions by their elective power. And this kind of popular control over government is what the Founding Fathers had always envisioned for America. James Madison wrote in The Federalist No. 49 that interpretive disputes over the Constitution could not be resolved "without an appeal to the people themselves, who, as grantors of the commission, can alone declare its true meaning and enforce its observance."[71] He emphasized again in The Federalist No. 51, "A dependence on the people is no doubt the primary control on the government."[72] This trust in the people to control government—to subordinate it to their will in the Constitution—is the essence of popular sovereignty in America.

The National Bank

After the Revolution of 1800, Republicans in power had an opportunity to repeal another law that many Americans believed was unconstitutional: the Bank Bill of 1791, which established the First Bank of the United States. Unlike the Sedition Act, however, the Bank Bill was not manifestly unconstitutional, and the nation had already participated in a vigorous debate over the bank's legality when it was first proposed in 1790.

Supporters of the bank in 1790—led by Treasury Secretary Alexander Hamilton—asserted that the bank was justified under the Constitution's Necessary and Proper Clause in Article I, section 8, which states that Congress shall have the power "[t]o make all Laws which shall be necessary and proper for carrying into Execution the foregoing Powers, and all other Powers vested by this Constitution in the Government of the United States, or in any Department or Officer thereof."[73] Hamilton argued that chartering a bank was a necessary and proper means to carry out Congress' constitutional duties to issue currency and regulate commerce.

In stark contrast, opponents of the bank—led by Congressman James Madison, Secretary of State Thomas Jefferson, and Attorney General Edmund Randolph—argued that Congress could not establish a national bank because no such enumerated power exists in the Constitution. Jefferson underscored the federal government's limited powers when he gave his "Opinion Against the Constitutionality of the National Bank" in 1791. He wrote:

> I consider the foundation of the Constitution as laid on this ground: That "all powers not delegated to the United States, by the Constitution, nor prohibited by it to the States, are reserved to the States or to the people." [quoting a draft of what became the Tenth Amendment] To take a single step beyond the boundaries thus specially drawn around the powers of Congress, is to take possession of a boundless field of power, no longer susceptible of any definition.[74]

The bank's opponents rejected the notion that Necessary and Proper Clause expanded Congress's power in any way. They also feared that the federal government might justify other powers not enumerated in the

Constitution by this clause. For example, Jefferson reasoned that such an expansive authority "would [make the federal government's] discretion, and not the Constitution, the measure of its powers."[75]

These concerns over a broad reading of the Necessary and Proper Clause echoed the fears that many Americans had expressed in earlier debates during the Constitution's ratification. Americans were so wary of this clause because they recognized that it could be interpreted to sanction any exercise of federal power, much to the detriment of state power and individual liberty. The federal government would be entirely without limitation if it were allowed to justify any power by asserting its necessity or propriety.

Ironically, in an effort to allay these fears and persuade apprehensive Americans to ratify the Constitution, it was Alexander Hamilton who assured the people in The Federalist No. 33 that the Necessary and Proper Clause was "perfectly harmless."[76] According to Hamilton (before ratification), the Necessary and Proper Clause was merely intended to ensure that Congress could use its natural legislative means—passing laws—to implement its limited powers. He wrote that "the "*means* to execute a *legislative* power [are] *laws*. . . . [T]he proper means of executing such a power [are] *necessary* and *proper* laws."[77] Essentially, the clause simply stated the obvious function of legislative power and no more. Given the asserted insignificance of the Necessary and Proper Clause, Hamilton had "perfect confidence that the constitutional operation of the intended government would be precisely the same" if the clause were left out of the Constitution altogether.[78] Hamilton mused that this superfluous clause was included in the Constitution as added assurance that federal power would not be weakened by the states—that it would be able to function by the operation of federal law.[79]

Despite his assurances to the American people that the impact of the Necessary and Proper Clause would remain insignificant, Hamilton later advocated a broad reading of the same clause to justify what many considered to be an expanse of federal power under the Bank Bill. His advocacy proved to be effective. Although President George Washington was at first hesitant about signing the bill, he ultimately sided with

Hamilton, and the Bank Bill became law. The new national bank began operating in 1791 under a 20-year charter that was set to expire in 1811.

Because the constitutionality of the Bank Bill had been decided by the people once already, and perhaps because its constitutionality was such a close question, Republicans chose not to repeal the law when they came into power in 1801. They instead decided to let the law expire a decade later—Republicans defeated a bill to renew the bank's charter in 1811. So after operating for twenty years, the controversial First Bank of the United States at last closed its doors, but not for long.

Many Republicans had a change of heart over the necessity of a national bank after the War of 1812 had begun—the federal government had difficulty financing the war, and it had no means to control inflation. Although President James Madison had vetoed banking legislation passed by Congress in 1814, he later conceded that a bank was needed. So in 1816, Madison signed a new bank bill into law, and the Second Bank of the United States began operating under another 20-year charter.

Not only was the new bank regarded as a necessity for the United States. It was also favored by a nationalist faction within the Republican Party—a faction that was largely composed of former Federalists, whose party had effectively dissolved by this time. Nationalists had risen in influence because the main priority of the dominant Republican Party during and after the War of 1812 was to preserve national unity and strength. Proponents of centralized power thus urged other Republicans to reestablish the national bank as a means to further that end.

The common political purpose that existed in America during and after the war worked to the advantage of the Republican Party. With so little partisan conflict, the Republican Party maintained its control of the federal government for some time. In fact, when James Monroe succeeded Madison as president in 1817, he began to preside over what became known as the "era of good feelings" for its reprieve from partisan hostility. Monroe worked to sustain national unity for political advantage, and his efforts paid off—he ran unopposed for reelection in 1820.

Despite their great political dominance during this era, many Republicans grew frustrated with the party for compromising its fundamental principles along the way. Thomas Jefferson particularly lamented the rise of nationalism within his party—a trend that he attributed to Federalists bearing the Republican name. In a letter written in 1822, Jefferson distinguished true Republicans from Federalists seeking to consolidate power in the national government, and he expressed his hope that all Federalists—however they called themselves—would fail politically. He wrote:

> An opinion prevails that there is no longer any distinction, that the Republicans and Federalists are completely amalgamated, but it is not so. The amalgamation is of name only, not of principle. All indeed call themselves by the name of Republicans, because that of Federalists was extinguished in the battle of New Orleans [the final battle in the War of 1812]. But the truth is that finding that monarchy is a desperate wish in this country, they rally to the point which they think next best, a consolidated government. Their aim is now therefore to break down the rights reserved by the Constitution to the states as a bulwark against that consolidation, the fear of which produced the whole of the opposition to the Constitution at its birth. Hence new Republicans in Congress, preaching the doctrines of the old Federalists, and the new nicknames of "Ultras" and "Radicals." But, I trust, they will fail under the new, as the old name, and that the friends of the real Constitution and Union will prevail against consolidation, as they have done against monarchism. I scarcely know myself which is most to be deprecated, a consolidation, or dissolution of the states. The horrors of both are beyond the reach of human foresight.[80]

Unfortunately for Jefferson and other like-minded Republicans, the nationalist faction within the Republican Party continued to grow, and it emerged victorious in the 1824 presidential election. In that race, the lone party was unable to unite behind a single candidate in its nominating caucus, so four individuals ran for president—each representing a different faction of the party. Republicans who sought to limit federal power favored Andrew Jackson. Although he won a plurality of the electoral votes, a majority is needed to become president. And when no candidate achieves an electoral majority, the Constitution directs the House of Representatives to decide the election. The House subsequently voted for John Quincy Adams—a former Federalist who was often regarded as "a Federalist-in-Republican clothing" for his nationalist policies.[81]

Adams' election so irritated traditional Republicans that they soon began to organize against him. Led by Martin Van Buren, a new generation of Republicans worked to restore the party's original commitment to the Founding Fathers' limited design of federal power. Van Buren understood that the ideological differences between Federalist-Republicans and traditional Republicans were so irreconcilable that they could never mix in one party. He wrote:

> [Party divisions between Federalists and Republicans can] be ascribed to the struggle between the two opposing principles that have been in active operation in this country from the closing scenes of the revolutionary war to the present day—the one seeking to absorb, as far as practicable, all power from its legitimate sources, and to condense it in a single head. The other, an antagonist principle, laboring as assiduously to resist the encroachments and limit the extent of executive authority. The former has grown out of a deep and settled distrust of the people and of the states. The antagonist principle has its origin in a jealousy of power, justified by all human experience. . . . The former is essentially the monarchical, the latter the democratical spirit, of society.[82]

By focusing on these stark ideological divisions, Van Buren was able to unite various factions of the Republican Party behind Andrew Jackson in the 1828 presidential election. These factions continued to operate under the banner of the Republican Party, but because Federalists had so tarnished the Republican name, Jackson's supporters commonly referred to themselves as "Jackson Men" or Jacksonians.

Stark political differences between the candidates surfaced throughout the 1828 presidential campaign. John Quincy Adams continued to stand for a strong central government, justified by a broad interpretation of the Constitution.[83] He and his Secretary of State, Henry Clay, had organized their supporters under the new National Republican Party in 1825, and they strove to unite the diverse regions of the country through a nationally-financed internal-improvements plan.

Jackson, on the other hand, rejected such an extension of federal power. Throughout the campaign, he called on the states to restrain federal power. He said on one occasion:

The state governments hold in check the federal, and must ever hold it in check, and the virtue of the people supported by the sovereign states, must prevent consolidation, and will put down that corruption engendered by executive patronage, wielded, as it has been lately, by executive organs to perpetuate their own power; the result of the present struggle between the virtue of the people and executive patronage will test the stability of our government, and I for one do not despair of the republic.[84]

Jackson believed that federal power under Adams was not serving the people as much as it was serving the whimsical desires of those in government. He further argued that Adams' national plan for internal improvements infringed upon the rights of the states and diminished their power that is so vital to the nation's survival. He said:

That this was intended to be a government of limited and specific, and not general powers must be admitted by all, and it is our duty to preserve for it the character intended by its framers. If experience points out the necessity for an enlargement of these powers, let us apply for it to those whose benefit it is to be exercised, and not undermine the whole system by a resort to constructions. . . . The great mass of legislation relating to our internal affairs was intended to be left where the federal convention found it—in the state governments. Nothing is clearer, in my view, than that we are chiefly indebted for the success of the Constitution under which we are now acting to the watchful and auxiliary operation of the state authorities. This is not the reflection of a day, but belongs to the most deeply rooted convictions of my mind. I cannot, therefore, too strongly or too earnestly, for my own sense of importance, warn you against all encroachments upon the legitimate share of state sovereignty. Sustained by its healthful and invigorating influence the federal system can never fail.[85]

Jackson recognized that liberty in America would not be secure if federal power were allowed to dominate over the states. The lesson of the Sedition Act of 1798 was not forgotten. Just as Jeffersonian Republicans stood against consolidated power then, "Jackson Men" invoked the "Spirit of '98" to rally the nation to return to its republican principles.[86]

The American people responded enthusiastically to this call for political change. Jackson soundly defeated Adams in the 1828 election, taking 56 percent of the popular vote and winning the electoral vote by a wide (more than 2-to-1) margin.

Although the national bank was little mentioned in the 1828 campaign, it received greater scrutiny after the election, for Jackson suspected it of colluding with his political opponents.[87] These suspicions of corruption were later confirmed when the bank's president extended him a special political opportunity. In exchange for an early renewal of the bank's charter, which was due to expire in 1836, the bank offered to assume the country's national debt to enable its full discharge before the end of Jackson's first term in office—an outcome that would have helped his bid for reelection.[88] But Jackson rejected the deal and became even more outspoken against the bank.

In his first State of the Union address, Jackson began arguing against an extension of the bank's charter even though it was not up for renewal for another seven years. He stated, "Both the constitutionality and the expediency of the law creating this bank are well questioned by a large proportion of our fellow citizens."[89] Jackson was not opposed to a national bank entirely. But he would only accept a bank that avoided the "constitutional difficulties" that characterized the current charter.[90] Specifically, Jackson believed that the existing bank was unconstitutional in its present form because Congress had no enumerated power under the Constitution to charter private corporations and exempt them from state taxation.

Jackson's argument against the bank was familiar, for it was the same argument that the State of Maryland made before the Supreme Court a decade earlier. Maryland had challenged the constitutionality of the national bank in *McCulloch v. Maryland* (1819) by asserting that the Constitution's silence on the subject of banks precluded the federal government from establishing such an entity. In essence, Congress could not charter a bank without a specific, enumerated grant of power in the Constitution.

Maryland's argument was unpersuasive in that case, however. The Supreme Court, with Federalist John Marshall still presiding as Chief Justice, upheld the constitutionality of the national bank. In his judicial decision, Marshall first suggested that the bank's history of legal sanction weighed in favor of its constitutionality. No matter what the Constitution says (or does not say), Marshall wrote that the practice of the federal government should receive "considerable" precedential value when determining constitutionality.[91]

Marshall further argued that Congress has an implied power to charter a national bank under the Necessary and Proper Clause. He wrote that Congress is free to implement all appropriate means—that it may pass all "necessary and proper" laws—that are intended to achieve certain constitutional ends. He stated, "Let the end be legitimate, let it be within the scope of the Constitution, and all means which are appropriate, which are plainly adapted to that end, which are not prohibited, but consist with the letter and spirit of the Constitution, are constitutional."[92] Because Congress was granted enumerated powers to lay and collect taxes, to borrow money, and to regulate commerce, Marshall decided that Congress could also charter a bank if it determined that such action was an appropriate means to fulfill those legitimate ends. And Marshall emphasized that Congress may choose whatever means that it prefers to fulfill those ends. He wrote, "To employ the means necessary to an end, is generally understood as employing *any means* calculated to produce the end."[93] Thus, as long as Congress could tie any federal action to some legitimate enumerated power, then the Supreme Court would have little reason to question its constitutionality.

Marshall's reading of the Necessary and Proper Clause was quite different from the interpretation that Hamilton gave in 1788 to assure all Americans of its insignificance—that it was "perfectly harmless."[94] Given the great concern that many Americans had over this clause during the ratification debates, Marshall should have recognized that the people did not intend to cede to Congress the unbridled legislative power that his opinion effectively granted it. Unmistakably, a power to employ unlimited means toward even the most limited end is still an unlimited power. As Madison explained in the Virginia Report of 1800, there is no difference "whether unlimited powers be exercised under the name unlimited powers, or be exercised under the name of unlimited means of carrying into execution limited powers."[95] Soon after Marshall's judgment was handed down, Republican Spencer Roane similarly wrote in the *Richmond*

Enquirer, "That man must be a deplorable idiot who does not see that there is no earthly difference between an *unlimited* grant of power, and a grant limited in its terms, but accompanied with *unlimited* means of carrying it into execution."[96]

Regardless of the perceived illogical reasoning in Marshall's opinion, the decision itself conferred some legitimacy on the national bank, further complicating Andrew Jackson's efforts in his first term to persuade others of its unconstitutionality. Nevertheless, he pressed on with his campaign against the bank. In his 1830 and 1831 State of the Union addresses to Congress, Jackson repeated his opposition to the bank as chartered, and he proposed in its stead an alternative that he thought would pass the test of constitutionality.[97] He recommended that a division of the Treasury Department replace the private bank and execute fewer financial functions.[98]

Congress responded to Jackson's request for new bank legislation in 1832, but the new bill merely extended the existing charter with few modifications.[99] Advocates of the national bank gambled that Jackson would not dare to veto the bill during an election year and risk losing voters who supported the bank, but Jackson surprised his opponents. He rejected the new banking bill in an unabashedly confrontational fashion and made the debate over the national bank the central issue in the 1832 election.

In his Bank Veto Message of July 10, 1832, President Jackson attacked the bank's asserted legitimacy and he discredited the Supreme Court's opinion in *McCulloch v. Maryland*. Jackson specifically criticized the Court's reliance on precedent as a basis to determine the bank's constitutionality. He wrote, "Mere precedent is a dangerous source of authority, and should not be regarded as deciding questions of constitutional power except where the acquiescence of the people and the states can be considered as well settled."[100] Jackson believed that the bank's constitutionality was far from settled, given that Congress had rejected the bank as often as it had approved it.[101] Precedent, therefore, could not be determinative of the bank's constitutionality.

Jackson also pointed out that the Supreme Court in *McCulloch v. Maryland* never actually "decided that all of the features of this corporation [were] compatible with the Constitution."[102] Although it articulated a broad enough reading of the Necessary and Proper Clause to justify a national bank, the Court actually deferred to Congress the responsibility to determine constitutionality—whether the establishment of the bank was necessary and proper. The Court had written:

> [W]here the law is not prohibited [by the Constitution], and is really calculated to effect any of the objects entrusted to the government, to undertake here to inquire into the degree of its necessity, would be to pass the line which circumscribes the judicial department, and to tread on legislative ground. This court disclaims all pretensions to such a power.[103]

Given the president's role in the legislative process to veto or sign a bill into law, Jackson accordingly interpreted the Supreme Court's decision as one that deferred to both political branches the authority to determine the bank's constitutionality. He wrote in his Veto Message:

> Under the decision of the Supreme Court, therefore, it is the exclusive province of Congress *and the President* to decide whether the particular features of this act are necessary and proper in order to enable the bank to perform conveniently and efficiently the public duties assigned to it as a fiscal agent, and therefore constitutional, or unnecessary and improper, and therefore unconstitutional.[104]

Jackson essentially reiterated what the Founding Fathers had earlier maintained: that each branch of the federal government had an independent duty to uphold the Constitution according to its own understanding of constitutionality. Jackson further assailed the idea that the political branches were beholden to the constitutional construction of the Court. He wrote of judicial supremacy:

> If the opinion of the Supreme Court covered the whole ground of this act, it ought not to control the coordinate authorities of this Government. The Congress, the Executive, and the Court must each for itself be guided by its own opinion of the Constitution. Each public officer who takes an oath to support the Constitution swears that he will support it as he understands it, and not as it is understood by others. It is as much the duty of the House of Representatives, of the Senate, and of the President to decide upon the constitutionality of any bill or resolution which may be

presented to them for passage or approval as it is of the supreme
judges when it may be brought before them for judicial decision.
The opinion of the judges has no more authority over Congress
than the opinion of Congress has over the judges, and on that
point the President is independent of both. The authority of the
Supreme Court must not, therefore, be permitted to control the
Congress or the Executive when acting in their legislative
capacities, but to have only such influence as the force of their
reasoning may deserve.[105]

Jackson's Veto Message inspired a vigorous debate in the Senate over
the finality of Supreme Court decisions. Senator Daniel Webster and other
advocates of judicial supremacy naturally denounced Jackson's Message
as reckless and unruly. In response, Senator Hugh White made the case for
popular constitutionalism in a speech that Jackson repeatedly cited for best
representing his administration's position on the issue.[106] White said:

> The honorable Senator [Webster] argues that the Constitution
> has constituted the Supreme Court a tribunal to decide great
> constitutional questions . . . and that when they have done so, the
> question is put at rest, and every other department of the
> government must acquiesce. This doctrine I deny. . . . [A]s an
> authority, [the Supreme Court] does not bind either the Congress
> or the President of the United States. If either of these co-
> ordinate departments is afterwards called upon to perform an
> official act, and conscientiously believes the performance of that
> act will be a violation of the Constitution, they are not bound to
> perform it, but, on the contrary, are as much at liberty to decline
> acting as if no such decision had been made. . . . If different
> interpretations are put upon the Constitution by the different
> departments, the people is the tribunal to settle the dispute. Each
> of the departments is the agent of the people, doing their
> business according to the powers conferred; and where there is a
> disagreement as to the extent of these powers, the people
> themselves, through the ballot-boxes, must settle it.[107]

Martin Van Buren later remarked that White's response—and
Jackson's position—was "the true view of the Constitution. . . . It [was]
one which was universally acquiesced in at the formation of the
government."[108] What the Founding Fathers proposed and the Constitution
supports, Van Buren wrote, is that the three branches of government "are

coordinate and independent of each other"—that they each have a duty "to judge for themselves in respect to the authority and requirements of the Constitution, without being controlled or interfered with by their co-departments."[109] He also emphasized that the people ultimately decide matters of constitutionally by their control over their representatives. Van Buren continued:

> It was upon [electorally accountable officials] that the entire political power of the federal government was intended to be conferred, and [it was] to the limited tenure by which they held their offices and to their direct responsibility to the people that the latter have always looked for the means to control their action. It is upon this swift and certain responsibility they have hitherto relied for their ability to bring the government back, without great delay, to the republican track designed for it by the Constitution, whenever it might be made to depart from it through the infidelity of their representatives.[110]

Van Buren showed that the Founding Fathers manifestly objected to the idea that a single branch of government was ever intended to dominate the others. He referred to The Federalist No. 48, in which Madison wrote, "'It is equally evident that [none of the three branches] ought to possess, directly or indirectly, an overruling influence over the others in the administration of their respective powers.'"[111] He again quoted Madison, who wrote in The Federalist No. 49, "'The several departments being perfectly coordinate by the terms of their common commission, neither of them, it is evident, can pretend to an exclusive or superior right of settling the boundaries between their respective powers.'"[112] Van Buren also drew attention to Hamilton's assurances in The Federalist Nos. 78 and 81 that the judicial power would remain weak. He stated:

> In Nos. 78 and 81, General Hamilton, admitting that "there is no liberty where the power of judging be not separated from the legislative and executive powers," shows at great length the comparative weakness of the judicial power, and the very slight probability that "the general liberty of the people can ever be endangered by that quarter."[113]

The Founding Fathers never intended the Constitution to empower one branch of government—especially the judicial branch—with a commanding authority over the other branches by its control of constitutional meaning. Van Buren asserted, "The provisions of the Constitution will be searched in vain for any which indicate a design on the part of its framers to give to one of the departments power to control the action of another in respect to its departmental duties under that instrument."[114]

Van Buren further reasoned that judicial supremacy could not have been intended by the Founding Fathers because it would so absurdly bind executive power. He wrote that the Constitution imposes on the president the "especial duty to take an oath to preserve and uphold the Constitution and prevent its violation."[115] Given this duty, Van Buren explained that the Constitution never could have been "intended to deny to him the right to withhold his assent from a [law] which he might conscientiously believe would [be unconstitutional], and to impose on him the necessity of outraging his conscience, by making himself a party to such a violation."[116] Such an absurd requirement imposed by the notion of judicial supremacy would effectively transform executive power into a blind ministerial duty. Van Buren was certain that the Constitution was not so ineptly designed. He wrote, "The Constitution, which was framed by great men, the form of which has been so much and so justly admired, is not so imperfect nor subject to such a reproach."[117]

Van Buren's knowledge of American history gave him confidence that judicial supremacy had no basis in the Constitution. He wrote, "The deeper the subject is looked into, the more apparent to all *bona fide* searchers for truth will become the fallacy of the principle which claims for the Supreme Court controlling power over the other departments in respect to constitutional questions."[118] Judicial supremacy was wholly incompatible with the Founding Fathers' design of a constitutional republic where the people rule over government. To place the judicial branch in control over all constitutional questions, Van Buren declared, "is nothing less than to divest the government of its republican features and to substitute in its place the control of an irresponsible judicial oligarchy—to make the Constitution a lie."[119]

Andrew Jackson shared the same understanding of the Constitution's design, and he endeavored to keep his presidential oath to preserve it. He so resolutely stood against judicial supremacy because he knew that the Supreme Court's loose interpretation of the Necessary and Proper Clause in *McCulloch v. Maryland* completely undermined the Founding Fathers' design of the federal government. Acceptance of the Court's holding that Congress could exercise unlimited means to carry out its constitutional ends would effectively transform the federal government's few and defined powers into an immeasurably broad authority over the states and the people. Jackson knew this was never intended, and he recognized that American liberty would be threatened by this kind of consolidated power. As he explained in his Bank Veto Message, the nation's freedom and vitality would always depend on decentralized power:

> Nor is our government to be maintained or our union preserved by invasions of the rights and powers of the several states. In thus attempting to make our general government strong we make it weak. Its true strength consists in leaving individuals and states as much as possible to themselves—in making itself felt, not in its power, but in its beneficence; not in its control, but in its protection; not in binding the states more closely to the center, but leaving each to move unobstructed in its proper orbit.[120]

Jackson's Bank Veto Message was not just an opportunity for him to disapprove of the Bank Bill or to lash out at the Supreme Court. Above all, it served as an appeal to the American people to support his constitutional understanding of the scope of federal power. Just as the Kentucky and Virginia Resolutions framed the 1800 presidential election, Jackson's Veto Message identified the key constitutional issues that the American people were to resolve in the 1832 election. And just as the American people rallied behind the Republican candidate in 1800, they favored the true Republican once again in 1832. (Jackson officially ran again as a Republican and received his nomination at the 1832 Republican Convention in Baltimore. But to differentiate themselves from the National Republicans, many traditional Republicans, or "Jackson Men," began referring to their party as the "Democratic Party," which later became the party's official name.[121]) Jackson won 219 of the 286 total electoral votes, crushing his opponent, Henry Clay of the National Republican Party.

Emboldened by his victory, Jackson used his electoral mandate to weaken the national bank. Even though the bank could still legally operate until 1836, Jackson withdrew all of the federal government's deposits in 1833 and placed them in various state-chartered banks.[122] (Jackson also removed his Treasury Secretary from office for protesting the withdrawal.[123]) By these actions, the operations of the national bank had effectively come to an end.

Opponents of the president were expectedly furious, but the American people continued to side with Jackson for his actions against the bank and his efforts to restrain federal dominance. The National Republican Party— which had reorganized as the Whig Party to, ironically, denote its opposition to Jackson's alleged kingly rule—formally censured Jackson in the Senate in 1834. But in the elections of 1836, the American people voted Jackson's newly-labeled Democratic Party into the majority in the Senate, and his censure was soon after expunged from the record.[124]

Moreover, the people made no attempt to renew the national bank's charter when it officially expired in 1836. They elected Martin Van Buren as president later that year, and he honored their continuing demand to limit federal power. In fact, the government operated without a national bank for the next 77 years, until President Woodrow Wilson signed into law the Federal Reserve Act of 1913, which established the central banking system that is still in operation today.

The controversy over the national bank in the 1830s ultimately stands for a period of American history in which popular constitutionalism prevailed. At a time when the nation was drifting toward nationalism, the American people renewed their founding principles and enforced the Constitution's limitations on federal power. Despite the national bank's prior formation and despite the Supreme Court's sanction of its establishment, the American people proved that they were not beholden to precedent, nor were they bound by the decision of the Court. By their rejection of the national bank, the American people affirmed their right to settle all constitutional controversies. They demonstrated their sovereign authority over government.

Slavery and Dred Scott v. Sandford

Decades later, popular constitutionalism prevailed once again in the nation's great controversy over slavery. In the late 1850's, divisions intensified over the spread of slavery in America as settlers populated its western territories. Slave-owners naturally sought to expand this wretched practice while abolitionists tried to stop its spread. What so exacerbated this popular divide, however, was the Supreme Court's attempt to bring finality to the debate. The Court's 1857 ruling in *Dred Scott v. Sandford* paved the way for slavery's expansion across the nation and completely undermined the efforts of those seeking to contain it. Strongly dissatisfied with the Court's decision, the ruling majority in America mobilized politically against it. In 1860, they elected a president who outright ignored the Court's opinion and instead implemented the people's constitutional understanding. In the end, the judicial decision that would have enslaved a people forever was emphatically overturned by the people, and the nation's founding principles were made universal at last.

The controversy over the expansion of slavery in the 1850's was such a galvanizing issue at the time that it entirely reshaped the political landscape. The nationalist Whig Party became divided over slavery and dissolved in 1856. The American Party, which had formed in the mid-1840s around immigration and naturalization concerns, also dissolved in 1856 due to divisions over slavery. The two remaining major parties of that day—the Democratic Party and Republican Party—consequently grew larger, standing on opposite sides of the slavery issue.

The Democratic Party was openly permissive of slavery's expansion in the western territories, mainly because slave-owners in the South comprised the base of the party. Southern Democrats clearly had an interest in the spread of slavery, and as they grew more agitated by the crescendo of cries for complete abolition, Northern Democrats increasingly tolerated slavery's expanse to appease them, hoping to avert civil war. Democrats ultimately passed the controversial Kansas-Nebraska Act of 1854 in an attempt to deflect the looming crisis. Designed by Democratic Senator Stephen Douglas of Illinois, the Act let settlers in the West decide whether or not they wanted to sanction the practice of slavery in their new state constitutions upon admission to the Union. Democrats effectively ignored the evil of slavery by deferring to the preferences of others.

The newly restored Republican Party, on the other hand, stanchly opposed the expansion of slavery. Reconstituted in 1854, the Republican Party brought together a variety of discordant interest groups whose members ultimately united on the containment of slavery and the enduring principles of the Declaration of Independence. Abraham Lincoln, who was instrumental in shaping the Republican Party, said in 1856, "Let us, in building our new party, make our cornerstone the Declaration of Independence; let us build on this rock, and the gates of hell shall not prevail against us."[125] Just as the Founding Fathers had based their independence from British oppression on Natural Law principles, the Republicans in the 1850s grounded their opposition to the spread of slavery on the same ideals. They declared in their party platform of 1856:

> That, with our Republican fathers, we hold it to be a self-evident truth, that all men are endowed with the inalienable right to life, liberty, and the pursuit of happiness, and that the primary object and ulterior design of our federal government were to secure these rights to all persons under its exclusive jurisdiction.[126]

The Declaration of Independence of course proclaimed that "all men are created equal, that they are endowed by their Creator with certain unalienable rights, that among these are life, liberty, and property."[127] While Democrats like Stephen Douglas suggested that this phrase was meant to apply only to "the white race alone, and not to the African," Republicans understood that its application was always intended to be universal.[128]

Although the Founding Fathers were unable to end slavery in their day, most of them—even many southerners—wished to see the practice discontinued forever in America. For example, Benjamin Franklin observed in 1773 that "a disposition to abolish slavery prevails in North America."[129] George Washington also wrote that "there is not a man living who wishes more sincerely than I do to see a plan adopted for the abolition of [slavery]."[130]

Natural Law philosophy, which prevailed during the revolutionary period, inspired an awakening to liberty for all, and the Founding Fathers especially sought to abolish slavery in accordance with those principles. Liberty and equality were gifts from God that no earthly power could unjustly deny. Nobody was born into servitude. As Thomas Jefferson wrote, "Under the Law of Nature, *all* men are born free."[131] Nature's God, wrote Luther Martin, "is equally Lord of all and [] views with equal eye the poor African slave and his American master."[132] Benjamin Rush similarly wrote that slavery is a "usurpation of the prerogative of the Great Sovereign of the universe who has solemnly claimed an exclusive property in the souls of men."[133]

The Founding Fathers' commitment to the eradication of slavery in America is best exemplified by the intentions of Henry Laurens, who served as the Fifth President of the Continental Congress. Laurens was a South Carolinian who once ran the largest slave-trading house in North America. He nevertheless sought to free his slaves as a matter of principle, despite the great obstacles and financial losses he would face in doing so. In a letter to his son in August 1776, Laurens wrote:

> You know, my dear son, I abhor slavery. I was born in a country where slavery had been established by British kings and parliaments, as well as by the laws of that country, ages before my existence. . . . In former days, there was no combating the prejudices of men supported by interest; the day, I hope is approaching, when, from principles of gratitude as well as justice, every man will strive to be foremost in showing his readiness to comply with the golden rule ["do unto others as you would have them do unto you," Matthew 7:12]. Not less than twenty thousand pounds sterling would all my Negroes produce, if sold at public auction tomorrow. I am not the man who enslaved them; they are indebted to Englishmen for that favor: nevertheless, I am devising means for manumitting many of them, and for cutting off the entail of slavery. Great powers oppose me,—the laws and customs of my country, my own and the avarice of my countrymen. What will my children say if I deprive them of so much estate? These are difficulties, but not insuperable. I will do as much as I can in my time, and leave the rest to a better hand.[134]

Notwithstanding such principled opposition to slavery, the Founding Fathers knew that abolition was impossible as long as the nation remained under British rule. As Laurens pointed out, the British Empire introduced and sustained slavery in America much to the disdain of the Founding

Fathers. George Mason also complained of this fact at the Constitutional Convention in Philadelphia. He said, "This infernal traffic originated in the avarice of British merchants. The British Government constantly checked the attempts of Virginia to put a stop to it."[135]

Because the British Government originated and supported slavery in America for so long, it soon became rooted in American traditions wherever it existed, impacting regional culture, law, and economic activity.[136] As time passed, slavery expanded in many regions—largely unchallenged because it had become such a societal norm. John Jay acknowledged this custom in a letter to an anti-slavery society in 1788. He wrote, "Prior to the great Revolution, the great majority . . . of our people had been so long accustomed to the practice and convenience of having slaves that very few among them even doubted the propriety and rectitude of it."[137]

Even those who had begun to question the legitimacy of slavery could do little about it before the Revolution. Whenever the American people had attempted to legally end slavery, the British government undermined those efforts by vetoing or repealing their laws. Benjamin Franklin wrote that "even the Virginia Assembly have petitioned the King for permission to make a law for preventing the importation of more [slaves] into that colony. This request, however, will probably not be granted as their former laws of that kind have always been repealed."[138] Thomas Jefferson also expressed his frustration with the king's regular vetoes of colonial anti-slavery measures. In his original draft of the Declaration of Independence, he wrote, "Determined to keep open a market where men should be bought and sold, [King George III] has prostituted his negative [veto power] for suppressing every legislative attempt to prohibit or restrain this execrable commerce."[139] Jefferson added that the king "has waged a cruel war against human nature itself, violating its most sacred rights of life and liberty in the persons of a distant people who never offended him, captivating and carrying them into slavery in another hemisphere, or to incur miserable death in their transportations thither."[140] Ending the evil of the slave trade, George Mason later said, "was one of the great causes of our separation from Great Britain."[141] Given the Americans' inability to end or weaken slavery under British rule, change could not be realized until independence was first achieved.

Even after declaring independence, however, a united effort to regulate slavery in the new nation was difficult to achieve because the individual states were sovereign over such matters—the Articles of Confederation created extremely limited national powers to effect any change. Consequently, most restrictions on slavery in the new nation developed within the individual states. For example, the Massachusetts Constitution of 1780 and the New Hampshire Constitution of 1783 abolished slavery altogether in those states. Pennsylvania in 1780 and Connecticut in 1784 passed gradual-emancipation laws that granted freedom to newborn slaves after they reached a certain age.[142] And many states, including some in the South, enacted laws that prohibited the slave trade.[143]

Although these state actions ending or regulating slavery fell short of the Founding Fathers' ultimate aspirations for the nation, the Founders understood that the abolition of slavery in America would not occur overnight. Total and immediate abolition was simply impracticable in that day, particularly in regions of the country where it had become so ingrained into the culture. Jefferson wrote:

> Where [slavery] is most deeply seated, there it will be slowest in eradication. In the northern states, it was merely superficial and easily corrected. In the southern, it is incorporated with the whole system and requires time, patience, and perseverance in the curative process.[144]

The Founding Fathers nevertheless exhibited their determined resolve to end slavery by implementing measures that were designed to nudge the nation toward total emancipation. An important policy that the Congress of the Confederation was able to unite behind was the prohibition on slavery in all national territories. The Northwest Ordinance of 1787 was designed to regulate the national lands northwest of the Ohio River and to mandate the eventual creation of new states from that region. Significantly, the law included a provision—first proposed by Jefferson in 1784—that prohibited slavery throughout the territory.[145] As a consequence of this provision, the Founding Fathers were able to contain slavery to the states where it was practiced so that the institution might fade away altogether as the nation would grow westward in freedom.

At the Philadelphia Convention of 1787, the Founding Fathers made further inroads against slavery's continuation by regulating and discouraging it in the new Constitution. For example, they gave to Congress the power to end the slave trade in 1808.[146] This was a vast improvement over the Articles of Confederation, which allowed states to carry on the slave trade indefinitely. Furthermore, the Founding Fathers placed a disability on slave states with respect to their representation in Congress. Congressional representation was apportioned according to state population, but slaves were counted as only three-fifths of their true number whereas free men were counted in full.[147] So the Constitution effectively encouraged emancipation by granting a two-fifths political advantage to states that were free.

Despite their desire to restrict slavery even more in the Constitution, the Founding Fathers had to make compromises in order to hold the union together. To be sure, they never would have achieved the Constitution's ratification had they placed any more restrictions on slavery in that document—southern states would not have joined the new government. And preserving the union was the primary goal of those who met at the Convention. James Madison warned his fellow Virginians in 1788 that if the union failed—if the southern states did not ratify the Constitution—then liberty for no one would be secure. He said:

> The southern states would not have entered into the union of America without the temporary permission of that [slave] trade; and if they were excluded from the union, the consequences might be dreadful to them and to us. . . . The union in general is not in a worse situation. Under the Articles of Confederation, [the slave trade] might be continued forever; but by this clause, an end may be put to it after twenty years. . . . Great as the evil is, a dismemberment of the union would be worse. If those states should disunite from the other states for not indulging them in the temporary continuance of this traffic, they might solicit and obtain aid from foreign powers.[148]

The Founding Fathers feared that disunion would give rise to military conflict and regular unrest in America, thus assuring that any experiment in liberty would be short-lived. So they compromised on slavery to preserve the union, and they hoped that this evil institution would dissolve in time.

The Founding Fathers anyway believed that the compromise worked in favor of freedom. At the Pennsylvania Ratifying Convention in 1787, James Wilson expressed his conviction that the ratification of the Constitution would effectively mark the beginning of the end of slavery in America:

> Under the present confederation, the states may admit the importation of slaves as long as they please; but by this article, after the year 1808, the Congress will have power to prohibit such importation, notwithstanding the disposition of any state to the contrary. I consider this as laying the foundation for banishing slavery out of this country; and though the period is more distant than I could wish, yet it will produce the same kind, gradual change, which was pursued in Pennsylvania. It is with much satisfaction I view this power in the general government, whereby they may lay an interdiction on this reproachful trade: but an immediate advantage is also obtained; for a tax or duty may be imposed on such importation, not exceeding ten dollars for each person; and this, sir, operates as a partial prohibition; it was all that could be obtained. I am sorry it was no more; but from this I think there is reason to hope, that yet a few years, and it will be prohibited altogether; and in the mean time, the new states which are to be formed will be under the control of Congress in this particular, and slaves will never be introduced amongst them.[149]

Wilson and others believed that total abolition of slavery would eventually come by constitutional amendment—after enough free states were admitted to the Union so that ratification of such a measure was possible.

Wilson's predictions about the end slavery under the new Constitution initially proved to be accurate. The First Congress of the United States passed, and President George Washington signed into law, a statute that gave full effect to the Northwest Ordinance, which had been in effect under the Articles of Confederation. The law guaranteed that all federal territories under the new government—and all new states admitted to the union—would remain free from slavery. In addition, New York and

New Jersey joined the other northern states in the common effort to eliminate slavery in America. They enacted gradual-emancipation laws in 1799 and 1804, respectively, modeled after those of Pennsylvania and Connecticut.

The Founding Fathers had successfully placed the nation on a course to realize their goal of abolishing slavery in America, and they cannot be faulted for failing to immediately reach that end. The means to that end was not always within their control, and they anyway faced a more pressing need to preserve the fledgling republic. Despite their many obstacles and challenges, however, many of the Founding Fathers—especially those in the South—still regretted that they could not do more to end slavery in their time. John Quincy Adams later spoke of their disappointment that slavery persisted, and also of their enduring optimism that it would eventually end. He said:

> The inconsistency of the institution of domestic slavery with the principles of the Declaration of Independence was seen and lamented by all the southern patriots of the Revolution; by no one with deeper and more unalterable conviction than by the author of the Declaration himself. No charge of insincerity or hypocrisy can be fairly laid to their charge. Never from *their* lips was heard one syllable of attempt to justify the institution of slavery. They universally considered it as a reproach fastened upon them by the unnatural step-mother country and they saw that before the principles of the Declaration of Independence, slavery, in common with every other mode of oppression, was destined sooner or later to be banished from the earth. Such was the undoubting conviction of Jefferson to his dying day. In the Memoir of His Life, written at the age of seventy-seven, he gave to his countrymen the solemn and emphatic warning that the day was not distant when they must hear and adopt the general emancipation of their slaves. "Nothing is more certainly written," said he, "in the book of fate, than that these people are to be free."[150]

The Founding Fathers did not see general emancipation in their lifetimes, but they set the nation on a course that, if maintained, would end with the abolition of slavery and the fulfillment of the nation's founding promise of equality. It would be the duty of future generations to keep the nation on that course to reach that end.

Unfortunately, the American people later strayed from that aim. Whereas the Founding Fathers worked to prevent the spread of slavery to federal territories under the Northwest Ordinance, subsequent generations undermined those efforts by passing the Missouri Compromise law of 1820 and the Kansas-Nebraska Act of 1854. Although the Missouri Compromise retained a prohibition on slavery in the new Louisiana Territory north of the 36° 30' parallel, it allowed slavery to expand into this territory south of that parallel and in the land of Missouri. More significantly, the Kansas-Nebraska Act removed all prohibitions on slavery in any federal territory. It allowed the settlers to decide if slavery would be permitted by their state constitutions upon admission to the union.

Not willing to let slavery bleed across the nation, Republicans in the 1850s recommitted themselves to the Founding Fathers' policy on slavery—they sought to place slavery on a path toward extinction by containing it within the states where it was practiced. Republican leader Abraham Lincoln reminded the people of "the position in which our fathers originally placed [slavery]—restricting it from the new territories where it had not gone, and legislating to cut off its source by the abrogation of the slave trade, thus putting the seal of legislation *against its spread*."[151] Like the Founding Fathers, Lincoln thought that by containing slavery, it would die away over time:

> I believe if we could arrest the spread [of slavery] and place it where Washington, and Jefferson, and Madison placed it, it *would be* in the course of ultimate extinction, and the public mind *would*, as for eighty years past, believe that it was in the course of ultimate extinction. The crisis would be past.[152]

The Republican Party embraced this strategy in its platform of 1856, resolving:

> [T]hat, as our Republican fathers, when they had abolished slavery in all our national territory, ordained that no person shall be deprived of life, liberty, or property, without due process of law [under the Fifth Amendment], it becomes our duty to maintain this provision of the Constitution against all attempts to

violate it for the purpose of establishing slavery in the territories of the United States by positive legislation, prohibiting its existence or extension therein. That we deny the authority of Congress, of a territorial legislation, of any individual, or association of individuals, to give legal existence to slavery in any territory of the United States, while the present Constitution shall be maintained.[153]

Republicans argued that black Americans in federal territories were free and possessed the same protections under the Constitution as any other American. They insisted that Congress was prohibited by the Fifth Amendment from depriving anyone in these territories of his life, liberty, or property without due process of law. And they asserted that a law such as the Kansas-Nebraska Act, which permitted the enslavement of a free people, was unquestionably unconstitutional. Republicans therefore stood against the Kansas-Nebraska Act. They stood against Democrats who supported or tolerated slavery in the federal territories. And after *Dred Scott v. Sandford* was decided in 1857, Republicans also stood against the Supreme Court.

Abolitionist attorneys initiated the lawsuit *Dred Scott v. Sandford* in 1853 in an attempt to free Dred Scott, his family, and other similarly situated slaves. Scott was born into slavery in Virginia and moved with his owner to Missouri—another slave state. But he later traveled with his owner to the Wisconsin Territory, which remained free under the Northwest Ordinance and the Missouri Compromise. After returning to Missouri with his owner, attorneys for Dred Scott sued for his freedom in federal court, arguing that Scott's presence in a free territory had emancipated him forever—the principle "once free, always free" had been recognized by many courts at the time, even in Missouri for a short while.[154] When the lower court decided that Scott was still a slave, Scott's attorney's appealed to the Supreme Court.

In a widely controversial and outright racist ruling, the Supreme Court dismissed the suit for lack of jurisdiction—it decided that black Americans had no right whatsoever to sue in federal court. In its opinion, the Court wrote that black Americans had always been "considered as a subordinate and inferior class of beings who had been subjugated by the dominant race, and, whether emancipated or not, yet remained subject to their authority."[155] According to the Court, black Americans were not "citizens" under the Constitution, and so they could "therefore claim none of the rights and privileges which that instrument provides for and secures to citizens of the United States."[156]

Not only did the Supreme Court dismiss Dred Scott's claim to freedom as immaterial, it further decided that Congress had no authority to prohibit slavery in any federal territory. It ruled the Missouri Compromise law unconstitutional for violating the Fifth Amendment, which ensures that "[n]o person shall . . . be deprived of life, liberty, or property, without due process of law."[157] Because the Court had already determined that the Constitution did not apply to black Americans, it conveniently ignored Dred Scott's claim of deprived liberty under the Fifth Amendment. The Court instead focused on the Fifth Amendment claim made by Scott's owner: that Dred Scott was his property, and the Missouri Compromise law deprived him of his property without due process of law. Siding with slave-owners everywhere, the Court wrote:

> [A]n act of Congress which deprives a citizen of the United States of his liberty or property merely because he came himself or brought his property into a particular territory of the United States, and who had committed no offence against the laws, could hardly be dignified with the name of due process of law.[158]

The Court struck down the Missouri Compromise and held that "neither Dred Scott himself, nor any of his family, were made free by being carried into this [free federal] territory."[159] A slave-owner could not be divested of his slave property no matter where in the country he might travel.

Republicans were outraged by the Court's decision because it so blatantly distorted constitutional history in reaching its judgment. For example, the Court asserted that the Founding Fathers, when they signed the Declaration of Independence, did not really mean what they said when they declared that "all men are created equal." The Court determined that it was "too clear for dispute" that black Americans were not meant to be included in that phrase, despite the Founding Fathers' unmistakable commitment to natural equality and their many statements in support of the eventual abolition of slavery.[160]

Moreover, the Court disregarded the clear language of the Constitution and the actions of the Founding Fathers when deciding whether Congress could regulate slavery in the federal territories. Article IV of the Constitution grants Congress the power to "make all needful rules and regulations respecting the territory or other property belonging to the United States."[161] And one of the first regulations that the First Congress of the United States imposed on the federal territories was a general prohibition on slavery in these lands. The Supreme Court nevertheless suggested that the Founding Fathers had misapplied congressional power by enacting that law—that the Founding Fathers somehow misunderstood the meaning of the Constitution that they had just created. The Court claimed to know better, and it expected the American people to submit to its ruling as the law of the land.

Republicans were especially concerned that the Supreme Court might follow its decision in *Dred Scott v. Sandford* with a similar ruling pertaining to state prohibitions on slavery in the North. It follows logically that if Congress cannot interfere with a slave-owner's property rights because they are constitutionally protected, then states may not either. Abraham Lincoln warned of this possibility in 1858:

> Put this and that together, and we have another nice little niche which we may ere long see filled with another Supreme Court decision, declaring that the Constitution of the United States does not permit a *state* to exclude slavery from its limits. . . .
>
> Such a decision is all that slavery now lacks of being alike lawful in all the states. Welcome or unwelcome, such decision is probably coming, and will soon be upon us, unless the power of the present political dynasty shall be met and overthrown. We shall lie down pleasantly dreaming that the people of Missouri are on the verge of making their state free, and we shall awake to the reality instead, that the Supreme Court has made Illinois a slave state.[162]

The Supreme Court's ruling in *Dred Scott v. Sandford* clearly agitated opponents of slavery, and it also triggered a national debate over the finality of that decision. Republicans and Democrats took opposing sides on the issue, and their differences became apparent during the prominent 1858 Lincoln-Douglas debates, which showcased the two rising leaders of their respective parties in a series of substantive political discussions over slavery and judicial supremacy.

Douglas became known as a strong proponent of judicial supremacy. Throughout the debates, Douglas criticized Lincoln for his many attacks on the Court and expressed his own submission to the Court's decisions. He said, "Mr. Lincoln goes for a warfare upon the Supreme Court of the United States because of their judicial decision in the *Dred Scott* case. I yield obedience to the decisions in that Court—to the final determination of the highest judicial tribunal known to our Constitution."[163] Douglas and other Democrats thus deferred to the Court's constitutional interpretation. They regarded its decision in *Dred Scott v. Sandford* as supreme and forever binding on all.

Conversely, Lincoln and the Republicans rejected judicial supremacy. Lincoln first conceded that Supreme Court rulings were binding on the actual parties involved in a case. He said, "We do not propose that when *Dred Scott* has been decided to be a slave by the court, we, as a mob, will decide him to be free."[164] But he was adamant that the judicial decision was not supreme and binding on the political branches of government—it did not become a political rule that was "binding on the members of Congress or the President to favor no measure that does not actually concur with the principles of that decision."[165] Lincoln and other Republicans believed that the people control constitutional meaning. If they disagree with the Court's constitutional interpretation, then they may assert their authority over government through the political branches to implement their understanding.

Throughout these debates, Lincoln sharply attacked Douglas' reverence of Supreme Court decisions. He warned that such blind devotion to judicial decrees would impose upon the people a continuing obedience to the Court, no matter how baseless its decisions might be. Lincoln said:

> [Stephen Douglas] sticks to a decision which forbids the people of a territory from excluding slavery, and he does so, not because he says it is right in itself—he does not give any opinion on that—but because it has been *decided by the court*; and being decided by the court, he is, and you are, bound to take it in your political action as *law*, not that he judges at all of its merits, but because a decision of the court is to him a "Thus saith the Lord."

He places it on that ground alone; and you will bear in mind that
thus committing himself unreservedly to this decision *commits
him to the next one* just as firmly as to this. He did not commit
himself on account of the merit or demerit of the decision, but it
is a "Thus saith the Lord." The next decision, as much as this,
will be a "Thus saith the Lord."[166]

Although Douglas became such a staunch advocate of judicial
supremacy after the *Dred Scott* case, Lincoln showed how hypocritical and
unprincipled his position really was. Douglas was not so deferential to
judicial reasoning in past cases—he actually commended the actions of
President Jackson when he defied the Court's ruling in *McCulloch v.
Maryland*. In fact, the Democratic Party took the position in its 1856
platform that the national bank was unconstitutional. Lincoln spoke of
Douglas' selectively deferential position:

I have said that I have often heard him approve of Jackson's
course in disregarding the decision of the Supreme Court
pronouncing the National Bank constitutional. . . . [H]e now
claims to stand on the Cincinnati [Democratic] platform, which
affirms that Congress *cannot* charter a National Bank, in the
teeth of that old standing decision that Congress *can* charter a
bank.[167]

Lincoln knew that the principled position on the finality of judicial
rulings was the one taken by the Founding Fathers—that the people are
capable of deciding all constitutional questions by their control of the
political branches of government. The Founding Fathers never intended to
give absolute control over constitutional meaning to a handful of unelected
and unrepresentative judges. They trusted the people to uphold the
Constitution themselves. Lincoln explained that this founding practice in
popular constitutionalism was later reaffirmed by Jeffersonian Republicans
and Jackson Men. But Douglas nevertheless remained obstinate in his
support of judicial supremacy after the *Dred Scott* decision. An
exasperated Lincoln lamented:

There is nothing that can divert or turn him away from this
decision. It is nothing that I point out to him that his great
prototype, General Jackson, did not believe in the binding force

of decisions. It is nothing to him that Jefferson did not so believe.[168]

No amount of reason could have persuaded Douglas and other Democrats to change their obedient submission to the Court because it so expediently served their political ends. Democrats in the South of course had a vested interest in the expansion of slavery in America. And Democrats in the North hoped that a judicial decision on slavery would remove that issue from political discussion—they were willing to turn a blind eye to slavery in exchange for political gain. Because the Court's decision in *Dred Scott* perfectly suited these objectives, Democrats naturally deferred to this ruling as authoritative and binding on all. And they officially committed themselves to these positions on slavery and judicial supremacy in their 1860 Democratic Party platform. In all disputes over slavery, Democrats resolved that they would "abide by the decision of the Supreme Court of the United states upon these questions of constitutional law."[169]

By their endorsement of *Dred Scott*, Democrats had the difficult task of defending the decision under the Constitution. Like the Court, Democrats had to stretch the meaning of the Constitution and subvert the moral truths set forth in the Declaration of Independence to justify this corrupt ruling. Like the Court, Democrats elevated a slave-owner's right to property over a slave's right to be free. Lincoln observed in 1859 that Democrats declared "the liberty of one man to be absolutely nothing when in conflict with another man's right to property."[170] Democrats assailed the ideal of natural equality. They distorted or outright disavowed the principles that formed the basis of liberty in America. Lincoln wrote:

> The principles of Jefferson are the definitions and axioms of a free society. And yet they are denied and evaded, with no small show of success. One [Democrat] dashingly calls them "glittering generalities." Another bluntly calls them "self-evident lies." And others insidiously argue that they apply to "superior races." These expressions, differing in form, are identical in object and effect—the supplanting the principles of free government, and restoring those of classification, caste, and legitimacy. They would light a convocation of crowned heads plotting against the people. They are the vanguard, the miners

and sappers of returning despotism. We must repulse them, or they will subjugate us.[171]

Lincoln recognized that liberty for all could never be guaranteed by those who denied it to others. It was clear to him that the apologists of slavery operated under the arbitrary rules of force and violence, not within the boundaries of Natural Law. For liberty to prevail in America, Lincoln advised that the people must "save the principles of Jefferson from total overthrow in this nation."[172] They had to restore the Natural Law ideals that Jefferson inscribed in the Declaration of Independence as the Founding Fathers' highest aspirations for the nation. Lincoln wrote:

> All honor to Jefferson—to the man, who, in the concrete pressure of a struggle for national independence by a single people, had the coolness, forecast, and capacity to introduce into a merely revolutionary document an abstract truth [on man's possession of natural rights], applicable to all men and all times, and so to embalm it there that today and in all coming days it shall be a rebuke and a stumbling-block to the very harbingers of reappearing tyranny and oppression.[173]

While the Declaration of Independence provided Lincoln and the Republicans the moral clarity to resist the spread of slavery in the West, they were unable to press for liberty in the South. Slavery in the existing states was still a constitutionally-protected practice. A complete prohibition on slavery everywhere in the nation would require a constitutional amendment, and such a measure had no hope of being ratified by the requisite number of states in that day. So despite their righteous opposition to slavery's expansion, Republicans knew that they could do nothing to end it completely. They could only do as the Founding Fathers did—prohibit the spread of slavery so that the nation might grow in freedom.

Republicans actually vowed not to impede slavery where it existed to allay the concerns of southerners. In their 1860 party platform, Republicans clearly broadcast their intention to leave slavery alone in the South. They resolved:

> That the maintenance inviolate of the rights of the states, and especially the right of each state to order and control its own domestic institutions according to its own judgment exclusively,

is essential to that balance of power on which the perfection and endurance of our political fabric depend; and we denounce the lawless invasion by armed force of the soil of any state or territory, no matter what pretext, as among the gravest of crimes.[174]

Republicans vowed to uphold the Constitution, even if that meant permitting slavery to continue in the South.

After Lincoln was sworn in as president, he further assured southerners that the Republican Party posed no threat to their practice of slavery. In his Inaugural Address, Lincoln promised that "the property, peace, and security of no section [of the United States] are to be in any wise endangered by the now incoming Administration."[175] He emphasized, "I have no purpose, directly or indirectly, to interfere with the institution of slavery in the states where it exists. I believe I have no lawful right to do so, and I have no inclination to do so."[176] Accepting that slavery in the South already was "implied constitutional law," Lincoln even offered his support for a proposed amendment that would have barred the federal government from ever interfering with slavery in those states.[177] Moreover, he affirmed his constitutional duty as president to facilitate the return of runaway slaves. In his address, Lincoln quoted from Article IV of the Constitution:

> "No person held to service or labor in one state, under the laws thereof, escaping into another, shall in consequence of any law or regulation therein be discharged from such service or labor, but shall be delivered up on claim of the party to whom such service or labor may be due."[178]

Lincoln hoped that his many assurances to southerners might quiet their concerns about his intentions as president and therefore avert secession and civil war. He made clear that, above all, he would faithfully support and defend the Constitution—even if he disagreed with some of its provisions.

Lincoln's commitment to the Constitution during his presidency proved to be unwavering. For instance, he continued to enforce the fugitive slave law even after the South had seceded and war had already begun. In 1862, jails in Washington, D.C. were filled with runaway slaves waiting to be claimed by their owners.[179] More significantly, he ignored repeated requests from his fellow Republicans and military leaders to emancipate the slaves in the South as the Civil War dragged on. He refrained from taking such action because he knew that he lacked the constitutional authority to do so. Only when he believed that emancipation was indispensable to the preservation of the Union did Lincoln finally give the order to free the slaves in rebel states. He later explained his rationale for his decision in a letter in 1864:

> I am naturally anti-slavery. If slavery is not wrong, nothing is wrong. I cannot remember when I did not so think and feel; and yet I have never understood that the presidency conferred upon me an unrestricted right to act officially upon this judgment and feeling. . . . I did understand, however, that my oath to preserve the Constitution to the best of my ability imposed upon me the duty of preserving, by every indispensable means, that government—that nation of which that Constitution was the organic law. . . . I felt that measures, otherwise unconstitutional, might become lawful, by becoming indispensable to the preservation of the Constitution, through the preservation of the nation. Right or wrong, I assumed this ground, and now avow it. When, early in the war, General Fremont attempted military emancipation, I forbade it, because I did not then think it an indispensable necessity. When a little later, General Cameron, then Secretary of War, suggested the arming of the blacks, I objected, because I did not yet think it an indispensable necessity. When, still later, General Hunter attempted military emancipation, I again forbade it, because I did not yet think the indispensable necessity had come. When, in March and May and July, 1862, I made earnest and successive appeals to the border states to favor compensated emancipation, I believed the indispensable necessity for military emancipation and arming the blacks would come, unless averted by that measure. They declined the proposition; and I was, in my best judgment, driven to the alternative of either surrendering the Union, and with it the Constitution, or of laying strong hand upon the colored element. I chose the latter.[180]

The Emancipation Proclamation was fundamentally a wartime measure, and it did not stop slavery in all of America. Its constitutional authority was based on Lincoln's war powers as Commander-in-Chief, and so the Proclamation could not be applied to the four slave states that did not secede: Delaware, Kentucky, Maryland, and Missouri. A constitutional amendment would still be necessary to end slavery everywhere in America once and for all.

While the Constitution's unambiguous sanction of slavery in the existing states was beyond all question, the great controversy in that day centered on its more indefinite terms concerning Congress' power to regulate the federal territories—what these provisions meant and whose interpretation was controlling.

From the very outset of his presidency, Lincoln made clear that he would always favor the constitutional understanding of the people over that of the Supreme Court when deciding constitutional questions. He explained in his First Inaugural Address that government could only continue in liberty if the will of the majority prevailed in such disputes:

> *May* Congress prohibit slavery in the [federal] territories? The Constitution does not expressly say. *Must* Congress protect slavery in the territories? The Constitution does not expressly say.
>
> From questions of this class spring all our constitutional controversies, and we divide upon them into majorities and minorities. If the minority will not acquiesce, the majority must, or the government must cease. There is no other alternative; for continuing the government, is acquiescence on one side or the other. If a minority, in such case, will secede rather than acquiesce, they make a precedent which, in turn, will divide and ruin them; for a minority of their own will secede from them, whenever a majority refuses to be controlled by such minority. For instance, why may not any portion of a new confederacy, a year or two hence, arbitrarily secede again, precisely as portions of the present Union now claim to secede from it? . . .
> . . .
>
> Plainly, the central idea of secession is the essence of anarchy. A majority, held in restraint by constitutional checks, and limitations, and always changing easily, with deliberate changes of popular opinions and sentiments, is the only true sovereign of a free people. Whoever rejects it, does of necessity fly to anarchy or to despotism. Unanimity is impossible; the rule of a minority as a permanent arrangement, is wholly inadmissible; so that rejecting the majority principle, anarchy, or despotism in some form, is all that is left.[181]

A majority held in restraint by the minority is the essence of tyranny, and it matters not whether the minority is a group of lawless citizens advocating secession or a group of judges claiming supremacy over constitutional meaning. Lincoln said in his Inaugural Address:

> [I]f the policy of the government upon vital questions affecting the whole people is to be irrevocably fixed by decisions of the Supreme Court, . . . [then] the people will have ceased to be their own rulers, having to that extent practically resigned their government into the hands of that eminent tribunal.[182]

For liberty to endure in America, Lincoln believed that the majority principle must survive. Whenever the Court's opinion on indefinite constitutional questions contradicts the conviction of the majority, it must be the people's will that prevails. Only then will they maintain their sovereignty over government.

The majority of Americans in the 1860s called upon Lincoln and the Republican Party to enforce their constitutional understanding and stop the spread of slavery in the West. And they did. Republicans ignored the Supreme Court's ruling in *Dred Scott v. Sandford*, which held that the government had no authority to regulate slavery in federal lands. In 1862, Republicans passed and Lincoln signed into law measures that abolished slavery in the western federal territories and in the District of Columbia.[183] Lincoln also rejected the Court's assertion that black Americans possessed no national citizenship rights under the Constitution. Through various federal regulations and through the issuance of national passports and patents to black Americans, Lincoln recognized their constitutional rights.[184] And when the southern states seceded, Republicans refused to let a minority of Americans in the South dissolve the nation into anarchy. They fought to preserve the Union—the legitimate government of the American majority—so that it might continue in liberty.

In that fight to save the republic, Republicans also found a new opportunity to at last fulfill the promises of liberty and equality set forth in the Declaration of Independence. Although they never intended to disturb slavery in the South upon taking control of government in 1861, once war was thrust upon them, Republicans came to realize that the only path toward lasting peace and freedom was to advance the cause of liberty for all, everywhere in the nation. At Gettysburg in 1863, Lincoln reminded the American people that "our fathers brought forth on this continent a new nation, conceived in liberty, and dedicated to the proposition that all men are created equal."[185] The United States would never endure going forward half slave and half free. Lincoln therefore called on the American people to rededicate themselves to those noble aspirations in the Declaration—to revive the founding ideals to extend liberty and justice for all. He called on the people to resolve that "this nation, under God, shall have a new birth of freedom; and that government of the people, by the people, and for the people shall not perish from the earth."[186]

The Fourteenth Amendment

After the Civil War ended, Republicans sought to reunite the nation under the Natural Law principles of the Declaration of Independence, and the Fourteenth Amendment became an important means to that end. It broadly defined American citizenship, ensuring that the Supreme Court's denial of rights to black Americans in *Dred Scott* was never mistaken as lawful. It eliminated the Constitution's three-fifths clause regarding congressional apportionment. And its language in Section 1 unmistakably prohibited the states from all forms of discrimination:

> No state shall make or enforce any law which shall abridge the privileges or immunities of citizens of the United States; nor shall any state deprive any person of life, liberty, or property, without due process of law; nor deny to any person within its jurisdiction the equal protection of the laws.[187]

Republicans hoped that the Fourteenth Amendment would finally force the nation to live up to its founding promise "that all men are created equal, that they are endowed by their Creator with certain unalienable rights, that among these are life, liberty, and the pursuit of happiness."[188]

Notwithstanding this intent, the imprecise wording of Section 1 soon led to misinterpretation and judicial abuse. The Supreme Court has since exploited the vague language of Section 1 to expand its jurisdiction and strike down state laws—even those that have nothing to do with racial equality—all because it considers them unfair. The Court has twisted the meaning of Section 1 to create a number of "rights" that were never even dreamed of by the amendment's framers—privacy rights, abortion rights, and gay/sodomy rights, to name a few. Its broad reading of the Fourteenth Amendment is nowhere near the framers' original design—a point that is made all the more clear by the context surrounding its ratification.

Of course, the Thirteenth Amendment came first. As the Civil War was drawing to a close, Republicans worked to permanently extend Lincoln's Emancipation Proclamation, and so they drafted the Thirteenth Amendment to the Constitution in 1864 to abolish slavery everywhere in the United States. Republicans needed a two-thirds majority vote in Congress just to propose the amendment to the states. But they had a relatively easy time achieving this result due to the war-time absence of southern congressional representatives who surely would have blocked the measure. Thus, the proposed Thirteenth Amendment passed through the Senate without difficulty in April 1864 by a vote of 38-6. And although the amendment initially failed to pass in the House—because many Democrats in the North still opposed the abolition of slavery—its passage became a foregone conclusion after Republicans dominated the 1864 elections. Given its inevitable passage, Lincoln convinced the outgoing Congressmen to reconsider and pass the amendment in their final lame-duck session. The Thirteenth Amendment passed in the House in January 1865 by a vote of 119-56.

Ratification in the states was a more cumbersome process, especially because the nation remained at war. The Constitution's three-fourths requirement for ratification meant that 27 of the entire 36 existing states in the Union needed to approve of the amendment, and only 25 states remained loyal or neutral to the Union. The ratification process in the North was relatively quick but not entirely successful. For instance, Democrats in New Jersey blocked the Thirteenth Amendment, along with the border states of Delaware and Kentucky. But the ratification process went on. By the time the war ended on April 9, 1865, 20 states had ratified the amendment, including the southern states of Virginia, Louisiana, and Tennessee. (The Virginia legislature that ratified the amendment was the representative body of Union loyalists that had regularly met throughout the war. The governments of Louisiana and Tennessee were those established under Lincoln's Reconstruction policy.) When Andrew

Johnson took over as president on April 15 after Lincoln's assassination, he forced the former Confederate states to abolish slavery in their new state constitutions, and he urged them to ratify the Thirteenth Amendment. The 27-state threshold for ratification was finally met in December 1865, and slavery had at last ended in the United States.

Many Americans believed that the Thirteenth Amendment would finally fulfill the promise of natural equality that the Founding Fathers had made in the Declaration of Independence. Republican Congressman Ebon Ingersoll said that the amendment would "secure to the oppressed slave his natural and God-given rights"—rights that were "as sacred in the sight of Heaven as those of any other race."[189] Abolitionist John Jay similarly believed that the Constitution had at last embraced natural equality. He wrote a letter to Supreme Court Justice Samuel Chase urging him and the Court to enshrine this foundational principle in constitutional law:

> The decision which I most wish to see pronounced by your Court is that the adopting of the [Thirteenth] Amendment abolishing slavery has destroyed the only exception recognized by the Constitution to the great principle of the Declaration of Independence, and that from the date of the adoption of the Amendment all persons black and white stand upon equal footing, that all state legislation establishing or recognizing distinctions of race or color are void.[190]

New York Attorney General John H. Martindale believed that, by removing slavery from the Constitution, the Thirteenth Amendment would abolish not just slavery, but all forms of racial discrimination. He wrote:

> There does not remain a logical argument on which to rest the exclusion of the native born black man from all the civil and political rights inherent in citizenship.
>
> No states, North or South, have the constitutional right to classify him and degrade him because he is black, any more than they have the constitutional right to classify and degrade white men.[191]

Despite this confidence that the Thirteenth Amendment would establish natural equality everywhere in America, it most certainly did not. Democratic legislatures in the South quickly passed Black Codes—discriminatory laws that limited the civil liberties of newly-freed slaves and controlled their freedom of movement. Black Americans could not vote, serve on juries, live in designated neighborhoods, or freely travel. Racial classifications pervaded the law everywhere in the South.

The Black Codes naturally inflamed public opinion in the North. After the long war over slavery, the former Confederate states in defeat were effectively reinstituting that unconstitutional practice under the guise of law. Republicans in Congress were particularly enraged by this defiance because they knew that upon reunification and eventual removal of the three-fifths clause from the Constitution, these recalcitrant southern states stood to gain more seats in Congress. One Illinois Republican feared that the "reward of treason will be increased representation."[192]

In response to the Black Codes, Republicans in Congress temporarily blocked southern representatives from joining the Congress—by failing to seat them—and they also passed the 1866 Civil Rights Act (CRA), which gave black Americans full legal equality in the nation. Although President Johnson vetoed the CRA because he believed it encroached upon state power, Congress overrode the veto, and the CRA became law. Questions about the constitutionality of the CRA still lingered, however, so Republicans proposed the Fourteenth Amendment a few months later—the amendment was practically identical to key provisions of the CRA, so it would remove all doubt about Congress' power to enact that law.

After Congress officially proposed the amendment in 1866, the states initially blocked its ratification—all but one of the former Confederate states (Tennessee) rejected the Fourteenth Amendment. So the amendment effort appeared to be unsuccessful, but Republicans then forced the amendment on the South by passing the Reconstruction Acts of 1867.

The Reconstruction Acts were composed of four statutes that imposed stringent restrictions on the southern states.[193] First of all, the Acts remilitarized the South—former Confederate state governments were placed under military control, the South was divided into five military districts, and martial law reigned once again.[194] (In response, southerners formed a number of paramilitary groups that aimed to suppress the black vote and intimidate Republicans candidates and office holders. Violent southern resistance and hostility thus continued via these various hate groups—including the Ku Klux Klan—that were aligned with the

Democratic Party.) The Reconstruction Acts also forced southern states to give voting rights to all men, regardless of race.[195] They required southern states to obtain congressional approval of their new state constitutions before they could be readmitted to the Union.[196] And most significantly, the Acts forced the former Confederate states to ratify the Fourteenth Amendment as a condition of readmission to the Union.[197] (The amendment was officially ratified the following year.)

The Fourteenth Amendment necessarily became one of the many terms of peace that was imposed upon southern states during the reconstruction. Professor William E. Nelson, an expert on Fourteenth Amendment law and history, explained:

> What was politically essential was that the North's victory in the Civil War be rendered permanent and the principles for which the war had been fought rendered secure, so that the South, upon readmission to full participation in the Union, could not undo them. The Fourteenth Amendment must be understood as the Republican Party's plan for securing the fruits both of the war and of the three decades of antislavery agitation preceding it.[198]

In this context, the Fourteenth Amendment was ratified, and its purpose is further discovered in various debates and speeches endorsing or opposing its approval.

The Fourteenth Amendment was designed to accomplish what the Thirteenth Amendment had failed to do: force state governments to operate under Natural Law principles. Thaddeus Stevens, the influential Republican who introduced the Fourteenth Amendment to the House, stated, "*All* men . . . created by the laws of nature and nature's God [were] equally endowed with the inalienable rights of life, liberty and the pursuit of happiness."[199] He explained that the Fourteenth Amendment would ensure that these founding principles were binding on not just the federal government, but on the states as well:

> I can hardly believe that any person can be found who will not admit that every one of these provisions [of the Fourteenth Amendment] is just. They are all asserted, in some form or another, in our Declaration or organic law. But the Constitution limits only the action of Congress, and is not a limitation on the States. This amendment supplies that defect, and allows

Congress to correct the unjust legislation of the states, so far that
the law which operates upon one man shall operate equally upon
all.[200]

Republican Senator Luke Poland explained that Section 1 of the
Fourteenth Amendment was a sensible measure because it simply aimed to
secure liberty and equality for all Americans by implementing the nation's
founding philosophy:

> Now that slavery is abolished, and the whole people of the
> nation stand upon the basis of freedom, it seems to me that there
> can be no valid or reasonable objection to the residue of the
> amendment: "Nor shall any state deprive any person of life,
> liberty, or property without due process of law, nor deny to any
> person within its jurisdiction the equal protection of the law."
>
> It is the very spirit and inspiration of our system of
> government, the absolute foundation upon which it was
> established. It is essentially declared in the Declaration of
> Independence and in all the provisions of the Constitution.
> Notwithstanding this, we know that state laws exist, and some of
> them of very recent enactment [Black Codes], in direct violation
> of these principles. Congress has already shown its desire and
> intention to uproot and destroy all such partial state legislation in
> the passage of what is called the Civil Rights [Act]. . . . It
> certainly seems desirable that no doubt should be left existing as
> to the power of Congress to enforce principles lying at the very
> foundation of all republican government if they be denied or
> violated by the States, and I cannot doubt that every Senator will
> rejoice in aiding to remove all doubt upon this power of
> Congress.[201]

Republican John Bingham, the congressman who drafted Section 1, urged
the American people to adopt the Fourteenth Amendment for its
commitment to natural equality. He urged them "to declare their purpose
to stand by the foundation principle of their own institutions, the absolute
equality of all citizens of the United States politically and civilly before
their own laws."[202]

Determined to secure natural equality for all Americans, the framers
wrote this general guarantee into the text of the Fourteenth Amendment.
Although the amendment's lack of substance would later frustrate judges
interpreting it, this was not the primary concern of its framers. Republicans

in that day needed to reunite the nation, and they sought to achieve this goal through familiar moral inspiration. Before the Civil War, Republicans were accustomed to speaking in broad terms of liberty and equality when advocating the abolition of slavery. After the war, they hoped that the same rousing language would engender respect for Natural Law and encourage reformation in the South. The framers of the Fourteenth Amendment, Professor Nelson wrote, served "primarily as statesmen and political leaders, not as legal draftsmen."[203] They designed the amendment not to "provide judges with a determinative text" but "to reaffirm the lay public's longstanding rhetorical commitment to general principles of equality, individual rights, and local self-rule."[204]

Hoping to realize these founding principles through the Fourteenth Amendment, the framers worked to approve of the amendment as quickly as they could. Republicans hoped to pass the amendment on to the states for ratification before southern congressmen were permitted to rejoin Congress and kill the amendment process. In a speech before Congress, Thaddeus Stevens explained why Republicans needed to work in haste:

> I do not pretend to be satisfied with [the Fourteenth Amendment]. And yet I am anxious for its speedy adoption, for I dread delay. The danger is that before any constitutional guards shall have been adopted, Congress will be flooded by rebels and rebel sympathizers. . . . Hence, I say, let us no longer delay; take what we can get now, and hope for better things in further legislation; in enabling acts or other provisions.[205]

While Republicans were ready to rush the Fourteenth Amendment through Congress, many Democrats tried to block the amendment on the fear that it would fundamentally alter the balance of power between the states and the national government. They warned that the amendment would obliterate the American tradition of local self-rule. Because the amendment's prohibitions on the states were left vague and undefined, state power would always remain uncertain and subject to federal interpretation. National standards and policies might abrogate local laws. Democratic Congressman Andrew J. Rogers opposed the amendment because he believed it would "take away the power of the states; . . . interfere with the internal police and regulations of the states; . . . [and] centralize a consolidated power in this federal government."[206] Democratic

Senator Willard Saulsbury argued that the amendment would make "state rights and state customs . . . yield to the decrees of a central despotism."[207] Alabama Governor Robert M. Patton also advised against ratification, fearing that the federal government would steal power traditionally reserved to the states:

> [Section 1 of the Fourteenth Amendment] would enlarge the judicial powers of the general government to such gigantic dimensions as would not only overshadow and weaken the authority and influence of the state courts, but might possibly reduce them to a complete nullity. It would give to the United States courts complete and unlimited jurisdiction over every conceivable case, however important or however trivial, which could arise under state laws. Every individual dissatisfied with the decision of a state court, might apply to a federal tribunal for redress. It matters not what might be the character of his case. . . . Upon a simple complaint that his rights, either of person or property, had been infringed, it would be the bounden duty of the tribunal to which he made his application to hear and determine his case. The granting of such an immense power as this over the state tribunals would, at the very best, subordinate them to a condition of comparative unimportance and insignificance.[208]

Democratic Congressman Michael Kerr similarly warned:

> [The Fourteenth Amendment] takes a long and fearful step toward the complete obliteration of state authority and the reserved and original rights of the states. It puts the local policy and officers, executive, ministerial, and judicial, of the states, at the mercy of the petty federal officers, who, under this bill, may be made to swarm over the whole country, exercising both ministerial and judicial functions, by arresting, examining, and imprisoning persons charged or suspected of having done any of the forbidden things under color of local laws or policy.[209]

An editorial titled "The Evils of Centralization" in the New York *Evening Post* observed that "liberty has never been secure without local and municipal institutions."[210] The kind of nationalism that Republicans were advancing under the Fourteenth Amendment, Democrats warned, would undermine liberty for all. Congressman Rogers suggested that the amendment would completely transform American government:

[The Fourteenth Amendment] saps the foundation of the government; it destroys the elementary principles of the states; it consolidates everything into one imperial despotism; it annihilates all the rights which lie at the foundation of the Union of the states, and which have characterized this government and made it prosperous and great during the long period of its existence. It will result in a revolution worse than that through which we have just passed; it will rock the earth like the throes of an earthquake, until its tragedy will summon the inhabitants of the world to witness its dreadful shock.[211]

Although the vague Fourteenth Amendment can be interpreted to grant broad national power to the federal government, Republicans had no intention to implement it in such despotic manner, and this original intent is vital to the amendment's meaning. Republicans merely intended to establish the same basic guarantees to all people, consistent with the republican design of American government. Republican Congressman John Bingham explained that the Fourteenth Amendment would not disrupt the traditional power held by the states. He said:

[T]his amendment takes from no state any right that ever pertained to it. No state ever had the right, under the forms of law or otherwise, to deny any freeman the equal protection of the laws or to abridge the privileges or immunities of any citizen of the Republic, although many of them have assumed and exercised the power, and that without remedy.[212]

Republican Congressman Frederick Woodbridge likewise stated that the Fourteenth Amendment "does not destroy the sovereignty of a state . . . . It does not even affect its sovereign rights, but merely keeps whatever sovereignty it may have in harmony with a republican form of government and the Constitution of the country."[213] Republican Senator Lot M. Morrill said that "the genius of republicanism is equality, impartiality of rights and remedies among all citizens . . . . The republican guarantee is that all laws shall bear upon all alike in what they enjoin and forbid, grant and enforce."[214]

In essence, the Fourteenth Amendment merely imposed upon the states the duty to treat all its citizens equally. Representative Thaddeus Stevens said that Section 1 required only that "the same laws must and shall apply to every mortal, American, Irishman, African, German or

Turk."[215] Republican Senator Lyman Trumbull also believed that the
Fourteenth Amendment was a simple guarantee of equality, not a charter
for the federal protection of fundamental rights.[216] In support of the 1866
Civil Rights Act, which had the same scope as Section 1, Trumbull stated
that the act would "in no manner interfere . . . with the municipal
regulations of any state which protects all alike in their rights of person
and property. It could have no operation in Massachusetts, New York,
Illinois, or most of the states of the Union."[217] As long as the states
guaranteed equal application of the law, Congressional enforcement of
equality would be completely unnecessary. A newspaper at the time
predicted that the act's "practical operation will probably be brief," and it
would be "a dead letter in a state if it is guilty of no injustice to any portion
of its inhabitants."[218] The act would apply only on "the lawless and
disobedient, the ungodly and sinners."[219] Congress would have broad
discretion to enforce equality in such "lawless" states. But once those
states corrected their ways, the effect of the new federal power would
cease, and their full lawmaking authority would be restored.

The expected temporary impact of the Fourteenth Amendment
comports with the understanding that it was more a peace treaty—to be
administered by Congress to secure the fruits of the North's victory in the
Civil War—than a legal document requiring precise definition.[220] The
framers were not so concerned about how the amendment might be
construed in the courts in the future. They were mainly focused on
reconstructing the South and unifying the people behind the nation's
founding principles. The Fourteenth Amendment simply empowered the
federal government to impose equality on the former Confederate states if
they did not willingly embrace it themselves.

The exercise of augmented federal power in times of crises was not
unforeseen by the Founding Fathers. Madison wrote, "The operations of
the federal government will be most extensive and important in times of
war and danger; those of the state governments, in times of peace and
security."[221] The Constitution anyway provided some flexibility in the
balance of power between the states and the national government. The
Founding Fathers had designed the American system of government to
serve as a double security to the people. Hamilton wrote that "the general

government will at all times stand ready to check the usurpations of the state governments, and [states] will have the same disposition towards the general government."[222] The American people held the scales of power in their hands, and it was their duty, Hamilton continued, "to preserve the constitutional equilibrium between the general and the state governments."[223] The people could augment the power of either government "by throwing themselves into either scale . . . . If their rights are invaded by either, they can make use of the other as the instrument of redress."[224]

Throughout the Civil War and Reconstruction, the use of augmented federal power was necessary to check the usurpations of state governments in the South. Instead of accepting political defeat in the elections of 1860, the southern states had blatantly ignored the will of the majority by seceding from the Union. And they continued to subvert the intent of the majority after the war by enacting Black Codes that ignored natural equality. Republicans consequently wielded the power of the federal government to restore the majority principle to popular government and to demand equality for all Americans.

Republicans all the while remained aware of their important obligation to restore the balance of power between the national and state governments. During the congressional debate on the Fourteenth Amendment, Republican Congressman Robert Hale acknowledged the immense growth of federal power. He said:

> I believe that the tendency in this country has been from the first too much toward the accumulation and strengthening of central federal power. During the last five years of war and rebellion, that tendency has necessarily and inevitably increased. It must always happen that, when the life of the nation is menaced, the strength and extent of central power will be augmented. In such emergencies, the nation arrogates to itself power which it never thought of possessing or exercising in time of peace. We have become habituated to yielding to such things as matters of inexorable necessity.[225]

Even though Hale fully supported the use of federal power to protect the liberty and rights of all Americans—black or white—he insisted that state power must always be maintained. He continued:

> [T]here are other liberties as important as the liberties of the
> individual citizen, and those are the liberties and rights of the
> states. I believe that whatever most clearly distinguishes our
> government from other governments in the extent of individual
> freedom and the protection of personal rights we owe to our
> decentralized system, to the fact that the functions of government
> with which the citizen has immediate relation are brought home
> to him, that he operates immediately upon him, instead of there
> being that long chain of communication which in a centralized
> government must extend from the fountain of power, whether
> despotic or republican, whether executive or legislative, to the
> citizen.[226]

States, when left alone, were surely capable of injustice—recent history had proved this. But Hale was certain that an unbridled centralized power could generate far greater evil because its impact would be more widespread. He therefore cautioned against the continued use of federal power after the southern states had been subdued and slavery had ended. He said, "Let us see that a more dangerous heresy [centralized power] be not allowed to rise in its place."[227]

At a time when increased federal power was necessary to secure the natural rights of all Americans, Republicans were clearly cognizant of the danger of centralized power—a danger that might be realized under a broad interpretation of the Fourteenth Amendment. Republicans therefore articulated a narrow reading of Section 1. The amendment would carry force only if states disrespected equal application of the law. Aimed primarily at the former Confederate states as a condition of peace, the Fourteenth Amendment and the federal powers that it created were expected to retreat from the South when equality was at last established. Republicans assumed that future Congresses, like theirs, would respect legitimate state rights and aim to restore constitutional equilibrium.[228]

Republicans never anticipated that the Supreme Court would later prevent that restoration by interpreting the Fourteenth Amendment in a way that indefinitely expanded federal power over the states. Yet in a number of cases since the Civil War, the Supreme Court has abused the broad language of the Fourteenth Amendment by arbitrarily inserting a number of individual rights into its guarantees. These decisions have resulted in the expansion of federal power, since any right that the Court determines is covered by Section 1 is removed from state control (because the amendment prohibits state action). As the Court has pulled new subject matter areas within its jurisdiction under the Fourteenth Amendment, the decentralized structure of the American government has been practically obliterated, making the restoration of constitutional equilibrium all the more difficult to achieve.

As the following examples illustrate, the Court's Fourteenth Amendment jurisprudence is hardly commendable. The Court has stripped the amendment of its original purpose. In its place, the Court has constructed an often inconsistent and incoherent body of case law that is practically incomprehensible to most Americans. And this muddled group of legal precedents is what the Court today regards as the supreme law of the land.

The Slaughterhouse Cases

The Supreme Court's problematic interpretation of the Fourteenth Amendment began with its 1873 decision in *The Slaughterhouse Cases*. At issue in the case was a Louisiana statute that centralized slaughterhouse operations in the city of New Orleans. The law forced butchers to close their independent slaughterhouses and rent space within a central location. A group of white butchers sued, arguing that the Fourteenth Amendment protected their right to exercise their trade independent of the regulated operations. They argued that a right to make a living was one of the privileges or immunities of American citizenship—a civil right that no state could abridge. The question for the Court to decide was whether such a right was protected under the Privileges or Immunities Clause of Section 1, which reads, "No State shall make or enforce any law which shall abridge the privileges or immunities of citizens of the United States."[229]

The Privileges or Immunities Clause was supposed to be the pivotal provision of the Fourteenth Amendment that recognized the substantive natural rights of all Americans. These rights would be shielded from all discriminatory laws by the guarantee of certain procedural protections found in the other two clauses of Section 1.[230] The Due Process Clause (no state shall "deprive any person of life, liberty, or property, without due process of law") would forbid judicial discrimination by assuring to every American the same access to the courts.[231] And the Equal Protection

Clause (no state shall "deny to any person within its jurisdiction the equal protection of the laws") would prohibit statutory discrimination by mandating uniformity in the law.[232]

This understanding of Section 1 was known to the Court in *Slaughterhouse*. One of the dissenting justices, Joseph Bradley, explained that the section was meant to protect the natural rights that have attached to American citizenship ever since the nation was founded. He wrote in his dissent, "The people of this country brought with them to its shores the rights of the enlightenment"—natural rights that "Blackstone classifie[d] as the absolute rights of individuals, to wit: the right of personal security, the right of personal liberty, and the right of private property."[233] Bradley pointed out that these fundamental rights were identified in the Declaration of Independence as the basic rights of American citizenship. And after the Civil War ended and the Fourteenth Amendment took effect, these privileges and immunities of citizenship could be denied to no one. All Americans from that moment on were "entitled to certain privileges and immunities as citizens" that every state had to "respect and maintain."[234] He wrote:

> Rights to life, liberty, and the pursuit of happiness are equivalent to the rights of life, liberty, and property. These are the fundamental rights which can only be taken sway by due process of law, and which can only be interfered with, or the enjoyment of which can only be modified, by lawful regulations necessary or proper for the mutual good of all; and these rights, I contend, belong to the citizens of every free government.[235]

Bradley recognized that the Privileges or Immunities Clause protected the natural rights of every American. And these rights could not be violated in an arbitrary or discriminatory manner, for the people were guaranteed due process and equal protection of the law by other provisions of Section 1.

Even the majority opinion in *Slaughterhouse* acknowledged this interpretation as the prevailing judicial understanding of the privileges and immunities of citizenship. It quoted the definition provided by a Supreme Court justice in an 1825 case:

> "[W]hat are the privileges and immunities of citizens in the several States? We feel no hesitation in confining these expressions to those privileges and immunities which are, in

their nature, fundamental; which belong, of right, to the citizens of all free governments; and which have, at all times, been enjoyed by the citizens of the several States which compose this Union, from the time of their becoming free, independent, and sovereign. What these fundamental principles are, it would perhaps be more tedious than difficult to enumerate. They may, however, be all comprehended under the following general heads: protection by the government; the enjoyment of life and liberty, with the right to acquire and possess property of every kind, and to pursue and obtain happiness and safety, subject, nevertheless, to such restraints as the government may justly prescribe for the general good of the whole."[236]

Instead of applying this common understanding of privileges and immunities, however, the Court glossed over it and formed out of nothing a new definition for the Principles or Immunities Clause. The Court decided that the clause protected only those rights that were exclusively related to the national government, such as the right to petition Congress, the right to protection on the high seas, and the right to use the navigable waters of the United States.[237] All other rights, if not protected elsewhere in the Constitution, could be regulated and restricted by the states.

The Supreme Court so narrowly defined the Privileges or Immunities Clause because it feared the consequences of an expansive federal power over the states. If the Court could invalidate a state law concerning local slaughterhouse operations under the pretence of a civil rights claim, then it could regulate virtually anything in America. The Court stated that the Privileges or Immunities Clause was never meant "to transfer the security and protection of all the civil rights . . . from the states to the federal government."[238] Such a broad interpretation of that clause, the Court wrote, would "radically change[] the whole theory of the relations of the state and federal governments to each other and of both these governments to the people."[239] It concluded that "no such results were intended by the Congress which proposed [this] amendment[], nor by the legislatures of the states which ratified [it]."[240] So the Court stripped the Privileges or Immunities Clause of its true meaning as a way to guard against excessive federal power. The state law in question in *Slaughterhouse* was upheld.

The problem with the Court's decision in this case was not its outcome. The framers of the Fourteenth Amendment by no means intended for Section 1 to protect a group of white butchers from any kind of state regulation. So the Court was correct to deny their claim and uphold the Louisiana statute.

The problem with the Court's decision was that it incorrectly assumed that the Court had the jurisdiction to even question the constitutionality of the Louisiana law. The American people gave the Court no new authority under the Fourteenth Amendment to invalidate state laws. So soon after the Court had bastardized the Constitution by its disgraceful decision in *Dred Scott*, the American people were not about to entrust to it a negative on all state laws. They instead empowered *Congress* with the authority to implement the Fourteenth Amendment. Section 5 clearly states that "Congress shall have the power to enforce, by appropriate legislation, the provisions of this article."[241] This amendment gave Congress—not the Court—the duty to protect the natural rights of all Americans from abuse by state governments.

The 1866 Civil Rights Act was Congress' first attempt to preserve the natural rights of black Americans. Although it preceded the Fourteenth Amendment, the CRA triggered the amendment process as a way to remove all doubt about Congress' power to protect the natural rights of black Americans after the Civil War. The CRA aimed to invalidate the discriminatory Black Codes in the South and specifically declared that:

> [Americans] of every race and color, without regard to any previous condition of slavery or involuntary servitude . . . shall have the same right, in every state and territory in the United States, to make and enforce contracts, to sue, be parties, and give evidence, to inherit, purchase, lease, sell, hold, and convey real and personal property, and to full and equal benefit of all laws and proceedings for the security of person and property, as is enjoyed by white citizens, and shall be subject to like punishment, pains, and penalties, and to none other, any law, statute, ordinance, regulation, or custom, to the contrary notwithstanding.[242]

Congress' clear intent behind the CRA, and the primary motivation behind the Fourteenth Amendment, was to secure the same rights for black Americans that every white American enjoyed. Anyone aggrieved by a discriminatory state law or regulation could file suit in federal court—or have an ongoing state court proceeding transferred to it—so that justice under the CRA could prevail. Anyone who violated this law faced punishment of imprisonment, fines, or both.[243]

Proper enforcement of the CRA would have effectively rendered any discriminatory state law null and void, so there was no need, nor was there any constitutional authority, for the Supreme Court to review state laws under the Fourteenth Amendment. The people, through their congressional representatives, were to determine the scope of that amendment; the Court's jurisdiction was meant to merely follow federal law. The Court still possessed its independent authority to decide whether a law like the CRA conformed to the spirit of the Fourteenth Amendment. But it had no power—no expanded jurisdiction under that amendment—to strike down state laws at will. Congress retained all constitutional authority to decide the best means to preserve the privileges and immunities of citizenship in America.

Despite this design, the Court's ruling in *Slaughterhouse* set a precedent for judicial encroachment of state and congressional power under the Fourteenth Amendment. Its review of the Louisiana slaughterhouse regulation—a law that had nothing to do with racial discrimination and violated no section of the CRA—encouraged subsequent Courts to scrutinize other state laws that had no relation to Congress' implementing measures under the Fourteenth Amendment.

The *Slaughterhouse* decision was also problematic because the Court's narrow reading of the Privileges or Immunities Clause rendered it a nullity. By glossing over the purpose of this provision in Section 1 to preserve natural equality for all, the Court stripped the Fourteenth Amendment of its original meaning. As a consequence, the Court thereafter developed the substance of Section 1 under the Due Process and Equal Protection Clauses. And because the Court had elevated textual meaning over original intent in *Slaughterhouse*, it all but assured that these other imprecise phrases would receive the same legalistic interpretation going forward.

Unrestrained by original intent and later unchallenged by the political branches, the Court was free to develop constitutional meaning for the Fourteenth Amendment. The Constitution soon became, as Jefferson long feared, "a mere thing of wax in the hands of the judiciary, which they may twist and shape into any form they please."[244] What follows is an introduction to the twisted form that the Court has since created out of the Fourteenth Amendment's Due Process and Equal Protection Clauses.

The Due Process Clause

The Due Process Clause of Section 1 has become one of the most malleable provisions in the Constitution thanks to the Court's broad construction of its terms. The clause, which prohibits all states from depriving "any person of life, liberty, or property, without due process of law," was intended to serve as a procedural barrier against judicial discrimination.[245] States could legally deprive select individuals of their natural rights—usually under criminal penalties such as capital punishment, imprisonment, or fines. But states could not deny any natural right without first affording their citizens due process of law—they had to give the accused a fair opportunity to present a defense before an unbiased judge or jury. The Due Process Clause merely assured every American the same legal process under the law, and this procedural guarantee is what due process had always been understood to mean. Alexander Hamilton wrote in 1787, "The words 'due process' have a precise technical import, and are only applicable to the process and proceedings of the courts of justice."[246]

To the Supreme Court, however, the Due Process Clause has come to mean so much more. Under the Court's broad interpretation of this provision, the Due Process Clause not only guarantees fair legal process; it also protects from state regulation certain fundamental rights as determined by the Court. The Court has essentially transformed this procedural provision into a substantive grant of individual rights—rights that state governments are bound to protect, even if they maintain fair legal proceedings for all. And the Court has been able to achieve this transformation with relative ease. Enabled by its precedent in *Slaughterhouse* to disregard the Fourteenth Amendment's original design, the Court has supplied new meaning to the Due Process Clause by broadly construing its text. In several judicial decisions since then, the Court has wielded this arbitrary and illegitimate legal doctrine, known as substantive due process, to shape constitutional meaning according to its own standard of fairness.

Substantive due process was introduced in constitutional law in the late nineteenth century when the Supreme Court decided a number of cases concerning the property rights of regulated industries. These cases had nothing to do with racial discrimination or legal procedure, but the Supreme Court nevertheless weighed in to give substance to the Due Process Clause. Specifically, the Court decided whether property rights were fundamental rights that states had to preserve. In *Munn v. Illinois* (1877), the Court determined that the right to property was fundamental under the Fourteenth Amendment, but not absolute.[247] It decided that a state could regulate private property as long as the property in question was "affected with a public interest."[248]

Although this ruling may have reflected the prevailing understanding of property rights in America, the Due Process Clause is clearly devoid of any language to support it. The Fourteenth Amendment makes no mention of any qualified right to property, and it grants no authority to the Court to even decide such a question. Yet the Court in *Munn* felt compelled to intervene and provide an answer that it determined was correct. In doing so, the Court created a single rule for the nation concerning the scope of a person's property rights. And it stripped state legislatures of their power to set these limits for themselves.

The Supreme Court claimed similar authority under the Due Process Clause to protect an individual's economic liberty from state regulation. In *Allgeyer v. Louisiana* (1897), the Court declared that no state could deprive any citizen of his fundamental right to contract. To justify this holding, the Court broadly interpreted "liberty" in the Fourteenth Amendment's Due Process Clause to include a number of fundamental rights. The Court wrote:

> The "liberty" mentioned in that amendment . . . is deemed to embrace the right of the citizen to be free in the enjoyment of all his faculties, to be free to use them in all lawful ways, to live and work where he will, to earn his livelihood by any lawful calling, to pursue any livelihood or avocation, and for that purpose to enter into all contracts which may be proper, necessary, and

essential to his carrying out to a successful conclusion the purposes above mentioned.[249]

The Court's definition of liberty in *Allgeyer* was so broad that it even encompassed a person's right to earn a living—the same right that it had previously rejected in *Slaughterhouse*. The sweeping impact of this construction of liberty enabled the Court to develop its doctrine of substantive due process virtually without limit. In subsequent cases, the Court aggressively scrutinized and often invalidated state laws that restricted, in any way, a person's economic liberty.

The Court's most significant Due Process Clause ruling pertaining to economic liberty came in 1905. In *Lochner v. New York*, the Court struck down a New York law that set an upper limit on the number of hours that a person could work in a bakery.[250] The law was designed to protect the health of bakers, and states had always enjoyed broad police powers to regulate the safety, health, and morals of their communities. But the Court claimed to hold a superior authority to determine the legitimacy of any state law. It argued that it was empowered to decide whether any law was "a fair, reasonable, and appropriate exercise of the police power of the state."[251] The Court in *Lochner* ultimately ruled that the New York law in question was an unreasonable exercise of state power—that the law unduly restricted the economic liberty of bakers by infringing upon their fundamental right to contract under the Due Process Clause. According to the Court, bakers were entitled to bargain and sell their labor as they wished and needed no special protection under the law.[252]

Substantive due process effectively enabled the Court to substitute its judgment for that of the people. Even if a state law had no discriminatory impact on the people, and even if the states provided equitable legal process, the Court decided that a state law could be held unconstitutional under the Due Process Clause if it failed to pass the Court's test of what was "fair, reasonable, and appropriate." The spurious doctrine of substantive due process thus empowered the Supreme Court to impose national legal standards in areas of law in which the federal government lacked any constitutional authority.

The Court asserted this paternalistic power not just over the states, but also over the political branches of the federal government. To justify this expansion of judicial authority over federal disputes, the Court interpreted the Fifth Amendment's Due Process Clause—"No person shall be . . . deprived of life, liberty, or property, without due process of law"[253]— according to the same doctrine that it had developed under the Fourteenth Amendment. (Because the Fourteenth Amendment applied only against the states, the Court had to use the Fifth Amendment to similarly restrain federal action.) Undeniably, had the Court bothered to look into original intent, it would have realized that the Founding Fathers who ratified the Bill of Rights never meant to empower the Court with such a domineering authority over the representative branches. But the Court instead employed a rigidly textual interpretation of the Fifth Amendment so that it could apply its arbitrary doctrine of substantive due process against the federal government. Consequently, the Court thereafter was free to invalidate any state or federal law in America that infringed upon an unwritten set of judicially-determined fundamental rights.

The Supreme Court's Due Process Clause rulings thus ushered in an era in the early twentieth century, known as the *Lochner* era, in which the Court invalidated numerous state and federal labor laws. These laws, which sought to regulate a variety of trades and industries, were largely the product of the populist progressive movement that influenced Democrats and Republicans alike. Progressives generally sought to impose social and economic reform on the nation by centralizing political control under guidance of administrators in government. But the Court would not permit such social and economic control.

The Court's prohibitions on any means to regulate economic activity naturally frustrated progressives, who believed that they were entitled to act virtually without limitation. Theodore Roosevelt, an early leader of the progressive movement and the founder of the Progressive Party in 1912, exemplified this privileged mentality in his autobiography. Roosevelt shared his belief that the Constitution was not a grant of limited, enumerated powers; it was instead meant to restrain the otherwise expansive powers of the federal government. He wrote of the philosophy that governed his presidency from 1901–09:

> [I insisted] upon the theory that the executive power was limited only by specific restrictions and prohibitions appearing in the

Constitution or imposed by the Congress under its constitutional powers. . . . My belief was that it was not only [the President's] right but his duty to do anything that the needs of the nation demanded unless such action was forbidden by the Constitution or by the laws. . . . I did not usurp power, but I did greatly broaden the use of executive power.[254]

After the Supreme Court blocked a number of efforts to expand administrative power (using its activist doctrine of substantive due process), progressives responded in kind by mobilizing against the Court. They demanded in their 1912 Progressive Party platform "such restriction of the courts as shall leave to the people the ultimate authority to determine fundamental questions of social welfare and public policy."[255] Although the progressive movement was undoubtedly antithetical to the founding principles for its aim to consolidate power in the national government, its opposition to judicial supremacy was not.

Theodore Roosevelt stood firmly against the Court's broad construction of the Fourteenth Amendment during his unsuccessful run for a third (nonconsecutive) term as president. In a speech in 1912, he invoked Abraham Lincoln's strong opposition to judicial supremacy. Lincoln had always insisted, Roosevelt explained, that that "the American people were the masters and not the servants of even the highest court in the land, and were thereby the final interpreters of the Constitution."[256] Roosevelt further stated that "the only tenable excuse" for taking a position in support of judicial supremacy "is the frank avowal that the people lack sufficient intelligence and morality to be fit to govern themselves."[257] Those who subscribe to judicial supremacy must necessarily believe "that the people have enough intelligence to frame and adopt a constitution, but not enough intelligence to apply and interpret the Constitution which they themselves have made."[258] Roosevelt concluded that "if the people are not to be allowed finally to interpret the fundamental law, [then] ours is not a popular government."[259]

Despite such impassioned cries against judicial supremacy, progressives failed to rouse the people against the Court. The United States was experiencing rapid economic growth in that day, and so the people were content with the Court's invalidation of restrictive legislative measures that threatened to disturb the largely free economic environment that was believed to have advanced such prosperity. As a consequence, the Court's doctrine of substantive due process remained the law of the land.

Once the economy soured during the Great Depression, however, progressives capitalized on the nation's widespread economic uncertainty to rally popular support against the Court in their effort to institute radical economic change. For example, President Franklin D. Roosevelt berated the Court throughout the 1930s for blocking much of his progressive agenda. (His New Deal economic programs were designed to, in his words, give Americans a "more equitable opportunity to share in the distribution of national wealth."[260]) In a speech in 1937, Roosevelt criticized the Court for its legalistic interpretation of the Constitution, saying, "The Constitution was a layman's document, not a lawyer's contract."[261] He argued that the Court's opinions on constitutionality were just opinions and were not binding on the other federal branches, which had independent authority to follow their interpretations of the Constitution. Roosevelt observed that, throughout American history, the people have followed this founding principle of departmental independence. He said, "[T]hey have respected as sacred *all* branches of their government. They have seen nothing *more* sacred about one branch than about either of the others."[262] Making the case for a political rejection of the Court's rulings, Roosevelt continued:

> [The people] can take cheer from the historic fact that every effort to construe the Constitution as a lawyer's contract rather than a layman's charter has ultimately failed. Whenever legalistic interpretation has clashed with the contemporary sense on great questions of broad national policy, ultimately the people and the Congress have had their way.[263]

Roosevelt sought to have his way as well, but he never challenged the Court by asserting executive independence. Instead, he proposed the Judiciary Procedures Reform Bill of 1937, which would have expanded the Court from 9 to 15 justices. The bill would have given Roosevelt the chance to appoint ideologically-friendly justices to the Court, resulting in a new majority that would have endorsed his policies. The proposed law soon became unnecessary, however.

Just 20 days after Roosevelt spoke on behalf of the bill, the Supreme Court caved to his pressure by reversing its position on substantive due process. In *West Coast Hotel v. Parrish* (1937), the Court decided that the Due Process Clause did not guarantee a fundamental right to contract after all. It wrote, "The Constitution does not speak of freedom of contract. It speaks of liberty and prohibits the deprivation of liberty without due process of law."[264] Recognizing that its doctrine of substantive due process was not supported by the Constitution, the Court suppressed its tendency to strike down state and federal laws that restrained economic liberty.

The Court in *West Coast Hotel* created a new deferential standard by which it would review all laws affecting economic freedom. To pass as constitutional, a law had to satisfy the Court's new definition of due process. It wrote, "[A] regulation which is reasonable in relation to its subject and is adopted in the interests of the community is due process."[265] The Court expounded upon this standard in *United States v. Carolene Products* (1938) by declaring that regulatory legislation carries "the assumption that it rests upon some rational basis within the knowledge and experience of the legislators."[266] The Court's subsequent application of "rational basis" scrutiny was essentially a rule of judicial restraint (or judicial acquiescence to progressive reform). As long as the Court could find some rational basis for the law in question—which it usually did for laws that merely regulated one's economic liberty—it would defer to the legislature's implicit opinion of constitutionality. Such deference allowed Roosevelt and the Democrats in Congress to enact all of their New Deal programs without fear that the Court would strike them down as unconstitutional.

The Equal Protection Clause

While the Supreme Court ceded constitutional authority over economic concerns to the political branches, it continued to assert interpretive control over laws that denied the equal rights of minorities. The Court in *Carolene Products* stated that it would exercise a "more searching judicial inquiry" for laws that evince "prejudice against discrete and insular minorities."[267] It would closely scrutinize state laws for prejudice under the Equal Protection Clause of the Fourteenth

Amendment, which says that no state shall "deny to any person within its jurisdiction the equal protection of the laws."[268]

The notion that the Supreme Court would serve as the protector of minority rights was dubious at best, given its long tendency to ignore the natural rights of black Americans. As already mentioned, the Court had stripped black Americans of all their rights in its controversial *Dred Scott* decision in 1856. And in the ensuing years, the Court's decisions fared no better.

The Supreme Court passed on an opportunity to take a firm stand against racial inequality in the *Civil Rights Cases* of 1883. At issue in that case was the federal Civil Rights Act (CRA) of 1875, which provided that "all persons within the jurisdiction of the United States shall be entitled to the full and equal enjoyment of the accommodations, advantages, facilities, and privileges of inns, public conveyances on land and water, theaters, and other places of public amusement."[269] This CRA was meant to invalidate Jim Crow laws passed by Democrats in the South—laws that forced private entities to provide segregated accommodations for black Americans. But the Court held that the CRA was unconstitutional.[270] Once again, the Court ignored the Fourteenth Amendment's original intent, which was to empower Congress with the means to establish natural equality for all Americans. The Court instead applied its legalistic reading of that amendment to strike down the federal law in question. It ruled that the Fourteenth Amendment outlawed discrimination by states only and did not apply to private individuals or organizations—even though private acts of discrimination were mandated by state law.

The Court's decision in the *Civil Rights Cases* was a major setback to equality in America, and the Republicans who passed the CRA could do nothing in response. Their once-dominant advantage in Congress had been eroded by Democrats ever since federal troops were withdrawn from the South in 1877 to end the Reconstruction. Democrats had quickly regained power in every southern state, and they reestablished their influence in Congress. Republicans therefore were unable to politically resist the Court's ruling, and segregation spread rapidly throughout the South as a result. Democrats enacted a variety of Jim Crow laws in their states, thereby stamping black Americans with a badge of inferiority by segregating their housing, employment, and public lives from other Americans.

Opponents of segregation were left with no other choice but to challenge the legality of Jim Crow laws. But the Supreme Court rebuffed that challenge in *Plessy v. Ferguson* (1896) by officially endorsing segregation as constitutional. The Court declared in *Plessy* that the Equal Protection Clause of the Fourteenth Amendment actually permitted the segregation of black Americans under state law.[271] It held that separate but equal accommodations for people of different races constituted equal protection of the law.

Racial segregation thus became the law of the land in America thanks to the Supreme Court. Segregation further expanded in law in the South. It emerged in practice in the North. And it even crept into the federal government during the Progressive Era—federal offices had been integrated since the end of the Civil War, but in 1913, Democratic President Woodrow Wilson allowed segregation to take hold in many executive departments.

Given the Supreme Court's shameful history of decisions that adversely impacted racial equality in America, the promise it made in *Carolene Products* to shield minorities from discriminatory laws could hardly be taken as credible. The Court's disgraceful decision in *Plessy* supporting segregation was still in force at the time. And it made yet another ruling in 1944 that enforced a racist restriction on minority rights.

In *Korematsu v. United States* (1944), the Supreme Court sanctioned the segregated internment of Japanese Americans during World War II.[272] Shortly after the attack on Pearl Harbor, Democratic President Franklin Roosevelt signed an executive order that forced Japanese Americans into concentration camps for the duration of the war. Fred Korematsu, a loyal American of Japanese descent, was one of those persons interned, and he sued unsuccessfully for his release.

The Supreme Court endorsed Roosevelt's discriminatory executive order in a 6-3 decision. Although the Court applied a higher level of scrutiny to the executive order—what the Court called "the most rigid scrutiny" for any legal restriction that curtailed minority rights—it still sanctioned the order.[273] The Court determined that there was a "pressing public necessity" for this racially targeted order.[274] It decided that national security interests amid war outweighed the individual rights of innocent and loyal Japanese Americans.

There truly was no basis for this ruling. First of all, there was almost no threat from Japanese Americans in that day. Roosevelt's legal team had deliberately withheld from the Court a key intelligence report showing that a vast majority of Japanese Americans were loyal to the United States and that those who were not were already in custody.[275] To scare the Court into a favorable ruling, Roosevelt's Solicitor General also made gross generalizations about Japanese Americans, saying they were disloyal and motivated by "racial solidarity."[276] Despite these dishonest and unethical tactics, for which the acting Solicitor General apologized in 2011, the Court still had no justifiable reason to uphold an executive order that criminalized an entire race of people. As Justice Robert Jackson explained in his dissent in that case, Korematsu was being confined solely because he was Japanese. He wrote:

> No claim is made that [Korematsu] is not loyal to this country. There is no suggestion that, apart from the matter involved here, he is not law-abiding and well disposed. Korematsu, however, has been convicted of an act not commonly a crime. . . . [He was convicted for being] the son of parents as to whom he had no choice, and [because he] belongs to a race from which there is no way to resign.[277]

Jackson was particularly concerned that the Court's sanction of a patently discriminatory order would set a dangerous precedent going forward. He continued:

> [O]nce a judicial opinion rationalizes such an order to show that it conforms to the Constitution, or rather rationalizes the Constitution to show that the Constitution sanctions such an order, the Court for all time has validated the principle of racial discrimination in criminal procedure and of transplanting American citizens. The principle then lies about like a loaded weapon, ready for the hand of any authority that can bring forward a plausible claim of an urgent need. Every repetition imbeds that principle more deeply in our law and thinking and expands it to new purposes. . . . A military commander may overstep the bounds of constitutionality, and it is an incident. But

if we review and approve, that passing incident becomes the
doctrine of the Constitution.[278]

The new constitutional doctrine that the Court effectively sanctioned in
Korematsu was, according to another dissenting justice, the "legalization
of racism."[279]

Despite this valid concern that the Court's ruling in *Korematsu* might
encourage similar acts of discrimination, it thankfully did not. No
succeeding president has ever followed the racist example set by Roosevelt
in rounding up an entire group of minorities and confining them to
internment camps. So the Court never again had to confront its appalling
decision in *Korematsu* that excused such action. But the decision stands as
yet another example of how the Court disregarded the natural rights of
minorities to achieve the outcome it desired—perhaps in acquiescence to
the dominating political influence of Roosevelt.

The Incorporation Doctrine (Limited Substantive Due Process)

While the Supreme Court apparently shied away from any
confrontation with Roosevelt, it showed more assertiveness against the
states. The Court steadily advanced against state power under a relatively
new judicial doctrine known as incorporation. Under this doctrine, the
Court incorporated various protections from the Bill of Rights into the
Fourteenth Amendment's Due Process Clause as a component of "liberty"
that no state could deny. By treating these restrictions on federal power as
fundamental rights protected by the Fourteenth Amendment, the Court
stole from the people their natural and constitutional authority to set the
boundaries of such rights in their state governments.

Undeniably, the Bill of Rights was never intended to prohibit state
action; it was meant only to limit federal power. The Supreme Court
acknowledged this fact in *Barron v. Baltimore* (1833), when it wrote,
"These amendments demanded security against the apprehended
encroachments of the general government—not against those of local
governments."[280]

The Court even reaffirmed this point just seven years after the
Fourteenth Amendment was ratified. At a time when the debates over the
amendment were fresh in the minds of the justices, the Court declared in
United States v. Cruikshank (1875), "[The Bill of Rights] was not intended

to limit the powers of state governments in respect to their own citizens, but to operate upon the national government alone."[281] When discussing the First Amendment, the Court in *Cruikshank* observed that the right of assembly was not a fundamental right of the people, but a mere limitation on federal power. It wrote:

> The particular amendment now under consideration assumes the existence of the right of the people to assemble for lawful purposes, and protects it against encroachment by Congress. The right was not created by the amendment; neither was its continuance guaranteed, except as against congressional interference. For their protection in its enjoyment, therefore, the people must look to the states. The power for that purpose was originally placed there, and it has never been surrendered to the United States.[282]

The people in their states retained all power to determine the scope of individual rights, and the Fourteenth Amendment did nothing to diminish that popular authority. As the Court in *Cruikshank* explained, the Fourteenth Amendment merely guaranteed to the people the equal application of the law:

> The Fourteenth Amendment prohibits a state from denying to any person within its jurisdiction the equal protection of the laws; but this provision does not . . . add anything to the rights which one citizen has under the Constitution against another. The equality of the rights of citizens is a principle of republicanism. Every republican government is in duty bound to protect all its citizens in the enjoyment of this principle, if within its power. That duty was originally assumed by the states, and it still remains there. The only obligation resting upon the United States is to see that the states do not deny the right. This the amendment guarantees, but no more. The power of the national government is limited to the enforcement of this guaranty.[283]

To the Court that endured the Civil War and the Reconstruction, it was perfectly clear that the Fourteenth Amendment did not extend the application of the Bill of Rights beyond the federal government.

Yet subsequent Courts decided otherwise. In a number of rulings over time, the Supreme Court selectively incorporated specific limitations in the Bill of Rights into the Fourteenth Amendment's Due Process Clause.

Limitations on federal power thus became limitations on state power just the same—limitations that were enforced by the Court.

The Court's incorporation doctrine was first applied to the First Amendment in 1925. That amendment clearly prohibited the federal government from restricting speech in any way—"Congress shall make no law . . . abridging the freedom of speech"[284]—but it placed no similar restriction on state authority. The people could regulate speech as they saw fit through their state governments. In *Gitlow v. New York* (1925), however, the Supreme Court decided that state governments also lacked power to restrict speech. It declared that "the freedom of speech . . . [is] among the fundamental personal rights and 'liberties' protected by the Due Process Clause of the Fourteenth Amendment."[285] In a single decision, the Court usurped from the people everywhere in the nation a power that had long been theirs. Power over speech, which was expressly denied to the federal government by the First Amendment, was brazenly claimed by the Court. From that moment on, the Court would regulate speech according to its arbitrary understanding of this new fundamental right.

The Court soon seized other state powers under its doctrine of incorporation. The power to regulate the press was taken in 1931 when the Court held that "liberty of the press . . . is within the liberty safeguarded by the Due Process Clause of the Fourteenth Amendment from invasion from state action."[286] The power to promote religion or religious education ended in 1947 when the Court incorporated the prohibition on religious establishment into the Due Process Clause.[287] Thereafter, religion would be wiped clean from public places everywhere, for the Court created new rules to restrict it, including:

> [N]either a state nor the federal government can set up a church. Neither can pass laws which aid one religion, aid all religions, or prefer one religion over another. . . . No tax in any amount, large or small, can be levied to support any religious activities or institutions, whatever they may be called, or whatever form they may adopt to teach or practice religion.[288]

The Court removed even more powers from the people in the 1960s, when Chief Justice Earl Warren led an activist majority to extend the incorporation doctrine. The Court incorporated certain Fourth Amendment prohibitions in cases decided in 1961, 1963, and 1964.[289] It incorporated provisions of the Fifth Amendment in 1964 and 1969.[290] It incorporated parts of the Sixth Amendment in 1963, 1965, 1967, and 1968.[291] And it incorporated the Eighth Amendment's prohibition on cruel and unusual punishment in 1962.[292]

In many respects, the Supreme Court's incorporation doctrine was a revival of the arbitrary authority that it once wielded during the *Lochner* era. Utilizing this doctrine, the Court overturned numerous state laws by exploiting the same broad interpretation of the Due Process Clause that the Lochner Court had exploited. The main difference, however, was that the incorporation doctrine was meant to be a much more limited form of substantive due process. The Court could no longer regard as a fundamental right anything that might fit into its broad definition of liberty, as it did in the *Lochner* era. It instead could search for fundamental rights only in the provisions of the first eight amendments to the Constitution.

In actuality, this apparent constraint on judicial activism was hardly a constraint at all. For instance, in *Griswold v. Connecticut* (1965), the Supreme Court applied the incorporation doctrine and claimed to find in the Bill of Rights a fundamental right to privacy that exists nowhere in the text of any amendment.[293] As expected, Court struck down the state law in question that did not comport with its sense of liberty.

The *Griswold* decision perfectly exhibits how the Court can so easily reshape the Constitution by stretching the meaning of its text. The Court in that case conceded that the right to privacy was not an express guarantee in the Bill of Rights, but it anyway decided that a right not mentioned could still be a fundamental right incorporated into the Due Process Clause to invalidate a state law. As long as the right was somewhere within the periphery of other guarantees, then that was enough for the Court to treat it as fundamental.

To support its assertion that the Bill of Rights includes a right to privacy, the Court in *Griswold* redefined the function and substance of various amendments to give the appearance that they were actually related to privacy. It inarticulately explained that the "specific guarantees in the Bill of Rights have penumbras, formed by emanations from those guarantees that help them give life and substance. Various guarantees create zones of privacy."[294] The Court said that the First Amendment was not just about the freedom of speech, press, religion, and assembly; it was also about the right to associate with others and to enjoy "privacy in one's associations."[295] The Third Amendment's prohibition against the quartering of soldiers was "another facet of that privacy."[296] The Fourth Amendment did not just protect and individual from unreasonable searches and seizures; it also created "a right to privacy, no less important than any other right carefully [and] particularly reserved to the people."[297] The Fifth Amendment's protection against self-incrimination actually enabled "the citizen to create a zone of privacy which government may not force him to surrender to his detriment."[298] The Court also suggested that a right to privacy was guaranteed by the Ninth Amendment, which reads, "The enumeration in the Constitution, of certain rights, shall not be construed to deny or disparage others retained by the people."[299]

The Court was plainly stretching the meaning of the Bill of Rights and disregarding the Constitution's original design. When the American people first adopted the Constitution, they granted to the federal government only those powers enumerated in the Constitution. The federal government—especially the Supreme Court—was supposed to play a limited role in the lives of most Americans as the scope of its power was narrow. And the additional prohibitions in the Bill of Rights served to underscore the limitations on federal power—they did not create fundamental rights. Furthermore, the Ninth Amendment was never meant to protect unenumerated rights, as the *Griswold* Court suggested. The people were to control the scope of their rights through the operation of their state governments—by crafting their state constitutions and enacting state and local laws. These reserved powers were expressly addressed in the Tenth Amendment, which the *Griswold* Court conspicuously ignored. It states, "The powers not delegated to the United States by the Constitution, nor prohibited by it to the states, are reserved to the States respectively, or to the people."[300]

Nevertheless, by recasting the Bill of Rights as being somehow related to privacy, the Court in *Griswold* decided that these amendments were always meant to empower the federal government with the authority to protect an individual's absolute right to privacy. The Court construed the Constitution as if the federal government possessed an expansive power over the people—as if the federal government, and particularly the Court, had the power to determine the content and scope of individual rights for the people. Consequently, the Court declared that the right to privacy—written nowhere in the Constitution—was a fundamental right. The Court incorporated that right against the states through the Fourteenth Amendment's Due Process Clause, and it has remained ensconced in constitutional law ever since.

The immediate impact of the *Griswold* opinion was insignificant. It invalidated a law that was practically unenforceable—it struck down a law that prohibited married couples from using contraceptives. But the decision continues to be so controversial today because it served as the foundational case upon which the constitutional protections for abortion and gay sodomy were based.

The Supreme Court in *Roe v. Wade* (1973) expanded the *Griswold* right to privacy to include abortion rights.[301] In this case, it struck down a Texas law that criminalized abortion except when necessary to save the life of the mother. The Court explained its rationale:

> This right of privacy, whether it be founded in the Fourteenth Amendment's concept of personal liberty and restrictions upon state action, as we feel it is, or, as the District Court determined, in the Ninth Amendment's reservation of rights to the people, is broad enough to encompass a woman's decision whether or not to terminate her pregnancy.[302]

Even though abortion laws regulate the *act* of terminating the life of a baby in the womb—a procedure that is not "private" in the ordinary usage of that word—the Court determined that this act was an extension of the woman's *decision* to terminate her pregnancy. And that decision, the Court held, was an extension of a person's fundamental right to privacy.

Although the Court recognized abortion rights as fundamental (being tied to privacy rights), it did not consider them absolute. The Court developed a new standard for abortion rights as follows. It applied its "strict scrutiny" standard of review to laws that restricted fundamental rights—in this case, a woman's fundamental right to have an abortion.

Under strict scrutiny, a law is upheld only if can be justified by a "compelling state interest" and is "narrowly drawn to express only the legitimate state interests at stake."[303] Texas argued that its law was motivated by "a compelling state interest in protecting life from and after conception."[304] The Court rejected this argument, however. It stressed that no consensus existed among doctors, philosophers, and theologians about the point at which life begins. Without consensus on this difficult question, the Court was not about to defer to "the theory of life" adopted by Texas when its law infringed a woman's fundamental right to abortion.[305] The Court decided that an abortion law, to be constitutional, must balance the state's interest in protecting "the potentiality of human life" against another interest in preserving "the health of the pregnant woman."[306]

With these competing interests in mind, the Court then constructed a trimester framework as a guide to states desiring to pass constitutional abortion laws. During the first trimester of a woman's pregnancy, states could not regulate abortion at all because in this trimester, a woman's "mortality in abortion may be less than the mortality in normal childbirth."[307] The Court determined that there could be no compelling interest for a state to regulate abortions during this trimester when the abortion procedure was statistically less dangerous to the health of the woman than childbirth—the life of the baby was of no concern to the Court during this period. In the second trimester, concern for the life of the baby was still irrelevant, but because the abortion procedure during this period was more dangerous to the mother, abortion laws were permitted as long as they "reasonably related to the preservation and protection of maternal health."[308] The interest in preserving the life of the baby would only prevail in the third trimester, for that was when the baby had "the capability of meaningful life outside the mother's womb," as determined by the Court.[309] During the third trimester, a state could prohibit abortion entirely, "except when it [was] necessary to preserve the life or health of the mother."[310]

According to Court, this trimester framework supporting abortion rights was precisely what the Constitution demanded. Although abortion rights exist nowhere in the text of the Constitution, the Court derived their constitutionality from a similarly nonexistent right to privacy that it had previously read into the Bill of Rights. The Court then incorporated abortion rights into the Due Process Clause so that its intricate trimester framework could be applied against the states. As for the Texas abortion law in question in *Roe*, the Court struck it down because it did not balance the various rights associated with each part of the trimester framework—it weighed too heavily on the side of the life of the baby.[311]

The Return of Substantive Due Process

Almost twenty years later in *Planned Parenthood of Southeastern Pa. v. Casey* (1992), the Supreme Court arbitrarily cast aside its trimester framework pertaining to abortion, but it still decided that "the essential holding of *Roe v. Wade* should be retained and once again reaffirmed."[312] The Court chose to discard its trimester framework, not because the Constitution makes no mention of it, but instead because it was no longer consistent with medical advances. A baby could survive outside the mother's womb much earlier in the pregnancy, and new abortion procedures reduced the risks to the health of the mother.

In place of the trimester framework, the Court in *Casey* decided that abortion rights would depend on the baby's viability—the point at which the baby would likely survive outside the womb. The Court allowed states to "restrict abortions after fetal viability, if the law contains exceptions for pregnancies which endanger the woman's life or health."[313] But before viability, a woman had the right "to choose to have an abortion . . . and to obtain it without undue interference from the State."[314] Because the Court never defined the exact point of viability, it retained maximum flexibility over the ultimate scope of abortion rights in America.

The Court in *Casey* made other notable changes to its holding in *Roe*. The Court invented a new standard to review laws that regulated abortion before viability. Instead of the "strict scrutiny" standard that required a balance of "compelling state interests," the Court applied a new "undue burden standard."[315] Under this standard, an abortion law would be ruled unconstitutional if "its purpose or effect is to place a substantial obstacle in the path of a woman seeking an abortion before the fetus attains viability."[316] The Court, of course—and not the people—would determine what a substantial obstacle is. Using this equally arbitrary standard, the

Court in *Casey* struck down portions of the Pennsylvania abortion law under review that it disliked.[317]

Significantly, the Court's decision in *Casey* also changed the justification upon which abortion rights were based. As mentioned before, the Court in *Roe* based abortion rights on the right to privacy that was incorporated from the Bill of Rights into the Due Process Clause. But the Court in *Casey* instead simply declared that abortion rights were fundamental rights by themselves. The Court announced that it was free to decide which rights fit into the word "liberty" in the Due Process Clause, just as the *Lochner* Court had done almost a century before. No longer would the Court be limited by the Bill of Rights, as it was under the doctrine of incorporation. Its only limitation going forward would be its own reasoned judgment. The Court wrote, "The inescapable fact is that adjudication of substantive due process claims may call upon the Court in interpreting the Constitution to exercise that same capacity which by tradition courts always have exercised: reasoned judgment. Its boundaries are not susceptible of expression as a simple rule."[318]

The *Casey* Court characterized its *Roe* decision as protecting more than a simple privacy right. It said, "*Roe* . . . may be seen not only as an exemplar of *Griswold* liberty but as a rule . . . of personal autonomy and bodily integrity."[319] The Court portrayed a "woman's right to make the ultimate decision" regarding abortion as a right that was fundamental to liberty itself.[320] It declared that "intimate and personal choices . . . central to personal dignity and autonomy, are central to the liberty protected by the Fourteenth Amendment. At the heart of liberty is the right to define one's own concept of existence, of meaning, of universe, and of the mystery of human life."[321] Such a broad definition of liberty would seemingly encompass any individual action that flows from a choice that is central to a person's idiosyncratic notion of existence. But the Court appeared less concerned about the broad scope of its definition of liberty than its aim to provide a solid constitutional basis for abortion rights.

The effect of *Roe* and *Casey*, aside from their protection of abortion rights, is that there is virtually no limit to the content of fundamental rights under the Fourteenth Amendment's Due Process Clause. If abortion rights can be sanctioned by their association with a questionable right to privacy as in *Roe*, or if they can be given their own constitutional justification under a broad right to personal autonomy as in *Casey*, then the Court can provide constitutional cover to anything within its "reasoned judgment."

The Supreme Court soon after gave constitutional protection to homosexual sodomy. In *Lawrence v. Texas* (2003), the Court struck down a Texas law that criminalized homosexual sodomy, deciding that it violated the broad right of personal liberty that the Court had developed in prior cases involving the Fourteenth Amendment's Due Process Clause.[322] The Court in *Lawrence* began its opinion by proclaiming, "Liberty presumes an autonomy of self that includes freedom of thought, belief, expression, and certain intimate conduct."[323] The Court emphasized, as it did in *Casey*, "that the protection of liberty under the Due Process Clause has a substantive dimension of fundamental significance in defining the rights of the person."[324] The Court further explained, "The *Casey* decision [] confirmed that our laws and tradition afford constitutional protection to personal decisions relating to marriage, procreation, contraception, family relationships, child rearing, and education. . . . [T]he Constitution demands [respect] for the autonomy of the person in making these choices."[325] Particularly for homosexuals, the Court declared, "Their right to liberty under the Due Process Clause gives them the full right to engage in their conduct without the intervention of the government."[326] As a consequence, the Court struck down the Texas law for infringing that broad fundamental right to liberty.

Curiously, the *Lawrence* Court did not apply its heightened "strict scrutiny" standard of review that it generally applies to laws impacting fundamental rights. Had it done so, Texas would have been forced to show a "compelling state interest" in enacting the homosexual sodomy law. The Court instead applied a lesser and more deferential standard of "rational basis review." Under this standard, Texas merely had to hypothesize some "legitimate government interest" to justify the law.

Texas argued that it had a legitimate government interest in regulating personal conduct that the people of Texas determined to be immoral and unacceptable. This was the same justification that the Supreme Court had accepted as legitimate in *Bowers v. Hardwick* (1986) just seventeen years earlier. In that case, the Court upheld a similar Georgia sodomy statute when the only basis for the law was "the presumed belief of a majority of the electorate in Georgia that homosexual sodomy [was] immoral and unacceptable."[327] The *Bowers* Court explained, "[L]aw . . . is constantly based on notions of morality, and if all laws representing essentially moral choices are to be invalidated under the Due Process Clause, the courts will be very busy indeed."[328]

The *Lawrence* Court overturned its decision in *Bowers*, however. It rejected Texas' justification for the law, ruling that there could be no rational basis for a law regulating homosexual conduct. It wrote, "The Texas statute furthers no legitimate state interest which can justify its intrusion into the personal and private life of the individual."[329]

By its ruling, the Court effectively imposed upon the people of Texas—and numerous other states having similar homosexual sodomy laws—its own notion of morality by recognizing a fundamental right to homosexual conduct in the Due Process Clause. As Justice Antonin Scalia noted in his dissent, the *Lawrence* Court's ruling "effectively decrees the end of all morals legislation."[330] Accordingly, "criminal laws against fornication, bigamy, adultery, adult incest, bestiality, and obscenity" that are based on similar notions of morality would also fail rational basis review because they, too, intrude upon an individual's liberty, as the Court defines it.[331] In the end, the Court's ruling in Lawrence enabled it to strike down any law based in morality. According to the Court, what is right or wrong under the law—what is acceptable behavior and what is not—is for the Court to decide and the nation to follow.

It bears repeating that the framers of the Fourteenth Amendment never intended to empower the Supreme Court in this way. After the Civil War, Republicans in Congress forced the Fourteenth Amendment on the defeated, yet defiant, Confederate states as a condition to reunification. The amendment gave power to the federal government, and specifically to Congress, to ensure that the nation's founding principle of natural equality was respected everywhere in the land. As long as rights were distributed equally in the states in accordance with Congress' implementing measures, the limited nature of the federal government would not change. The people would retain all authority to determine the content and scope of their rights through their state governments. The objective of the Fourteenth

Amendment was to end discrimination in the South, not to consolidate power over every individual right in the federal government—particularly in its only unelected branch.

The Supreme Court has clearly neglected the spirit of the Fourteenth Amendment by its unbounded interpretation of liberty in the Due Process Clause. The Court has since reshaped the Fourteenth Amendment according to its own notion of fairness, and it has effectively become the super-legislature that it claimed it was not in *Griswold*. It wrote in that opinion, "We do not sit as a super-legislature to determine the wisdom, need, and propriety of laws that touch economic problems, business affairs, or social conditions."[332]

To this day, the Supreme Court continues to construe the Fourteenth Amendment's Due Process Clause in a way that empowers it to define the content and scope of individual rights for every person in America. Recently in *McDonald v. Chicago* (2010), the Court incorporated the Second Amendment's right to bear arms into the Due Process Clause, forcing upon all states a single legal standard pertaining to gun rights—a standard defined by the Court, of course.[333] This ruling, when viewed alongside *Lawrence*, demonstrates that no matter where an issue falls on the political spectrum (gun rights and homosexual sodomy rights are typically at polar opposites), the Court deems itself to be the only authority in the nation that is competent enough to decide what laws are best for all.

Modern Judicial Supremacy

The Supreme Court's paternalistic control over society today exists mainly because the people have let it encroach upon their governing authority. But the Court has done much in the last half century to convince the American people that its reading of the Constitution is binding on all in the land. To some degree, the people's obedience to the Court is a result of its relentless assertion that it is the supreme interpreter of constitutional meaning. Although this claim is wholly contrived—judicial supremacy has been rejected time and again throughout American history—new generations of Americans have come to accept the Court's revisionist account of the past.

The Court began constructing its false narrative in *Cooper v. Aaron* in 1958.[334] In this decision, the activist Warren Court glossed over constitutional history and insisted that it was always meant to be the final arbiter of constitutional meaning. It revived its controversial decision in *Marbury v. Madison* (1803) to support its spurious claim that judicial supremacy has been the rule ever since the nation's founding. The Court wrote in *Cooper*:

> It is necessary only to recall some basic constitutional propositions which are *settled doctrine*. Article VI of the Constitution makes the Constitution the "supreme law of the land." In 1803, Chief Justice Marshall, speaking for a unanimous Court, referring to the Constitution as "the fundamental and paramount law of the nation," declared in the notable case of *Marbury v. Madison* that "It is emphatically the province and duty of the judicial department to say what the law is." *This decision declared the basic principle that the federal judiciary is supreme in the exposition of the law of the Constitution, and that principle has ever since been respected by this Court and the country as a permanent and indispensable feature of our constitutional system.* It follows that the interpretation of the Fourteenth Amendment enunciated by this Court . . . is the supreme law of the land.[335]

The suggestion that judicial supremacy has been respected by the nation "as a permanent and indispensable feature of our constitutional system" and that it is "settled doctrine" is a gross misrepresentation of history. A review of the prominent constitutional controversies previously discussed—involving the Sedition Act, the national bank, and slavery—makes it clear that the people have controlled constitutional meaning in many divisive cases throughout time.

Even the *Marbury* decision itself was practically rejected by the people. Prior to that decision, President Jefferson had placed the Court on notice that he might ignore an unfavorable opinion.[336] He and the Republicans who controlled government after the Revolution of 1800 were not about to submit to the dictates of the Court concerning constitutional questions—they were prepared to exercise their independent authority under the Constitution and let the people pass final judgment on their actions. Aware of Jefferson's confidence in his interpretive independence, the Court in *Marbury* chose to avoid a constitutional controversy by dismissing the case on jurisdictional grounds. So despite its authoritative language, the *Marbury* decision had no impact on executive action, and it most certainly was not embraced by the people, as the Court in *Cooper* suggested. If the *Marbury* decision stands for anything, it demonstrates judicial weakness, not judicial supremacy.

Yet the Supreme Court after *Cooper* continued to misrepresent the significance of *Marbury* to build upon its claim of judicial supremacy. The following sample of cases reveals that the Court repeatedly asserted its authority over constitutional meaning—perhaps hoping that repetition of a falsehood might make it true. In *Baker v. Carr* (1962), the Court stated that "constitutional interpretation . . . is a responsibility of this Court as the *ultimate interpreter* of the Constitution."[337] The Court in *United States v. Nixon* (1974) suggested that constitutional interpretation is a function of judicial power and is exclusive to the Court. Invoking *Marbury*, the Court wrote, "We therefore reaffirm that it is the province and duty of this Court 'to say what the law is.'"[338] In *Goldwater v. Carter* (1979), the Court expressed its concern that political disputes over constitutional meaning might bring "the federal government . . . to a halt."[339] It therefore determined that the role of the Court, as expressed in *Marbury*, was "to provide a resolution pursuant to our duty 'to say what the law is.'"[340] The Court in *Thompson v. Oklahoma* (1988) wrote that "the task of interpreting the great, sweeping clauses of the Constitution ultimately falls on us [and] has been for some time an accepted principle of American jurisprudence. See *Marbury v. Madison* ('It is emphatically the province and duty of the judicial department to say what the law is')."[341]

To supply more apparent credibility to the idea of judicial supremacy, the Court in subsequent cases cited not only to *Marbury*, but also to the aforementioned cases that derived their authority from *Marbury*. For example, the Court in *Miller v. Johnson* (1995) listed the following citations to declare interpretive superiority over the executive branch:

> See, *e.g., United States v. Nixon* (judicial power cannot be shared with Executive Branch); *Marbury v. Madison* ("It is emphatically the province and duty of the judicial department to say what the law is"); cf. *Baker v. Carr* (Supreme Court is "ultimate interpreter of the Constitution"); *Cooper v. Aaron*

("permanent and indispensable feature of our constitutional system" is that "the federal judiciary is supreme in the exposition of the law of the Constitution").[342]

The Court in *United States v. Morrison* (2000) took the same approach as *Miller* and in fact cited to that case, among others, for support:

> It is thus a "'permanent and indispensable feature of our constitutional system'" that "'the federal judiciary is supreme in the exposition of the law of the Constitution.'" *Miller v. Johnson* (quoting *Cooper v. Aaron*). No doubt the political branches have a role in interpreting and applying the Constitution, but ever since *Marbury* this Court has remained the ultimate expositor of the constitutional text. As we emphasized in *United States v. Nixon*, "[I]n the performance of assigned constitutional duties each branch of the Government must initially interpret the Constitution, and the interpretation of its powers by any branch is due great respect from the others. . . . Many decisions of this Court, however, have unequivocally reaffirmed the holding of *Marbury* . . . that '[i]t is emphatically the province and duty of the judicial department to say what the law is.'"[343]

Under the Court's reasoning, anything that it repeats in its case law over time must be authoritative, not because it is right, but simply because it once said so.

The Supreme Court often applies this common law tradition of precedent to guide its reasoning. Under this judicial doctrine, courts generally apply rules or principles established in prior decisions to new cases having similar issues or facts. As a consequence, past decisions are often treated as authoritative law, and judges regularly cite to them, no matter how unreasonable or faulty they may be.

Not only does the tradition of precedent guide judicial reasoning, but it also influences legal education and practice in America. Aspiring lawyers are taught to respect any case that the Supreme Court regards as precedential, including *Marbury v. Madison*, which is typically the very first case presented in any constitutional law class in America. Because the Court's prior case law is so important to judicial decision making, it often forms the basis upon which most legal arguments are made. Whether an old case helps or hurts a lawyer's argument, as long as the Court treats it as precedential, then a lawyer must also. Given this trained deference to judicial decisions, it is not surprising to find within the legal profession a common reverence for the Court as the ultimate arbiter of constitutional meaning.

Alexis de Tocqueville took note of this peculiarity in his book, *Democracy in America*. Because the tradition of precedent so pervasively controlled legal reasoning, Tocqueville observed that lawyers were not being trained to reason. They were instead being trained to follow "the opinions of others."[344] He wrote that the willingness of the "American lawyer to forswear his own interpretation in favor of that of his forbears—indeed, the need to subject his thinking to a kind of servitude—must make the legal mind more timid in its habits and more static in its inclinations."[345] Tocqueville continued, "This type of legal mind [] seems indifferent to the spirit and attentive only to the letter of the law and [] would sooner relinquish reason and humanity than venture beyond its limits."[346]

This kind of legalistic understanding of the Constitution is what frustrated President Franklin Roosevelt so much in the 1930s. Constitutional meaning was never intended to be controlled by the legalistic practices and doctrines of the Court; it was meant to be controlled by the people. Roosevelt of course reminded the people that their constitutional interpretation had always prevailed against the Court's throughout history. He said, "Whenever legalistic interpretation has clashed with contemporary sense on great questions of broad national policy, ultimately the people and Congress have had their way."[347]

Yet the Supreme Court has its way with the Constitution today, and it does so with contempt for the people. The Court's professed supremacy over constitutional meaning is evidently driven by its complete lack of faith in the political process. Its close oversight of every political act—thanks to its broad and arbitrary reading of the Fourteenth Amendment—ultimately forces the people to bend to its will. The Court essentially rules under an elitist idea that the people are incapable of ruling themselves; that the democratic process is messy, self-interested, impulsive, and unfair; and that an impartial and apolitical body like the Court is necessary to check the power of the insensitive political majority. In essence, the Court believes that the alleged vices of the political process can only be corrected by the supposed counter-majoritarian virtue of judicial reasoning.

Jack Balkin, a constitutional law professor at Yale, described this elitist judicial philosophy as a "progressivist sensibility" that embodies "an inflated sense of superiority over ordinary people, disdain for popular values, [and] fear of popular rule."[348] Roberto Unger, a professor at Harvard Law School, similarly wrote that "discomfort with democracy" is one of the "dirty little secrets of contemporary jurisprudence."[349] He explained:

> The discomfort with democracy shows up in every area of contemporary legal culture: in the ceaseless identification of restraints upon majority rule, rather than of restraints upon the power of dominant minorities, as the overriding responsibility of judges and jurists; . . . in the single-minded focus upon the higher judges and their selection as the most important part of democratic politics; . . . and, occasionally, in the explicit treatment of party government as a subsidiary last-ditch source of legal evolution, to be tolerated when none of the more refined modes of legal resolution applies. Fear and loathing of the people always threaten to become the ruling passions of this legal culture.[350]

This kind of elitist mentality is nothing new in America. As discussed earlier, an aristocratic movement existed during the founding era. James Madison captured the patronizing attitude of this anti-republican group in 1792 when he contrasted its beliefs against those of republicans like himself. While republicans believed that "the people themselves" were the best stewards of liberty in America, anti-republicans believed that "[t]he people are stupid, suspicious, [and] licentious. They cannot safely trust themselves. When they have established government, they should think of nothing but obedience, leaving the care of their liberties to their wiser rulers."[351]

One of these anti-republicans was Alexander Hamilton, who had once advocated a government ruled by an elite group of individuals. When his aristocratic philosophy was politically rejected, he and others who shared a similar distrust of popular rule placed their faith in the Supreme Court. They hoped that this unelected body might subdue the people by sitting in judgment of every political action. Martin Van Buren wrote of this elitist aspiration:

> The want of a proper respect for the people, as has been often said, was Hamilton's great misfortune. If he could have felt otherwise, he would have been a Republican. This distrust of the capacity and disposition of the masses, which had been the bane of his life, retained its hold upon his strong mind and ardent feelings when he bequeathed it to his political disciples, and it has been the shibboleth of their tribe ever since. . . . [P]roud of their social position, their fear of the popular will, and desire to escape from popular control, instead of being lessened, is increased by the advance of the people in education and knowledge. Under no authority do they feel their interests to be safer than under that which is subject to the judicial power, and in no way could their policy be more effectually promoted than by taking power from those departments of the government over which the people have full control, and accumulating it in that over which they may fairly be said to have none.[352]

Although judicial supremacy over political action was never realized in early American history, it has since materialized in the modern era. The Supreme Court can review and invalidate any law made by any legislature that fails its arbitrary tests for constitutionality. In the Court's view, the political branches are so inept at serving the people's interests that it must fill that void. Writing for the Court in 1986, Justice William Brennan advised that "the Court must be ever mindful of its *primary role* as the protector of the citizen."[353] The Court views itself as a guardian of the people—protecting the people from themselves.

The Court's paternalistic care for the people is not limited to United States citizens. In *Boumediene v. Bush* (2008), the Court held that its jurisdiction applies to, and constitutional rights are extended to, foreign terrorists captured on the battlefield and held in captivity on foreign soil (at Guantanamo Bay, Cuba).[354] Although prior rulings suggested that the Court lacks jurisdiction over such alien enemy combatants, the Court twisted the meaning of those decisions to broaden its authority over the political branches.[355]

The Court's opinion in *Boumediene* was driven by its manifest distrust of political power unchecked by the judicial branch. The five

Justices who spoke for the majority of the Court suggested that the political branches should never be permitted to act on their own constitutional interpretation without judicial oversight.[356] Such freedom, the Court said, was contrary to *Marbury* and would "lead[] to a regime in which Congress and the President, not this Court, say 'what the law is.'"[357] Justice Scalia in his dissent touched on the motivation behind the Court's ruling when he wrote, "What drives today's decision is . . . an inflated notion of judicial supremacy."[358] Scalia opined that the Court had to rule against the political branches "because otherwise we would not be supreme."[359]

Notwithstanding the controversial nature of the *Boumediene* ruling—it gave foreign terrorists the same legal protections as American citizens—the political branches never challenged its validity. President George W. Bush made clear that he strongly disagreed with the decision, but he simultaneously promised that the executive branch would "abide by the Court's decision."[360] Members of Congress likewise obeyed the ruling.

This kind of reflexive political subservience to the Court has been all too common in modern times. In fact, the political branches have not challenged judicial supremacy since the 1980s, and even then, the challenge was brief and soon withdrawn.

In that brief confrontation in 1986, Attorney General Edwin Meese (serving under President Ronald Reagan) suggested that the Court's opinions were not the "supreme law of the land" and that each branch of government held an equal responsibility to interpret the Constitution and act accordingly.[361] The *New York Times* quickly attacked Meese for "making a calculated assault on the idea of law in this country: on the role of judges as the balance wheel in the American system."[362] In response to criticism such as this, Meese amended his remarks, later conceding that the Court's decisions "are the law of the land"—that they "do indeed have general applicability and deserve the greatest respect from all Americans."[363]

Ever since then, the Supreme Court has enjoyed near universal political acquiescence to its control over constitutional meaning.[364] A perfect example of the kind of submissive attitude that predominates within the political branches today is found in a speech made by

Democratic Senator Patrick Leahy, who said in 2001 on the floor of the Senate:

> As a member of the bar of the Court, as a U.S. Senator, as an American, I, of course, respect the decisions of the Supreme Court as being the ultimate decision of law for our country. And, as an American, I accept any of their decisions as the ultimate interpretation of our Constitution, whether I agree or disagree.[365]

Senator Leahy completely surrendered all constitutional judgment to the Court, despite being completely frustrated with its arbitrary and patronizing rulings. In the same speech, he complained that there was never "a more activist Supreme Court than the current one," he complained that "the Supreme Court [has] paid little heed to the view of either democratic branch of our government," and he complained of the Court's "arrogant disregard of the U.S. Congress" and its "feeling that the Congress is somehow unable . . . to express the will of the people or uphold the Constitution."[366] Despite these many objections, Leahy dutifully obeyed the Court, for he lives by the rule that the Court controls constitutional meaning.

Most politicians today are no different. Like Senator Leahy, they regard the Court as the supreme interpreter of constitutional meaning. Whenever constitutional questions arise, they patiently wait on the Court for answers. And whatever the Court decides, they reflexively obey.

When the Court's decisions are so controlling, the Constitution's original meaning and history are practically irrelevant. A case like *Marbury v. Madison* is no longer understood in the context of republicanism and popular sovereignty that reigned throughout most of American history; it is instead understood in the context of the Court's revisionist account of that history, beginning with its 1958 decision in *Cooper v. Aaron*. The Fourteenth Amendment is no longer interpreted in the context of the tumultuous Reconstruction Era or in the context of Natural Law principles that inspired it; the amendment is instead construed according to the Court's determination of what its language means—what the Court believes is fundamental to liberty or due process. In practice, the Court's various legal doctrines and precedential decisions affect constitutionality more than the Constitution itself.

This is not how the Founding Fathers intended the republic to function. They never meant to give the only unelected branch of government absolute control over constitutional meaning. The three branches of government were designed to be separate and coequal so that each branch could act according to its independent interpretation of the Constitution. And should any conflict ever arise over constitutional meaning, the people could resolve the matter by their elective power over government.

Popular constitutionalism was the design for American government, and time and again throughout history, popular constitutionalism prevailed. Whether or not elected officials were called upon to defy unconstitutional judicial decisions, the American people supported politicians who were confident in their ability to do so.

They supported Thomas Jefferson, who was adamantly opposed to judicial supremacy. He wrote, "[T]he opinion which gives to the judges the right to decide what laws are constitutional, and what not, not only for themselves in their own sphere of action, but for the legislature and executive also, in their spheres, would make the judiciary a despotic branch."[367]

They supported James Madison, who strongly rejected the idea that the judicial "department draws from the constitution greater powers than another, in marking out the limits of the powers of the several departments."[368] He wrote, "I do not see that any one of these independent departments has more right than another to declare their sentiments on [constitutionality]."[369]

The people supported Andrew Jackson, who believed that the Supreme Court's rulings had no automatic obligatory effect on the political branches. He wrote, "The authority of the Supreme Court must not . . . be permitted to control the Congress or the Executive . . . but to have only such influence as the force of their reasoning may deserve."[370]

They supported Martin Van Buren, who warned of the dangers of judicial supremacy:

> [T]o place the fidelity to the federal Constitution . . . under the supervision of that [judicial] department, is nothing less than to divest the government of its republican features and to substitute

in its place the control of an irresponsible judicial oligarchy—to make the Constitution a lie, and turn to mockery its most formal provisions, designed to secure to the people a control over the action of the government under its authority.[371]

They supported Abraham Lincoln, who knew that judicial supremacy would put an end to America's experiment in self-government and liberty. He said:

[I]f the policy of the government upon vital questions affecting the whole people is to be irrevocably fixed by decisions of the Supreme Court, . . . [then] the people will have ceased to be their own rulers, having to that extent practically resigned their government into the hands of that eminent tribunal.[372]

The people supported Theodore Roosevelt, who argued that "the American people [are] the masters and not the servants of even the highest court in the land, and [are] thereby the final interpreters of the Constitution."[373] He added, "[I]f the people are not to be allowed finally to interpret the fundamental law, [then] ours is not a popular government."[374]

And the American people supported Franklin Roosevelt, who saw "nothing more sacred about [the judicial] branch than about either of the others."[375] He pointed out that the people's understanding of the Constitution has always prevailed over the Court's in every major constitutional question throughout history. He said, "Whenever [the Court's] legalistic interpretation has clashed with the contemporary sense on great questions of broad national policy, ultimately the people and the Congress have had their way."[376]

Altogether, the Founding Fathers and succeeding generations of political leaders kept faith with the American people by rejecting judicial supremacy. They refused to let an elite judicial body impose on the people its arbitrary constitutional interpretation. They recognized that, because the people are the source of all governing power, their view of constitutionality must always prevail.

Although the current political class has since lost sight of this republican principle, it remains to be seen whether it is lost forever. It remains to be seen whether elected officials will ever act with confidence on the people's behalf to uphold their sense of constitutionality; whether judicial supremacy will ever be rejected; whether a government ordained and established by "We the People" will ever operate by its intended republican form; whether popular constitutionalism will prevail once again.

5

ON ECONOMIC LIBERTY

To the Founding Fathers, economic liberty was a central component of individual liberty. For if the American people were unable to pursue the occupations of their choosing, if they were forced to comply with overbearing government regulations, or if they were subject to burdensome taxation, then freedom would be a fallacy no matter how politically liberated they might be. American liberty therefore depended not only on decentralized political power, but also on a free market in which the people were largely left alone by government to follow their interests in pursuit of happiness.

The economic philosophy of the Founding Fathers was greatly influenced by the writings of Adam Smith—a Scottish moral philosopher and economist whose book, *An Inquiry into the Nature and Causes of the Wealth of Nations*, promoted free market principles and laid the foundation for modern economic theory. Published in 1776, *The Wealth of Nations* was widely read—particularly by many of the Founding Fathers, including George Washington, Benjamin Franklin, John Adams, Thomas Jefferson, Alexander Hamilton, James Madison, and John Jay.[1] Franklin actually met with Adam Smith in person and became an early advocate of free trade.[2] Jefferson also thought highly of Smith and his ideas. He wrote, "[O]n the subjects of money and commerce, Smith's *Wealth of Nations* is the best book to be read."[3]

The premise of Smith's economic theory in *The Wealth of Nations* is that the twin forces of self-interest and competition in a free market optimize the distribution of labor, resources, and products in society to the maximum benefit of all. Although self-interest is often regarded as one of man's baser instincts, Smith recognized that this innate quality is the underlying force in all commercial transactions. Self-interest—or the drive for financial gain—is what motivates individuals to supply products or services to others. He wrote, "It is not from the benevolence of the butcher, the brewer, or the baker that we expect our dinner, but from their regard to their self-interest. We address ourselves, not to their humanity, but to their self-love, and never talk to them of our necessities, but of their advantages."[4] In a free market, good ultimately emerges as the byproduct of self-interest.[5]

In a free market, efficiencies result from competition. No individual can extract exorbitant profits from others in the marketplace when other self-interested actors may freely join the in the same commercial activity and compete for market share. Moreover, self-interested actors in a free market continually seek out efficiencies to lower costs in a competitive environment, and these efficiencies drive down prices to the benefit of all consumers. As a consequence of self-interest and competition, a diverse set of goods can be produced at the lowest possible cost.

Importantly, free market capitalism provides an adaptability that fosters societal progress far better than central government planning. As the wants of society evolve, any individual in a free market can supply new products or services to satisfy those demands—motivated, of course, by profit. A large bureaucratic system could never advance so quickly or efficiently to keep up with the drivers of a free market. And just as capitalism encourages creative innovation, it also allows for creative destruction, which is the termination of economic activities that are no longer desired by the market.[6] When demand is lacking for certain products or services, profits disappear, and operations in these markets eventually cease. No individual, company, or industry is sheltered from these market forces, as they might be if supported and sustained by government. The superior adaptability of free markets therefore ensures that economic activity is always productive and efficient to best satisfy the wants of the people.

The beauty of the free market system is that it is impartial, self-regulating, and free. The people have the broadest economic liberty to pursue their interests in commerce, yet they remain disciplined by other competitors. If output, prices, or wages stray from their socially ordained levels, then market forces provide the necessary correction—not some bureaucratic authority whose response is likely untimely, unproductive, or unfair.[7] And because the anonymous pressures of the market are felt by all participants equally, success can be achieved by anyone who merits it. A free market does not discriminate by race, color, sex, or creed—only by achievement.

Particularly because free market capitalism coincides with the precepts of Natural Law, it became the favored economic system of the Founding Fathers. Thomas Paine pointed out that the best economic laws were those that followed Natural Law:

> All the great laws of society are Laws of Nature. Those of trade and commerce, whether with respect to the intercourse of individuals or of nations, are laws of mutual and reciprocal interests. They are followed and obeyed, because it is the interest of the parties to do so, and not on account of any formal laws their governments may impose or interpose.[8]

James Madison also believed that a free market economic system best suited the American people, given their strong claim to natural liberty and their ability to make sound economic decisions for themselves. He wrote:

> I have always concurred in the general principle that the industrious pursuits of individuals ought to be left to individuals, as most capable of choosing and managing them. And this policy is certainly most congenial with the spirit of a free people, and is particularly due to the intelligent and enterprising citizens of the United States.[9]

The Founding Fathers recognized that a free market system was optimal not only in principle but also in practice. Understanding that free markets maximize societal wealth, Jefferson wrote that the United States, and all other countries, "would gain by setting commerce at perfect liberty."[10] Hamilton described some of the national benefits that would result from a free market economy in America when he wrote:

An unrestrained intercourse between the states themselves will advance the trade of each, by an interchange of their respective productions, not only for the supply of reciprocal wants at home, but for exportation to foreign markets. The veins of commerce in every part will be replenished, and will acquire additional motion and vigor from a free circulation of the commodities of every part. Commercial enterprise will have much greater scope, from the diversity in the productions of different states.[11]

Given these practical benefits of a free market economy, the Founding Fathers naturally promoted this system in the United States.

Immediately after the Revolutionary War, however, the Founding Fathers had no power to establish this economic system, and they anticipated the problems that the new nation would have without it. Under the Articles of Confederation then in operation, the national government was too weak to enforce free trade, and many states at the time were biasing their laws in favor of their local residents. The Founding Fathers feared that this kind of protectionism might impede national economic development and divide the nation going forward. Hamilton warned what would come of the new nation if the states did not unite under a national government with the power to remove these obstacles to free trade. He wrote in The Federalist No. 7:

The competitions of commerce would be another fruitful source of contention. The states less favorably circumstanced would be desirous of escaping from the disadvantages of local situation, and of sharing in the advantages of their more fortunate neighbors. Each state, or separate confederacy, would pursue a system of commercial polity peculiar to itself. This would occasion distinctions, preferences and exclusions, which would beget discontent. The habits of intercourse, on the basis of equal privileges, to which we have been accustomed from the earliest settlement of the country, would give a keener edge to those causes of discontent, than they would naturally have, independent of this circumstance. . . . The spirit of enterprise, which characterizes the commercial part of America, has left no occasion of displaying itself unimproved. It is not at all probable that this unbridled spirit would pay much respect to those regulations of trade, by which particular states might endeavor to secure exclusive benefits to their own citizens. The infractions of these regulations on one side, the efforts to prevent and repel them on the other, would naturally lead to outrages, and these to reprisals and wars.[12]

Restrictive economic regulations in one state would beget restrictive economic regulations in other states, and dissention and conflict would ensue.

To avoid a heavily regulated economic environment driven by local interests, national economic unity had to be achieved. So the Founding Fathers proposed in the new Constitution that the federal government assume power over interstate commerce. They wrote in the Commerce Clause of the Constitution that Congress shall have power "[t]o regulate commerce with foreign nations, and among the several states."[13]

The Founding Fathers intended the Commerce Clause to be narrowly interpreted, just like other provisions in the Constitution that limited federal power. The aim of the Commerce Clause was not to give Congress an overbearing regulatory authority over all commerce in the nation— states would retain exclusive power to regulate commerce that was completely local. The Commerce Clause was simply meant to give Congress the means to establish free trade among the states, to break down barriers to interstate trade, and to set a national economic policy to compete with other nations.

While the Founding Fathers aimed for perfect economic liberty everywhere, they knew that national economic policy had to be pragmatic. They had to account for economic risks to national security and the practical reality that foreign nations often engaged in anticompetitive trade practices. Some exceptions to free trade principles had to be made, therefore, given the country's national security concerns and the market biases that were introduced by foreign governments. Madison wrote that the "true question to be decided . . . is, what are the exceptions to the rule [of free trade], not incompatible with its generality, and what the reasons justifying them?"[14]

For instance, Congress may have an interest in promoting certain domestic industries that manufacture war supplies. The national security interest is plain: military readiness is impacted by war supply production capabilities. The national financial interest is also clear: the premium that the United States might pay for domestic war supplies in times of peace might still be cheaper than the tax imposed on foreign war supplies in times of war. Madison expounded on this point:

> Were there a certainty of perpetual peace, and, still more, a universal freedom of commerce, the theory might hold good without exception, that government should never bias individuals in the choice of their occupations. But such a millennium has not yet arrived; and experience shows that if peace furnishes supplies from abroad cheaper than they can be made at home, the cost in war may exceed that at which they could be afforded at home; whilst it cannot be expected that a home provision will be undertaken in war, if the return of peace is to break down the undertakers.[15]

To promote the domestic manufacture of war supplies, Madison recommended a tariff on foreign war supplies at a level "that could be afforded in peace in order to avoid the tax imposed by war."[16]

The Founding Fathers supported other tariffs to promote the growth of the American economy under the new constitutional government. In his 1791 "Report on Manufactures," Alexander Hamilton (who was Treasury Secretary at the time) proposed to the First Congress of the United States a variety of tariffs that were designed to shield young American industries from foreign competition until they matured and were able to compete unsubsidized.[17]

Madison (a Congressman at the time) generally regarded tariffs like these as legitimate "exceptions to the principle of free industry."[18] They were "cases in which there could be a scarce doubt that a manufacture once brought into activity would support itself and be profitable to the nation."[19] Madison agreed that certain exceptions to free trade with foreign nations were permissible in order to grow American industry.

Madison was more suspicious of federal actions that altered the domestic competitive environment. He believed that the federal government had no business picking winners and losers in private industry by its special support to certain individuals or entities. He was particularly watchful of Federalists in that day who seemed willing to "convert the [free trade] exceptions to the rule, and [to] make the government a general supervisor of individual concerns. The length to which they push their system is involving it in complexities and inconsistencies, which can hardly fail to end in great modifications if not a total miscarriage [of American government]."[20] Madison recommended that the government "in every doubtful case . . . should forbear to intermeddle [in domestic industry], and that particular caution should be observed where one part of the community would be favored at the expense of another."[21] Madison recognized that excessive government intervention in private industry would only lead to favoritism and corruption. And he believed that an intrusive, regulatory government would likely benefit only the wealthy and politically-connected. He explained:

> Every new regulation concerning commerce or revenue, or in any manner affecting the value of different species of property, presents a new harvest to those who watch the change and can trace its consequences; a harvest reared not by themselves, but by the toils and cares of the great body of their fellow-citizens. This is a state of things in which it may be said with some truth that laws are made for the few, and not the many.[22]

Affluent special interests would benefit from excessive regulation not only because of their superior ability to adapt to costly regulatory changes. They also would benefit by their greater capacity to influence legislatures to craft regulations in their favor. Concentrated special interest groups can exert far greater pressure over the legislative process than the widely-dispersed and unorganized public interest. Given this added influence, any restrictive regulation or subsidy would likely operate to the exclusive benefit of those groups advocating it.

The Founding Fathers naturally advised against industry subsidies and other kinds of needless commercial meddling. For example, Paine warned against government intervention in the market, since government tends to "act[] by partialities of favor and oppression, [and] it becomes the cause of the mischiefs it ought to prevent."[23] Hamilton wrote in The Federalist No. 35 that "the most productive system of finance will always be the least burdensome."[24] Washington similarly recommended:

> [O]ur commercial policy should hold an equal and impartial hand: neither seeking nor granting exclusive favors or preferences; consulting the natural course of things; diffusing

and diversifying by gentle means the streams of commerce, but
forcing nothing; establishing with powers so disposed; in order
to give trade a stable course.[25]

Jefferson also stressed that, "to make us a happy and prosperous people,"
government "shall restrain men from injuring one another, shall leave
them otherwise free to regulate their own pursuits of industry and
improvement, and shall not take from the mouth of labor the bread it has
earned. This is the sum of good government."[26] The Founding Fathers
understood that excessive commercial regulation would cultivate a corrupt
and tyrannical central government. As a consequence, they insisted that
Congress' commercial regulatory power always remain limited.

Through much of American history, the Commerce Clause was rarely
employed to restrictively regulate trade. The political branches for some
time used the Commerce Clause in the limited manner that the Founding
Fathers had intended. They used it to remove all barriers to interstate trade
and to eliminate protectionism among the states. In fact, up until the
1930s, the Supreme Court was seldom called upon to decide cases
regarding the extent of Congress' power under the Commerce Clause,
since Congress rarely regulated commerce in an overbearing manner.[27]

This changed as progressivism took hold in the early twentieth
century. Congress began to regulate economic activity throughout the
nation in an overly restrictive manner—it wielded the commerce power in
a way that it was never meant to be used. Instead of using its power under
the Commerce Clause to remove limitations on interstate trade, Congress
began to rely on it as justification for new regulations and requirements on
industry, even if these mandates actually impeded the fluid working of the
market and had little direct impact on interstate trade.

The Supreme Court initially resisted these bold assertions of national
power by invalidating or limiting commercially-restrictive legislation. For
example, in *Hammer v. Dagenhart* (1918), the Court struck down a federal
statute that prevented the products of child labor from being traded across
state lines.[28] Although the law's intent to prevent children from being
exploited for work was noble, the Court held that Congress had no power
under the Commerce Clause to regulate working conditions, which were
entirely local concerns. It declared, "The Commerce Clause was not

intended to give to Congress a general authority to equalize [working] conditions."[29] Even if the products produced by child labor "were intended for interstate commerce transportation," the Court explained, it did not "make their production subject to federal control under the commerce power."[30] According the Court, Congress could only regulate commercial activities that had a direct impact on interstate commerce—local working conditions were too far removed to be the subject of federal regulation. The Court added that the Commerce Clause "was not intended to destroy the local power always existing and carefully reserved to the states in the Tenth Amendment to the Constitution."[31]

The Supreme Court continued to oppose restrictive regulation into the early 1930s. In *A. L. A. Schechter Poultry Corp. v. United States* (1935), the Court invalidated a portion of the 1933 National Industrial Recovery Act (NIRA), which created an administrative agency to impose "codes of fair competition" on various trades and industries throughout the nation.[32] The codes prohibited child labor, they granted the right of collective bargaining, they required many businesses to institute a 40-hour work week, they set a federal minimum wage, and, for some businesses, they also set the minimum number of workers that must be employed.[33]

The NIRA was intended to reduce unemployment that was ballooning during the Great Depression by transforming private industry into regulated markets controlled by government. In his speech to Congress recommending passage of the NIRA, President Franklin Roosevelt argued for a "great cooperative movement throughout all industry in order to obtain wide reemployment."[34] Existing federal antitrust laws, which had prohibited monopolies, would be suspended under the NIRA so that companies could collude to draft industry-wide codes of fair competition "under the guidance of the government."[35] Roosevelt said that government must exercise a "rigorous licensing power" to force all companies to participate and to ensure that members of the movement were not undersold by "selfish competitors unwilling to join in such a public-spirited endeavor."[36] Roosevelt essentially aimed to replace the free market system with a restrictive licensing system in which the government would assign power to members of various industries. Designed to benefit jobless Americans, the NIRA would benefit industry too. After signing the

NIRA into law, Roosevelt assured participating businesses "of a reasonable profit" for their cooperation with government—no matter how well or poorly they were operated.[37] Crony capitalism thus became established in law until the Court completely rejected it.

In a unanimous decision, the Court in *Schechter Poultry* invalidated the "codes of fair competition" in the NIRA because they had no direct affect on interstate commerce.[38] The Court indicated that it would not stand in the way of restrictive regulations, but such regulations at least had to relate to interstate commerce to pass its test for constitutionality. It decided that labor conditions were local matters having only an indirect and attenuated impact on interstate commerce, so Congress had no authority to regulate them under the Commerce Clause. The Court wrote, "Activities local in their immediacy do not become interstate and national because of distant repercussions. . . . To find immediacy or directness here is to find it almost everywhere."[39] The Court also dismissed the argument that the fallout from the Great Depression justified more comprehensive intervention by the federal government. The Court instead reaffirmed the limited nature of federal power:

> Extraordinary conditions do not create or enlarge constitutional power. The Constitution established a national government with powers deemed to be adequate, as they have proved to be both in war and peace, but these powers of the national government are limited by the constitutional grants. Those who act under these grants are not at liberty to transcend the imposed limits because they believe that more or different power is necessary. Such assertions of extraconstitutional authority were anticipated and precluded by the explicit terms of the Tenth Amendment—"The powers not delegated to the United States by the Constitution, nor prohibited by it to the States, are reserved to the States respectively, or to the people."[40]

Finally, the Court in *Schechter Poultry* rejected the government's paternalistic argument that a nationalized economic system under the management of the federal government was the most effective and efficient way to resolve economic problems. The Court refuted the legitimacy of such consolidated power, writing, "It is not the province of the Court to consider the economic advantages or disadvantage of such a centralized system. It is sufficient to say that the Federal Constitution does not provide for it."[41]

Undeterred by the Court's ruling, President Roosevelt and Democrats in Congress—just three months after the *Schechter Poultry* decision—enacted a new law regulating the coal industry. The Bituminous Coal Conservation Act created new coal industry regulations establishing fair competition standards to replace those that were enacted under the unconstitutional NIRA.[42] The new codes empowered a coal commission to form coal production standards, to set employee wages and hours, and to fix coal prices. Although mining companies were not obligated to follow the commission's regulations, they were coerced into doing so—mining companies that obeyed the commission would pay a small 2.5% tax on coal while companies that disregarded the new regulations would pay a much larger 15% tax.[43]

The fact that this new regulatory scheme was in some sense voluntary was immaterial to the Supreme Court when it decided the law's constitutionality. In *Carter v. Carter Coal Co.* (1936) the Court invalidated the Coal Conservation Act for the same reasons that it invalidated the NIRA codes: labor laws were local concerns for the states to regulate.[44] The Court also struck down the law because it deemed the mining industry itself to be a local industry that could not be regulated by Congress at all under the Commerce Clause. Mining fundamentally is production, and, according to the Court, "Production is not commerce."[45]

To further support its holding, the Court in *Carter Coal* wrote at length about the limited nature of federal power. It stressed that the government's constitutional limitations were made "absolutely certain by the Tenth Amendment. This amendment, which was seemingly adopted with prescience of just such contention as the present, disclosed the widespread fear that the national government might, under the pressure of a supposed general welfare, attempt to exercise powers which had not been granted."[46] The Court explained that "the framers intended that no such assumption [of power] should ever find justification in the organic act [the Constitution], and that if, in the future, further powers seemed necessary they should be granted by the people in the manner they had provided for amending that act."[47] Because the states had absolute control over those powers reserved to them, any expansion of the powers of the national government would "to some extent detract[] from or invade[] the power of the states."[48] The Court underscored the importance of preventing the federal government from intruding upon state powers "in order to preserve the fixed balance intended by the Constitution."[49] It wrote:

> The determination of the Framers Convention and the ratifying conventions to preserve complete and unimpaired state self-government in all matters not committed to the general government is one of the plainest facts which emerge from the history of their deliberations. And adherence to that determination is incumbent equally upon the federal government and the states. State powers can neither be appropriated, on the one hand, nor abdicated, on the other. As this court said in *Texas v. White*, "the preservation of the states, and the maintenance of their governments, are as much within the design and care of the Constitution as the preservation of the Union and the maintenance of the national government. The Constitution, in all its provisions, looks to an indestructible Union, composed of indestructible states."[50]

The Court in *Carter Coal* understood that the Commerce Clause was not intended to give to Congress a broad regulatory power over all commercial activity in the nation. Such a power would effectively strip state governments of their natural authority over local concerns. The Court therefore blocked the federal government from embarking upon a course of action that was certain to bring about an illegitimate imbalance of power—an imbalance, the Court noted, that was intolerable to the Founding Fathers and the Americans who ratified the Constitution. It wrote:

> Every journey to a forbidden end begins with the first step, and the danger of such a step by the federal government in the direction of taking over the powers of the states is that the end of the journey may find the states so despoiled of their powers, or—what may amount to the same thing—so relieved of the responsibilities which possession of the powers necessarily enjoins, as to reduce them to little more than geographical subdivisions of the national domain. It is safe to say that, if, when the Constitution was under consideration, it had been

thought that any such danger lurked behind its plain words, it would never have been ratified.[51]

Although the Court firmly resisted the federal government's encroachment against state powers in cases like *Dagenhart* (1918), *Schechter Poultry* (1935), and *Carter Coal* (1936), its resistance did not last for long. In 1937, the Court ended its opposition to President Roosevelt's economic legislation. Coincidentally, the Court's shift came after Roosevelt had proposed the Judiciary Procedures Reform Bill of 1937—a bill that would have increased the size of the Court from 9 to 15 justices, giving Roosevelt the chance to achieve an ideologically-friendly majority on the Court. Whether the bill actually precipitated the Court's reversal remains unclear, but what is absolutely certain is that the Court thereafter began to sanction an unlimited federal regulatory power.

In *NLRB v. Jones & Laughlin Steel Corp.* (1937), the Court decided that the National Labor Relations Act—a federal labor law—was constitutional. Under past judicial doctrine, all federal labor laws were held unconstitutional because they regulated the relationship between managers and employees—a purely local relationship. And even many industries such as production and manufacturing escaped federal regulation because their activities were considered to be intrastate, not interstate, commerce.

Yet under the Court's new test for constitutionality, the Commerce Clause would permit almost any kind of federal regulation against any industry or business in the nation. The Court decided that a federal law would always be constitutional under the Commerce Clause if the activities that it regulated had a "close and substantial relation to interstate commerce."[52] The Court wrote, "Although activities may be intrastate in character when separately considered, if they have such a close and substantial relation to interstate commerce that their control is essential or appropriate to protect that commerce from burdens and obstructions, Congress cannot be denied the power to exercise that control."[53] The Court decided that labor relations at any company in the nation could be controlled by the federal government. It permitted the executive branch to paternalistically oversee the bargaining process between labor and management and adjudicate any relevant dispute that may arise locally in the workplace.

Emboldened by this decision, Congress and the President soon after passed the Fair Labor Standards Act (FLSA) of 1938 to regulate the manufacturing industry. The FLSA set a national minimum wage, set the maximum number of hours an employee could work in a given week, and prohibited child labor. The FLSA was similar in many respects to the federal child labor law that the Supreme Court previously found unconstitutional in *Hammer v. Dagenhart* (1918). But the Court this time upheld the labor law by expressly overruling that case in *United States v. Darby* (1941).

The Court in *Darby* applied its new Commerce Clause test for constitutionality—whether the activities regulated had a "close and substantial relation to interstate commerce"—to uphold the FLSA.[54] The Court acknowledged that "manufacture is not, of itself, interstate commerce."[55] But because the "shipment of goods interstate is such commerce," the Court wrote, there was enough of a relationship with interstate commerce for Congress to regulate intrastate matters like child labor, employee salary, and working hours.[56]

Even though the commerce power had long been understood as a limited power to remove barriers to trade between the states, the Court in *Darby* adopted the new progressive understanding that the Commerce Clause permitted paternalistic, restrictive regulations of anything related to economic activity. The Court wrote, "The power to regulate commerce is the power to prescribe the rule by which commerce is governed. It extends not only to those regulations which aid, foster and protect the commerce, but embraces those which prohibit it."[57]

For support, the Court twisted the meaning of its precedent. It cited an 1824 case, *Gibbons v. Ogden*, in which Chief Justice John Marshall wrote that Congress' commerce power "is complete in itself, may be exercised to its utmost extent, and acknowledges no limitations other than are prescribed in the Constitution."[58] The *Gibbons* case, however, was never about Congress' power to restrictively regulate commerce—it was about Congress' power to remove barriers to trade. The Court in *Gibbons* used the Commerce Clause to invalidate a protectionist New York state law, not to sanction a restrictive federal regulation. Notwithstanding that purpose to support free trade, the *Darby* Court redefined its past decisions to assert that Congress all along had the power to regulate intrastate matters under the Commerce Clause, no matter how much it encroached upon state power.

The *Darby* Court in fact dismissed state power by stripping the Tenth Amendment of any meaning whatsoever. It stated that its decision was "unaffected by the Tenth Amendment, which provides: 'The powers not delegated to the United States by the Constitution, nor prohibited by it to the States, are reserved to the States respectively, or to the people.'"[59] The Court disregarded its own strong defense of the Tenth Amendment just five years earlier in *Carter Coal* and suggested that the amendment was no longer valid—that it was merely "declaratory of the relationship between the national and state governments as it had been established by the Constitution *before* the amendment."[60] In other words, the amendment was simply an historical account of the balance of power before it was adopted, and it did not guarantee the same relationship going forward. The Court went on to say that the purpose of the Tenth Amendment was simply "to allay fears that the new national government might seek to exercise powers not granted, and that states might not be able to exercise fully their reserved powers."[61] Essentially, the Court suggested that the Tenth Amendment was just an expedient means for proponents of the Constitution to inspire broader confidence in the new federal government—that it was meant to give superficial assurance to Americans who sought to limit federal powers without actually providing a substantive guarantee.

It is astonishing that the Court could render the Tenth Amendment entirely meaningless and also imply that James Madison and other framers of that amendment participated in a grand ruse against the American people to build support for the new government. Yet this is the kind of activist constitutional interpretation that became more common as time passed. The Court would start with a desired outcome in mind and then reshape constitutional meaning as necessary to reach that end.

In *Darby* and in other commerce cases at the time, the Court clearly construed the Constitution in a way that sanctioned President Roosevelt's economic agenda. The Court even endorsed Roosevelt's most invasive extension of the federal commerce power in *Wickard v. Filburn* in 1942.[62] This case challenged the Agricultural Adjustment Act (AAA) of 1938, which set quotas for agricultural production. The AAA was meant to subsidize farmers by artificially raising crop prices under the quotas. Roosevelt said that the AAA would, among other things, "assure to agriculture a fair share of an increasing national income."[63]

A similar law was declared unconstitutional by the Court in 1936 in *United States v. Butler* for violating the Tenth Amendment.[64] The Court in *Butler* held that the law "invade[d] the reserved rights of the states" because it aimed "to regulate and control agricultural production, a matter beyond the powers delegated to the federal government."[65] The Court remarked that the Founding Fathers never intended, by the Commerce Clause, to give "power to the Congress to tear down the barriers, to invade the states' jurisdiction, and to become a parliament of the whole people, subject to no restrictions save such as are self-imposed."[66]

Six years later, however, the Court decided otherwise. In *Wickard*, the Court again cited the 1824 case *Gibbons v. Ogden* to support its endorsement of a broad federal regulatory power. It suggested that Chief Justice Marshall "made emphatic the embracing and penetrating nature of this [commerce] power by warning that effective restraints on its exercise must proceed from political, rather than from judicial, processes."[67] As noted earlier, Marshall in *Gibbons* construed the Commerce Clause broadly with respect to Congress' power to *remove* barriers to trade; he never addressed whether Congress had a power to impose restrictions on all aspects of commerce, both interstate and intrastate. The Court in *Wickard* again disregarded that distinction and endorsed a federal regulatory power that was virtually without limit.

Remarkably, the Court in *Wickard* declared that Congress could regulate practically anything—even local, non-commercial activities. It declared, "[E]ven if [an] activity be local, and though it may not be regarded as commerce, it may still, whatever its nature, be reached by Congress if it exerts a substantial economic effect on interstate commerce."[68] The only condition that a regulation had to pass to be deemed lawful by the Court was that it exerted a substantial economic effect on interstate commerce. Yet this was hardly a condition at all, since the Court in *Wickard* held that even a "trivial" effect on interstate commerce passed the test for constitutionality.

In *Wickard*, Roscoe Filburn was the farmer who challenged the constitutionality of the quota limitations set forth in the AAA. He operated a small dairy farm in Ohio as his primary business, but he also raised small amounts of wheat for his livestock, for home consumption, and for local sale. Filburn's wheat allotment under the AAA in 1941 was 222 bushels, but he harvested 461 bushels that year.[69] Because he exceeded the AAA quota, the Department of Agriculture assessed Filburn a penalty and later sued him after he refused to pay.

The Supreme Court acknowledged that the additional wheat that Filburn harvested had a "trivial" economic impact, but it nevertheless held that it was substantial enough for federal regulation. The Court wrote, "That [Filburn's] own contribution to the demand for wheat may be trivial by itself is not enough to remove him from the scope of federal regulation."[70] Even if Filburn had grown his wheat exclusively for his own consumption—and did not even enter it into the stream of commerce—the Court suggested that the federal regulation would still apply. It declared, "It can hardly be denied that a factor of such volume and variability as home-consumed wheat would have a substantial influence on price and market conditions."[71] The Court reasoned that "[h]ome-grown wheat . . . competes with wheat in commerce," and so individuals who grew their own wheat would escape having to pay the higher, artificially-maintained prices for wheat that Congress and the president were hoping to achieve under the AAA.[72] The Court thus disregarded Filburn's claim to economic liberty and instead declared that it was Congress' role to determine who would benefit under regulation and who would not. It wrote:

> It is of the essence of regulation that it lays a restraining hand on the self-interest of the regulated, and that advantages from the regulation commonly fall to others. The conflicts of economic interest between the regulated and those who advantage by it are wisely left under our system to resolution by the Congress under its more flexible and responsible legislative process.[73]

The ultimate consequence of the Court's ruling in *Wickard* was that any desired regulation under the Commerce Clause would pass as constitutional. The Court would uphold a federal regulation even if the underlying regulated activity was not regarded as commerce and even if its economic impact was trivial. So the Supreme Court effectively withdrew from constitutional review of the federal government's restrictions on commerce.

Without the Court blocking his way, President Roosevelt could fully implement his regulatory economic program at last. He could establish in America the administrative authority that had long been the ideal of past advocates of centralized power. It was the same kind of aristocratic arrangement that Hamilton sought to establish in the founding era. And it was the same progressive plan that had eluded President Woodrow Wilson when the Democratic Party last controlled the executive branch.

The progressive, transformational change that Roosevelt sought for the federal government was no secret to the American people. Years before, at the 1932 Democratic National Convention, Roosevelt rededicated himself and the Democratic Party to Wilson's failed progressive aims. He said:

> Let us now and here highly resolve to resume the country's interrupted march along the path of real progress, of real justice, of real equality for all of our citizens, great and small. Our indomitable leader in that interrupted march is no longer with us, but there still survives today his spirit. Many of his captains, thank God, are still with us, to give us wise counsel. Let us feel that in everything we do there still lives with us, if not the body, the great indomitable, unquenchable, progressive soul of our Commander-in-Chief, Woodrow Wilson.[74]

Roosevelt's plan to implement progressive change required a profound consolidation of power in the national government. Under this elitist governing philosophy, intelligent central planners needed all necessary authority to regulate the economy and distribute the advantages that flowed from those regulations as they deemed best for all. Contrary to the Founding Fathers' decentralized design of governmental power in America, Roosevelt proposed, "We must merge, we must consolidate subdivisions of government."[75]

Roosevelt exploited the existing economic crisis to justify a broad expansion of federal executive power. He was certain that the executive branch of the federal government was "the only governmental agency with sufficient power and credit" to guide the nation out of the economic crisis and meet the needs of the American people going forward.[76] In his First Inaugural Address, he said:

> It is to be hoped that the normal balance of executive and legislative authority may be wholly adequate to meet the unprecedented task before us. But it may be that an unprecedented demand and need for undelayed action may call for temporary departure from that normal balance of public procedure. . . . I shall ask the Congress for the one remaining instrument to meet the [economic] crisis—broad executive power to wage a war against the emergency, as great as the power that would be given to me if we were in fact invaded by a foreign foe.[77]

Roosevelt was confident that congressional grants of authority would confer all the constitutional legitimacy that he needed to fundamentally transform the executive branch into an all-powerful national administrative body.

The national government would be all-powerful, but it would also be good. Roosevelt sought to create "a new relationship between government and people" that was based on an appeal to "the ideal of the public interest."[78] The people might have to surrender much of their liberty to government in this relationship, but the more powerful national government would serve them with greater benevolence, fairness, and competence. Roosevelt said that government would become "the representative and the trustee of the public interest" composed of "essentially democratic institutions."[79] A progressive government would provide "the intelligent care of population throughout our nation, in accordance with an intelligent distribution of the means of livelihood for that population."[80]

Roosevelt particularly believed that the federal government had a duty to care for the needy and protect the weak. He adamantly asserted that "the federal government has always had and still has a continuing responsibility for the broader public welfare."[81] Having complete faith in the national government as a force for good—almost a holy institution to progressive politicians—Roosevelt based his New Deal economic program upon what he called a "simple moral principle."[82] Describing this principle, he said, "[T]he welfare and the soundness of a nation depend first upon what the great mass of the people wish and need; and second, whether or not they are getting it."[83] Americans could religiously depend on the national government to provide for them, Roosevelt said, because from that moment on, government would "live[] in a spirit of charity."[84] Government would provide a "more equitable opportunity to share in the distribution of national wealth"[85] and "advance the lot of the average American citizen."[86]

In order for the federal government to distribute a more equitable share of national wealth to all Americans, it must first have the means to collect that wealth from those who have it. For most of American history, the federal government lacked any power to target the income of wealthy individuals. But that limitation was removed during the Progressive Era when Americans ratified the Sixteenth Amendment, which gave the national government the means to tax any source of personal income in the nation.

Adopted in 1913, the Sixteenth Amendment was motivated in part by the rising national deficit after the economic recession of 1907. But it also coincided with the progressive idea that the national government could be transformed into an instrument for social justice—progressives viewed the national government as an agent for social good. Accordingly, they believed that it was incumbent upon all citizens to provide the national government with the financial backing necessary to achieve their progressive aims, and the national income tax would assist in that endeavor. Progressives therefore encouraged other Americans to sacrifice their property for the greater good. Referring to the income tax as a "most just and equitable tax," one advocate of the Sixteenth Amendment said, "Men should contribute to the needs of the state as God has prospered them."[87]

The Founding Fathers shared no similar faith in the goodness of government. Thomas Paine believed that "government, even in its best state, is but a necessary evil; in its worst state an intolerable one."[88] He was adamant that those who exalted government did so not because government was good. They did so purely to entice others to financially support the corrupt excesses of government at all costs. He wrote, "It can only be by blinding the understanding of man, and making him believe that government is some wonderful mysterious thing, that excessive revenues are obtained. . . . It is the popery of government; a thing kept up to amuse the ignorant and quiet them into taxes."[89]

Progressives, without question, acclaimed the wonders of government in support of the income tax, but others supported the Sixteenth Amendment for more practical reasons. Some Republicans supported the tax as an alternative means to raise revenue only when necessity required it. For example, Republican Senator Norris Brown believed that income tax would be helpful "in national emergencies" or "when necessary to the life of the republic."[90] He said in 1910, "Whether the power shall be exercised, when it shall be exercised, or whether it shall be exercised at all, are other questions entirely aside from the question of whether the government shall be vested or stripped of the power."[91] Many such proponents of the national income tax simply sought to empower the national government with the option to impose the tax, and they stressed that its use would likely be infrequent and its impact small.

Despite such assurances, it was not long before the federal government began imposing the income tax as a regular source of revenue. Less than two months after the Sixteenth Amendment was ratified, President Wilson summoned a special session of Congress to advocate a change in revenue policy. He wanted to sharply reduce the nation's tariffs and establish a national income tax to make up for the lost revenue. The nation was not at war, and there was no national emergency. The Democratic-controlled Congress adopted Wilson's proposed Revenue Act of 1913, and Wilson signed the first income tax bill into law later that year.

The federal income tax initially had a minimal impact on most Americans. Many individuals were exempted from the tax, and most of those who were taxed fell into the lowest tax bracket of 1 percent.[92] The highest tax rate at the time was 7 percent.[93]

But these low tax rates and the small income tax base quickly grew. By 1918—just five years after the Sixteenth Amendment was ratified—the lowest tax rate increased to 6 percent.[94] Significantly, the tax exemption level was decreased to below the median income, so many more individuals were forced to pay the income tax.[95] And the top income earners were hardest hit—their tax rate jumped from 7 percent in 1913 to 77 percent in 1918.[96] Although the higher tax rates were precipitated by the nation's entry into World War I in 1917, they continued well after the war had ended in 1918. President Wilson kept the highest tax rate at 73 percent throughout the remainder of his second term, which ended in 1921.[97]

While high tax rates are undoubtedly oppressive to some, any income tax is authoritarian to all. To enforce the income tax, the federal government must snoop into the financial affairs of every American citizen to determine their earnings and other personal circumstances that factor into the level of tax. This intrusive requirement is one reason why the Founding Fathers never allowed the federal government to tax personal income in the first place. Not only did they leave the income tax out of the Constitution, the Founding Fathers also expressly prohibited this kind of ubiquitous federal power under the Fourth Amendment, which keeps Americans "secure in their persons, houses, papers, and effects."[98]

Given the constitutional limitations on federal power, the Founding Fathers favored consumption taxes—tariffs and sales taxes—as the best way for the federal government to raise money. No coercive informational requirements about the citizens are necessary to impose these taxes. Consumption taxes are also the most equitable kind of taxes because every citizen can independently determine his level of tax by moderating his own consumption. Hamilton explained how consumption taxes maximize American liberty:

> The amount to be contributed by each citizen will in a degree be at his own option, and can be regulated by an attention to his resources. The rich may be extravagant, the poor can be frugal. And private oppression may always be avoided by a judicious selection of objects proper for such impositions.[99]

Another benefit of the consumption tax is that, unlike the income tax, it does not penalize productivity. Like the other Founding Fathers, Thomas Jefferson staunchly opposed any measure that discouraged industriousness, saying that "a wise and frugal government . . . shall not take from the mouth of labor the bread it has earned."[100] He further wrote:

> To take from one, because it is thought his own industry and that of his fathers has acquired too much, in order to spare to others, who, or whose fathers, have not exercised equal industry and skill, is to violate arbitrarily the first principle of association, "the guarantee to everyone the free exercise of his industry and the fruits acquired by it."[101]

The Founding Fathers believed that the consumption tax would leave American people free in their economic pursuits, and it would also serve as a natural restraint on federal power. Hamilton explained in The Federalist No. 21 that any attempt by the national government to overburden the people with taxes would be self-defeating:

> It is a signal advantage of taxes on articles of consumption, that they contain in their own nature a security against excess. They prescribe their own limit; which cannot be exceeded without defeating the end proposed—that is, an extension of the revenue. . . . If duties are too high they lessen the consumption— the collection is eluded; and the product to the treasure is not so great as when they are confined within proper and moderate bounds. This forms a complete barrier against any material oppression of the citizens, by taxes of this class, and is itself a natural limitation of the power of imposing them.[102]

While a natural restraint on federal power is inherent in the consumption tax, no such limit exists under the income tax, thus allowing a despotic governmental control over the people to form. As already noted, under the income tax, the federal government must exercise an invasive and coercive power to ensure that all citizens are complying with the tax. In addition to this encroaching power, the government exerts complete control over all earnings in the nation. When the government determines how much of a person's income that it allows him to keep—by the rate at which income is taxed—it in principle controls all of that income. The Supreme Court wrote in 1874 that a government holding "the property of its citizens, subject at all times to the absolute disposition and unlimited control of even the most democratic depository of power, is after all but a despotism. It is true it is a despotism of the many, . . . but it is none the less a despotism."[103]

The Sixteenth Amendment therefore provided the national government a powerful—if not despotic—tool to bring about the kind of redistributive change that Franklin Roosevelt hoped to accomplish during his presidency. The income tax authorized the national government to collect money from any individual or entity and in whatever amount it desired.

As a proponent of consolidated administrative power, Roosevelt favored higher taxation so that the federal government could wield greater discretion over the utilization of the nation's resources. In fact, at the 1932 Democratic National Convention, Roosevelt expressed his frustration with prior Republican administrations for lowering the rates of taxation after Wilson left office. In the time of economic expansion between Wilson's departure from office and the Great Depression, national wealth had increased, but Roosevelt lamented that "very little of it was taken by taxation to the beneficent government of those years."[104] Although tax rates were raised in the year prior to his inauguration, Roosevelt quickly expanded the tax base once in office and continued to raise taxes throughout his presidency. He increased the tax burden on lower-income earners by reducing personal exemptions and by eliminating the earned income tax credit.[105] And he consistently raised taxes on higher-income earners—their tax rates rose from 63 percent in 1932, to 79 percent in 1936, to 81 percent in 1940, to 88 percent in 1942, and finally to 90 percent in 1944.[106]

The income tax to some degree gave the federal government a power to level economic conditions of its citizens, but complete redistributive power did not exist until the government could spend national wealth with impunity. Roosevelt's New Deal social programs were designed to enable such discretionary spending, but until 1937, the Supreme Court had prevented the federal government from funding social welfare programs. For example, in 1935, the Supreme Court invalidated the Railroad Retirement Act (RRA), which created a federally managed pension program for railroad employees.[107] Under the RRA, pensions for retirees were funded by railroad companies and working employees—workers would contribute 2 percent of their total compensation and the companies had to double that amount.[108] The Court held that this federally-mandated program was unconstitutional as an uncompensated taking under the Fifth Amendment, as a deprivation of property without due process of law under the Fifth Amendment, and as an unauthorized use of the commerce power under the Commerce Clause. The Court characterized the RRA as an attempt by the national government "to impose by sheer fiat" a social welfare program that exceeded its limited authority in the Constitution.[109]

Despite the adverse ruling regarding the RRA, the Democrats enacted a similar and more sweeping social welfare program later that year. They passed the 1935 Social Security Act (SSA), which remains in force today, to provide direct federal assistance to unemployed workers, to the elderly, to children, and to the poor. Like the RRA, the SSA funds various social welfare programs by taxing current employees. All employees in the nation must pay the Federal Insurance Contributions Act tax, or payroll tax, which funds current beneficiaries under the SSA.

The SSA essentially created a wealth redistribution plan that masqueraded as a social insurance policy. Individuals would have no legal right to collect on the payroll taxes that they paid to the government, yet the taxes would in some form appear as payments on an annuity that would accumulate until retirement age or financial hardship. Even President Roosevelt acknowledged that the purpose of the regressive payroll tax was simply to create the illusion of a guaranteed benefit—an illusion that would ensure the longevity of this social welfare program. He said:

> [T]hose taxes were never a problem of economics. They are politics all the way through. We put those payroll taxes there so as to give the contributors a legal, moral, and political right to collect their pensions and their unemployment benefits. With those taxes in there, no damn politician can ever scrap my social security program.[110]

At a public policy level, therefore, it was imperative that the SSA be regarded as a social insurance policy for it to last.

From a constitutional point of view, however, the SSA could not be cast as an insurance policy, for the federal government has no power under the Constitution to act as an insurer for all Americans. Consequently, when the Roosevelt administration defended the SSA before the Supreme Court, it was forced to confess the truth about the social security program: individuals had no guaranteed benefit under the SSA. The law's taxing and spending functions were wholly separate from each other. Individuals who paid payroll taxes earned no right to receive government benefits in the future. The Supreme Court in *Helvering v. Davis* (1937) observed, "The proceeds of both [employee and employer payroll] taxes are to be paid into the Treasury like internal revenue taxes generally, and are not earmarked in any way."[111] The Court therefore upheld the SSA's taxing function as a mere exercise of Congress' general taxing powers.

The SSA's spending provisions for various welfare programs were more difficult to justify under the Constitution. After all, the Constitution does not provide for the redistribution of national wealth. James Madison explained that "the government of the United States is a definite government, confined to specified objects. It is not like the state governments, whose powers are more general. Charity is no part of the legislative duty of the government."[112] Samuel Adams similarly wrote, "The utopian schemes of leveling [redistributing wealth] and a community of goods, are as visionary and impractical as those which vest all property in the Crown. [These ideas] are arbitrary, despotic, and, in our government, unconstitutional."[113]

Despite the certain unconstitutionality of federal welfare spending, the Supreme Court upheld the SSA's spending provisions in *Steward Machine Co. v. Davis* (1937).[114] This decision came after the Court had already begun endorsing other broad extensions of federal power, so its deference to Roosevelt's arbitrary system of wealth redistribution was not out of the ordinary. But its decision in *Steward Machine* was noteworthy for transforming yet another clause in the Constitution into an unlimited grant of federal power.

Specifically, the Court exploited the phrase "general welfare" in Article I, section 8, to justify the federal government's broad spending authority. This section states that "Congress shall have power to lay and collect taxes, duties, imposts, and excises, to pay the debts and provide for the common defense and general welfare of the United States."[115] The

Court in *Steward Machine* interpreted this clause as a broad grant of power to Congress to tax and spend however it wanted, as long as it exercised that authority to provide for the general welfare. The Court even asserted that social welfare spending was widely accepted as a constitutional function of the federal government, particularly in a time of crisis. It wrote, "It is too late today for the argument to be heard with tolerance that, in a crisis so extreme, the use of the moneys of the nation to relieve the unemployed and their dependents is a use for any purpose narrower than the promotion of the general welfare."[116]

Apparently, it was too late for the Court to even consider its recent decisions to the contrary. Just two years before its decision in *Steward Machine*, the Court pointed out that constitutional powers do not change in economic crises. It emphasized in *Schechter Poultry* (1935), "Extraordinary conditions do not create or enlarge constitutional power."[117] And just one year before, in *Carter Coal* (1936), the Court argued that Congress could not spend solely to promote the "general welfare." Rather, it could only spend to exercise the enumerated powers granted by the Constitution. It wrote:

> The [constitutional] convention . . . carefully limited the powers which it thought wise to entrust to Congress by specifying them, thereby denying all others not granted expressly or by necessary implication. It made no grant of authority to Congress to legislate substantively for the general welfare, and no such authority exists, save as the general welfare may be promoted by the exercise of the powers which are granted.[118]

The Founding Fathers made this point abundantly clear. The "general welfare" reference in the Constitution did not give Congress a license to spend at will under the guise of providing for the general welfare. Congress could only spend in support of those powers enumerated in the Constitution. Thomas Jefferson explained:

> [Federal representatives] are not to do anything they please to provide for the general welfare . . . . [G]iving a distinct and independent power [to Congress] to do any act they please which may be good for the Union would render all the preceding and subsequent enumerations of power completely useless. It would reduce the whole instrument to a single phrase, that of instituting

a Congress with power to do whatever would be for the good of the United States; and, as they would be the sole judges of the good or evil, it would be also a power to do whatever evil they please.[119]

Madison similarly argued, "I cannot undertake to lay my finger on that article of the Constitution which grants a right to Congress of expending, on objects of benevolence, the money of their constituents."[120] He continued, "If Congress can do whatever in their discretion can be done by money, and will promote the general welfare, the government is no longer a limited one, possessing enumerated powers, but an indefinite one, subject to particular exceptions."[121]

The Founding Fathers designed the Constitution to preserve a free nation, not to sanction a welfare state in which politicians can redistribute private property according to their notions of fairness. The nation was built upon Natural Law principles, and the Founding Fathers understood that the preservation of property rights was paramount to enduring liberty. They believed in Locke's statement that the "great and chief end" of government "is the preservation of property."[122] If this fundamental purpose of government were ignored, then the consequences would be severe. John Adams wrote, "The moment the idea is admitted into society that property is not as sacred as the laws of God, and that there is not a force of law and public justice to protect it, anarchy and tyranny commence."[123] He further declared, "Property must be secured or liberty cannot exist."[124] Benjamin Franklin and Samuel Adams similarly wrote that those in government "have no right to seek and take what they please; by this, . . . they would soon become absolute masters, despots, and tyrants."[125] James Madison stated that government was "instituted to protect property of every sort," and that this purpose could not be achieved "where the property, which a man has in his personal safety and personal liberty, is violated by arbitrary seizures of one class of citizens for the service of the rest."[126] Madison also said:

> It is sufficiently obvious, that persons [] and property are the two great subjects on which governments are to act; and that the rights of persons, and the rights of property, are the objects, for the protection of which government was instituted. These rights cannot well be separated. The personal right to acquire property,

which is a natural right, gives to property, when acquired, a right to protection as a social right.[127]

Property rights were so significant to the Founding Fathers because they also served as the driving force of the American economy. They were, and still are, central to free market theory. Economic progress depends on the twin forces of self-interest and competition, and these forces grow weak if property rights are not secure. Man's self-interested drive for profit is subverted if he cannot keep what he has created. And the competitive drive of others is subdued if they are routinely given what they do not earn. Montesquieu once observed:

> The effect of wealth in a country is to inspire every heart with ambition: that of poverty is to give birth to despair. The former is excited by labor the latter is soothed by indolence.
>
> Nature is just to all mankind, and repays them for their industry: she renders them industrious by annexing rewards in proportion to their labor. But if an arbitrary prince should attempt to deprive the people of nature's bounty, they would fall into a disrelish of industry; and then indolence and inaction must be their only happiness.[128]

The Founding Fathers made similar observations concerning the importance of private property rights. Benjamin Franklin wrote:

> In my youth I travelled much, and I observed in different countries, that the more public provisions were made for the poor, the less they provided for themselves, and of course became poorer. And, on the contrary, the less was done for them, the more they did for themselves, and became richer.[129]

Franklin wrote a friend in England, "I have long been of your opinion, that your legal provision for the poor is a very great evil, operating as it does to the encouragement of idleness."[130] He contended, "I am for doing good to the poor, but I differ in opinion of the means. I think the best way of doing good to the poor, is not making them easy in poverty, but leading or driving them out of it."[131] James Wilson recognized that private property rights benefitted not just man, but also property itself. He explained, "By exclusive property, the productions of the earth and the means of subsistence are secured and preserved, as well as multiplied. What belongs to no one is wasted by everyone. What belongs to one man in particular is the object of his economy and care."[132] The Founding Fathers had separately observed what Adam Smith instructed in *The Wealth of Nations*: property rights inspire productive human behavior and encourage property conservation or improvement. By protecting these rights, society's resources are most efficiently allocated to the benefit of all.

For some time, the Supreme Court respected private property rights as a matter of principle and as a tenet of constitutional law. In a 1795 decision, the Court wrote:

> No man would become a member of a community in which he could not enjoy the fruits of his honest labor and industry. The preservation of property, then, is a primary object of the social compact. . . . The legislature, therefore, had no authority to make an act divesting one citizen of his freehold, and vesting it in another, without a just compensation. It is inconsistent with the principles of reason, justice and moral rectitude; it is incompatible with the comfort, peace and happiness of mankind; it is contrary to the principles of social alliance in every free government; and lastly, it is contrary to the letter and spirit of the Constitution.[133]

The Court recognized that taking property from one and giving it to another is theft, whether done privately by an individual or publicly by the government. It denounced such wealth redistribution schemes in an 1874 decision, writing, "To lay with one hand the power of the government on the property of the citizen, and with the other to bestow it upon favored individuals . . . is none the less a robbery because it is done under the forms of law and is called taxation."[134] In a speech to the New York Bar Association in 1921, Justice George Sutherland expounded on the importance of property rights to liberty and the rule of law in society. He said:

> [T]he individual [] has three great rights, equally sacred from arbitrary interference: the right to his life, the right to his liberty, the right to his property. . . . [T]he three rights are so bound together as to be essentially one right. To give a man his life but deny him his liberty, is to take from him all that makes his life worth living. To give him his liberty but take from him the property which is the fruit and badge of his liberty, is to still leave him a slave. . . . If the time shall ever come in this country,

as it has already come in poor distracted Russia [under Lenin], when the property of rich or poor may be taken by the hand of arbitrary authority, liberty and property will depart together, and the rule of law, so far as these rights are concerned, will have ceased to be.[135]

Despite the Supreme Court's repeated recognition that property rights were protected by the Constitution and central to American liberty, its sudden reversal in 1937 permitted the federal government to begin redistributing private wealth in America. There remained no legal barrier to federal spending of any kind. The government could make direct payments to select individuals just as easily as it could provide for the common defense.

While the Supreme Court surely neglected its responsibility to defend the Constitution's original limited design, it is important to remember that the progressive transformation of America was not judicially mandated—it was politically decided. President Roosevelt wanted the Court to defer to his judgment of constitutionality, not because he believed that his interpretation was correct, but because he could stretch the Constitution's broad language so far that it would cover virtually any federal action. Roosevelt once described the Constitution as "the most marvelously elastic compilation of rules of government ever written."[136]

After receiving the judicial deference he wanted in 1937, Roosevelt needed only to secure the support of the people to carry out his progressive designs. And this proved easy to do. The nation's shaken confidence in the economy at the time made the people open to new political ideas. More significantly, Roosevelt's success in marginalizing his opposition drove many Americans to support his cause. Roosevelt smeared his political opponents as "the resolute enemy within our gates."[137] Those who did not support the "wholesome and proper" power of the national government were denounced as uncaring, undemocratic, and unscrupulous opportunists who sought "power for themselves [and] enslavement for the public."[138] Roosevelt criticized all who championed America's traditions respecting private property rights and limited federal powers, saying, "In vain they seek to hide behind the Flag and the Constitution."[139] Roosevelt later warned amid war that if America ever returned to the political "'normalcy' of the 1920's" when Republicans were in power, "then it is certain that even though we shall have conquered our enemies on the battlefields abroad, we shall have yielded to the spirit of Fascism here at home."[140]

Roosevelt's persistent attacks on Republicans helped build a lasting Democratic majority in America. He was reelected to unprecedented third and fourth terms in office. But Roosevelt's political impact was even more enduring in Congress. The Democratic Party went on to control the House of Representatives between 1930 and 1994 for all but four years. Because all federal spending bills originate in the House, the Democratic majority was able to ensure that Roosevelt's social welfare programs were fully supported by the national treasury throughout most of the twentieth century.

In fact, the large size of the federal government today is mainly the product of the administrative state that Roosevelt created in the 1930s. Over the course of Roosevelt's presidency, over 100 new federal agencies or offices were created to administer labor practices, agriculture, theater, banking, music, housing, mining, insurance, community planning, emergency management, construction, labor union representation, navigation, fertilizer manufacturing, communication, shipping, securities, securities exchanges, and much, much more. The once-limited federal government quickly became an unrestrained centralized power that dominated the nation in so many social and economic concerns.

While unprecedented in America, Roosevelt's progressive transformation of the federal government in many ways mirrored the Marxist ideological change that was taking place in Europe at the time. Roosevelt himself noted the similarities. Speaking to his Secretary of the Interior in 1933, he acknowledged that "what we are doing in this country were some of the things that were being done in Russia and even some of the things that were being done under Hitler in Germany. But we are doing them in a more orderly way."[141] In fact, the chief Nazi newspaper, *Volkischer Beobachter*, repeatedly praised "Roosevelt's adoption of National Socialist strains of thought in his economic and social policies" and "the development toward an authoritarian state" based on the "demand that collective good be put before individual self-interest."[142]

Philosophically, Roosevelt shared the same fundamental belief upon which Marxist political ideology was based: he believed that property rights were created by laws of government, not laws of nature. Karl Marx wrote in *The Communist Manifesto* that capitalist laws were merely constructs of the propertied class—he argued that a "selfish misconception [] induces [the capitalist] to transform into eternal laws of nature and reason the social forms springing from [his] present mode of production and form of property."[143] Similarly, Roosevelt rejected the Natural Law principle that private property rights are unalienable, stating that "economic laws are not made by nature. They are made by human beings."[144]

Roosevelt also embraced the Marxist belief that wealthy individuals had exploited new technologies and self-serving legal structures to secure their influence over government. Karl Marx introduced this idea as follows:

> We see, therefore, how the modern bourgeoisie [capitalist] is itself the product of a long course of development, of a series of revolutions in the modes of production and of exchange. Each step in the development of the bourgeoisie was accompanied by a corresponding political advance of that class. . . . [T]he bourgeoisie has at last, since the establishment of modern industry and of the world market, conquered for itself, in the modern representative state, exclusive political sway. The executive of the modern state is but a committee for managing the common affairs of the whole bourgeoisie.[145]

Roosevelt likewise complained about the propertied "economic royalists" in America who developed "new uses of corporations, banks and securities, new machinery of industry and agriculture, of labor and capital" to subject the common man to their will.[146] According to Roosevelt, these capitalist leaders used their dominant positions in society to influence the government for their own political and financial gain. He said:

> It was natural and perhaps human that the privileged princes of these new economic dynasties, thirsting for power, reached out for control over government itself. They created a new despotism and wrapped it in the robes of legal sanction. In its service new mercenaries sought to regiment the people, their labor, and their property.[147]

Roosevelt and Marx each sought to dismantle the legal structures that they believed were responsible for society's economic inequalities and power imbalances. They differed only in the degree to which capitalist principles should be overthrown.

Marx sought the complete transformation of a capitalist society into a communist state by the elimination of private property rights, which were central to the capitalist system. He believed that class distinctions and their resulting antagonisms would disappear only when complete economic equality was achieved—when private property rights were entirely eliminated in society.[148] Marx said that "the theory of the Communists may be summed up in the single sentence: Abolition of private property."[149] A communal spirit and utopian society would result once all property and all means of production were "concentrated in the hands of a vast association of the whole nation."[150] To achieve this end in a modern capitalist society, Marx recommended a steady advance against property rights in order to disrupt and ultimately undermine the capitalist system:

> [I]n the beginning, this [communist goal] cannot be effected except by means of despotic inroads on the rights of property, and on the conditions of bourgeois production; by means of measures, therefore, which appear economically insufficient and untenable, but which, in the course of the movement, outstrip themselves, necessitate further inroads upon the old social order, and are unavoidable as a means of entirely revolutionizing the mode of production.[151]

Different countries would require different inroads or measures to implement this societal transformation, but Marx identified some policies that would be generally applicable in all nations, including, "A heavy progressive or graduated income tax;" "abolition of all rights of inheritance;" "centralization of credit in the hands of the state, by means of a national bank with state capital and an exclusive monopoly;" "centralization of the means of communication and transport in the hands of the state;" "extension of factories and instruments of production owned by the state;" and "free education for all children in public schools."[152]

Although Roosevelt pursued similar policies to construct a centralized administrative state, he never intended to reach the extreme political end that Marx envisioned. He never set out to abolish private property altogether. What Roosevelt wanted instead was control. He sought to empower the federal government with an unlimited regulatory potential so that government could alter the distribution of national wealth in society. As a force for good, government would remedy economic inequalities in society by regulating industries and individuals alike.

Believing that free markets were inherently bad, Roosevelt promoted a centrally-planned economy that was directed by the federal government. No longer would self-interest operate in an unregulated and competitive environment, for Roosevelt believed that "a selfish and greedy people cannot be free."[153] Going forward, the national government would supervise, steer, or control all economic activity in America. The nation could only prosper, Roosevelt claimed, "by [government] ordering society as to assure to the masses of men and women reasonable security and hope for themselves and for their children."[154] In his First Inaugural Address, Roosevelt informed the American people that he would command this aggressive, almost militaristic, reordering of society. He said:

> [I]f we are to go forward, we must move as a trained and loyal army willing to sacrifice for the good of a common discipline, because without such discipline no progress is made, no leadership becomes effective. We are, I know, ready and willing to submit our lives and property to such discipline, because it makes possible a leadership which aims at a larger good. . . . I assume unhesitatingly the leadership of this great army.[155]

Roosevelt essentially proposed a new social compact for America. The people would cede their economic liberty to the national government in exchange for the promise of fairness and economic security. In 1934, Roosevelt reflected on the sweeping impact of his new economic plan. He said, "[A]s a result of our action, we have demanded of many citizens that they surrender certain licenses to do as they please in their business relationships; but we have asked this in exchange for the protection which the state can give."[156]

Although the national government was meant to serve the greater good, the new powers that it wielded were undeniably despotic. Remarkably, the Fascist Italian leader Benito Mussolini observed striking similarities between Roosevelt's economic programs and those he instituted in Italy. In a review of Roosevelt's 1933 book, *Looking*

Forward, which outlined the major reforms of his New Deal program, Mussolini wrote:

> The question is often asked in America and in Europe just how much "Fascism" the American President's [New Deal] program contains. . . . Reminiscent of Fascism is the principle that the state no longer leaves the economy to its own devices, having recognized that the welfare of the economy is identical with the welfare of the people. Without question, the mood accompanying this sea change [in America] resembles that of Fascism.[157]

Roosevelt himself acknowledged the domineering federal authority that his policies created. In his 1936 State of the Union Address, Roosevelt proudly spoke of the "new instruments of public power" that were being created to prevent a return to "individualism" in America.[158] These instruments of power were so authoritative that Roosevelt regarded the national government as "[o]ur resplendent economic autocracy."[159] And he acknowledged that the national government had become so powerful that it could "provide shackles for the liberties of the people."[160] Former-President Herbert Hoover observed in 1940:

> There has been a gigantic and insidious building up of personal power of the President during these two terms [1933–1940]. The President himself admits these powers provide shackles upon liberty which may be dangerous. Many of these extraordinary powers have been obtained under claims of emergencies which proved not to exist or to have expired. Despite many promises, there has been no return of these dangerous powers or the unused powers, or those which proved futile or for which emergencies have passed.[161]

Despite the immense control that the federal government possessed over the American people, Roosevelt remained confident that a centrally-managed economy was best for the nation. He viewed the American people as helpless victims of powerful, moneyed interests, and his remedy for this perceived injustice was to subject every individual to the power of the national government. Notions of fairness would trump individual liberty, and those in power would determine what was right. Over the course of his presidency, Roosevelt's policies manifested his sense of economic justice, but his vision for America became clear when promoted "a second Bill of Rights" for America in 1944, which included:

> The right to a useful and remunerative job in the industries or shops or farms or mines of the nation; The right to earn enough to provide adequate food and clothing and recreation; The right of every farmer to raise and sell his products at a return which will give him and his family a decent living; The right of every businessman, large and small, to trade in an atmosphere of freedom from unfair competition and domination by monopolies at home or abroad; The right of every family to a decent home; The right to adequate medical care and the opportunity to achieve and enjoy good health; The right to adequate protection from the economic fears of old age, sickness, accident, and unemployment; The right to a good education.[162]

These proposed entitlements could not be realized without further expanding national power over the economy and individual liberty. But what was so extraordinary about the second Bill of Rights was not just its intended radical transformation of American government, but also Roosevelt's plan to bring about this change. Roosevelt made no effort whatsoever to incorporate these rights into the Constitution by the amendment process. He instead believed that the national government already possessed all the power it needed to carry out these political aims. He asserted in 1944, "*We have accepted*, so to speak, a second Bill of Rights under which a new basis of security and prosperity can be established for all regardless of station, race or creed."[163] Essentially, all that was necessary to guarantee these rights to the people was the political will to implement and sustain them. Roosevelt simply committed the nation's dominant central authority to this set of progressive political principles—principles that he believed should forever govern the nation going forward.

Although the second Bill of Rights was a political goal, many progressives wanted the Supreme Court to insert these rights in the Constitution by judicial decree. And for some time, the Court acted toward that end. Harvard Law Professor Cass Sunstein observed, "In the 1960s, the nation was rapidly moving toward accepting a second Bill, not through constitutional amendment but through the Supreme Court's interpretations of the existing Constitution."[164] The activist Warren Court continued to find new rights in the Constitution that brought the nation ever closer to Roosevelt's aim. And progressives relentlessly pressed the Court to go even further. Sunstein noted, for example, that "prominent academic commentators insisted that the Court should find a constitutional right to minimum welfare guarantees."[165]

The Court never fully accepted the second Bill of Rights, however. Its momentum toward that end ultimately stalled in 1969 when Republican Richard Nixon assumed the presidency. During his first term in office, Nixon filled four vacancies on the Court, including the seat of retiring Chief Justice Earl Warren. As a consequence of these appointments, the Court became much less progressive and activist. Its constitutional interpretation no longer encompassed the radical entitlements of Roosevelt's second Bill of Rights. Professor Sunstein remarked that, had there been "a relatively small shift in the [1968] presidential vote, the American Constitution might well have been understood to create a wide range of social and economic rights."[166] Sunstein believed that the Court would have eventually succeeded in reading the second Bill of Rights into the Constitution had a Democrat controlled the judicial nominating process during this time.

While many progressives in the 1960s counted on the Supreme Court to impose their will on the nation, others later recognized that political action was necessary to realize the kind of transformative change that Roosevelt envisioned for America. The Court could not accomplish this feat alone, no matter how activist it might be. After all, the Court's authority is largely derived from popular support for its opinions. It may stretch the meaning of the Constitution to justify existing progressive laws, but the Court is less inclined to radically expand federal powers in the absence of federal legislation out of concern for its own legitimacy. Many progressives understood that the Court was more comfortable endorsing or acquiescing to radical social policy enacted by Congress under the guise of its commerce power—something the Court had done repeatedly since the 1930s.

Barack Obama, for example, questioned the usefulness of legal action in the 1960s as a means to bring about progressive change in America. In an interview in 2001, Obama pointed out that the Warren Court was unwilling to make that final leap to insert positive economic rights into the Constitution, much to his frustration. He said:

> The Supreme Court never ventured into the issues of redistribution of wealth and [the] sort of more basic issues of political and economic justice in this society. And to that extent as radical as I think people tried to characterize the Warren Court, it wasn't that radical. It didn't break free from the essential constraints that were placed by the Founding Fathers in the Constitution, as least as it's been interpreted, and [the] Warren Court interpreted it in the same way: that, generally, the Constitution is a charter of negative liberties, [it] says what the states can't do to you, [it] says what the federal government can't do to you, but it doesn't say what the federal government or the state government must do on your behalf. And that hasn't shifted.[167]

Because the Court seemed unwilling to insert progressive rights into the Constitution, Obama thought the civil rights movement in the 1960s would have been better off disregarding the Court altogether—he actually criticized the movement for being "so Court-focused."[168] Obama said that "one of the, I think, the tragedies of the civil rights movement . . . was [its] tendency to lose track of the political and community organizing activities on the ground that are able to put together the actual coalitions of power through which you bring about redistributive change."[169]

Like Roosevelt, Obama believed that there already existed enough regulatory authority in the federal government for it to implement various progressive aims. All that remained to radically change the nation—to "fundamentally transform[] the United States of America," as he later promised during the 2008 presidential election[170]—was the political momentum necessary to direct the powerful federal government. (Incidentally, upon taking office in 2009, President Obama appointed Professor Sunstein—who regarded Franklin Roosevelt as the greatest leader in American history and authored *The Second Bill of Rights: FDR's Unfinished Revolution and Why We Need It More Than Ever*[171]—to the position of Administrator of the Office of Information and Regulatory Affairs, also known as the "Regulatory Czar.")

The importance of political power in America was validated in 2005, when the Supreme Court once again sanctioned Congress' broad, if not unlimited, commerce power. In *Gonzales v. Raich*—a case involving the legitimacy of the 1970 Controlled Substance Act—the Court affirmed the government's power to regulate nearly any activity, even those that were purely local and noncommercial.[172] Specifically, the Court affirmed the federal government's power to criminalize homegrown medicinal marijuana, which was legal under California law.

To support its endorsement of this sweeping federal power, the Court reached back to its 1942 holding in *Wickard v. Filburn*, which had given President Roosevelt all the authority he needed to construct any kind of regulation he desired. Using that case as authority, the Court wrote in 2005, "*Wickard* thus establishes that Congress can regulate purely intrastate activity that is not itself 'commercial,' in that it is not produced for sale, if it concludes that failure to regulate that class of activity would undercut the regulation of the interstate market in that commodity."[173] By this reasoning, anything that is grown or produced in America, whether or not it is sold, undercuts the broader market for some commodity in commerce. In effect, the Court pronounced that the federal government's regulatory power is virtually without limit.

As Justice Clarence Thomas argued in his dissent in *Gonzales*, the Founding Fathers never meant to grant the federal government this kind of sweeping power over the people. Such power, he wrote, is completely "at odds with the constitutional design."[174] Thomas suggested that the Court's interpretation of the Commerce Clause was so absurdly expansive and contrary to the Founding Fathers' intent that it rendered their guarantees of limited government utterly meaningless. He wrote:

> If the majority is to be taken seriously, the federal government may now regulate quilting bees, clothes drives, and potluck suppers throughout the 50 states. This makes a mockery of [James] Madison's assurance to the people of New York that the "powers delegated" to the federal government are "few and defined," while those of the states are "numerous and indefinite."[175]

Justice Thomas had previously warned that the Court's misguided and overly-broad interpretation of the Commerce Clause would only embolden politicians to further expand federal power. He wrote in *United States v. Morrison* (2000) that the Court's application of the Commerce Clause in recent times has been "inconsistent with the original understanding of the Congress' and with this Court's early Commerce Clause cases. By continuing to apply this rootless and malleable standard, however circumscribed, the Court has encouraged the federal government to persist in its view that the Commerce Clause has virtually no limits."[176] Thomas then predicted, "Until this Court replaces its existing Commerce Clause jurisprudence with a standard more consistent with the original understanding, we will continue to see Congress appropriating state police powers under the guise of regulating commerce."[177]

The Court's ruling in *Gonzales v. Raich*, which sustained these rulings, did nothing to restore the Constitution's original limits. It instead reassured Congress that the Court would continue to sanction practically any law under the Commerce Clause—that politicians could brandish federal regulatory power however they so desired. In effect, the Court paved the way for subsequent expansions of federal power, including one of the largest in American history.

In 2010, President Obama and Democrats in Congress, with no Republican support, passed the controversial Patient Protection and Affordable Care Act (ACA).[178] The ACA was so divisive because it imposed on every American the mandatory obligation to buy health insurance—anyone refusing to buy insurance would face a penalty for noncompliance. So for the first time in history, the federal government claimed a power to regulate individual *inactivity* under the Commerce Clause under the theory that inactivity itself affects interstate commerce. All Americans would be forced into the heavily-regulated market for health insurance—they would be forced to buy something against their will—simply because Democrats so desired and directed.

In response to the ACA's authoritarian nature, many states quickly sued to block its implementation, and their legal challenges focused in large part on the constitutionality of the individual mandate. The Obama Administration defended the mandate primarily under the Commerce Clause and alternatively under Congress' taxing power. Because the appellate courts in various jurisdictions reached different outcomes, and because the cases touched on novel constitutional issues, the Supreme Court sought to resolve the matter once and for all in *NFIB v. Sebelius* in 2012.

On the Commerce Clause question, five justices argued in two separate opinions that the ACA was unconstitutional.[179] Chief Justice John Roberts explained in his opinion why he rejected the Obama Administration's commerce power claim:

> Construing the Commerce Clause to permit Congress to regulate individuals precisely *because* they are doing nothing would open a new and potentially vast domain to congressional authority. . . . The Framers gave Congress the power to *regulate* commerce, not to *compel* it . . . . The Commerce Clause is not a general license to regulate an individual from cradle to grave, simply because he will predictably engage in particular transactions. Any police power to regulate individuals as such, as opposed to their activities, remains vested in the states.[180]

The other justices who found the ACA unconstitutional on these grounds (Antonin Scalia, Anthony Kennedy, Clarence Thomas, and Samuel Alito) wrote in a separate dissenting opinion that the Commerce Clause had been stretched far enough and could not accommodate the regulation of inactivity. Using the Court's most expansive ruling in *Wickard v. Filburn* to illustrate, they wrote:

> To go beyond [*Wickard*], and to say the *failure* to grow wheat (which is not an economic activity, or any activity at all) nonetheless affects commerce and therefore can be federally regulated, is to make mere breathing in and out the basis for federal prescription and to extend federal power to virtually all human activity.[181]

Although the four dissenting justices clearly agreed with the Chief Justice on the outer boundary of the Commerce Clause, they curiously did not join in his opinion.[*] Consequently, there was no official majority that spoke for the Court on this issue, which means that their expressed opinions on the

---

[*] The prevailing theory as to why Scalia, Kennedy, Thomas, and Alito did not join in Roberts' opinion is that they were annoyed by his abrupt change in position on the overall constitutionality of the ACA. Reportedly, Roberts initially sided with the dissenters but later chose to uphold the law under Congress' taxing power.[182]

commerce power hold no precedential value to guide future judicial decisions on similar coercive laws.

In effect, the Court's ruling in *NFIB v. Sebelius* did nothing to rein in excessive federal power under the Commerce Clause. Rather, it maintained the status quo. It preserved in full the Court's past rulings on the commerce power—decisions that were overly permissive of Congress' ability to regulate any commercial or noncommercial activity in the nation. The continued use of these illegitimate precedents prompted Justice Thomas to once again express his deep frustration with the Court's Commerce Clause jurisprudence. In a separate dissenting opinion in *NFIB* on this issue, he wrote:

> I adhere to my view that "the very notion of a 'substantial effects' test under the Commerce Clause is inconsistent with the original understanding of Congress' powers and with this Court's early Commerce Clause cases." . . . As I have explained, the Court's continued use of that test "has encouraged the federal government to persist in its view that the Commerce Clause has virtually no limits." The government's unprecedented claim in this suit that it may regulate not only economic activity but also *inactivity* that substantially affects interstate commerce is a case in point.[183]

The Court may have properly applied its Commerce Clause precedent in *NFIB* to stop further damage to this provision of the Constitution. But this deferential legal precedent, which alone is a distortion of the Constitution, invites this kind of legislative abuse. As Justice Thomas reiterated, until the Court commits itself to upholding the Constitution's original design, such abuse will surely continue.

Moreover, because of the Court's ruling in *NFIB*, politicians seeking to radically expand federal power have a new constitutional basis for their oppressive regulatory schemes. While the Court blocked the ACA's individual mandate under the Commerce Clause, it found the mandate constitutional under Congress' taxing power. The Court thus sanctioned the federal regulation of inactivity under the guise of a tax. Chief Justice Roberts, who wrote for the majority, indicated some discomfort with his own opinion when he wrote, "If it is troubling to interpret the Commerce Clause as authorizing Congress to regulate those who abstain from commerce, perhaps it should be similarly troubling to permit Congress to impose a tax for not doing something."[184] But he and the other activist justices who joined in his opinion nevertheless declared that the ACA's individual mandate penalty "may reasonably be characterized as a tax" and that "the Constitution permits such a tax."[185]

Nothing could be further from the truth. It is utterly preposterous for the Court to claim that the individual mandate is a tax when it was never called a tax in the statute nor characterized as one during the debates leading up to its enactment. In fact, Democrats were stubbornly opposed to this characterization when selling the ACA to the American people. For example, when President Obama was asked in 2009 whether the individual mandate was a tax, he retorted, "No. That's not true . . . [It] is absolutely not a tax increase."[186] When asked again if he rejected the ACA's characterization as a tax, Obama repeated, "I absolutely reject that notion."[187] He said in the same interview, "[Y]ou can't just make up that language and decide that that's called a tax increase."[188]

Yet the Supreme Court did just that. It recast the ACA as a tax to serve the judicial outcome it desired. As the four dissenting justices pointed out, the Court effectively "rewr[o]te the statute to be what it is not."[189]

Even worse, the Court's revisionist ruling circumvented the political process required by the Constitution to pass any tax. The Constitution demands in Article I, section 7, "All bills for raising revenue shall originate in the House of Representatives."[190] The ACA, however, originated in the Senate. And it is questionable whether the American people would have even supported this $4 billion-per-year tax increase had the ACA been proposed to them as such.[191] The four dissenting justices expounded on these points:

> Taxes have never been popular, see, e.g., Stamp Act of 1765, and in part for that reason, the Constitution requires tax increases to originate in the House of Representatives. See Art. I, §7, cl. 1. That is to say, they must originate in the legislative body most accountable to the people, where legislators must weigh the need for the tax against the terrible price they might pay at their next election, which is never more than two years off. The Federalist No. 58 "defend[ed] the decision to give the origination power to

the House on the ground that the Chamber that is more accountable to the people should have the primary role in raising revenue." *United States* v. *Munoz-Flores*, 495 U. S. 385, 395 (1990). We have no doubt that Congress knew precisely what it was doing when it rejected an earlier version of this legislation that imposed a tax instead of a requirement-with-penalty. See Affordable Health Care for America Act, H. R. 3962, 111th Cong., 1st Sess., §501 (2009); America's Healthy Future Act of 2009, S. 1796, 111th Cong., 1st Sess., §1301. Imposing a tax through judicial legislation inverts the constitutional scheme, and places the power to tax in the branch of government least accountable to the citizenry.[192]

The Court was clearly intent upon upholding the ACA in spite of the Constitution, for it actually treated the individual mandate as a *penalty*, not a tax, where necessary in its duplicitous ruling. Specifically, the Court held that the mandate was a penalty when another law, the Anti-Injunction Act, potentially barred its ruling altogether. The Anti-Injunction Act requires anyone who challenges a tax to do so only after it is assessed—to pay the tax first and then sue for a refund. Had the Court treated the individual mandate as a tax for the purpose of this law, then it would have been unable to rule on the ACA's constitutionality until the mandate becomes enforceable in 2014. But the Court conveniently held that the individual mandate in this specific instance was a penalty and not a tax. The four dissenters wrote in exasperation:

> The government and those who support its position on this point make the remarkable argument that [the individual mandate] is not a tax for purposes of the Anti-Injunction Act, but it is a tax for constitutional purposes. . . . That carries verbal wizardry too far, deep into the forbidden land of the sophists.[193]

Even if the Court had correctly decided that the ACA's individual mandate was a tax for constitutional purposes (after first deeming it a penalty for purposes of the Anti-Injunction Act), it still had to determine whether the Constitution permits such a tax. As Chief Justice Roberts wrote, "any tax must still comply with other requirements in the Constitution."[194]

The federal government's taxing power is limited by the Constitution to the following uses. Congress may enact "duties, imposts, and excises," under Article I, section 8, provided that these taxes are "uniform throughout the United States."[195] These include tariffs and taxes on the sale or production of goods. Congress may tax income under the Sixteenth Amendment—this includes all income earned or received from any source. Finally, Congress may impose a "capitation, or other direct, tax" under Article I, section 9, provided that the tax is apportioned among the states.[196]

The ACA's individual mandate qualifies as none of these taxes. It is not a duty, impost, or excise tax, since these taxes apply to those who actively engage in commerce, not those who withhold their participation in it. And it is not an income tax, since individuals are not generating income by choosing not to buy health insurance. The only taxing authority that remains to justify the individual mandate is the capitation or direct tax. But the Chief Justice discussed this tax at length in his majority opinion in *NFIB* and concluded, "A tax on going without health insurance does not fall within any recognized category of direct tax. It is not a capitation."[197]

Because there was no true constitutional basis for the individual mandate, the Court instead made one up. Chief Justice Roberts wrote:

> [O]ur Constitution protects us from federal regulation under the Commerce Clause so long as we abstain from the regulated activity. But from its creation, the Constitution has made no such promise with respect to taxes. See Letter from Benjamin Franklin to M. Le Roy (Nov. 13, 1789) ("Our new Constitution is now established . . . but in this world nothing can be said to be certain, except death and taxes").[198]

Notice that the authority Roberts cites here is not the Constitution or any interpretation of its meaning. Rather, he rests his claim—that any kind of tax is permissible under the Constitution—on a quote from Benjamin Franklin that was blatantly pulled out of context. In the quoted letter, Benjamin Franklin was not discussing Congress' constitutional taxing power at all. He was instead making a point about the uncertain longevity of the American Constitution. His full statement reads, "Our new Constitution is now established, and has an appearance that promises permanency; but in this world nothing can be said to be certain, except death and taxes."[199]

In its desperate search for anything else that might justify the ACA's individual mandate, the Court also pointed out that Congress has long used its taxing power to "encourage buying something."[200] It wrote, "Tax incentives already promote, for example, purchasing homes and professional education."[201] While these benefits or inducements may influence individual behavior in commerce, they do not penalize inactivity like the ACA does—Americans are not taxed separately for not buying a home or not going to college. So these comparisons are wholly irrelevant for failing to address the constitutional issue at the heart of the ACA: Congress' power to mandate the purchase of a commodity. In truth, the Court could not look to the Constitution to justify the ACA because the Constitution confers no power on Congress to enact such a law.

By validating this vast overreaching of federal authority, the Supreme Court in *NFIB v. Sebelius* demonstrated once again that the people cannot rely on this institution to uphold their Constitution. Its justices are not the "faithful guardians of the Constitution" or the "bulwarks of a limited Constitution against legislative encroachments," as Alexander Hamilton assured they would be in The Federalist No. 78.[202] Ever since the Court first caved to political pressure during the Great Depression, it has continued to authorize the expansion of regulatory power in America. In matters affecting the people's economic liberty, the Court has continued to defer to Congress—it has sanctioned progressive plans to transform the United States into a centralized administrative state. Chief Justice Roberts snidely wrote in the opening of *NFIB*, "It is not our job to protect the people from the consequences of their political choices."[203] Apparently, their job is not to preserve the Constitution and the protections it affords but to distort its meaning to justify federal law.

Of course, the Chief Justice is correct in the sense that it is ultimately the people's responsibility to keep their elected representatives in check. The growth of federal power over time was not the Court's doing. The people have let their own government encroach on their liberty by succumbing to the false hopes of progressive ideas.

In the 1930s, Franklin Roosevelt was able to fundamentally transform the nature of the federal government because he convinced new generations of Americans that free market economics and limited government were relics of bygone days. He held the private sector responsible for the economic stagnation and high unemployment that lasted throughout the Great Depression. He argued that the failings of the private sector necessitated government intervention to stabilize the economy and put Americans back to work. He claimed that his economic policies, which would increase federal spending and regulatory power, were best for the American people. And he assured the nation that government could be trusted as a force for good—to manage the economy and bring about economic justice in society.

Since that time, the people have continued to empower government as a force for good, even though it is now known that Roosevelt was wrong in so many ways. Economic studies of the Depression era reveal that the federal government—not the private sector—was largely responsible for the nation's economic collapse in that day. Many studies also show that Roosevelt's progressive policies did nothing to stimulate the economy or create jobs; the New Deal actually extended that economic crisis.

Economist Milton Friedman, who won the 1976 Nobel Prize in Economics for his analysis of monetary history, attributed the onset of the Great Depression to the federal government's failed monetary policy. He wrote:

> The fact is that the Great Depression, like most other periods of severe unemployment, was produced by government mismanagement rather than by any inherent instability of the private economy. A governmentally established agency—the Federal Reserve System—had been assigned responsibility for monetary policy. In 1930 and 1931, it exercised this responsibility so ineptly as to convert what otherwise would have been a moderate contraction into a major catastrophe.[204]

Friedman's analysis of the Great Depression was later validated by the Chairman of the Federal Reserve, Ben Bernanke, who served under Presidents George W. Bush and Barack Obama. At an event honoring Friedman in 2002, Bernanke said, "[B]ecause of institutional changes and misguided doctrines [of the Federal Reserve], the banking panics of the Great Contraction were much more severe and widespread than would have normally occurred during a downturn. . . . Regarding the Great Depression, you're right. We did it. We're very sorry."[205]

After causing the Great Depression by sharply contracting the money supply in the United States from 1929 to 1933, the Federal Reserve at last reversed its destructive course, and productivity grew as a result. On the basis of the Federal Reserve's expansionary policy alone, economists Leonard Rapping and Nobel Laureate Robert Lucas calculated that the American economy should have recovered by 1935.[206] But the actual recovery did not come until 1943.

The reason for this delayed economic recovery was clear to economists Harold Cole and Lee Ohanian: Roosevelt's restrictive New Deal policies were a heavy burden on the economy. Cole explained in 2004:

> President Roosevelt believed that excessive competition was responsible for the Depression by reducing prices and wages, and by extension reducing employment and demand for goods and services. So he came up with a recovery package that would be unimaginable today, allowing businesses in every industry to collude without the threat of antitrust prosecution and workers to demand salaries about 25 percent above where they ought to have been, given market forces. The economy was poised for a beautiful recovery, but that recovery was stalled by these misguided policies.[207]

Cole and Ohanian later wrote, "The goal of the New Deal was to get Americans back to work. But the New Deal didn't restore employment. In fact, there was even less work on average during the New Deal than before FDR took office."[208] In the end, Roosevelt's forceful regulatory response to the Great Depression proved to be counterproductive to economic recovery. Despite the government's best efforts to stimulate the economy, Cole and Ohanian showed that "the recovery would have been very rapid had the government not intervened."[209]

In spite of these findings, the powerful federal government has continued to disturb natural market forces, much to the detriment of economic stability and prosperity. Recently, the government's inept monetary policy and market interference helped create the 2008 financial crisis, which is considered to be the worst economic crisis since the Great Depression.

Economist John Taylor identified the Federal Reserve's monetary policy as primary cause of the housing boom in the mid-2000s, which was soon after followed by a bust that "led to defaults, the implosion of the mortgages and mortgage-related securities at financial institutions, and resulting financial turmoil."[210] He wrote:

> The Fed held its target interest rate, especially in 2003–2005, well below known monetary guidelines that say what good policy should be based on historical experience. Keeping interest rates on the track that worked well in the past two decades, rather than keeping rates so low, would have prevented the boom and the bust. Researchers at the Organization for Economic Cooperation and Development have provided corroborating evidence from other countries: The greater the degree of monetary excess in a country, the larger was the housing boom.[211]

Because the Federal Reserve maintained such low interest rates throughout the 2000s, investors seeking higher yields gravitated towards riskier securities, including mortgage-backed securities and collateralized debt obligations. As the demand for these new securities grew, so did the demand for mortgages. And thanks to progressive social policies, mortgage lenders were able to satisfy that demand by abandoning traditional underwriting standards (e.g., verifying income or assets, requiring a down payment, or assuring the applicant's ability to make payments).

Banks had long utilized these traditional underwriting standards to confirm that a borrower could repay a loan—they were sensible measures that any rational business would apply to avoid financial loss. But the federal government in the 1990s decided that these underwriting standards were somehow discriminatory against minorities. So it forced banks to relax these "outdated" standards by changing regulations that governed the banking industry.[212] Specifically, the Clinton Administration in 1995 made regulatory changes to the 1977 Community Reinvestment Act (CRA) to force banks to use "innovative or flexible" lending practices that addressed the needs of low- and moderate-income borrowers.[213] Banks could no longer base their underwriting standards on criteria meant to find qualified borrowers and limit defaults. Banks had to plainly show that they were making a certain number of loans to low- and moderate-income borrowers.[214]

The relaxed underwriting standards and new lending practices that were mandated by the CRA soon expanded across the entire mortgage market. Any borrower could take advantage of these more flexible loan options, and they did. Between 2001 and 2006, the share of all mortgage originations comprising of traditional 30-year fixed rate mortgages was nearly cut in half.[215] Quick access to large amounts of credit on very favorable terms—often with no money down and at very low interest rates—gave borrowers more purchasing power than ever before. More Americans bought homes. And given the availability of cheap credit, more Americans bought homes that were previously beyond their price range. As a consequence, real estate values grew higher and higher.

When the housing bubble finally burst with sweeping repercussions on the economy, politicians were quick to blame the banks for greedily pushing risky loans on the American people. But the banking industry, which happens to be one of the most heavily-regulated industries in America, did not independently create these faulty loans. They were the product of the government's interference in the mortgage market. Economist Stan Liebowitz wrote in 2008, "From the current hand-wringing, you'd think that the banks came up with the idea of looser underwriting standards on their own, with regulators just asleep on the job. In fact, it was the regulators who relaxed these standards—at the behest of community groups and 'progressive' political forces."[216]

The federal government's meddling in the free market, combined with its inept monetary policy, created the conditions for economic disaster in America. But progressive politicians have continued to ignore these causes. They have since asserted that even more regulations are necessary to avert a similar crisis in the future. And by their control of Congress and the presidency in 2010, Democrats successfully acted on these beliefs.

That year, not only did President Obama sign into law the 2,400-page health care reform bill discussed earlier, but he also signed into law a sweeping 2,300-page regulatory reform bill that he referred to as "the toughest financial reform since the ones we created in the aftermath of the

Great Depression."[217] Democrat Congresswoman Carolyn Maloney said in support of the bill, "The goal is to prevent what happened from happening again. We had regulations after the Great Depression that gave us 50 years of prosperity. This will help give us another 50 years."[218]

This reflexive tendency to turn to government for a regulatory solution to a problem—in spite of its historical failings—is typical in politics today. Ever since the federal government assumed its sweeping power over any commercial or noncommercial activity in the nation, debates over the constitutionality of such power have diminished in time. The question that is asked is not whether government may act in a given case, but what its action might be. For many politicians, the government's long exercise of a restrictive, regulatory power has alone justified its continuing legitimacy. And for progressives, especially, that precedential authority provides an opportunity to further stretch the scope of federal power.

The Founding Fathers recognized that illegitimate, precedential actions could have a damaging effect on liberty over time. James Madison observed that, throughout world history, "there have been more instances of the abridgment of the freedom of the people by the gradual and silent encroachments of those in power than by violent and sudden usurpations."[219] Thomas Jefferson recognized that the people's willingness to tolerate minute reductions to their liberty is what makes precedential authority so lasting. He wrote, "[A]ll experience has shown that mankind are more disposed to suffer, while evils are sufferable, than to right themselves by abolishing the forms to which they are accustomed."[220] This conditioned acceptance of illegitimate action makes precedential measures so difficult to change. Thomas Paine wrote, "[A] long habit of not thinking a thing *wrong*, gives it a superficial appearance of being *right*, and raises at first a formidable outcry in defense of custom."[221]

Paine was particularly critical of any government that based its authority on precedent. He proclaimed:

> Government by precedent, without any regard to the principle of the precedent, is one of the vilest systems that can be set up. . . .
>
> Either the doctrine of precedents is policy to keep man in a state of ignorance, or it is a practical confession that wisdom degenerates in governments as governments increase in age, and

can only hobble along by the stilts and crutches of precedents. How is it that the same persons who would proudly be thought wiser than their predecessors appear at the same time only as the ghosts of departed wisdom? How strangely is antiquity treated! To answer some purposes it is spoken of as the times of darkness and ignorance, and to answer others, it is put for the light of the world.[222]

The Founding Fathers recognized that certain precedential actions could erode liberty over time by conditioning the people to subordinate their reason to custom. So they advised the American people to remain alert to any government action that expanded its authority, no matter how insignificant that increase in power might be. Paine cautioned, "In numerous instances, the precedent ought to operate as a warning and not as an example"—it must "be shunned instead of imitated."[223] Madison similarly warned in 1785:

> [I]t is proper to take alarm at the first experiment on our liberties. We hold this prudent jealousy to be the first duty of citizens and one of the noblest characteristics of the late revolution. The freemen of America did not wait until usurped power had strengthened itself by exercise, and entangled the question in precedents. They saw all the consequences in the principle, and they avoided the consequences by denying the principle. We revere this lesson too much, soon to forget it.[224]

Decades later, Madison again warned of precedential advances by government, restating that American independence was based on the people's recognition and rejection of such illegitimate authority. He wrote:

> The people of the U.S. owe their independence and their liberty, to the wisdom of descrying in the minute tax of 3 pence on tea, the magnitude of the evil comprised in the precedent. Let them exert the same wisdom, in watching against every evil lurking under plausible disguises, and growing up from small beginnings.[225]

Undeniably, the current power wielded by the federal government grew up from small beginnings. Progressives have persistently nudged the nation along a path toward a more paternalistic centralized government. And the American people—especially younger generations—have increasingly grown accustomed to the government's broad authority by its regular application of that power. As a consequence of this conditioning, the federal government's complex income tax code, burdensome regulations, and numerous welfare programs have practically become permanent fixtures of American society.

As noted before, the federal government once had no power to tax income at all. Even after the Sixteenth Amendment was ratified in 1913, the tax was meant to have a narrow reach or to be used only as an emergency measure. Yet the federal income tax code now surpasses 67,000 pages and touches every kind of productive activity in the nation, costing Americans at least $225 billion in compliance costs each year.[226]

The federal government's regulatory power clearly grew up from small beginnings. The Commerce Clause was formerly used to break down barriers to free trade, not to impose restrictions and regulations on all kinds of commercial and noncommercial activity. Federal regulation was practically nonexistent during the founding era, but it "began in earnest in the 1930s," according to the Office of Management and Budget.[227] The volume of federal regulations now exceeds 163,000 pages, burdening Americans with hidden taxes for compliance that total over $1.75 trillion each year.[228]

The federal government's power to redistribute wealth also grew out of nothing. The Constitution confers no redistributive power on the federal government, and, not surprisingly, total federal spending on social welfare programs was zero for much of American history. But as progressivism grew in the twentieth century—and especially after the Supreme Court twisted constitutional meaning to give complete spending discretion to Congress in the 1930s—limits on federal spending eventually disappeared. Federal spending on social welfare programs now totals over $2 trillion each year and comprises close to 60 percent of the federal budget—more than double the government's spending on national defense.[229]

The Founding Fathers never meant to create such a domineering central government in America. They shared no similar faith with monarchists in their day (or progressives of today) that an authoritarian bureaucracy could best care for the interests of the people. They believed instead that the American people were better off when government mainly left them alone in their economic pursuits. They were confident that the ingenuity and generosity of the American people could provide for the diverse wants of society better than any central authority.

Informed by history, their own experiences, and Adam Smith's free market economic theory, the Founding Fathers designed the federal government to be limited in power so that the nation would prosper in liberty. James Madison argued that "the industrious pursuits of individuals ought to be left to individuals," for they were "most capable of choosing and managing them" and such a policy was "most congenial with the spirit of a free people."[230] Alexander Hamilton wrote that free trade was "perceived and acknowledged by all enlightened statesmen to be the most useful as well as the most productive source of national wealth."[231] He stated that the American economy would most benefit by an "unrestrained intercourse between the states."[232] Thomas Jefferson also was confident that the United States "would gain by setting commerce at perfect liberty."[233] He said that good government "shall leave [the people] otherwise free to regulate their own pursuits of industry and improvement, and shall not take from the mouth of labor the bread it has earned."[234] George Washington advised:

> [O]ur commercial policy should hold an equal and impartial hand: neither seeking nor granting exclusive favors or preferences; consulting the natural course of things; diffusing and diversifying by gentle means the streams of commerce, but forcing nothing; establishing with powers so disposed; in order to give trade a stable course.[235]

By exercising federal power in support of free trade, the Founding Fathers assured that the government's limited role in the economy would remain aligned with its primary purpose to preserve private property—consistent with Natural Law precepts. As John Locke wrote, "the great and chief end" of government "is the preservation of [private] property."[236] Madison similarly declared:

> It is sufficiently obvious, that persons [] and property are the two great subjects on which governments are to act; and that the rights of persons, and the rights of property, are the objects, for the protection of which government was instituted. These rights cannot well be separated. The personal right to acquire property,

which is a natural right, gives to property, when acquired, a right
to protection as a social right.[237]

Madison recognized that government was "instituted to protect property of
every sort," and that this purpose could not be achieved "where the
property, which a man has in his personal safety and personal liberty, is
violated by arbitrary seizures of one class of citizens for the service of the
rest."[238]

Notwithstanding this fundamental purpose of American government,
private property is not secure today. The federal government wields an
arbitrary power over private property through the income tax and its
unbounded regulatory authority. Those in power determine how much
income to take from the people through arbitrary taxation. Those in power
determine who benefits from government's access to other people's money
through arbitrary welfare spending. Those in power promote favored
industries, businesses, and special interest groups through preferential
regulations and tax breaks. And those in power encumber all forms of
commercial activity with a labyrinth of bureaucratic rules and regulations
that inhibits economic freedom.

The federal government's sweeping power over private property
undeniably exceeds the bounds of the Constitution and Natural Law. The
Founding Fathers never designed the nation's commerce and taxing
authority to be so broad that government could morph into such an
omnipotent centralized power. And they certainly had no intention to
create a government that could disregard the people's natural rights
endowed by God in order to distribute economic benefits promised by
politicians.

The Founding Fathers recognized that liberty could not endure in
America when property rights were so abused. John Adams wrote,
"Property must be secured or liberty cannot exist."[239] When the
government fails to preserve private property—when its laws do not
comport with Natural Law—it rules by force and coercion. And the
Founders knew that the rise of an arbitrary, autocratic power over property
in America would soon mark the end of liberty for all. Adams warned,
"The moment the idea is admitted into society that property is not as

sacred as the laws of God, and that there is not a force of law and public justice to protect it, anarchy and tyranny commence."[240]

That moment took place in America long ago, and that idea still persists in government today. Tyranny, once begun, continues.

6

ON TYRANNY

At the close of the Constitutional Convention in 1787, Benjamin Franklin left Independence Hall in Philadelphia and was soon after met on the street by a woman eager for news from the convention. She asked him what kind of government the Founding Fathers had created, and Franklin candidly responded, "A republic, if you can keep it."[1] Despite the Constitution's foundation in liberty, the Founding Fathers knew that a free republic was not forever guaranteed. For liberty to last in America, the people had to diligently guard their liberty against government's innate tendency toward tyranny.

John Locke defined tyranny as "the exercise of power beyond right"—the use of power "not for the good of those who are under it, but for [one's] own private separate advantage."[2] He explained that tyranny arises when the bounds of Natural Law are exceeded. It exists when "the governor, however entitled, makes not the law, but his will, the rule; and [when] his commands and actions are not directed to the preservation of the properties of his people, but the satisfaction of his own ambition, revenge, covetousness, or any other irregular passion."[3] Fundamentally, a tyrannical power exists when those in government—no matter what kind of government is instituted—wield an arbitrary power over the natural rights of the people.

Locke considered it "a mistake" to think that tyranny "is proper only to monarchies."[4] He explained that "wherever the power that is put in any hands for the government of the people and the preservation of their properties is applied to other ends and made use of to impoverish, harass, or subdue them to the arbitrary and irregular commands of those that have it, [then] it presently becomes tyranny, whether those that thus use it are one or many."[5] Tyranny, therefore, can emerge in any form of government, including a representative republic.

A republic can be just as tyrannical as an autocratic dictatorship if its elected representatives hold an arbitrary power over the people's natural rights. Although the people in such a republic may vote abusive politicians out of office, voting rights matter little to tyranny as long as government retains this broad power. Thomas Paine explained, "It is not because a part of the government is elective, that makes it less a despotism, if the persons so elected possess afterwards, as a parliament, unlimited powers. Election in this case becomes separated from representation, and the candidates are candidates for despotism."[6]

The Founding Fathers in fact acknowledged that tyranny might arise one day in America. Thomas Jefferson wrote of the historical tendency of those in power to nudge their nations ever closer toward despotism. He said, "[E]xperience hath shown, that even under the best forms [of government], those entrusted with power have, in time, and by slow operations, perverted it into tyranny."[7] Jefferson made no exception for the new American government under the Constitution when he wrote, "The natural progress of things is for liberty to yield and government to gain ground."[8] Benjamin Franklin likewise observed that "there is a natural inclination in mankind to kingly government."[9] He predicted "that the government of these [United] States may in future times end in monarchy."[10] James Monroe also feared that liberty might give way to tyranny in America, as it had in all governments throughout history. He observed:

> [H]ow prone all human institutions have been to decay; how subject the best-formed and most wisely organized governments have been to lose their checks and totally dissolve; how difficult it has been for mankind, in all ages and countries, to preserve their dearest rights and best privileges, impelled as it were by an irresistible fate of despotism.[11]

Monroe believed that the relevant question was not whether, but when, tyranny might emerge in America. He said that, unless the United States was somehow "exempted from the fate of other nations," then the same despotic fate would come to America "sooner or later."[12]

The Founding Fathers of course designed the Constitution with the aim of extending liberty into the future. To that end, they limited the federal government's scope of authority in the Constitution so that power could not be concentrated in a single governing body. Madison wrote that "the general government is not to be charged with the whole power of making and administering laws. Its jurisdiction is limited to certain enumerated objects."[13] The Constitution was designed to maintain the dual sovereignty of the federal and state governments. The power of the federal government would be supreme within its designated sphere of authority, and that of the states within their respective areas of control. Joseph Story explained in *Commentaries on the Constitution*:

> [T]he powers of the general government will be, and indeed must be, principally employed upon external objects, such as war, peace, negotiations with foreign powers, and foreign commerce. . . . The powers on the states, on the other hand, extend to all objects, which, in the ordinary course of affairs, concern the lives, and liberties, and property of the people, and the internal order, improvement, and prosperity of the state.[14]

Alexander Hamilton wrote in The Federalist No. 32 that "the state governments would clearly retain all the rights of sovereignty which they before had, and which were not, by [the Constitution], *exclusively* delegated to the United States."[15] He emphasized that "the states must, by every rational man, be considered as essential component parts of the Union; and therefore the idea of sacrificing the former to the latter is totally inadmissible."[16]

This unique kind of federalism allowed the American people to balance state power against national power to guard against the abuse that often results from a consolidated government. Thomas Jefferson wrote that "the states can best govern our home concerns and the general government our foreign ones. I wish . . . never to see all offices transferred to Washington, where, further withdrawn from the eyes of the people, they

may more secretly be bought and sold as at market."[17] Jefferson further
observed:

> Our country is too large to have all its affairs directed by a single
> government. Public servants at such a distance, and from under
> the eye of their constituents, must, from the circumstance of
> distance, be unable to administer and overlook all the details
> necessary for the good government of the citizens; and the same
> circumstance, by rendering detection impossible to their
> constituents, will invite public agents to corruption, plunder and
> waste.[18]

Jefferson feared, "[W]hen all government, domestic and foreign, in little as
in great things, shall be drawn to Washington as the center of all power, it
will render powerless the checks provided of one government on
another."[19] He based this prediction on historical examples, noting that
"the generalizing and concentrating [of] all cares and powers into one
body" had "destroyed the liberty and the rights of man in every
government which [had] ever existed under the sun."[20] To avoid a similar
fate in America, the people had to maintain strong state and local
governments, and the federal government had to respect the clear
constraints on its authority in the Constitution. American liberty could be
preserved, Jefferson advised, as long as the national government remained
limited—its power restrained "by the chains of the Constitution."[21]

The Constitution successfully restrained federal power for some time.
When Tocqueville visited America in 1831, he attributed its enduring
liberty in part to the limitations imposed on the national government. He
wrote, "Since the sovereignty of the Union is hobbled and incomplete, the
exercise of that sovereignty poses no danger to liberty."[22] Even though the
federal government was "omnipotent in its own sphere," it could not be
repressive in all matters that affected the people, for its scope of authority
was confined by the Constitution.[23] The United States remained free, he
concluded, "because of the relatively small number of issues with which
its government [was] concerned."[24]

Tocqueville believed that centralized power would always disserve
the people in any society. He said, "No central power, no matter how
enlightened or intelligent one imagines it to be, can by itself embrace all
the details of life of a great people."[25] This inability to account for the

varied interests of the people is especially true in "large, centralized nations, [where] lawmakers are obliged to give the laws a uniform character that does not comport with the diversity of places and customs."[26] The people, who must then bend to the requirements of general laws that ineffectively serve them, soon become conditioned to follow the detailed edicts of government. In time, Tocqueville wrote, society devolves into "a state of administrative somnolence," where the people become apathetic and increasingly dependent upon the competence and fate of government itself.[27]

Tocqueville was so convinced of this degenerative effect on society because he witnessed it firsthand in Europe. In *Democracy in America*, Tocqueville described how Europeans living under centralized governments had become indifferent and detached from their communities—how they had lost all interest in "the fortunes of their village, the safety of their streets, and the fate of their church and its vestry."[28] Tocqueville added:

> They think that such things have nothing to do with them, that they belong to a powerful stranger called "the government." They enjoy these goods as tenants, without a sense of ownership, and never give a thought to how they might be improved. They are so divorced from their own interests that even when their own security and that of their children is finally compromised, they do not seek to avert the danger themselves but cross their arms and wait for the nation as a whole to come to their aid. Yet as utterly as they sacrifice their own free will, they are no fonder of obedience than anyone else. They submit, it is true, to the whims of a clerk, but no sooner is force removed than they are glad to defy the law as a defeated enemy. Thus one finds them ever wavering between servitude and license.
>
> When a nation has reached this point, it must either change its laws and mores or perish, for the well of public virtue has run dry: in such a place one no longer finds citizens but only subjects.[29]

The degenerative effect of centralized power is no different wherever it is found, and Tocqueville believed that American society would atrophy just the same if centralization were ever to occur in the United States. He warned:

> If the ruling power in America . . . enjoyed not only the right to issue orders of all kinds but also the capability and habit of carrying out those orders; if it not only laid down general principles of government but also concerned itself with the details of applying those principles; and if it dealt not only with the country's major interests but also descended to the limit of individual interests, then liberty would soon be banished from the New World.[30]

At a time when the promise of democracy was spreading around the world, Tocqueville actually believed that most democracies would end in despotism as a result of centralized government. He was "convinced . . . that no nation is more likely to succumb to the yoke of administrative centralization than one whose social state is democratic."[31] And so he predicted that liberty would remain the rare exception to the norm of tyranny in the world. He said, "In the democratic centuries that are about to begin, I think that individual independence and local liberties will always be a product of art. Centralization will be the natural form of government."[32]

In any democratic society, a tyrannical, centralized government does not rise by force. Rather, it forms by the assent of the people in their impassioned pursuit of equality. Tocqueville explained that the people's innate drive for equality can lead a society to two utterly disparate outcomes: "one leads men directly to independence . . . while the other leads by a longer, more hidden, but also more certain path to servitude."[33]

The path toward independence is traversed when the people show respect for natural equality—the idea that all people are born equal before God with the same natural rights to life, liberty, and property. When the guarantees of equality are properly limited to these natural rights, the coercive force of government remains similarly limited. The people are free to realize their fullest potential and pursue their respective paths towards happiness without government barring the way. Moreover, when government is prohibited from leveling all conditions in the name of equality, the people must rely on their own industriousness to satisfy any inclination for parity with others. To match the skills or achievements of those who stand above them, the people recognize that they must independently improve themselves, for *they* are the masters of their destiny—not some distant, centralized power. Tocqueville wrote that this "manly and legitimate passion for equality [] spurs all men to wish to be strong and esteemed. This passion tends to elevate the lesser to the rank of the greater."[34]

A more corrupt passion for equality can have just the opposite effect, however. Tocqueville wrote that "one also finds in the human heart a depraved taste for equality, which impels the weak to want to bring the strong down to their level, and which reduces men to preferring equality in servitude to inequality in freedom."[35] When a nation gives in to this decadent passion to guide its governance, the idea of equality as a tenet of liberty becomes perverted into an instrument of governmental control. In this sense, equality is less about the individual guarantee of natural rights and more about the common assurance of economic parity—a utopian idea that can only be achieved if government has the power to force it on the people. If the people pursue this dream, then they must inevitably surrender their liberty to a domineering force. They may become more equal, but they certainly become less free.

The extent of a nation's freedom, therefore, is largely driven by the people's moderation of their passion for equality. Properly controlled, this passion can sustain liberty. But if unchecked, it can give rise to tyranny. As Tocqueville wrote, the fate of democracy ultimately depends on the people, who must "decide whether equality will lead them into servitude or liberty, enlightenment or barbarism, prosperity or misery."[36]

Tocqueville predicted that centralization and despotism would eventually dominate in most democracies due to the seductive power of equality, not from any popular loathing of liberty. He observed that the people do not "naturally despise liberty; on the contrary, they have an instinctive taste for it."[37] In fact, people in democracies "seek [liberty] out, love it, and suffer if deprived of it."[38] Yet Tocqueville was certain that "liberty is not the principle and constant object of their desire."[39] The people instead worship equality "with a love that is eternal" because it is always there to console them when they fail in liberty.[40] He explained, "They lunge toward liberty with an abrupt impulse or sudden effort and, if they fail to achieve their goal, resign themselves to their defeat. But nothing could satisfy them without equality, and, rather than lose it, they would perish."[41] Tocqueville despairingly wrote:

> No use telling people that such blind surrender to an exclusive passion jeopardizes their most cherished interests: they are deaf. No use pointing out to them that liberty slips through their fingers while their attention is focused elsewhere: they are blind, or, rather, in all the world they see only one good worth coveting.[42]

They see only equality, and they would endlessly pursue it with "an ardent, insatiable, eternal, invincible passion. They want equality in liberty, and if they cannot have it, they want it still in slavery. They will suffer poverty, servitude, and barbarity, but they will not suffer aristocracy."[43]

The people would go to such lengths to establish complete equality because of its ever growing addictive force. Once governmental power is wielded in the name of equality in one circumstance, the people will call for it in others. Tocqueville wrote that the more equal the people become under the authority of government, "the more unbearable the sight of inequality. Hence it is natural for love of equality to grow steadily with equality itself; by satisfying it, one fosters its growth."[44]

Given the people's innate and ever intensifying passion for equality, centralization and tyranny can rise in a democracy without much prodding. In fact, proponents of centralized power need only to feed these impulses to advance their cause. Tocqueville wrote, "Any central power that follows [man's] natural instincts loves equality and encourages it, because equality markedly facilitates, extends, and secures the action of such a power."[45] And as centralized power strengthens, the more tyrannical it can become, for Tocqueville explained that "when all the prerogatives of government are already vested in a single power, it is difficult for that power to refrain from entering into the details of administration, and over the long run there will be no shortage of opportunities to do so."[46] Consequently, a centralized and tyrannical government can form in a democratic society assisted only by the people's depraved passion for equality. Tocqueville wrote, "A democratic government therefore increases its prerogatives simply by enduring. Time works in its favor. Every accident redounds to its benefit. Individual passions aid it unwittingly, and we can say that the older a democratic society is, the more centralized its government becomes."[47] He further emphasized, "The most important, and in a sense the only necessary condition for centralizing public power in a democratic society is to love equality or to make a show of loving it. Thus the science of despotism . . . can be reduced, as it were, to a single principle."[48]

Once centralized power has formed in democracy, it maintains its dominance over the people by manipulating them into continued obedience. It claims to rule on their behalf. Tocqueville observed, "There is nothing so irresistible as a tyrannical power that issues orders in the people's name."[49] He described how a centralized government generally "loves what the citizens love, and it naturally hates what they hate. This community of feeling, which in democratic nations constantly unites each individual with the sovereign in an identical frame of mind, establishes a secret and permanent sympathy between them."[50] This superficial bond effectively sustains the government's hold on the people. By playing on their passions, centralized government effectively nudges the people into compliance.

Tocqueville was certain that this kind of paternalistic political demagoguery would have a much more damaging effect on the people than the kind of terror historically employed by past forms of tyranny. When democratic government claims to serve the people, many will blindly support it. Yet those who oppose this professed benevolent institution can be easily maligned as enemies of the common man—they can be silenced into subservience. Tocqueville believed that such political ostracism would have a more direct and debilitating impact on the soul than ever before, making democratic despotism all the more dangerous to the people. He wrote:

> Princes made violence a physical thing, but today's democratic republics have made it as intellectual as the human will it seeks to coerce. Under the absolute government of one man, despotism tried to reach the soul by striking crudely at the body; and the soul, eluding such blows, rose gloriously above it. Tyranny in democratic republics does not proceed in the same way, however. It ignores the body and goes straight for the soul. The master no longer says: "You will think as I do or die." He says: "You are free not to think as I do. You may keep your life,

your property, and everything else. But from this day forth you shall be as a stranger among us. You will retain your civic privileges, but they will be of no use to you. For if you seek the votes of your fellow citizens, they will withhold them, and if you seek only their esteem, they will feign to refuse even that. You will remain among men, but you will forfeit your rights to humanity. When you approach your fellow creatures, they will shun you as one who is impure. And even those who believe in your innocence will abandon you, lest they, too, be shunned in turn. Go in peace, I will not take your life, but the life I leave you with is worse than death."[51]

Not only does centralized power in democracy seek to ostracize its opponents, but it also aims to divide the people against themselves in order to extend its rule over the nation. Tocqueville wrote that tyranny cannot be resisted "in a country where individuals are weak and no common interest binds them together."[52] Consequently, democratic despotism actually "looks upon the isolation of men as the surest guarantee of its own duration and ordinarily does all it can to ensure that isolation."[53] Tocqueville observed that equality and despotism naturally "complement and assist each other to disastrous effect."[54] He explained:

Equality places men side by side without a common bond to hold them together. Despotism raises barriers between them to keep them apart. The former disposes them not to think of their fellow men, and the latter makes a kind of public virtue of indifference.

Despotism, dangerous at all times, is therefore particularly to be feared in democratic centuries.[55]

Despite his ominous warnings about democratic despotism, Tocqueville had hope for the United States. In fact, he was very optimistic about America's prospects for liberty because the people so far had resisted the temptations of tyranny. He observed, "No one in the United States has yet dared to propose the maxim that everything is permitted in the interest of society—a wicked maxim that seems to have been invented in an age of liberty to legitimize all the tyrants of the future."[56]

Yet Tocqueville knew that tyranny was still possible in America, and he made an even more sinister warning about the fate of the nation should tyranny ever take hold there. He predicted, "without fear of contradiction,"

that "if a democratic republic like the one in the United States" ever
succumbed to "administrative centralization, [] where both custom and law
had absorbed its influence, [then] that country would come to know a
despotism more intolerable than any that has ever existed in Europe's
absolute monarchies."[57]

In an effort to illuminate the dangers of centralized power that could
form in democratic nations like the United States, Tocqueville described in
detail his vision of this new kind of despotism:

> I see an innumerable host of men, all alike and equal, endlessly
> hastening after petty and vulgar pleasures with which they fill
> their souls. Each of them, withdrawn into himself, is virtually a
> stranger to the fate of all the others. For him, his children and
> personal friends comprise the entire human race. As for the
> remainder of his fellow citizens, he lives alongside them but
> does not see them. He touches them but does not feel them. He
> exists only in himself and for himself, and if he still has a family,
> he no longer has a country.
>
> Over these men stands an immense tutelary power, which
> assumes sole responsibility for securing their pleasure and
> watching over their fate. It is absolute, meticulous, regular,
> provident, and mild. It would resemble paternal authority if only
> its purpose were the same, namely, to prepare men for manhood.
> But on the contrary, it seeks only to keep them in childhood
> irrevocably. It likes citizens to rejoice, provided they think only
> of rejoicing. It works willingly for their happiness but wants to
> be the sole agent and only arbiter of that happiness. It provides
> for their security, foresees and takes care of their needs,
> facilitates their pleasures, manages their most important affairs,
> directs their industry, regulates their successions, and divides
> their inheritances. Why not relieve them entirely of the trouble of
> thinking and the difficulty of living?
>
> Every day it thus makes man's use of his free will rarer and
> more futile. It circumscribes the action of the will more
> narrowly, and little by little robs each citizen of the use of his
> own faculties. Equality paved the way for all these things by
> preparing men to put up with them and even to look upon them
> as a boon.
>
> The sovereign, after taking individuals one by one in his
> powerful hands and kneading them to his liking, reaches out to
> embrace society as a whole. Over it he spreads a fine mesh of

uniform, minute, and complex rules, through which not even the most original minds and most vigorous souls can poke their heads above the crowd. He does not break men's wills but softens, bends, and guides them. He seldom forces anyone to act but consistently opposes action. He does not destroy things but prevents them from coming into being. Rather than tyrannize, he inhibits, represses, saps, stifles, and stultifies, and in the end he reduces each nation to nothing but a flock of timid and industrious animals, with the government as its shepherd.[58]

Despite the apparent paradox of democratic despotism—that the sovereign people would allow themselves to be subdued by a government that they control—Tocqueville reiterated that this oppressive state arises at the behest of the people. Despotism can creep into democracy with relative ease when it is attached to their will. He wrote:

> I have always believed that this kind of servitude—the regulated, mild, peaceful servitude that I have just described— could be combined more easily than one might imagine with some of the external forms of liberty, and that it would not be impossible for it to establish itself in the shadow of popular sovereignty itself.[59]

The people, eager to satisfy their depraved desire for equality, would sanction the rise of a strong, centralized authority that aimed to level all conditions. And they would justify their deference to this despotic authority by their elective power to choose their leaders. In effect, the people would comfort themselves in tyranny by their outward appearance of control over government. Tocqueville observed:

> Our contemporaries are constantly wracked by two warring passions: they feel the need to be led and the desire to remain free. Unable to destroy either of these contrary instincts, they seek to satisfy both at once. They imagine a single, omnipotent, tutelary power, but one that is elected by the citizens. They combine centralization with popular sovereignty. This gives them some respite. They console themselves for being treated as wards by imagining that they have chosen their own protectors. Each individual allows himself to be clapped in chains because he sees that the other end of the chain is held not by a man or a class but by the people themselves.

In this system citizens emerge from dependence for a moment
to indicate their master and then return to it.

There are many people nowadays who adjust quite easily to a
compromise of this kind between administrative despotism and
popular sovereignty and who believe that they have done enough
to guarantee the liberty of individuals when in fact they have
surrendered that liberty to the national government. That is
enough for me. The nature of the master matters far less to me
than the fact of obedience.[60]

Like John Locke and Thomas Paine before him, Tocqueville understood
that voting rights do not make an unlimited governing power any less
despotic. Whether tyranny springs from the force of one ruler or the
passion of many, it compels subservience to authority all the same.

As the people grow conditioned to such subservience, Tocqueville
anyway believed that electoral power would become insignificant in time.
He wrote:

In vain will you ask the same citizens whom you have made so
dependent on the central government to choose representatives
of that government from time to time. This use of their freedom
to choose—so important yet so brief and so rare—will not
prevent them from slowly losing the ability to think, feel, and act
on their own and thus from sinking gradually beneath the level
of humanity.

. . .

It is indeed difficult to imagine how men who have entirely
renounced the habit of managing their own affairs could be
successful in choosing those who ought to lead them. It is
impossible to believe that a liberal, energetic, and wise
government can ever emerge from the ballots of a nation of
servants.[61]

When the people are so conditioned to servitude, Tocqueville predicted
that democracy would not long endure, for "[t]he vices of those who
govern and the imbecility of the governed would quickly bring about its
ruin."[62]

When American liberty is measured against this model of democracy
in decline, it becomes clear that the United States today is no longer the
bastion of freedom that Tocqueville observed in his day. The United States
is no longer a decentralized federal republic where, he wrote, "the right to

apply [the law] is divided among so many hands."[63] As a consequence of the many radical changes to federal power that were progressively implemented over time, the American people today are now controlled by a large, central government and its intricate web of rules and regulations. They periodically send new representatives to Washington, D.C., but they must evermore bend to the will of the federal government—they must yield to an unlimited, arbitrary power that continues to advance against their liberty.

The United States is drifting along the same destructive course that Tocqueville so presciently warned against, as exemplified by the federal government's latest and most radical expansion of autocratic power: the 2010 Patient Protection and Affordable Care Act (ACA).[64] As discussed earlier, the ACA was pushed on the nation by President Obama and Democrats in Congress, and it extended federal power well beyond the limits of the Constitution by imposing upon every person in the nation the mandatory obligation to purchase private health insurance. In addition, the ACA created so many new burdensome regulations that its complete implementation would be drawn out well into the future—many of its provisions would take effect in 2014 or later.[65] Democrat Representative John Dingell candidly explained why the ACA's protracted execution was necessary. He said that "it takes a long time to do the necessary administrative steps that have to be taken to put the legislation together *to control the people.*"[66]

The 2,400-page bill created a new regulatory system that was so complex that some members of Congress did not even bother reading the bill before passing it. Even the Chairman of the House Judiciary Committee, Democrat Representative John Conyers, refused to read the legislation, explaining, "What good is reading the bill if it's [two] thousand pages and you don't have two days and two lawyers to find out what it means after you read the bill?"[67]

Nevertheless, Democrats worked to build popular support for this massive regulatory scheme, using the same political tactics that Tocqueville predicted would prevail under an authoritarian democratic government: they played on the passions of the people. They argued that the federal government's new controlling and coercive powers were necessary to better serve the interests of the people—that government would shield the people from the evils of private industry. President Obama in 2009 said that the main purpose of the health care reform bill was to protect Americans from devious private insurance companies. He explained that "the idea behind reform [is that] we reform the insurance industries so they can't take advantage of you."[68] Nancy Pelosi, the Democratic Speaker of the House at the time, described insurance companies as "immoral" and "villains" for their alleged fleecing of the American people, and said, "They have had a good thing going for a long time at the expense of the American people and the health of our country."[69]

Democrats also tried to weaken and isolate popular opposition to the bill. Americans who demonstrated against health care reform were smeared as selfish, uncaring, irrational, and even racist.[70] House Democrat John Dingell actually compared opponents of the bill to "Ku Klux Klan folks and white supremacists and folks in white sheets and other things running around causing trouble."[71]

Beneath all the demagoguery, however, there was no constitutional basis for the bill. When Democrats in Congress were questioned about its constitutionality, their responses varied from ignorance to complete indifference, as if the Constitution was an afterthought—if it even entered their minds at all—when advocating the ACA. For example, Representative Phil Hare was asked to cite the section of the Constitution that allowed the individual mandate, and he replied, "I don't worry about the Constitution on this. . . . I care more about the people dying every day who don't have health care."[72] Senator Daniel Akaka conceded that the Constitution "in particular" did not cover the individual mandate, saying, "It's not covered in that respect."[73] Akaka nevertheless defended the ACA anyway, stammering, "But in ways to help citizens in our country to live a good life, let me say it that way, is what we're trying to do, and in this case, we're trying to help them with their health."[74] Senator Ben Nelson proclaimed ignorance of the Constitution when he was asked about the individual mandate's validity. He said, "Well, you know, I don't know that I'm a constitutional scholar. So, I, I'm not going to be able to answer that question."[75] Senator Kent Conrad also admitted that he was unqualified to assess the ACA's constitutionality. When asked if he knew from where in the Constitution the authority for the mandate came, he replied, "No, but I'll refer you to the legal counsel for the Senate, and they're the ones that lead there as the full legal basis for the individual mandate—and I assume it's in the Commerce Clause."[76]

When Representative Steny Hoyer, the House Majority Leader, was asked about the ACA's constitutionality, he at least could answer with conviction, although his response was ill-informed. Hoyer justified the bill under the Constitution's "general welfare" phrase in Article I, section 8 ("The Congress shall have power to lay and collect taxes, duties, and excises, to pay the debts and provide for the common defense and general welfare of the United States.").[77] He said, "Well, in promoting the general welfare, the Constitution obviously gives broad authority to Congress to effect that end. The end that we're trying to effect is to make health care affordable, so I think clearly this is within our constitutional responsibility."[78] In other words, Hoyer suggested that any act that is intended to help the American people is permitted by the Constitution. Or in Tocqueville's words, Hoyer "propose[d] the maxim that everything is permitted in the interest of society—a wicked maxim that seems to have been invented in an age of liberty to legitimize all the tyrants of the future."[79] Although Hoyer acknowledged that the Constitution did not grant Congress an unbounded power, he could not say where its power ended. Nor did he seem to care. When asked about the outer boundary of congressional power, Hoyer deferred to Court, saying, "I'm sure the Court will find a limit."[80]

Yet it did not. As mentioned before, when the Supreme Court ruled on the constitutionality of the ACA in *NFIB v. Sebelius*, it upheld the individual mandate as an acceptable use of Congress' taxing power, thereby sanctioning an unrestrained regulatory authority cloaked as a tax. Chief Justice Roberts actually justified this unlimited legislative power using the same flawed reasoning as Hoyer. He wrote in *NFIB* that Congress may lay and collect taxes to "'provide for the . . . general welfare of the United States.' Put simply, Congress may tax and spend. This grant gives the federal government considerable influence even in areas where it cannot directly regulate."[81]

Put simply, Congress has no such authority to tax and spend at will. The Constitution's reference to "general welfare" in Article I, section 8, was never meant to stand alone as a broad grant of federal power to do anything in the interest of society. James Madison insisted in The Federalist No. 41 that it was an "absurdity" to suggest that Congress' taxing and spending powers were unlimited by that phrase when the Constitution identified in the very same sentence—"not even separated by a longer pause than a semicolon"—the specific, narrow powers of the federal government.[82] He explained, "Nothing is more natural or common than first to use a general phrase, and then to explain or qualify it by a recital of particulars."[83] Congress' ability to tax and spend was to be confined by the enumerated powers that immediately followed that general phrase. Madison emphasized that the Constitution granted Congress no general power to tax and spend, saying, "I cannot undertake to lay my finger on that article of the Constitution which grants a right to Congress of expending, on objects of benevolence, the money of their constituents."[84] Madison later wrote, "If Congress can do whatever in their discretion can be done by money, and will promote the general welfare, the government is no longer a limited one, possessing enumerated powers, but an indefinite one, subject to particular exceptions."[85] Thomas Jefferson similarly argued:

> [Federal representatives] are not to do anything they please to provide for the general welfare . . . . [G]iving a distinct and independent power [to Congress] to do any act they please which may be good for the Union would render all the preceding and subsequent enumerations of power completely useless. It would reduce the whole instrument to a single phrase, that of instituting a Congress with power to do whatever would be for the good of the United States; and, as they would be the sole judges of the good or evil, it would be also a power to do whatever evil they please.[86]

The great fear of this kind of sweeping, arbitrary power was not that the federal government might begin to rule over the people wickedly and harshly, using brute force. No representative body elected by the people and acting so cruelly would remain in power for long. The Founding Fathers more intently feared that the people's natural power, once surrendered to the federal government, would be lost forever. They feared losing their liberty to an autocratic centralized power in the United States—an outcome that would completely undermine the purpose for which the Revolution was waged. Madison emphasized in 1788, quoting Thomas Jefferson, "'An *elective despotism* was not the government we fought for.'"[87]

What the Founding Fathers fought for was a self-government that would respect Natural Law. They declared their natural equality under God, but they never suggested that equality should be stretched to the extreme. James Wilson proclaimed that the "natural rights and duties of man belong equally to all," but he added that individuals differed greatly "with regard to virtue, talents, taste, and acquirements."[88] The people were equal in natural rights, but they were equal in no other respect—a point that Abraham Lincoln later emphasized in a speech on the Declaration of Independence. Lincoln said that the Founding Fathers surely "intended to include *all* men [in their proclamation of natural equality], but they did not mean to declare all men equal *in all respects*. They did not mean to say all men were equal in color, size, intellect, moral development, or social capacity."[89] Rather, "[t]hey defined with tolerable distinctness in what they did consider all men created equal—equal in certain inalienable rights, among which are life, liberty, and the pursuit of happiness."[90]

The Founding Fathers were careful to make this distinction because they understood that a depraved passion for equality could be so dangerous to liberty. History informed them that democracies were particularly vulnerable to the influence of passion and demagoguery in politics—that reason and order in a democracy were often overpowered by the fleeting demands of unruly factions. James Madison observed in The Federalist No. 55, "In all very numerous assemblies, of whatever character composed, passion never fails to wrest the scepter from reason. Had every Athenian citizen been a Socrates, every Athenian assembly would still have been a mob."[91] Madison explained in The Federalist No. 10:

> [S]uch democracies have ever been spectacles of turbulence and contention; have ever been found incompatible with personal security or the rights of property; and have in general been as short in their lives as they have been violent in their deaths. Theoretic politicians, who have patronized this species of

government, have erroneously supposed that by reducing mankind to a perfect equality in their political rights, they would, at the same time, be perfectly equalized and assimilated in their possessions, their opinions, and their passions.[92]

The Founding Fathers recognized that perfect equality is impossible to achieve in liberty, for any utopian system requires a domineering force to level all conditions—and the kind of equality then achieved is equality in misery and servitude to government.

Given the people's innate passion for equality, however, the Founders knew that liberty in America would continually be in peril if this passion were unrestrained in society. In an article titled, "The Dangers of American Liberty," Fisher Ames (a representative in the First United States Congress) described the menace that the Founding Fathers hoped to avoid in constructing a government that was based on the democratic models of the past. He wrote:

> The danger obviously was, that a species of government, in which the people choose all the rulers, and then, by themselves, or ambitious demagogues pretending to be the people, claim and exercise an effective control over what is called the government, would be found on trial no better than a turbulent, licentious democracy. The danger was, that their best interests would be neglected, their dearest rights violated, their sober reason silenced, and the worst passions of the worst men not only freed from legal restraint, but invested with public power. The known propensity of a democracy is to licentiousness which the ambitious call, and ignorant believe to be liberty.
>
> The true great object, then, of political wisdom in framing our Constitution, was to guard against licentiousness, that inbred malady of democracies, that deforms their infancy with grey hairs and decrepitude.[93]

To prevent these destructive passions from tainting politics in America, the Founding Fathers designed the national government to be republican in form—and they mandated in the Constitution a republican government for every state admitted to the Union.[94] They hoped, Ames wrote, "that a federal republic of states might subsist."[95] James Madison believed that a republic, compared to a pure democracy, could more effectively resist factions of citizens "who are united and actuated by some common impulse of passion, or of interest, adverse to the rights of other citizens, or to the permanent and aggregate interests of the community."[96] He reasoned that the smaller legislature in a republic might yield a more trusted and able representative body that is more dedicated to preserving the blessings of liberty.[97]

Notwithstanding this calculated republican design, the Founding Fathers still knew that the people's depraved passions could be exploited to undermine liberty in America. As James Madison said, "The essence of government is power; and power, lodged as it must be in human hands, will ever be liable to abuse."[98] He understood that a cunning politician's "base and selfish measures" could be easily "masked by pretexts of public good and apparent expediency."[99] Demagoguery could disguise a politician's corruption by "veiling his selfish views under the professions of public good and [by] varnishing his sophistical arguments with the glowing colors of popular eloquence."[100] Alexander Hamilton also warned the American people about politicians who might abuse the people's passions for political gain. He advised the people to beware of politicians who promise a more equitable and caring government if empowered to effect it, for such demagoguery might seduce the masses into submission to government and pave the way toward tyranny. He wrote in The Federalist No. 1:

> [A] dangerous ambition more often lurks behind the specious mask of zeal for the rights of the people, than under the forbidding appearance of zeal for the firmness and efficiency of government. History will teach us that the former has been found a much more certain road to the introduction of despotism than the latter, and that of those men who have overturned the liberties of republics, the greatest number have begun their career by paying an obsequious court to the people, commencing demagogues and ending tyrants.[101]

Joseph Story also wrote in *Commentaries on the Constitution*, "Republics are created by the virtue, public spirit, and intelligence of the citizens. They fall when the wise are banished from the public councils, because they dare to be honest; and [when] the profligate are rewarded, because they flatter the people in order to betray them."[102]

The corrupting influence of passion and demagoguery in politics had long been known as the Achilles' heel of democratic governments. Montesquieu wrote in 1748, "The principle of democracy is corrupted not only when the spirit of equality is extinct, but likewise when [the people] fall into a spirit of extreme equality."[103] He noted that Greek historian and political philosopher, Xenophon (430–354 B.C.), made one of the earliest accounts of this depraved passion for equality. Montesquieu chronicled:

> We find in Xenophon's *Banquet* a very lively description of a republic in which the people abused their equality. Each guest gives in his turn the reason why he is satisfied [by extreme equality]. "Content I am," says Chamides, "because of my poverty. When I was rich, I was obliged to pay my court to informers, knowing I was more liable to be hurt by them than capable of doing them harm. The republic constantly demanded some new tax of me, and I could not decline paying. Since I have grown poor, I have acquired authority; nobody threatens me; I rather threaten others. I can go or stay where I please. The rich already rise from their seats and give me the way. I am a king; I was before a slave. I paid taxes to the republic, now it maintains me. I am no longer afraid of losing, but I hope to acquire."[104]

Montesquieu then instructed, "The people fall into this misfortune when those [politicians] in whom they confide, desirous of concealing their own corruption, endeavor to corrupt them. To disguise their own ambition, they speak to them only of the grandeur of the state; to conceal their own avarice, they incessantly flatter theirs."[105] Politicians play on the passions of the people to grow their own authority at the expense of the nation.

As this corrupt passion spreads in society, politicians grow more wasteful and extravagant in order to satisfy the arbitrary wants of the people and to maintain their hold on power. Montesquieu predicted that this passion would corrupt government completely and ultimately ruin it. He wrote:

> The corruption will increase among the corruptors, and likewise among those who are already corrupted. The people will divide the public money among themselves, and, having added the administration of affairs to their indolence, will be for blending their poverty with the amusements of luxury. But with

their indolence and luxury, nothing but the public treasure will be able to satisfy their demands.

We must not be surprised to see their suffrages given for money. It is impossible to make great largesses to the people without great extortion: and to compass this, the state must be subverted. The greater the advantages they seem to derive from their liberty, the nearer they approach towards the critical moment of losing it.[106]

This kind of deceit and abuse, if unchecked would lead a republic to the same destructive end as any depraved democracy. Thomas Paine believed that any government "made up of a band of parasites living in luxurious indolence out of the public taxes" would surely deteriorate.[107] He wrote, "When once such a vicious system is established, it becomes the guard and protection of all inferior abuses."[108] A republic so tainted by licentiousness would continue in corruption toward its eventual ruin.

The Founding Fathers recognized that they could not prevent the new American republic from reaching this end. Although they made great efforts to guard against this outcome by limiting federal power in the Constitution, they knew that it was ultimately up to the people to preserve their liberty—the republic was theirs to keep. In a letter in 1802, Thomas Jefferson expressed his hope that the American people would always "prevent the government from wasting the labors of the people under the pretense of taking care of them."[109] He hoped that the people might reject politicians who seek to expand the power and extravagance of government in the name of the people and at the expense of their liberty. But by 1824, Jefferson regretfully assessed, "I think we have more machinery of government than is necessary—too many parasites living on the labor of the industrious."[110]

What the Founding Fathers considered excessive and wasteful then is undoubtedly trivial today. The federal government—once composed of the Departments of State, War, and the Treasury—now includes 439 departments and agencies that operate at great cost to the American taxpayer.[111] By its virtually unlimited (and unconstitutional) scope of power, the federal government today expends enormous sums of money on countless ineffective programs. To illustrate, Republican Senator Tom Coburn published a "Wastebook" in 2011 that detailed some of the federal government's exorbitant and unnecessary outlays made that year, including:

- $200 million to subsidize prosperous industry groups, cooperatives, and corporations;
- $168 million for a duplicative Housing and Urban Development neighborhood revitalization initiative;
- $30 million to spur sales and employment in Pakistan;
- $17.8 million in aid to China (America's largest debtor);
- $15 million for the infamous Alaskan "bridge to nowhere" that may never be constructed (bringing the total spent on this project to over $65 million);
- $12 million to help industries in Pakistan use less energy;
- $10 million to an arts organization in Pakistan to create "130 episodes of an indigenously produced *Sesame Street*;"
- $9.49 million to help foreign nations promote sustainable forest management;
- $5.18 million for a steamboat history museum in Louisiana;
- $2 million for a wine exhibition and culinary center in Washington state;
- $1.35 million for an entrepreneurship initiative in Barbados;
- $765,000 to study how college students use mobile devices for social networking;
- $606,000 to study how the internet impacts sexual behavior; and, most incredibly,
- $593,000 to study why chimpanzees throw feces.[112]

These wasteful expenses are just a small sample of the unnecessary federal spending that regularly occurs today, and they actually pale in comparison to the large amount of money spent on the federal government's social welfare programs, which consume almost two-thirds of the entire federal budget.[113] Under the pretense of taking care of the people, the government spends and spends money on programs that have no basis in the Constitution. And to make matters worse, the federal government spends and spends money that it does not have.

As the federal government's vast regulatory powers and wasteful spending drive the nation toward despotism and ruin, its ever rising national debt accelerates it toward that end. In fact, the national debt has grown so large in recent years that the Comptroller General of the United States (the nation's chief auditor) warned in 2010 that "the federal government is on an unsustainable long-term fiscal path."[114] This path is easy to track. When George W. Bush was inaugurated as president in January 2001, the national debt totaled $5.7 trillion.[115] Eight years later, the debt climbed to $10.6 trillion.[116] And after just three and a half years under President Barack Obama—who as a candidate promised "net spending cuts" to reign in government deficits—the national debt rose to $15.9 trillion in July 2012.[117]

The sheer magnitude of the national debt today is distressing alone, but its true danger to the nation's economic health becomes apparent when compared to the nation's gross domestic product (GDP). GDP is the market value of all the goods and services produced by a nation in a given period of time, and it is often used as a general indicator of national wealth. By measuring national debt against GDP, the government's financial leverage is determined and can be reliably compared against historical data. Low debt-to-GDP ratios generally indicate that government has the financial capacity to pay off its debt. High debt-to-GDP ratios signal a nation's risk of insolvency, especially when sustained over time. Given the nation's very high debt-to-GDP ratios off late—94 percent in 2010 and over 100 percent in 2011 and 2012—there is valid cause for alarm over the government's financial health.[118]

Throughout much of American history, such soaring debt-to-GDP ratios were rare, as shown in the following chart. In fact, for the first 144 years under the Constitution—until Franklin Roosevelt became president in 1933—no ratio exceeded the 1791 high of 37 percent, which resulted from Congress' assumption of all state debts incurred during the Revolutionary War.[119] The federal government during this long period often avoided large deficit spending unless it was necessary to fund the nation's wars. Moreover, there existed little tolerance for a perpetual national debt, particularly during the founding era.

The Founding Fathers considered lasting public debt to be a dire threat to liberty. Benjamin Franklin generally observed that "when you run in debt, you give to another power over your liberty."[120] Given the adverse impact that debt can have on freedom, Thomas Jefferson advised, "To preserve our independence, we must not let our rulers load us with perpetual debt. We must make our election between economy and liberty, or profusion and servitude."[121] Jefferson regarded fiscal restraint to be "among the first and most important of republican virtues, and public debt as the greatest of the dangers to be feared."[122]

The Founding Fathers believed that sustained public debts were not only dangerous to liberty, but also unjust because they restricted the freedom of future generations. They forced upon posterity the obligation to repay. Naturally, the Founding Fathers staunchly advocated the reduction and elimination of all public debts so that liberty would long endure in America. Thomas Paine suggested that anyone who "run[s] the next generation into debt . . . use[s] them meanly and pitifully."[123] George Washington advised, "No pecuniary consideration is more urgent than the regular redemption and discharge of the public debt."[124] In his Farewell Address, he instructed the nation "to discharge the debts which unavoidable wars may have occasioned, [and to avoid] ungenerously throwing upon posterity the burthen which we ourselves ought to bear."[125]

Thomas Jefferson similarly pledged, "[W]e shall all consider ourselves unauthorized to saddle posterity with our debts, and morally bound to pay them ourselves; and consequently within what may be deemed the period of a generation, or the life [expectancy] of the majority."[126] He later added, "The principle of spending money to be paid by posterity, under the name of funding, is but swindling futurity on a large scale."[127] And James Madison regarded the federal government's large debts as "evils which ought to be removed as fast as honor and justice will permit."[128] He also believed that the government should not spend "without knowing whether the ways and means can be provided." Incurring debt without a plan to pay it off, he warned, "would be rash and unjustifiable"—"it would be hazarding the public faith in a manner contrary to every idea of prudence."[129]

Given their great disfavor of an enduring national debt, the Founding Fathers committed themselves to paying it down. As a consequence of their fiscal discipline, the nation's debt-to-GDP ratio steadily declined over time from its initial high of 37 percent and fell below 10 percent by 1809. Increased spending associated with the War of 1812 drove the ratio back up to 16 percent, but the government soon after curtailed its spending and placed the debt-to-GDP ratio on a downward trend once again. The national debt was at last paid off, albeit momentarily, in 1835.[130]

Although the debt has never since reached zero, succeeding generations exercised fiscal restraint for some time and carried large deficits only in times of war. Remarkably, the debt-to-GDP ratio remained below 3 percent from 1832 until the Civil War began in 1861. Spending to fund the war and the nation's reconstruction forced the debt-to-GDP ratio up to 33 percent in 1869, but it gradually fell thereafter as the economy grew and the debt was again paid down. From 1890 to 1917, the ratio stayed near or below 10 percent. Deficit spending during World War I again drove the debt-to-GDP ratio higher—it reached 35 percent in 1919. But in each year of the following decade, the government reduced the national debt so that the nation's debt-to-GDP ratio fell back to 16 percent by 1929.[131]

The onset of the Great Depression, not surprisingly, had an adverse impact on the nation's debt-to-GDP ratio. Tax receipts dwindled, forcing the federal government to take on more debt. And economic production fell sharply—by 1932, the nation's GDP had declined by 43 percent from its high in 1929. Consequently, the nation's debt-to GDP ratio jumped to 33 percent just before Franklin Roosevelt took over as president.[132]

Notably, throughout Roosevelt's election campaign, he had promised to control federal spending and balance the budget once in office. In fact, he blamed Republican President Herbert Hoover for recklessly spending the people's money, saying in 1932, "I accuse the present Administration of being the greatest spending Administration in peace times in all our history."[133] Roosevelt declared, "I regard reduction in federal spending as one of the most important issues of this campaign."[134]

Yet throughout his long presidency, not once did Roosevelt balance the federal budget. In fact, in just four years, Roosevelt's spending more than doubled that of the Hoover Administration, increasing federal outlays from $4.27 billion to $9.17 billion. And in just eight years, Roosevelt added more to the national debt than all the previous presidents combined, raising the debt from $19 billion in 1932 to $43 billion in 1940. The nation's debt-to-GDP ratio during this eight-year period of peace increased to record levels between 39 percent and 44 percent.[135]

After the United States entered World War II in 1941, the nation's debt-to-GDP ratio soared even higher. Sharp increases in military spending created large deficits that greatly expanded the national debt. Military spending during the war peaked at $94 billion—up from prewar averages of $2 billion each year—and accounted for 88 percent of all federal spending. These outlays no doubt were required to win the war, but they drove the nation's debt-to-GDP ratio up to 116 percent by 1945 and 121 percent the following year.[136]

After the war ended, necessary cuts in military spending brought the federal budget back into balance. Unlike the efforts during the founding era, however, no plan was instituted to pay off the national debt, which had grown to $259 billion in 1945. The debt was reduced slightly to $252 billion in 1948, but it has never since been lower. In fact, from that time to the present day, the total national debt has been reduced only three times (in 1951, 1956, and 1957), and each of those reductions was miniscule—the debt decreased by a mere fraction of one percent. In every other year since then, the national debt has grown larger and more burdensome to manage.[137]

Notwithstanding the nation's mounting debt since World War II, its debt-to-GDP ratio actually fell for some time due to steady economic expansion (the nation's GDP grew at a faster rate than the national debt). From its high of 121 percent in 1946, the debt-to-GDP ratio dropped to 88 percent in 1950, 70 percent in 1953, 50 percent in 1963, 40 percent in 1966, and 32 percent in 1974.[138]

But the growth of government debt soon outpaced economic expansion once again, and the nation's debt-to-GDP ratio climbed higher as a consequence. It reached 40 percent in 1984, 50 percent in 1987, 60 percent in 1991, and 67 percent in 1995. After a slight decline to 56 percent by 2001, the debt-to-GDP ratio again grew to 60 percent in 2003, 69 percent in 2008, 83 percent in 2009, 94 percent in 2010, 100 percent in 2011, and, most recently, 101 percent in 2012.[139]

It is worth emphasizing that these exceptionally high debt-to-GDP ratios of late were not created by a faltering economy. Since 1950, the United States economy has grown every single year except in 2009 when it contracted by only two percent. And that economic downturn was nothing like the economic collapse that occurred between 1929 and 1932 when the economy contracted by 43 percent, forcing the nation's debt-to-GDP ratio to double during that time. The American economy has been solid over the last half century, and so the nation's deteriorating economic health can only be attributed to undisciplined deficit spending.[140]

Furthermore, the nation's regular deficit spending in the modern era cannot be attributed to national security concerns. Unlike the level of military spending in World War II that eclipsed all other spending at 88 percent of the federal budget, defense spending since 1974 has averaged only 26 percent of the entire budget, as shown in the following chart. Even when the United States was fighting in two wars in Afghanistan and Iraq in the mid-2000s, three-quarters of the federal budget was still dedicated to non-defense spending. Therefore, defense spending is not main driver of the nation's soaring national debt. Rather, it is reckless non-defense spending, mainly due to costly social welfare programs that were first instituted by President Franklin Roosevelt.[141]

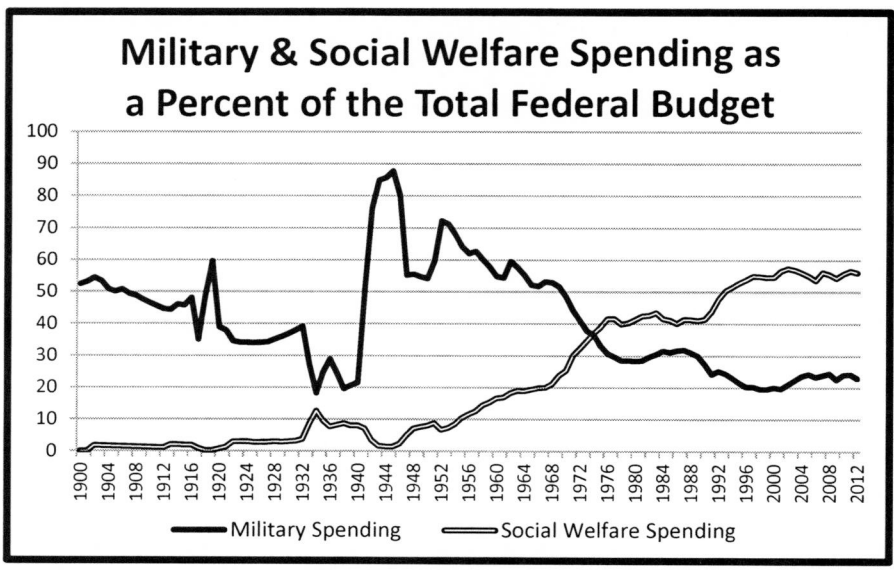

It is no coincidence that social welfare spending grew after Franklin Roosevelt transformed the federal government into a progressive national state. Prior to the twentieth century, not a single dime of federal revenues was spent on social welfare programs. Even after progressivism had taken hold in the early 1900s and the federal government began spending on social welfare programs, such spending could not reach the levels desired by progressives as long as the Supreme Court continued to enforce the Constitution's limitations on federal power. But after Roosevelt was elected president, he implemented his unconstitutional New Deal economic plan without delay in 1933. Unfazed by the Court's prior rulings, he quickly transformed the federal government into an expansive administrative state. And as mentioned before, the Court eventually reversed its decisions on the limits of federal power under pressure from Roosevelt and effectively sanctioned the inauguration of a new paternalistic government for the nation—a government that would become ever more expensive to operate over time.

Roosevelt's increases in social welfare spending were significant. He nearly tripled social welfare spending in one year and more than quadrupled it in two years. Roosevelt continued to increase social welfare spending throughout his presidency, even as deficits soared during the war.

And by 1945, social welfare spending was ten times as high as it was before Roosevelt took office.[142]

Since Roosevelt's presidency, social welfare spending has grown even more. The social welfare programs that Roosevelt instituted were later expanded to cover a wider base of individuals. New welfare programs were also enacted, such as Medicare and Medicaid in 1965, which further stretched the federal budget. Total social welfare spending reached 30 percent of all federal spending by 1971. It grew to 40 percent in 1976, 50 percent in 1993, and 57 percent in 2011—more than doubling the amount spent on national defense.[143]

Social welfare spending is projected to rise even higher in the future, further aggravating the nation's financial problems. If nothing is done to fundamentally change this trend, then the federal government will be so overwhelmed by debt that its solvency will not last. The Comptroller General warned in 2010:

> [T]he present value of projected scheduled [welfare] benefits exceeds earmarked revenues for social insurance programs (e.g., Social Security and Medicare) by about $46 trillion over the next 75-year period. . . . Absent a change in policy, under this scenario, the interest costs on the growing debt together with spending on major entitlement programs could absorb 92 cents of every dollar of federal revenue in 2019. Clearly, this is not sustainable.[144]

The federal government's fiscal problems are becoming so great that they could severely destabilize the nation. Even the military has taken notice of this threat. The Chairman of the Joint Chiefs of Staff—the top military officer at the Pentagon—declared in September 2011 that "the single, biggest threat to our national security is our debt."[145]

These dire warnings have gone unheeded by many politicians, however—especially by those in the Democratic Party. For example, in the face of financial ruin, President Obama proposed a budget for 2012 that would have added a projected record $1.65 trillion to the national debt for that fiscal year. (Remarkably, Obama referred to his budget as a "down payment" on fiscal responsibility.[146] Usually, down payments involve a reduction of total debt, not a record increase of it.) Under Obama's 2012 budget, which was rejected by Congress, the nation's most expensive

social welfare programs—Social Security, Medicare, and Medicaid—
would have grown by 79 percent through 2021, and the total national debt
would have risen to $26.3 trillion by 2021.[147] The interest on the debt
alone by then would have approached $1 trillion each year—an amount
that Obama's own Treasury Secretary, Timothy Geithner, conceded was
"unsustainable."[148] Little changed in Obama's 2013 budget, and Geithner
again confessed before Congress that the proposed levels of social welfare
spending were unsustainable. He said, "Even if Congress were to enact
this budget, we would be left with—in the outer decades as millions of
Americans retire—what are still unsustainable commitments in Medicare
and Medicaid."[149] Despite acknowledging that the proposed budgets would
lead the nation toward financial disaster, the Obama Administration
continued to press Congress to pass them anyway.

Unfortunately, this total disregard for the future is completely
common among depraved factions in a democracy. When passion
overcomes reason in political discourse, lasting responsibilities always
give way to momentary comforts—prudence gives way to licentiousness.
Tocqueville wrote, "[U]nder the tumultuous conditions of democracy, . . .
the present looms large; it hides the future, which fades from view, and
men no longer wish to think beyond tomorrow."[150] And when the people
are no longer restrained by a common morality, Tocqueville added, "they
lapse easily into that state of complete and brutish indifference to the
future that is only too consistent with certain instincts of the human
species."[151] Such is the way for any democratic movement that derives its
power from the corrupt passions of the people.

Such is the way for progressivism. For over a century, progressives in
America have used demagoguery to steadily consolidate power in the
federal government, promising a more utopian society if empowered to
effect it. They have inflamed passions for equality, arguing that
government ought to level all conditions to best provide for the people.
They have fundamentally transformed the federal government, much to the
detriment of future generations. The federal government—originally
designed to preserve American liberty for all time—now aims to satisfy
the fleeting wants of the people today, no matter what the cost may be
tomorrow.

It should come as no surprise, then, that progressives in government continue to ignore the catastrophic consequences of their political actions. Progressive policies are not based in reason or practicality. Progressivism is, and always has been, a populist movement that derives its power from the passions of the people. It is based on the fanciful idea that government can be all things to all people—that government can meet the needs of every person, everywhere. It is a movement that deceives the people into submission to government with promise after promise of benevolence and generosity. Progressivism is fundamentally corrupt. It is a bankrupt ideology that will ultimately bankrupt government itself.

Progressivism continues to nudge the United States down a predictable and perilous path toward potential ruin—a course that the Founding Fathers tried in earnest to avoid. At the Constitutional Convention in 1787, the Founding Fathers set out to create a government for America that would long endure in liberty. To that end, they limited federal power in the Constitution to inhibit the rise of a corrupt, centralized government. They created in the Constitution a federal republic that offered the best hope to preserve liberty for generations to come. But they also knew that the ultimate responsibility to safeguard freedom in America rested with the people themselves. The republic they established would endure in liberty so long as the people preserved its limited constitutional design—a condition that Benjamin Franklin made clear at the close of the Constitutional Convention, for he warned the American people that the republic would last only "if you can keep it."[152]

By any measure, the republic has not been well maintained. The federal government's scope of authority has since grown beyond all limits in the Constitution. Countless federal taxes and restrictive regulations suppress economic activity. Wasteful federal spending incessantly persists. The national debt rises ever higher without any plan to pay it down. Special interest groups hold undue influence over government, and corruption pervades throughout. Politics is dominated by demagoguery, for empty political promises continue unabated. And many Americans readily submit to federal control, seduced by the idea that a benevolent government will manage their cares, fulfill their wants, and bring about total equality in society.

America today is much unlike the republic that the Founding Fathers created. In many ways, it resembles the depraved, dependent state envisioned by Tocqueville in his forecast of democratic despotism. It increasingly resembles past failed democracies that James Madison labeled "spectacles of turbulence and contention . . . [that] have in general been as short in their lives as they have been violent in their deaths."[153]

Undeniably, the American republic has departed the path of lasting liberty that was set by the Founding Fathers. And until its course is finally reversed, the nation's trend toward tyranny will continue. Freedom will be fleeting and potentially lost for all time. As John Adams wrote at the dawn of the Revolutionary War, "[A] constitution of government, once changed from freedom, can never be restored. Liberty, once lost, is lost forever."[154] Time is running out on American liberty, and there are no second chances once tyranny takes hold.

7

ON REVOLUTION

It is necessary for every *American*, with becoming energy to endeavor to stop the dissemination of principles evidently destructive of the cause for which they have bled. It must be the combined virtue of the rulers and of the people to do this, and to rescue and save their civil and religious rights from the outstretched arm of tyranny, which may appear under any mode or form of government.

—*Mercy Otis Warren, 1805*[1]

When the people have no other recourse against a tyrannical government—one that betrays its true purpose to secure life, liberty, and property—revolution is justified under Natural Law. The people may form, by popular consent, a new government that respects the natural boundaries of its power. John Locke explained:

[W]henever the legislators endeavor to take away and destroy the property of the people, or to reduce them to slavery under arbitrary power, they put themselves into a State of War with the people, who are thereupon absolved from any further obedience, and are left to the common refuge, which God hath provided for all men against force and violence. Whenever, therefore, the legislative shall transgress this fundamental rule of society and, either by ambition, fear, folly or corruption, endeavor to grasp themselves, or put into the hands of any other, absolute power over the lives, liberties, and estates of the people; by this breach of trust they forfeit the power the people had put into their hands for quite contrary ends, and it devolves to the people, who have a right to resume their original liberty and, by the establishment of a new legislative (such as they shall think fit), provide for their own safety and security, which is the end for which they are in society.[2]

Locke emphasized that individuals enter into society and institute government to preserve their natural rights. Whenever this end is "manifestly neglected, or opposed" by government, he wrote, then "the trust must necessarily be forfeited, and the power devolve into the hands of those that gave it, who may place it anew where they shall think best for their safety and security."[3] The people may "remove or alter" government when it violates Natural Law.[4]

The Founding Fathers justified the American Revolution by making the same appeal to higher authority. They inscribed in two revolutionary documents the basic precepts of Natural Law and the grounds upon which the people could assert their inherent power over government. The Virginia Declaration of Rights of 1776 stated:

That all men are by nature equally free and independent and have certain inherent rights, of which, when they enter into a state of society, they cannot, by any compact, deprive or divest their posterity; namely, the enjoyment of life and liberty, with the means of acquiring and possessing property, and pursuing and obtaining happiness and safety. . . . That government is, or ought to be, instituted for the common benefit, protection, and security of the people, nation, or community; of all the various modes and forms of government, that is best which is capable of producing the greatest degree of happiness and safety and is most effectually secured against the danger of maladministration; and that, when any government shall be found inadequate or contrary to these purposes, a majority of the community hath an indubitable, inalienable, and indefeasible right to reform, alter, or abolish it, in such manner as shall be judged most conducive to the public weal.[5]

The Founding Fathers soon after pronounced the following truths to be "self-evident" in the Declaration of Independence:

[T]hat all men are created equal, that they are endowed by their Creator with certain unalienable rights, that among these are life, liberty, and the pursuit of happiness. That to secure these rights, governments are instituted among men, deriving their just powers from the consent of the governed, That whenever any form of government becomes destructive to these ends, it is the right of the people to alter or to abolish it, and to institute new government, laying its foundation on such principles and organizing its powers in such form, as to them shall seem most likely to effect their safety and happiness.[6]

By these declarations, the Founding Fathers unequivocally asserted the people's natural claim to liberty. And they proclaimed their inalienable right to resist government that defies Natural Law.

Given the long list of abuses by the British monarch that were detailed in the Declaration of Independence, the American people had every right to revolt under Natural Law. But not every American believed that revolution was prudent at the time. Some were content with their restricted freedoms, and others profited by their loyalty to the British government. Many Americans, therefore, were willing to tolerate arbitrary injustices in tyranny to avoid certain peril in war.

The Founding Fathers recognized, however, that corruption and injustice would only grow in time under the absolute power of a distant, centralized government. They knew that the American people would have to resist tyranny by force at some time in the future if they did not fight for independence in their day. Thomas Paine wrote, "[U]ntil an independence is declared, the Continent will feel itself like a man who continues putting off some unpleasant business from day to day, yet knows it must be done, hates to set about it, wishes it over, and is continually haunted with the thoughts of its necessity."[7]

The Founding Fathers were unwilling to postpone an inevitable war for independence simply to avoid the burden associated with it, and they pilloried those who refused to join the cause for liberty. In 1775, Benjamin Franklin condemned those who surrendered to tyranny in the name of peace. He wrote, "They that can give up essential liberty to purchase a little temporary safety, deserve neither liberty nor safety."[8] Later that year, Patrick Henry famously declared, "Is life so dear or peace so sweet as to be purchased at the price of chains and slavery? Forbid it, Almighty God. I know not what course others may take, but as for me, give me liberty or give me death!"[9] Samuel Adams said in 1776, "Shame on the men who can court exemption from present trouble and expense at the price of their own posterity's liberty!"[10] And Thomas Paine most harshly criticized these loyalists, or Tories. In late 1776, he wrote, "Every Tory is a coward, for a servile, slavish, self-interested fear is the foundation of Toryism; and a man under such influence, though he may be cruel, never can be brave."[11] Paine called on the American people to fight for independence to spare future generations from unavoidable war. He wrote:

> I once felt all that kind of anger, which a man ought to feel, against the mean principles that are held by the Tories: A noted one, who kept a tavern at Amboy, was standing at his door, with as pretty a child in his hand, about eight or nine years old, as most I ever saw, and after speaking his mind as freely as he thought was prudent, finished with this unfatherly expression, *"Well! give me peace in my day."* Not a man lives on the continent but fully believes that a separation must some time or other finally take place, and a generous parent should have said, *"If there must be trouble, let it be in my day that my child may have peace;"* and this single reflection, well applied, is sufficient to awaken every man to duty. Not a place upon earth might be so happy as America. Her situation is remote from all the wrangling world, and she has nothing to do but to trade with them. A man may easily distinguish in himself between temper and principle, and I am as confident, as I am that GOD governs the world, that America will never be happy till she gets clear of foreign dominion. Wars, without ceasing, will break out till that period arrives, and the continent must in the end be conqueror; for though the flame of liberty may sometimes cease to shine, the coal never can expire.[12]

The Founding Fathers' impatience for independence was well justified. When revolution is necessary for liberty to prevail—when war for independence is inevitable—any delay is counterproductive to that end. The longer that tyranny is tolerated, the greater is the precedential force against which succeeding generations must fight in the future. Tyranny must be opposed at all times, therefore, not only when it matures, but also as it develops. Thomas Jefferson advised, "The time to guard against corruption and tyranny is before they shall have gotten hold of us. It is better to keep the wolf out of the fold, than to trust to drawing his teeth and talons after he shall have entered."[13]

The importance of early resistance to tyranny was previously stressed by John Locke, who wrote:

> [T]he state of mankind is not so miserable that they are not capable of using this remedy [of dissolving government] till it be too late to look for any. To tell people they may provide for themselves, by erecting a new legislative, when by oppression, artifice, or being delivered over to a foreign power, their old one is gone, is only to tell them they may expect relief when it is too late and the evil is past cure. This is in effect no more than to bid them first to be slaves and then to take care of their liberty; and when their chains are on, tell them they may act like freemen. This, if barely so, is rather mockery than relief; and men can never be secure from tyranny if there be no means to escape it till they are perfectly under it: And therefore it is, that they have not only a right to get out of it but to prevent it.[14]

Despite this inherent right to resist oppressive government, Locke recognized that there would always be those (like the Tories during the American Revolution) who would accept and excuse tyranny in the name of peace. Even "when illegal attempts are made upon their liberties or properties," he wrote, these people would still acquiesce to authority. They would give way to government, believing that any resistance might lay a "foundation for rebellion," sanction disobedience, "occasion civil wars," and become "so destructive to the peace of the world."[15] Locke considered such reasoning absurd, for he countered:

> They may as well say upon the same ground, that honest men may not oppose robbers or pirates, because this may occasion disorder or bloodshed. If any mischief comes in such cases, it is not to be charged upon him who defends his own right, but on him that *invades* his neighbors. If the innocent honest man must quietly quit all he has for peace sake to him who will lay violent hands upon it, I desire it may be considered, what a kind of peace there will be in the world, which consists only in violence and rapine; and which is to be maintained only for the benefit of robbers and oppressors. Who would not think it an admirable peace between the mighty and the mean, when the lamb, without resistance, yielded his throat to be torn by the imperious wolf?[16]

Peace in the presence of tyranny is nothing more than subservience to an unnatural, arbitrary power. It is a state in which the people readily forfeit their claim to liberty and consign themselves to servitude.

The Founding Fathers understood that liberty, not peace alone, was the true object worth pursuing. After the British government had trampled on the people's natural rights and ignored their many pleas for justice, the Founding Fathers called for independence, not obedience. They urged the people to refuse the allure of tranquility in tyranny and instead fight for their right to be free.

The American people proclaimed independence from Great Britain under the authority of Natural Law, and these revolutionary ideals ultimately formed the basis of all government in America. The same principles set forth in the Declaration of Rights and the Declaration of Independence were even written into the text of many state constitutions. For example, the Pennsylvania Constitution of 1776, which Benjamin Franklin assisted in drafting, stated:

> That all men are born equally free and independent, and have certain natural, inherent and inalienable rights, amongst which are, the enjoying and defending life and liberty, acquiring, possessing and protecting property, and pursuing and obtaining happiness and safety. . . . That government is, or ought to be, instituted for the common benefit, protection and security of the people, nation or community; and not for the particular emolument or advantage of any single man, family, or soft of men, who are a part only of that community, And that the community hath an indubitable, unalienable and indefeasible right to reform, alter, or abolish government in such manner as shall be by that community judged most conducive to the public weal.[17]

The Constitution of New York of 1777 included a complete copy of the Declaration of Independence in its preamble as a "cogent and conclusive" basis upon which to justify independence from the "tyrannical and oppressive" King and Parliament of Great Britain.[18] John Adams, Samuel Adams, and James Bowdoin later wrote in the Massachusetts Constitution (which was ratified in 1780 and is the oldest surviving written constitution in the world) the following declaration of the people's natural power over government:[19]

> All men are born free and equal, and have certain natural, essential, and unalienable rights; among which may be reckoned the right of enjoying and defending their lives and liberties; that of acquiring, possessing, and protecting property; in fine, that of seeking and obtaining their safety and happiness. . . . Government is instituted for the common good; for the protection, safety, prosperity and happiness of the people; and not for the profit, honor, or private interest of any one man, family, or class of men: Therefore the people alone have an incontestable, unalienable, and indefeasible right to institute government; and to reform, alter, or totally change the same, when their protection, safety, prosperity, and happiness require it.[20]

These revolutionary principles continued to guide the Founding Fathers even after independence was finally achieved in 1783. Mindful that government must always work to secure the people's natural rights into the future, they soon recognized that the existing national government—formed amid war under the Articles of Confederation—was inadequate and potentially destructive to that end. In 1787, when they were called upon by the Congress of the Confederation to devise ways to improve upon the Articles, they did not propose amendments to the Congress, as they were instructed to do. They instead designed and presented to the American people an entirely new constitution. Because the new constitution called for ratification by only 9 of the 13 states, it was technically illegal under the Articles of Confederation, which required unanimous consent to ratify any amendment. But the Founding Fathers once again appealed to the higher authority of Natural Law to justify their action. They called on the American people to exercise their natural power over government by replacing their unrepresentative and ineffective Congress with a new national body that would better preserve their natural rights. The people of course accepted this new social contract and officially ratified the Constitution of the United States in 1788.

Unlike the Articles of Confederation, which was essentially a treaty of independent states—or a "league of friendship," as it was described in the Articles—the Constitution formed a more representative national government in America.[21] It gave the people political control over the new federal government to ensure that the laws respected their will. It also provided a means for amendment so that the people could reform government whenever they deemed necessary.

When the people in any society wield such control over government, liberty is theirs to preserve. If government grows corrupt and infringes upon their natural rights, the people have no one but themselves to blame, for they decide who acts as their temporary stewards of government. They control their constitution and the laws. They hold the power to restore their rights.

In any representative government established by consent and truly powered by the people, violent revolution is no longer justified under Natural Law. Rather, it is illegal. John Locke wrote:

> [W]hoever . . . lays the foundation for *overturning* the constitution and frame of *any just government*, is guilty of the greatest crime, I think, a man is capable of, being answer for all those mischiefs of blood, rapine, and desolation, which the breaking to pieces of governments bring on a country. And he who does it, is justly to be esteemed the common enemy and pest of mankind; and is to be treated accordingly.[22]

Revolting against a representative republic does nothing to further the cause of liberty, for the people already have within their power the means to peaceably change their government according to their will.

The U.S. Constitution, ordained and established by "We the People of the United States," created a just government for the American people and foreclosed all violent means to reform it.[23] Alexander Hamilton explained in 1788:

> If the federal government should overpass the just bounds of its authority and make a tyrannical use of its powers, the people, whose creature it is, must appeal to the standard they have formed, and take such measures to redress the injury done to the Constitution as the exigency may suggest and prudence justify.[24]

The Founding Fathers expected the people to correct any injustice or breach of the Constitution through political action, not through force or civil disobedience. Thomas Jefferson believed that political education "is the true corrective of abuses of constitutional power."[25] Thomas Paine likewise advised in 1792:

> It is better to obey a bad law, making use at the same time of every argument to show its errors and procure its repeal, than forcibly to violate it; because the precedent of breaking a bad law might weaken the force, and lead to a discretionary violation of those which are good.[26]

Paine regarded political action as the only legitimate way to reform law in a representative republic. He also considered it to be the most honorable course to take. Paine wrote, "It may be considered as an honor to the animal faculties of man to obtain redress by courage and danger, but it is far greater honor to the rational faculties to accomplish the same object by reason, accommodation, and general consent."[27]

Ever since the Constitution was ratified, the American people have followed this course. In a number of constitutional controversies throughout history, the people mobilized politically to resist government abuses of power. Whether seeking to repeal unconstitutional laws passed by Congress or to reject unconstitutional rulings handed down by the Court, the people used the political process to assert their authority over government. In this way, the people brought revolution to government, but it was revolution in principle, not practice, advanced by reason, not force.

The Revolution of 1800 was the first popular uprising against those in government who neglected the Constitution. After Federalists had passed the Sedition Act in 1798 to restrict free speech, Thomas Jefferson and James Madison led the newly-formed Republican Party to restore the Constitution's limits on federal power. Their political victory in the 1800 elections was so sweeping that Jefferson later compared it to the revolution that had occurred a quarter century before. He wrote, "The Revolution of 1800 was as real a revolution in the principles of our government as that of 1776 was in its form; not effected, indeed, by the sword, as that, but by the rational and peaceable instrument of reform, the suffrage of the people."[28]

Years later, Andrew Jackson called on the American people to renew the same foundational ideals to enforce the Constitution's limits on federal power. He said, "That this was intended to be a government of limited and specific, and not general, powers must be admitted by all, and it is our duty to preserve for it the character intended by its framers."[29] Jackson also sought to enforce the Constitution's limits as understood by the people, not the Supreme Court. When the controversy over the national bank resurfaced in his first term, he stood against the Court's ruling, which had sanctioned the constitutionality of that institution. In his reelection campaign, Jackson invoked the "Spirit of 1798" to inspire confidence in the people's power over constitutional meaning, just as Madison and Jefferson had done in their time.[30] By his reelection, that revolutionary spirit prevailed once more.

And in the divisive controversy over the expansion of slavery, the people reclaimed their command over the Constitution yet again to live out the nation's revolutionary ideals. When the Supreme Court declared that black Americans had no rights under the Constitution, Abraham Lincoln and the newly-reformed Republican Party boldly rejected that decision in defense of natural equality. Their task, Lincoln wrote, was to "save the principles of Jefferson from total overthrow in this nation."[31] They had to restore the founding truths that Jefferson inscribed in the Declaration of Independence by asserting their control over the Constitution. Lincoln reminded the people in that day that Presidents Jackson and Jefferson "did not believe in the binding force of [judicial] decisions."[32] Like them, Lincoln understood that the people had the final say over constitutional meaning—popular sovereignty was never meant to be subordinate to the whims of government or the dictates of the Court. He declared, "The people of these United States are the rightful masters of both congresses and the courts, not to overthrow the Constitution, but to overthrow the men who pervert the Constitution."[33] The American people elected Lincoln as president to overturn the Supreme Court's twisted reading of the Constitution. They restored their primacy over government, and they preserved the founding principles that made liberty possible for all.

Similar political action is needed again today, for these principles have been lost in time. Few in government respect, or even know, the limits of their power. Politicians pass arbitrary laws and regulations to control businesses and individuals alike. They expand costly social welfare programs in the name of fairness and equality. And when their authority under the Constitution is questioned, they almost reflexively defer to the Court, ready to submit to its opinion even if it conflicts with their own.

More than ever, there needs to be a revolution in American government—a revolution by political action to restore the principles upon which the United States was founded. Montesquieu long ago advised, "When once a republic is corrupted, there is no possibility of remedying any of the growing evils, but by removing the corruption and restoring its lost principles; every other correction is either useless or a new evil."[34] This is the only way for the American people to arrest the rise of centralized power and recover their liberty at last.

After a century of diminishing freedoms and rising debt under progressive policies, there is no question that revolutionary action must be taken. And given the success of past "revolutions" in America, there is no doubt that the people can achieve a similar result today. The only uncertainty that remains is whether the people have the determination to act on their founding ideals—whether they will revolt against a growing authoritarian power and win their independence again.

Ultimately, it is up to the American people to decide their destiny, and it has always been this way ever since the founding generation freed themselves from British rule. At the close of the Revolutionary War in 1783, George Washington wrote of this unique opportunity. In a letter to the governors of the newly-independent states, Washington marveled at the many blessings that befell the American people, and he expressed great hope for their prospects in freedom. Although liberty was not forever guaranteed, Washington pointed out that the people controlled their fate—liberty was theirs to maintain. He wrote:

> The citizens of America, placed in the most enviable condition, as the sole lords and proprietors of a vast tract of continent, comprehending all the various soils and climates of the world, and abounding with all the necessaries and conveniences of life, are now, by the late satisfactory pacification, acknowledged to be possessed of absolute freedom and independence. They are from this period to be considered as the actors on a most conspicuous theatre, which seems to be peculiarly designated by Providence for the display of human greatness and felicity. Here they are not only surrounded with everything which can contribute to the completion of private and

domestic enjoyment; but heaven has crowned all its other blessings by giving a fairer opportunity for political happiness than any other nation has ever been favored with. Nothing can illustrate these observations more forcibly, than a recollection of the happy conjuncture of times and circumstances under which our republic assumed its rank among the nations. The foundation of our empire was not laid in the gloomy age of ignorance and superstition, but at an epocha when the rights of mankind were better understood and more clearly defined than at any former period. The researches of the human mind after social happiness have been carried to a great extent; the treasures of knowledge, acquired by the labors of philosophers, sages, and legislators through a long succession of years, are laid open for our use; and their collected wisdom may be happily employed in the establishment of our forms of government. The free cultivation of letters; the unbounded extension of commerce; the progressive refinement of manners; the growing liberality of sentiment; and above all, the pure and benign light of revelation; have had a meliorating influence on mankind, and increased the blessings of society. At this auspicious period, the United States came into existence as a nation; and, if their citizens should not be completely free and happy, the fault will be entirely their own.[35]

EPILOGUE

Our political foundation was based on certain moral truths—that life, liberty, and property are inalienable rights endowed to us by God. It was based on the idea that government is instituted by our consent to preserve these natural rights. It was based on the theory that we, the people, can govern ourselves within the boundaries of Natural Law.

These common ideals were written into the Declaration of Independence, not only to justify political separation from Great Britain, but also to state unequivocally the common principles that prevailed in America. Thomas Jefferson wrote in 1825:

> This was the object of the Declaration of Independence. Not to find out new principles, or new arguments, never before thought of, not merely to say things which had never been said before; but to place before mankind the common sense of the subject, in terms so plain and firm as to command their assent, and to justify ourselves in the independent stand we are compelled to take. Neither aiming at originality of principle or sentiment, nor yet copied from any particular and previous writing, it was intended to be an expression of the American mind, and to give to that expression the proper tone and spirit called for by the occasion.[1]

While the Declaration proclaimed the fundamental principles that defined our American identity, the Constitution gave structure to American government based on that philosophy. As Thomas Paine wrote, "Government is nothing more than a national association acting on the principles of society."[2] The Constitution created a framework that would enable us to live in liberty by the precepts of Natural Law. It established a system of government that best conformed to our cherished American ideals.

As the implementing force of our founding philosophy and as the supreme law of the land, the Constitution has long served as a barrier to tyranny in America. Throughout much of our history, whenever liberty came under assault—whether by proponents of centralized administrative power or by advocates of judicial supremacy—the people stood behind the Constitution in defense of the principles it was designed to preserve. With confidence in their collective authority over government, the people resisted the rise of despotism in America. They sustained their liberty by upholding the Constitution and the Laws of Nature.

Past generations have sacrificed dearly to preserve these fundamental blessings of liberty, but that responsibility now falls on us. Are we ready to take on this duty? And can we fulfill it? When future generations look back upon history to our moment in time, what will they see in our stewardship of American liberty? Will they find a people drifting further from freedom—lost in the soothing words of a demagogue, willingly ceding power to government? Will they find a people mindlessly following the dictates of judicial or administrative authority? Or will they find a people who rejected the false premise that a nation of followers can also be free? Will they find a people who stood up for their rights and reclaimed their sovereignty—a people who defended the Constitution and Laws of Nature? As we find in past generations, will they find the greatness of America in us?

If we seek to preserve liberty for posterity, then we cannot maintain our current political course—forward marks the direction toward our nation's destruction. We must instead turn back toward our founding ideals. We must return to the principles that set us free. It is the only way to restore our command over government, and it is the only way to save our republic for generations to come.

This was the course set by our Founding Fathers, and this was the course that Abraham Lincoln urged the people to return to as the only way to preserve American liberty. At an 1837 Young Men's Lyceum in

Springfield, Illinois, Lincoln gave a speech on "The Perpetuation of Our Political Institutions." He was only 27 years old at the time and unknown in national politics. But he showed a deep understanding of the threats to American liberty and the principles that would sustain it—principles that would later guide his presidency in his effort to save the Union from dissolution. In his sincere (and in many ways prophetic) remarks, Lincoln proposed a renewed commitment to the Constitution and the rule of law. Just as the Founding Fathers fought in support of the Declaration of Independence as the basis of their liberty, Lincoln called on the people to uphold the Constitution as the surest guardian of those ideals. He said:

> In the great journal of things happening under the sun, we, the American people, find our account running under date of the nineteenth century of the Christian era. We find ourselves in the peaceful possession of the fairest portion of the earth as regards extent of territory, fertility of soil, and salubrity of climate. We find ourselves under the government of a system of political institutions conducing more essentially to the ends of civil and religious liberty than any of which the history of former times tells us. We, when mounting the stage of existence, found ourselves the legal inheritors of these fundamental blessings. We toiled not in the acquisition or establishment of them; they are a legacy bequeathed us by a once hardy, brave, and patriotic, but now lamented and departed, race of ancestors. Theirs was the task (and nobly they performed it) to possess themselves, and through themselves us, of this goodly land, and to uprear upon its hills and valleys a political edifice of liberty and equal rights; 'tis ours only to transmit these—the former unprofaned by the foot of an invader, the latter undecayed by the lapse of time and untorn by usurpation—to the latest generation that fate shall permit the world to know. This task, gratitude to our fathers, justice to ourselves, duty to posterity, and love for our species in general, all imperatively require us faithfully to perform.
>
> How, then, shall we perform it? At what point shall we expect the approach of danger? By what means shall we fortify against it? Shall we expect some transatlantic military giant to step the ocean and crush us at a blow? Never! All the armies of Europe, Asia, and Africa combined, with all the treasure of the earth (our own excepted) in their military chest, with a Bonaparte for a commander, could not by force take a drink from the Ohio, or make a track on the Blue Ridge in a trial of a thousand years.

At what point, then is the approach of danger to be expected? I answer, If it ever reach us, it must spring up amongst us; it cannot come from abroad. If destruction be our lot, we must ourselves be its author and finisher. As a nation of free men, we must live through all time, or die by suicide.

. . .

I know the American people are much attached to their government; I know they would suffer much for its sake; I know they would endure evils long and patiently before they would ever think of exchanging it for another,—yet, notwithstanding all this, if the laws be continually despised and disregarded, if their rights to be secure in their persons and property are held by no better tenure than the caprice of a mob, the alienation of their affections from government is the natural consequence; and to that, sooner or later, it must come.

Here, then, is one point at which danger may be expected.

The question recurs, "How shall we fortify against it?" The answer is simple. Let every American, every lover of liberty, every well-wisher to his posterity, swear by the blood of the Revolution, never to violate in the least particular the laws of the country, and never to tolerate their violation by others. As the patriots of seventy-six did to the support of the Declaration of Independence, so to the support of the Constitution and the Laws let every American pledge his life, his property, and his sacred honor—let every man remember that to violate the law is to trample on the blood of his father, and to tear the charter of his own and his children's liberty. Let reverence for the laws be breathed by every American mother to the lisping babe that prattles on her lap; let it be taught in schools, in seminaries, and in colleges; let it be written in primers, spelling-books, and in almanacs; let it be preached from the pulpit, proclaimed in legislative halls, and enforced in courts of justice. And, in short, let it become the political religion of the nation.[3]

At a time when government has grown well beyond its natural and constitutional limits, let us recommit to our founding ideals. Let us live by the philosophy that secures our liberty. Let the American Ideology guide our nation once again.

THE DECLARATION OF INDEPENDENCE

Adopted on July 4, 1776

When, in the course of human events, it becomes necessary for one people to dissolve the political bands which have connected them with another, and to assume among the powers of the earth, the separate and equal station to which the laws of nature and of nature's God entitle them, a decent respect to the opinions of mankind requires that they should declare the causes which impel them to the separation.

We hold these truths to be self-evident, that all men are created equal, that they are endowed by their Creator with certain unalienable rights, that among these are life, liberty and the pursuit of happiness. That to secure these rights, governments are instituted among men, deriving their just powers from the consent of the governed. That whenever any form of government becomes destructive to these ends, it is the right of the people to alter or to abolish it, and to institute new government, laying its foundation on such principles and organizing its powers in such form, as to them shall seem most likely to effect their safety and happiness. Prudence, indeed, will dictate that governments long established should not be changed for light and transient causes; and accordingly all experience hath shown that mankind are more disposed to suffer, while evils are sufferable, than to right themselves by abolishing the forms to which they are accustomed. But when a long train of abuses and usurpations, pursuing invariably the same object evinces a design to reduce them under absolute despotism, it is their right, it is their duty, to throw off such government, and to provide new guards for their future security. --Such has been the patient sufferance of these colonies; and such is now the necessity which constrains them to alter their former systems of government. The history of the present King of Great Britain is a history of repeated injuries and usurpations, all having in direct object the establishment of an absolute tyranny over these states. To prove this, let facts be submitted to a candid world.

He has refused his assent to laws, the most wholesome and necessary for the public good.

He has forbidden his governors to pass laws of immediate and pressing importance, unless suspended in their operation till his assent should be obtained; and when so suspended, he has utterly neglected to attend to them.

He has refused to pass other laws for the accommodation of large districts of people, unless those people would relinquish the right of representation in the legislature, a right inestimable to them and formidable to tyrants only.

He has called together legislative bodies at places unusual, uncomfortable, and distant from the depository of their public records, for the sole purpose of fatiguing them into compliance with his measures.

He has dissolved representative houses repeatedly, for opposing with manly firmness his invasions on the rights of the people.

He has refused for a long time, after such dissolutions, to cause others to be elected; whereby the legislative powers, incapable of annihilation, have returned to the people at large for their exercise; the state remaining in the meantime exposed to all the dangers of invasion from without, and convulsions within.

He has endeavored to prevent the population of these states; for that purpose obstructing the laws for naturalization of foreigners; refusing to pass others to encourage their migration hither, and raising the conditions of new appropriations of lands.

He has obstructed the administration of justice, by refusing his assent to laws for establishing judiciary powers.

He has made judges dependent on his will alone, for the tenure of their offices, and the amount and payment of their salaries.

He has erected a multitude of new offices, and sent hither swarms of officers to harass our people, and eat out their substance.

He has kept among us, in times of peace, standing armies without the consent of our legislature.

He has affected to render the military independent of and superior to civil power.

He has combined with others to subject us to a jurisdiction foreign to our constitution, and unacknowledged by our laws; giving his assent to their acts of pretended legislation:

For quartering large bodies of armed troops among us:

For protecting them, by mock trial, from punishment for any murders which they should commit on the inhabitants of these states:

For cutting off our trade with all parts of the world:

For imposing taxes on us without our consent:

For depriving us in many cases, of the benefits of trial by jury:

For transporting us beyond seas to be tried for pretended offenses:

For abolishing the free system of English laws in a neighboring province, establishing therein an arbitrary government, and enlarging its boundaries so as to render it at once an example and fit instrument for introducing the same absolute rule in these colonies:

For taking away our charters, abolishing our most valuable laws, and altering fundamentally the forms of our governments:

For suspending our own legislatures, and declaring themselves invested with power to legislate for us in all cases whatsoever.

He has abdicated government here, by declaring us out of his protection and waging war against us.

He has plundered our seas, ravaged our coasts, burned our towns, and destroyed the lives of our people.

He is at this time transporting large armies of foreign mercenaries to complete the works of death, desolation and tyranny, already begun with circumstances of cruelty and perfidy scarcely paralleled in the most barbarous ages, and totally unworthy the head of a civilized nation.

He has constrained our fellow citizens taken captive on the high seas to bear arms against their country, to become the executioners of their friends and brethren, or to fall themselves by their hands.

He has excited domestic insurrections amongst us, and has endeavored to bring on the inhabitants of our frontiers, the merciless Indian savages, whose known rule of warfare, is undistinguished destruction of all ages, sexes and conditions.

In every stage of these oppressions we have petitioned for redress in the most humble terms: our repeated petitions have been answered only by repeated injury. A prince, whose character is thus marked by every act which may define a tyrant, is unfit to be the ruler of a free people.

Nor have we been wanting in attention to our British brethren. We have warned them from time to time of attempts by their legislature to extend an unwarrantable jurisdiction over us. We have reminded them of the circumstances of our emigration and settlement here. We have appealed to their native justice and magnanimity, and we have conjured them by the ties of our common kindred to disavow these usurpations, which, would inevitably interrupt our connections and correspondence. They too have been deaf to the voice of justice and of consanguinity. We must, therefore, acquiesce in the necessity, which denounces our separation, and hold them, as we hold the rest of mankind, enemies in war, in peace friends.

We, therefore, the representatives of the United States of America, in General Congress, assembled, appealing to the Supreme Judge of the world for the rectitude of our intentions, do, in the name, and by the authority of the good people of these colonies, solemnly publish and declare, that these united colonies are, and of right ought to be free and independent states; that they are absolved from all allegiance to the British Crown, and that all political connection between them and the state of Great Britain, is and ought to be totally dissolved; and that as free and independent states, they have full power to levy war, conclude peace, contract alliances, establish commerce, and to do all other acts and things which independent states may of right do. And for the support of this declaration, with a firm reliance on the protection of Divine Providence, we mutually pledge to each other our lives, our fortunes and our sacred honor.

New Hampshire: *Josiah Bartlett, William Whipple, Matthew Thornton*
Massachusetts: *John Hancock, Samuel Adams, John Adams, Robert Treat Paine, Elbridge Gerry*
Rhode Island: *Stephen Hopkins, William Ellery*
Connecticut: *Roger Sherman, Samuel Huntington, William Williams, Oliver Wolcott*
New York: *William Floyd, Philip Livingston, Francis Lewis, Lewis Morris*
New Jersey: *Richard Stockton, John Witherspoon, Francis Hopkinson, John Hart, Abraham Clark*
Pennsylvania: *Robert Morris, Benjamin Rush, Benjamin Franklin, John Morton, George Clymer, James Smith, George Taylor, James Wilson, George Ross*
Delaware: *Caesar Rodney, George Read, Thomas McKean*
Maryland: *Samuel Chase, William Paca, Thomas Stone, Charles Carroll of Carrollton*
Virginia: *George Wythe, Richard Henry Lee, Thomas Jefferson, Benjamin Harrison, Thomas Nelson, Jr., Francis Lightfoot Lee, Carter Braxton*
North Carolina: *William Hooper, Joseph Hewes, John Penn*
South Carolina: *Edward Rutledge, Thomas Heyward, Jr., Thomas Lynch, Jr., Arthur Middleton*
Georgia: *Button Gwinnett, Lyman Hall, George Walton*

THE UNITED STATES CONSTITUTION

Adopted on September 17, 1787; Ratified on June 21, 1788

We the People of the United States, in Order to form a more perfect Union, establish Justice, insure domestic Tranquility, provide for the common defence, promote the general Welfare, and secure the Blessings of Liberty to ourselves and our Posterity, do ordain and establish this Constitution for the United States of America.

Article I

Section 1. All legislative Powers herein granted shall be vested in a Congress of the United States, which shall consist of a Senate and House of Representatives.

Section 2. The House of Representatives shall be composed of Members chosen every second Year by the People of the several States, and the Electors in each State shall have the Qualifications requisite for Electors of the most numerous Branch of the State Legislature.

No Person shall be a Representative who shall not have attained to the age of twenty five Years, and been seven Years a Citizen of the United States, and who shall not, when elected, be an Inhabitant of that State in which he shall be chosen.

Representatives and direct Taxes shall be apportioned among the several States which may be included within this Union, according to their respective Numbers, which shall be determined by adding to the whole Number of free Persons, including those bound to Service for a Term of Years, and excluding Indians not taxed, three fifths of all other Persons. The actual Enumeration shall be made within three Years after the first Meeting of the Congress of the United States, and within every subsequent Term of ten Years, in such Manner as they shall by Law direct. The Number of Representatives shall not exceed one for every thirty Thousand, but each State shall have at Least one Representative; and until such enumeration shall be made, the State of New Hampshire shall be entitled to chuse three, Massachusetts eight, Rhode-Island and Providence Plantations one, Connecticut five, New-York six, New Jersey four, Pennsylvania eight, Delaware one, Maryland six, Virginia ten, North Carolina five, South Carolina five, and Georgia three.

When vacancies happen in the Representation from any State, the Executive Authority thereof shall issue Writs of Election to fill such Vacancies.

The House of Representatives shall chuse their Speaker and other Officers; and shall have the sole Power of Impeachment.

Section 3. The Senate of the United States shall be composed of two Senators from each State, chosen by the Legislature thereof, for six Years; and each Senator shall have one Vote.

Immediately after they shall be assembled in Consequence of the first Election, they shall be divided as equally as may be into three Classes. The Seats of the Senators of the first Class shall be vacated at the Expiration of the second Year, of the second Class at the

Expiration of the fourth Year, and the third Class at the Expiration of the sixth Year, so that one third may be chosen every second Year; and if Vacancies happen by Resignation, or otherwise, during the Recess of the Legislature of any State, the Executive thereof may make temporary Appointments until the next Meeting of the Legislature, which shall then fill such Vacancies.

No Person shall be a Senator who shall not have attained to the Age of thirty Years, and been nine Years a Citizen of the United States and who shall not, when elected, be an Inhabitant of that State for which he shall be chosen.

The Vice President of the United States shall be President of the Senate, but shall have no Vote, unless they be equally divided.

The Senate shall chuse their other Officers, and also a President pro tempore, in the Absence of the Vice President, or when he shall exercise the Office of President of the United States.

The Senate shall have the sole Power to try all Impeachments. When sitting for that Purpose, they shall be on Oath or Affirmation. When the President of the United States is tried, the Chief Justice shall preside: And no Person shall be convicted without the Concurrence of two thirds of the Members present.

Judgment in Cases of Impeachment shall not extend further than to removal from Office, and disqualification to hold and enjoy any Office of Honor, Trust or Profit under the United States: but the Party convicted shall nevertheless be liable and subject to Indictment, Trial, Judgment and Punishment, according to Law.

Section 4. The Times, Places and Manner of holding Elections for Senators and Representatives, shall be prescribed in each State by the Legislature thereof; but the Congress may at any time by Law make or alter such Regulations, except as to the Places of chusing Senators.

The Congress shall assemble at least once in every Year, and such Meeting shall be on the first Monday in December, unless they shall by Law appoint a different Day.

Section 5. Each House shall be the Judge of the Elections, Returns and Qualifications of its own Members, and a Majority of each shall constitute a Quorum to do Business; but a smaller Number may adjourn from day to day, and may be authorized to compel the Attendance of absent Members, in such Manner, and under such Penalties as each House may provide.

Each House may determine the Rules of its Proceedings, punish its Members for disorderly Behaviour, and, with the Concurrence of two thirds, expel a Member.

Each House shall keep a Journal of its Proceedings, and from time to time publish the same, excepting such Parts as may in their Judgment require Secrecy; and the Yeas and Nays of the Members of either House on any question shall, at the Desire of one fifth of those Present, be entered on the Journal.

Neither House, during the Session of Congress, shall, without the Consent of the other, adjourn for more than three days, nor to any other Place than that in which the two Houses shall be sitting.

Section 6. The Senators and Representatives shall receive a Compensation for their Services, to be ascertained by Law, and paid out of the Treasury of the United States. They shall in all Cases, except Treason, Felony and Breach of the Peace, be privileged from Arrest during their Attendance at the Session of their respective Houses, and in going to and returning from the same; and for any Speech or Debate in either House, they shall not be questioned in any other Place.

No Senator or Representative shall, during the Time for which he was elected, be appointed to any civil Office under the Authority of the United States, which shall have been created, or the Emoluments whereof shall have been increased during such time: and no Person holding any Office under the United States, shall be a Member of either House during his Continuance in Office.

Section 7. All Bills for raising Revenue shall originate in the House of Representatives; but the Senate may propose or concur with Amendments as on other Bills.

Every Bill which shall have passed the House of Representatives and the Senate, shall, before it become a Law, be presented to the President of the United States; if he approve he shall sign it, but if not he shall return it, with his Objections to that House in which it shall have originated, who shall enter the Objections at large on their Journal, and proceed to reconsider it. If after such Reconsideration two thirds of that House shall agree to pass the Bill, it shall be sent, together with the Objections, to the other House, by which it shall likewise be reconsidered, and if approved by two thirds of that House, it shall become a Law. But in all such Cases the Votes of both Houses shall be determined by Yeas and Nays, and the Names of the Persons voting for and against the Bill shall be entered on the Journal of each House respectively. If any Bill shall not be returned by the President within ten Days (Sundays excepted) after it shall have been presented to him, the Same shall be a Law, in like Manner as if he had signed it, unless the Congress by their Adjournment prevent its Return, in which Case it shall not be a Law.

Every Order, Resolution, or Vote to which the Concurrence of the Senate and House of Representatives may be necessary (except on a question of Adjournment) shall be presented to the President of the United States; and before the Same shall take Effect, shall be approved by him, or being disapproved by him, shall be repassed by two thirds of the Senate and House of Representatives, according to the Rules and Limitations prescribed in the Case of a Bill.

Section 8. The Congress shall have Power To lay and collect Taxes, Duties, Imposts and Excises, to pay the Debts and provide for the common Defence and general Welfare of the United States; but all Duties, Imposts and Excises shall be uniform throughout the United States;

To borrow Money on the credit of the United States;

To regulate Commerce with foreign Nations, and among the several States, and with the Indian Tribes;

To establish an uniform Rule of Naturalization, and uniform Laws on the subject of Bankruptcies throughout the United States;

To coin Money, regulate the Value thereof, and of foreign Coin, and fix the Standard of Weights and Measures;

To provide for the Punishment of counterfeiting the Securities and current Coin of the United States;

To establish Post Offices and post Roads;

To promote the Progress of Science and useful Arts, by securing for limited Times to Authors and Inventors the exclusive Right to their respective Writings and Discoveries;

To constitute Tribunals inferior to the supreme Court;

To define and punish Piracies and Felonies committed on the high Seas, and Offences against the Law of Nations;

To declare War, grant Letters of Marque and Reprisal, and make Rules concerning Captures on Land and Water;

To raise and support Armies, but no Appropriation of Money to that Use shall be for a longer Term than two Years;

To provide and maintain a Navy;

To make Rules for the Government and Regulation of the land and naval Forces;

To provide for calling forth the Militia to execute the Laws of the Union, suppress Insurrections and repel Invasions;

To provide for organizing, arming, and disciplining, the Militia, and for governing such Part of them as may be employed in the Service of the United States, reserving to the States respectively, the Appointment of the Officers, and the Authority of training the Militia according to the discipline prescribed by Congress;

To exercise exclusive Legislation in all Cases whatsoever, over such District (not exceeding ten Miles square) as may, by Cession of particular States, and the Acceptance of Congress, become the Seat of the Government of the United States, and to exercise like Authority over all Places purchased by the Consent of the Legislature of the State in which the Same shall be, for the Erection of Forts, Magazines, Arsenals, dock-Yards, and other needful Buildings;--And

To make all Laws which shall be necessary and proper for carrying into Execution the foregoing Powers, and all other Powers vested by this Constitution in the Government of the United States, or in any Department or Officer thereof.

Section 9. The Migration or Importation of such Persons as any of the States now existing shall think proper to admit, shall not be prohibited by the Congress prior to the Year one thousand eight hundred and eight, but a Tax or duty may be imposed on such Importation, not exceeding ten dollars for each Person.

The Privilege of the Writ of Habeas Corpus shall not be suspended, unless when in Cases of Rebellion or Invasion the public Safety may require it.

No Bill of Attainder or ex post facto Law shall be passed.

No Capitation, or other direct, Tax shall be laid, unless in Proportion to the Census or Enumeration herein before directed to be taken.

No Tax or Duty shall be laid on Articles exported from any State.

No Preference shall be given by any Regulation of Commerce or Revenue to the Ports of one State over those of another: nor shall Vessels bound to, or from, one State, be obliged to enter, clear or pay Duties in another.

No Money shall be drawn from the Treasury, but in Consequence of Appropriations made by Law; and a regular Statement and Account of Receipts and Expenditures of all public Money shall be published from time to time.

No Title of Nobility shall be granted by the United States: And no Person holding any Office of Profit or Trust under them, shall, without the Consent of the Congress, accept of any present, Emolument, Office, or Title, of any kind whatever, from any King, Prince, or foreign State.

Section 10. No State shall enter into any Treaty, Alliance, or Confederation; grant Letters of Marque and Reprisal; coin Money; emit Bills of Credit; make any Thing but gold and silver Coin a Tender in Payment of Debts; pass any Bill of Attainder, ex post facto Law, or Law impairing the Obligation of Contracts, or grant any Title of Nobility.

No State shall, without the Consent of the Congress, lay any Imposts or Duties on Imports or Exports, except what may be absolutely necessary for executing it's inspection Laws: and the net Produce of all Duties and Imposts, laid by any State on Imports or Exports, shall be for the Use of the Treasury of the United States; and all such Laws shall be subject to the Revision and Controul of the Congress.

No State shall, without the Consent of Congress, lay any Duty of Tonnage, keep Troops, or Ships of War in time of Peace, enter into any Agreement or Compact with another State, or with a foreign Power, or engage in War, unless actually invaded, or in such imminent Danger as will not admit of delay.

Article II

Section 1. The executive Power shall be vested in a President of the United States of America. He shall hold his Office during the Term of four Years, and, together with the Vice President, chosen for the same Term, be elected, as follows:

Each State shall appoint, in such Manner as the Legislature thereof may direct, a Number of Electors, equal to the whole Number of Senators and Representatives to which the State may be entitled in the Congress: but no Senator or Representative, or Person holding an Office of Trust or Profit under the United States, shall be appointed an Elector.

The Electors shall meet in their respective States, and vote by Ballot for two Persons, of whom one at least shall not be an Inhabitant of the same State with themselves. And they shall make a List of all the Persons voted for, and of the Number of Votes for each; which List they shall sign and certify, and transmit sealed to the Seat of the Government of the United States, directed to the President of the Senate. The President of the Senate shall, in the Presence of the Senate and House of Representatives, open all the Certificates, and the Votes shall then be counted. The Person having the greatest Number of Votes shall be the President, if such Number be a Majority of the whole Number of Electors appointed; and if there be more than one who have such Majority, and have an equal Number of Votes, then the House of Representatives shall immediately chuse by Ballot one of them for President; and if no Person have a Majority, then from the five highest on the List the said House shall in like Manner chuse the President. But in chusing the President, the Votes shall be taken by States, the Representation from each State having one Vote; A quorum for this Purpose shall consist of a Member or Members from two thirds of the States, and a Majority of all the States shall be necessary to a Choice. In every Case, after the Choice of the President, the Person having the greatest Number of Votes of the Electors shall be the Vice President. But if there should remain two or more who have equal Votes, the Senate shall chuse from them by Ballot the Vice President.

The Congress may determine the Time of chusing the Electors, and the Day on which they shall give their Votes; which Day shall be the same throughout the United States.

No Person except a natural born Citizen, or a Citizen of the United States, at the time of the Adoption of this Constitution, shall be eligible to the Office of President; neither shall any Person be eligible to that Office who shall not have attained to the Age of thirty five Years, and been fourteen Years a Resident within the United States.

In Case of the Removal of the President from Office, or of his Death, Resignation, or Inability to discharge the Powers and Duties of the said Office, the Same shall devolve on the Vice President, and the Congress may by Law provide for the Case of Removal, Death, Resignation or Inability, both of the President and Vice President, declaring what Officer shall then act as President, and such Officer shall act accordingly, until the Disability be removed, or a President shall be elected.

The President shall, at stated Times, receive for his Services, a Compensation, which shall neither be encreased nor diminished during the Period for which he shall have been elected, and he shall not receive within that Period any other Emolument from the United States, or any of them.

Before he enter on the Execution of his Office, he shall take the following Oath or Affirmation:--"I do solemnly swear (or affirm) that I will faithfully execute the Office of President of the United States, and will to the best of my Ability, preserve, protect and defend the Constitution of the United States."

Section 2. The President shall be Commander in Chief of the Army and Navy of the United States, and of the Militia of the several States, when called into the actual Service of the United States; he may require the Opinion, in writing, of the principal Officer in each of the executive Departments, upon any Subject relating to the Duties of their respective Offices, and he shall have Power to grant Reprieves and Pardons for Offences against the United States, except in Cases of Impeachment.

He shall have Power, by and with the Advice and Consent of the Senate, to make Treaties, provided two thirds of the Senators present concur; and he shall nominate, and by and with the Advice and Consent of the Senate, shall appoint Ambassadors, other public Ministers and Consuls, Judges of the supreme Court, and all other Officers of the United States, whose Appointments are not herein otherwise provided for, and which shall be established by Law: but the Congress may by Law vest the Appointment of such inferior Officers, as they think proper, in the President alone, in the Courts of Law, or in the Heads of Departments.

The President shall have Power to fill up all Vacancies that may happen during the Recess of the Senate, by granting Commissions which shall expire at the End of their next Session.

Section 3. He shall from time to time give to the Congress Information of the State of the Union, and recommend to their Consideration such Measures as he shall judge necessary and expedient; he may, on extraordinary Occasions, convene both Houses, or either of them, and in Case of Disagreement between them, with Respect to the Time of Adjournment, he may adjourn them to such Time as he shall think proper; he shall receive Ambassadors and other public Ministers; he shall take Care that the Laws be faithfully executed, and shall Commission all the Officers of the United States.

Section 4. The President, Vice President and all civil Officers of the United States, shall be removed from Office on Impeachment for, and Conviction of, Treason, Bribery, or other high Crimes and Misdemeanors.

Article III

Section 1. The judicial Power of the United States, shall be vested in one supreme Court, and in such inferior Courts as the Congress may from time to time ordain and establish. The Judges, both of the supreme and inferior Courts, shall hold their Offices during good Behaviour, and shall, at stated Times, receive for their Services, a Compensation, which shall not be diminished during their Continuance in Office.

Section 2. The judicial Power shall extend to all Cases, in Law and Equity, arising under this Constitution, the Laws of the United States, and Treaties made, or which shall be made, under their Authority;--to all Cases affecting Ambassadors, other public Ministers and Consuls;--to all Cases of admiralty and maritime Jurisdiction;--to Controversies to which the United States shall be a Party;--to Controversies between two or more States;--between a State and Citizens of another State;--between Citizens of different States;--between Citizens of the same State claiming Lands under Grants of different States, and between a State, or the Citizens thereof, and foreign States, Citizens or Subjects.

In all Cases affecting Ambassadors, other public Ministers and Consuls, and those in which a State shall be Party, the supreme Court shall have original Jurisdiction. In all the other Cases before mentioned, the supreme Court shall have appellate Jurisdiction, both as to Law and Fact, with such Exceptions, and under such Regulations as the Congress shall make.

The Trial of all Crimes, except in Cases of Impeachment, shall be by Jury; and such Trial shall be held in the State where the said Crimes shall have been committed; but when not committed within any State, the Trial shall be at such Place or Places as the Congress may by Law have directed.

Section 3. Treason against the United States, shall consist only in levying War against them, or in adhering to their Enemies, giving them Aid and Comfort. No Person shall be convicted of Treason unless on the Testimony of two Witnesses to the same overt Act, or on Confession in open Court.

The Congress shall have Power to declare the Punishment of Treason, but no Attainder of Treason shall work Corruption of Blood, or Forfeiture except during the Life of the Person attainted.

Article IV

Section 1. Full Faith and Credit shall be given in each State to the public Acts, Records, and judicial Proceedings of every other State. And the Congress may by general Laws prescribe the Manner in which such Acts, Records, and Proceedings shall be proved, and the Effect thereof.

Section 2. The Citizens of each State shall be entitled to all Privileges and Immunities of Citizens in the several States.

A Person charged in any State with Treason, Felony, or other Crime, who shall flee from Justice, and be found in another State, shall on Demand of the executive Authority of the State from which he fled, be delivered up, to be removed to the State having Jurisdiction of the Crime.

No Person held to Service or Labour in one State, under the Laws thereof, escaping into another, shall, in Consequence of any Law or Regulation therein, be discharged from such Service or Labour, but shall be delivered up on Claim of the Party to whom such Service or Labour may be due.

Section 3. New States may be admitted by the Congress into this Union; but no new States shall be formed or erected within the Jurisdiction of any other State; nor any State be formed by the Junction of two or more States, or Parts of States, without the Consent of the Legislatures of the States concerned as well as of the Congress.

The Congress shall have Power to dispose of and make all needful Rules and Regulations respecting the Territory or other Property belonging to the United States; and nothing in this Constitution shall be so construed as to Prejudice any Claims of the United States, or of any particular State.

Section 4. The United States shall guarantee to every State in this Union a Republican Form of Government, and shall protect each of them against Invasion; and on Application of the Legislature, or of the Executive (when the Legislature cannot be convened) against domestic Violence.

Article V

The Congress, whenever two thirds of both Houses shall deem it necessary, shall propose Amendments to this Constitution, or, on the Application of the Legislatures of two thirds of the several States, shall call a Convention for proposing Amendments, which, in either Case, shall be valid to all Intents and Purposes, as Part of this Constitution, when ratified by the Legislatures of three fourths of the several States, or by Conventions in three fourths thereof, as the one or the other Mode of Ratification may be proposed by the Congress; Provided that no Amendment which may be made prior to the Year One thousand eight hundred and eight shall in any Manner affect the first and fourth Clauses in the Ninth Section of the first Article; and that no State, without its Consent, shall be deprived of its equal Suffrage in the Senate.

Article VI

All Debts contracted and Engagements entered into, before the Adoption of this Constitution, shall be as valid against the United States under this Constitution, as under the Confederation.

This Constitution, and the Laws of the United States which shall be made in Pursuance thereof; and all Treaties made, or which shall be made, under the Authority of the United States, shall be the supreme Law of the Land; and the Judges in every State shall be bound thereby, any Thing in the Constitution or Laws of any State to the Contrary notwithstanding.

The Senators and Representatives before mentioned, and the Members of the several State Legislatures, and all executive and judicial Officers, both of the United States and of the several States, shall be bound by Oath or Affirmation, to support this Constitution; but no religious Test shall ever be required as a Qualification to any Office or public Trust under the United States.

Article VII

The Ratification of the Conventions of nine States, shall be sufficient for the Establishment of this Constitution between the States so ratifying the Same.

* * * * * * *

Done in Convention by the Unanimous Consent of the States present the Seventeenth Day of September in the Year of our Lord one thousand seven hundred and Eighty seven and of the Independence of the United States of America the Twelfth. In witness whereof We have hereunto subscribed our Names,

George Washington--*President and deputy from Virginia*

New Hampshire: *John Langdon, Nicholas Gilman*
Massachusetts: *Nathaniel Gorham, Rufus King*
Connecticut: *William Samuel Johnson, Roger Sherman*
New York: *Alexander Hamilton*
New Jersey: *William Livingston, David Brearly, William Paterson, Jonathan Dayton*
Pennsylvania: *Benjamin Franklin, Thomas Mifflin, Robert Morris, George Clymer, Thomas FitzSimons, Jared Ingersoll, James Wilson, Gouverneur Morris*
Delaware: *George Read, Gunning Bedford, Jr., John Dickinson, Richard Bassett, Jacob Broom*
Maryland: *James McHenry, Daniel of Saint Thomas Jenifer, Daniel Carroll*
Virginia: *John Blair, James Madison, Jr.*
North Carolina: *William Blount, Richard Dobbs Spaight, Hugh Williamson*
South Carolina: *John Rutledge, Charles Cotesworth Pinckney, Charles Pinckney, Pierce Butler*
Georgia: *William Few, Abraham Baldwin*

* * * * * * *

Amendment I (1791)

Congress shall make no law respecting an establishment of religion, or prohibiting the free exercise thereof; or abridging the freedom of speech, or of the press; or the right of the people peaceably to assemble, and to petition the Government for a redress of grievances.

Amendment II (1791)

A well regulated Militia, being necessary to the security of a free State, the right of the people to keep and bear Arms, shall not be infringed.

Amendment III (1791)

No Soldier shall, in time of peace be quartered in any house, without the consent of the Owner, nor in time of war, but in a manner to be prescribed by law.

Amendment IV (1791)

The right of the people to be secure in their persons, houses, papers, and effects, against unreasonable searches and seizures, shall not be violated, and no Warrants shall issue, but upon probable cause, supported by Oath or affirmation, and particularly describing the place to be searched, and the persons or things to be seized.

Amendment V (1791)

No person shall be held to answer for a capital, or otherwise infamous crime, unless on a presentment or indictment of a Grand Jury, except in cases arising in the land or naval forces, or in the Militia, when in actual service in time of War or public danger; nor shall any person be subject for the same offence to be twice put in jeopardy of life or limb; nor shall be compelled in any criminal case to be a witness against himself, nor be deprived of life, liberty, or property, without due process of law; nor shall private property be taken for public use, without just compensation.

Amendment VI (1791)

In all criminal prosecutions, the accused shall enjoy the right to a speedy and public trial, by an impartial jury of the State and district wherein the crime shall have been committed, which district shall have been previously ascertained by law, and to be informed of the nature and cause of the accusation; to be confronted with the witnesses against him; to have compulsory process for obtaining witnesses in his favor, and to have the Assistance of Counsel for his defence.

Amendment VII (1791)

In Suits at common law, where the value in controversy shall exceed twenty dollars, the right of trial by jury shall be preserved, and no fact tried by a jury, shall be otherwise re-examined in any Court of the United States, than according to the rules of the common law.

Amendment VIII (1791)

Excessive bail shall not be required, nor excessive fines imposed, nor cruel and unusual punishments inflicted.

Amendment IX (1791)

The enumeration in the Constitution, of certain rights, shall not be construed to deny or disparage others retained by the people.

Amendment X (1791)

The powers not delegated to the United States by the Constitution, nor prohibited by it to the States, are reserved to the States respectively, or to the people.

Amendment XI (1795)

The Judicial power of the United States shall not be construed to extend to any suit in law or equity, commenced or prosecuted against one of the United States by Citizens of another State, or by Citizens or Subjects of any Foreign State.

Amendment XII (1804)

The Electors shall meet in their respective states, and vote by ballot for President and Vice-President, one of whom, at least, shall not be an inhabitant of the same state with themselves; they shall name in their ballots the person voted for as President, and in distinct ballots the person voted for as Vice-President, and they shall make distinct lists of all persons voted for as President, and of all persons voted for as Vice-President, and of the number of votes for each, which lists they shall sign and certify, and transmit sealed to the seat of the government of the United States, directed to the President of the Senate;--The President of the Senate shall, in the presence of the Senate and House of Representatives, open all the certificates and the votes shall then be counted;--The person having the greatest number of votes for President, shall be the President, if such number be a majority of the whole number of Electors appointed; and if no person have such majority, then from the persons having the highest numbers not exceeding three on the list of those voted for as President, the House of Representatives shall choose immediately, by ballot, the President. But in choosing the President, the votes shall be taken by states, the representation from each state having one vote; a quorum for this purpose shall consist of a member or members from two-thirds of the states, and a majority of all the states shall be necessary to a choice. And if the House of Representatives shall not choose a President whenever the right of choice shall devolve upon them, before the fourth day of March next following, then the Vice-President shall act as President, as in the case of the death or other constitutional disability of the President.14 --The person having the greatest number of votes as Vice-President, shall be the Vice-President, if such number be a majority of the whole number of Electors appointed, and if no person have a majority, then from the two highest numbers on the list, the Senate shall choose the Vice-President; a quorum for the purpose shall consist of two-thirds of the whole number of Senators, and a majority of the whole number shall be necessary to a choice. But no person constitutionally ineligible to the office of President shall be eligible to that of Vice-President of the United States.

Amendment XIII (1865)

Neither slavery nor involuntary servitude, except as a punishment for crime whereof the party shall have been duly convicted, shall exist within the United States, or any place subject to their jurisdiction.

Congress shall have power to enforce this article by appropriate legislation.

Amendment XIV (1868)

1: All persons born or naturalized in the United States, and subject to the jurisdiction thereof, are citizens of the United States and of the State wherein they reside. No State shall make or enforce any law which shall abridge the privileges or immunities of citizens of the United States; nor shall any State deprive any person of life, liberty, or property, without due process of law; nor deny to any person within its jurisdiction the equal protection of the laws.

2: Representatives shall be apportioned among the several States according to their respective numbers, counting the whole number of persons in each State, excluding Indians not taxed. But when the right to vote at any election for the choice of electors for President and Vice President of the United States, Representatives in Congress, the Executive and

Judicial officers of a State, or the members of the Legislature thereof, is denied to any of the male inhabitants of such State, being twenty-one years of age,15 and citizens of the United States, or in any way abridged, except for participation in rebellion, or other crime, the basis of representation therein shall be reduced in the proportion which the number of such male citizens shall bear to the whole number of male citizens twenty-one years of age in such State.

3: No person shall be a Senator or Representative in Congress, or elector of President and Vice President, or hold any office, civil or military, under the United States, or under any State, who, having previously taken an oath, as a member of Congress, or as an officer of the United States, or as a member of any State legislature, or as an executive or judicial officer of any State, to support the Constitution of the United States, shall have engaged in insurrection or rebellion against the same, or given aid or comfort to the enemies thereof. But Congress may by a vote of two-thirds of each House, remove such disability.

4: The validity of the public debt of the United States, authorized by law, including debts incurred for payment of pensions and bounties for services in suppressing insurrection or rebellion, shall not be questioned. But neither the United States nor any State shall assume or pay any debt or obligation incurred in aid of insurrection or rebellion against the United States, or any claim for the loss or emancipation of any slave; but all such debts, obligations and claims shall be held illegal and void.

5: The Congress shall have power to enforce, by appropriate legislation, the provisions of this article.

Amendment XV (1870)

The right of citizens of the United States to vote shall not be denied or abridged by the United States or by any State on account of race, color, or previous condition of servitude.

The Congress shall have power to enforce this article by appropriate legislation.

Amendment XVI (1913)

The Congress shall have power to lay and collect taxes on incomes, from whatever source derived, without apportionment among the several States, and without regard to any census or enumeration.

Amendment XVII (1913)

1: The Senate of the United States shall be composed of two Senators from each State, elected by the people thereof, for six years; and each Senator shall have one vote. The electors in each State shall have the qualifications requisite for electors of the most numerous branch of the State legislatures.

2: When vacancies happen in the representation of any State in the Senate, the executive authority of such State shall issue writs of election to fill such vacancies: Provided, That the legislature of any State may empower the executive thereof to make temporary appointments until the people fill the vacancies by election as the legislature may direct.

3: This amendment shall not be so construed as to affect the election or term of any Senator chosen before it becomes valid as part of the Constitution.

Amendment XVIII (1919)

1: After one year from the ratification of this article the manufacture, sale, or transportation of intoxicating liquors within, the importation thereof into, or the exportation thereof from the United States and all territory subject to the jurisdiction thereof for beverage purposes is hereby prohibited.

2: The Congress and the several States shall have concurrent power to enforce this article by appropriate legislation.

3: This article shall be inoperative unless it shall have been ratified as an amendment to the Constitution by the legislatures of the several States, as provided in the Constitution, within seven years from the date of the submission hereof to the States by the Congress.

Amendment XIX (1920)

The right of citizens of the United States to vote shall not be denied or abridged by the United States or by any State on account of sex.

Congress shall have power to enforce this article by appropriate legislation.

Amendment XX (1933)

1: The terms of the President and Vice President shall end at noon on the 20th day of January, and the terms of Senators and Representatives at noon on the 3d day of January, of the years in which such terms would have ended if this article had not been ratified; and the terms of their successors shall then begin.

2: The Congress shall assemble at least once in every year, and such meeting shall begin at noon on the 3d day of January, unless they shall by law appoint a different day.

3: If, at the time fixed for the beginning of the term of the President, the President elect shall have died, the Vice President elect shall become President. If a President shall not have been chosen before the time fixed for the beginning of his term, or if the President elect shall have failed to qualify, then the Vice President elect shall act as President until a President shall have qualified; and the Congress may by law provide for the case wherein neither a President elect nor a Vice President elect shall have qualified, declaring who shall then act as President, or the manner in which one who is to act shall be selected, and such person shall act accordingly until a President or Vice President shall have qualified.

4: The Congress may by law provide for the case of the death of any of the persons from whom the House of Representatives may choose a President whenever the right of choice shall have devolved upon them, and for the case of the death of any of the persons from whom the Senate may choose a Vice President whenever the right of choice shall have devolved upon them.

5: Sections 1 and 2 shall take effect on the 15th day of October following the ratification of this article.

6: This article shall be inoperative unless it shall have been ratified as an amendment to the Constitution by the legislatures of three-fourths of the several States within seven years from the date of its submission.

Amendment XXI (1933)

1: The eighteenth article of amendment to the Constitution of the United States is hereby repealed.

2: The transportation or importation into any State, Territory, or possession of the United States for delivery or use therein of intoxicating liquors, in violation of the laws thereof, is hereby prohibited.

3: This article shall be inoperative unless it shall have been ratified as an amendment to the Constitution by conventions in the several States, as provided in the Constitution, within seven years from the date of the submission hereof to the States by the Congress.

Amendment XXII (1951)

1: No person shall be elected to the office of the President more than twice, and no person who has held the office of President, or acted as President, for more than two years of a term to which some other person was elected President shall be elected to the office of the President more than once. But this article shall not apply to any person holding the office of President when this article was proposed by the Congress, and shall not prevent any person who may be holding the office of President, or acting as President, during the term within which this article becomes operative from holding the office of President or acting as President during the remainder of such term.

2: This article shall be inoperative unless it shall have been ratified as an amendment to the Constitution by the legislatures of three-fourths of the several states within seven years from the date of its submission to the states by the Congress.

Amendment XXIII (1961)

1: The District constituting the seat of government of the United States shall appoint in such manner as the Congress may direct: A number of electors of President and Vice President equal to the whole number of Senators and Representatives in Congress to which the District would be entitled if it were a state, but in no event more than the least populous state; they shall be in addition to those appointed by the states, but they shall be considered, for the purposes of the election of President and Vice President, to be electors appointed by a state; and they shall meet in the District and perform such duties as provided by the twelfth article of amendment.

2: The Congress shall have power to enforce this article by appropriate legislation.

Amendment XXIV (1964)

1. The right of citizens of the United States to vote in any primary or other election for President or Vice President, for electors for President or Vice President, or for Senator or Representative in Congress, shall not be denied or abridged by the United States or any state by reason of failure to pay any poll tax or other tax.

2. The Congress shall have power to enforce this article by appropriate legislation.

Amendment XXV (1967)

1: In case of the removal of the President from office or of his death or resignation, the Vice President shall become President.

2: Whenever there is a vacancy in the office of the Vice President, the President shall nominate a Vice President who shall take office upon confirmation by a majority vote of both Houses of Congress.

3: Whenever the President transmits to the President pro tempore of the Senate and the Speaker of the House of Representatives his written declaration that he is unable to discharge the powers and duties of his office, and until he transmits to them a written declaration to the contrary, such powers and duties shall be discharged by the Vice President as Acting President.

4: Whenever the Vice President and a majority of either the principal officers of the executive departments or of such other body as Congress may by law provide, transmit to the President pro tempore of the Senate and the Speaker of the House of Representatives their written declaration that the President is unable to discharge the powers and duties of his office, the Vice President shall immediately assume the powers and duties of the office as Acting President.

Thereafter, when the President transmits to the President pro tempore of the Senate and the Speaker of the House of Representatives his written declaration that no inability exists, he shall resume the powers and duties of his office unless the Vice President and a majority of either the principal officers of the executive department or of such other body as Congress may by law provide, transmit within four days to the President pro tempore of the Senate and the Speaker of the House of Representatives their written declaration that the President is unable to discharge the powers and duties of his office. Thereupon Congress shall decide the issue, assembling within forty-eight hours for that purpose if not in session. If the Congress, within twenty-one days after receipt of the latter written declaration, or, if Congress is not in session, within twenty-one days after Congress is required to assemble, determines by two-thirds vote of both Houses that the President is unable to discharge the powers and duties of his office, the Vice President shall continue to discharge the same as Acting President; otherwise, the President shall resume the powers and duties of his office.

Amendment XXVI (1971)

1: The right of citizens of the United States, who are 18 years of age or older, to vote, shall not be denied or abridged by the United States or any state on account of age.

2: The Congress shall have the power to enforce this article by appropriate legislation.

Amendment XXVII (1992)

No law varying the compensation for the services of the Senators and Representatives shall take effect until an election of Representatives shall have intervened.

NOTES

INTRODUCTION

1. Alexis de Tocqueville, *Democracy in America* (The Library of America, 2004) (1835), 13.
2. *Ibid.*, 32.
3. *Ibid.*, 364.
4. *Ibid.*

CHAPTER 1 – ON NATURAL LAW

1. St. George Tucker, *William Blackstone's Commentaries with Notes*, Vol. 2 (Philadelphia: William Young Birch and Abraham Small, 1803), 129.
2. Declaration of Independence.
3. Thomas Jefferson, "Letter to Samuel Adams Wells," May 12, 1819, in *The Jefferson Cyclopedia* (John P. Foley, ed., Funk & Wagnalls, 1900), 245.
4. John Locke, *Two Treatises of Government* (Peter Laslett ed., Cambridge University Press, 2008) (1698), 215.
5. *Ibid.*, 143.
6. *Ibid.*, 162.
7. *Ibid.*, 172–74.
8. *Ibid.*, 190.
9. Thomas Paine, "Rights of Man," in *Common Sense, Rights of Man, and Other Essential Writings of Thomas Paine* (Signet Classics 2003) (1776), 167 (emphasis in original).
10. *Ibid.*, 232 (emphasis in original).
11. *Ibid.*, 248.
12. *Ibid.*
13. *Ibid.*, 248–49 (emphasis in original).
14. Quincy Wright, *The Control of American Foreign Relations* (The MacMillan Company, 1922), 363.
15. John Adams, *Boston Gazette*, Sep. 5, 1763, in *The Works of John Adams* (Charles F. Adams, ed., 1851), 438.
16. Samuel Adams, *Boston Gazette*, Feb. 27, 1769, in *The Writings of Samuel Adams*, Vol. 1 (Harry Alonzo Cushing, ed., G.P. Putnam's Sons, 1904), 317 (quoting Blackstone).
17. Samuel Adams and Benjamin Franklin, "The Report of the Committee of Correspondence to the Boston Town Meeting," Nov. 20, 1772.
18. George Washington, "Fairfax County Resolves," Jul. 18, 1774.
19. Thomas Jefferson, "A Summary View of the Rights of British America," Jul. 1774, in *The Papers of Thomas Jefferson* (Julian P. Boyd et al., ed., Princeton University Press, 1950).
20. Declaration and Resolves of the First Continental Congress, Oct. 14, 1774.

21. Alexander Hamilton, "The Farmer Refuted," Feb. 23, 1775, in *The Founders' Constitution*, Vol. 1 (The University of Chicago Press, 2000), 91.
22. Declaration of Independence.
23. *Ibid.*
24. *Ibid.*
25. John Locke, *Two Treatises of Government*, 271.
26. *Ibid.*
27. *Ibid.*, 270.
28. *Ibid.*, 271.
29. *Ibid.*, 284.
30. St. George Tucker, *William Blackstone's Commentaries with Notes*, Vol. 2, 129.
31. *Ibid.*, 133.
32. *Ibid.*, Vol. 3, 3.
33. *Ibid.*, 4.
34. John Locke, *Two Treatises of Government*, 291.
35. Ibid., 306.
36. *Ibid.*, 269.
37. St. George Tucker, *William Blackstone's Commentaries with Notes*, Vol. 2, 125 (emphasis added).
38. *Ibid.*
39. Adams and Franklin, "The Report of the Committee of Correspondence," (emphasis added).
40. John Locke, *Two Treatises of Government*, 306.
41. *Ibid.*, 271.
42. *Ibid.*
43. *Ibid.*, 272.
44. *Ibid.*, 323–24.
45. *Ibid.*
46. *Ibid.*
47. *Ibid.*
48. *Ibid.*, 326.
49. *Ibid.*, 350.
50. *Ibid.*
51. Alexander Hamilton, James Madison, and John Jay, *The Federalist Papers* (Bantam Classic 2003) (1787–88), 316.
52. Thomas Paine, "Common Sense," in *Common Sense, Rights of Man, and Other Essential Writings of Thomas Paine* (Signet Classics 2003) (1776), 5.
53. John Locke, *Two Treatises of Government*, 350.
54. *Ibid.*, 350–51.
55. *Ibid.*, 353.
56. *Ibid.*, 344.
57. St. George Tucker, *William Blackstone's Commentaries with Notes*, Vol. 1, Appendix, 8.
58. Adams and Franklin, "The Report of the Committee of Correspondence."
59. Declaration of Independence.
60. John Locke, *Two Treatises of Government*, 348 (emphasis in original).
61. *Ibid.*, 349.
62. *Ibid.*, 332.
63. *Ibid.*
64. Adams and Franklin, "The Report of the Committee of Correspondence."
65. *Ibid.*
66. John Quincy Adams, Jubilee of the Constitution Address, Apr. 30, 1839.
67. Thomas Jefferson, "A Summary View of the Rights of British America," July 1774, in *The Papers of Thomas Jefferson* (Julian P. Boyd et al., ed., Princeton University Press, 1950).
68. John Dickinson, "An Address," in *The Political Writings of John Dickinson* Vol. 1 (Wilmington, Bonsal and Niles, 1801), 111.
69. Alexander Hamilton, "The Farmer Refuted."
70. John Adams, "Thoughts on Government," 1776, in *The Political Writings of John Adams* (George A. Peek, Jr., ed., Hackett Publishing Company 2003), 96.
71. Charles de Montesquieu, *The Spirit of the Laws* (F. Neumann ed., Hafner Press, 1949) (1748), 1.

72. Thomas Paine, "Age of Reason," in *Common Sense, Rights of Man, and Other Essential Writings of Thomas Paine* (Signet Classics 2003) (1776), 365.
73. *Ibid.*
74. Thomas Jefferson, "Letter to John Adams," Apr. 11, 1823, in *The Jefferson Cyclopedia* (John P. Foley, ed., Funk & Wagnalls, 1900), 248.
75. James Wilson, "Lectures on Law," 129.
76. Benjamin Franklin, "A Lecture on the Province of God in the Government of the World," in *The Works of Benjamin Franklin*, Vol. 2 (Jared Sparks, ed., Boston: Tappan, Whittemore, and Mason, 1836), 526.
77. David Barton, "The Founding Fathers on Creation and Evolution," *Wallbuilders*, 2008, http://www.wallbuilders.com/LIBissuesArticles.asp?id=7846#R8.
78. *Ibid.*
79. *Ibid.*
80. Charles Darwin, *The Autobiography of Charles Darwin, 1809-1882* (Nora Barlow, ed., London: Collins, 1958), 92–93.
81. Declaration of Independence.
82. John Locke, *Two Treatises of Government*, 278.
83. *Ibid.*, 279.
84. *Ibid.*
85. *Ibid.*, 280.
86. Samuel Adams, *Boston Gazette*, Feb. 27, 1769 (quoting Blackstone).
87. Adams and Franklin, "The Report of the Committee of Correspondence."
88. James Wilson, "Of the Natural Rights of Individuals," in *The Works of The Honorable James Wilson*, Vol. 2 (Bird Esquire, ed., Philadelphia: Lorenzo Press, 1804), 496.
89. Alexander Hamilton, "A Full Vindication," Dec. 15, 1774, in *The Works of Alexander Hamilton*, Vol. 1 (Henry Cabot Lodge, ed., New York: G.P. Putnam's Sons, 1904), 12.
90. John Adams, *Boston Gazette*, Sep. 5, 1763, in *The Works of John Adams* (Charles F. Adams, ed., 1851), 438.
91. John Locke, *Two Treatises of Government*, 280.
92. *Ibid.*
93. *Ibid.*, 281.
94. Montesquieu, *The Spirit of the Laws*, 133.
95. *Ibid.*
96. St. George Tucker, *William Blackstone's Commentaries with Notes*, Vol. 5, 66.
97. *Ibid.*, 67.
98. *Ibid.*, 68.
99. *Ibid.*
100. *Ibid.*
101. *Ibid.*, 71.
102. John Witherspoon, "Speech to Congress," Jan. 8, 1778, in *American eloquence: a collection of speeches and addresses*, Vol. 1 (Frank Moore, ed., New York: Appleton and Company, 1857), 300.
103. Thomas Jefferson, "Letter to George Washington," Apr. 28, 1793, in *The Works of Thomas Jefferson* (New York: Cosimo, Inc., 2009) (1904), 285–86.
104. *Ibid.*, 286.
105. *Ibid.*
106. *Ibid.*
107. George Washington, "First Annual Message to Congress," Jan. 8, 1790.
108. Benjamin Franklin, "Letter to Thomas Cushing," Jan. 5, 1773, in *Memoirs of Benjamin Franklin* (Philadelphia: McCarty & Davis, 1834), 281.
109. Benjamin Franklin, "Paper on the Present States of the Province of Pennsylvania," in *Poor Richard Day by Day* (Philadelphia: George W. Jacobs, 1917), 102.
110. Thomas Jefferson, "Letter to James Monroe," Jul. 11, 1790, in *The Jefferson Cyclopedia* (John P. Foley, ed., Funk & Wagnalls, 1900), 685.
111. Thomas Paine, "Rights of Man," in *Common Sense, Rights of Man, and Other Essential Writings of Thomas Paine*, 266.
112. St. George Tucker, *William Blackstone's Commentaries with Notes*, Vol. 1, 4 Appendix Note A.
113. Declaration of Independence.

CHAPTER 2 – ON AMERICAN GOVERNMENT

1. Charles de Montesquieu, *The Spirit of the Laws* (Franz Neumann ed., Hafner Press, 1949) (1748), 126.
2. *Ibid.*
3. Alexander Hamilton, James Madison, and John Jay, *The Federalist Papers* (Bantam Classic 2003) (1787–88), 267.
4. *Ibid.*, 77.
5. *Ibid.*, 283–84.
6. *Ibid.*, 181 (emphasis in original).
7. Thomas Jefferson, "Letter to Joseph C. Cabell," 1816, in Joseph Story, *Commentaries on the Constitution of the United States*, Vol. 1 (Boston: Little Brown and Company, 1873), 194.
8. U.S. Constitution, Article II, § 1.
9. U.S. Constitution, Article I, § 3. This process was changed by the Seventeenth Amendment to popular election.
10. Hamilton, Madison, and Jay, *The Federalist Papers*, 282.
11. *Ibid.*
12. *Ibid.*, 49.
13. *Ibid.*, 96.
14. *Ibid.*
15. *Ibid.*, 281.
16. *Ibid.*, 280.
17. Alexander Hamilton, "Speech on the Constitution Resumed," Jun. 21, 1788, *The Works of Alexander Hamilton*, Vol. 2 (New York: Haskell House Publishers, 1904), 28.
18. Hamilton, Madison, and Jay, *The Federalist Papers*, 162–63.
19. *Ibid.*, 180.
20. *Ibid.*, 163.
21. *Ibid.*, 285–86.
22. Montesquieu, *The Spirit of the Laws*, 150.
23. James Madison, "Speech to the Virginia State Convention," in *Debates of the Virginia State Convention of 1829-30* (Richmond: Ritchie & Cook, 1830), 537.
24. Hamilton, Madison, and Jay, *The Federalist Papers*, 317.
25. Montesquieu, *The Spirit of the Laws*, 152.
26. *Ibid.*
27. *Ibid.*
28. John Locke, *Two Treatises of Government* (Peter Laslett ed., Cambridge University Press, 2008) (1698), 355–56.
29. U.S. Constitution, Article I, § 1 (emphasis added).
30. Alexander Hamilton, "The Farmer Refuted," in *The Papers of Alexander Hamilton*, Vol. 1 (Harold C. Syrett, ed., New York: Columbia University Press, 1961), 87 (quoting William Blackstone, *Commentaries on the Laws of England* (Philadelphia: Robert Bell, 1771)).
31. James Wilson, "Of the General Principles of Law and Obligation," in *The Works of the Honorable James Wilson*, Vol. 1 (Bird Wilson, ed., Philadelphia: Lorenzo Press, 1804), 104–05.
32. Rufus King, "Letter to C. Gore," Feb. 17, 1820, in *The Life and Correspondence of Rufus King*, Vol. 6 (Charles R. King, ed., New York: G. P. Putnam's Sons, 1900), 276.
33. Thomas Jefferson, "Note on Crimes Bill," 1779, in *The Jefferson Cyclopedia* (John P. Foley, ed., Funk & Wagnalls, 1900), 486.
34. Robin v. Hardaway, General Court of Virginia, Apr. 1772.
35. Samuel Adams and Benjamin Franklin, "The Report of the Committee of Correspondence to the Boston Town Meeting," Nov. 20, 1772.
36. Theophilus Parsons, "On the Adoption of the Federal Constitution," Jan. 9, 1788, in *Debates and Proceedings in the Convention of the Commonwealth of Massachusetts*, Vol. 2 (Boston: William White, 1856), 265.
37. Locke, *Two Treatises of Government*, 360.
38. *Ibid.*, 363.
39. Benjamin Franklin, "Emblematical Representations," in *The Works of Benjamin Franklin*, Vol. 4 (Jared Sparks, ed., Boston: Hilliard, Gray, and Company, 1837), 457 (emphasis in original).

40. Benjamin Rush, "Letter to David Ramsay," 1788, in *The Letters of Benjamin Rush*, Vol. 1 (L. H. Butterfield, ed., Princeton: Princeton University Press for the American Philosophical Society, 1951) 454.
41. Hamilton, Madison, and Jay, *The Federalist Papers*, 349.
42. U.S. Constitution, Article I, § 2.
43. U.S. Constitution, Article I, § 8.
44. U.S. Constitution, Article I, § 9.
45. Hamilton, Madison, and Jay, *The Federalist Papers*, 349–50.
46. Locke, *Two Treatises of Government*, 364–65.
47. U.S. Constitution, Article II, § 3.
48. U.S. Constitution, Article II, § 3.
49. U.S. Constitution, Article II, § 1.
50. Locke, *Two Treatises of Government*, 375.
51. *Ibid.*, 377.
52. U.S. Senate, Reports, Committee on Foreign Relations, vol. 8, p. 24. (Feb. 15, 1816).
53. U.S. Constitution, Article II, § 1.
54. Hamilton, Madison, and Jay, *The Federalist Papers*, 420 (emphasis in original).
55. St. George Tucker, *William Blackstone's Commentaries with Notes*, Vol. 1 (Philadelphia: William Young Birch and Abraham Small, 1803), 62.
56. Montesquieu, *The Spirit of the Laws*, 75.
57. Hamilton, Madison, and Jay, *The Federalist Papers*, 478 (emphasis in original).
58. *Ibid.*, 472.
59. *Ibid.*, 324.
60. *Ibid.*, 476.
61. *Ibid.*, 477.
62. *Ibid.*, 473, 475.
63. Eugene W. Hickok, Jr., "Introduction," in *The Bill of Rights: Original Meaning and Current Understanding*, Vol. 1 (Eugene W. Hickok, Jr. ed., University Press of Virginia, 1999), 1.
64. James Madison, "Speech in Congress," Jun. 8, 1789, in *Selected Writings of James Madison* (Ralph Ketcham, ed., Hackett Publishing Company Inc., 2006) 170.
65. Hamilton, Madison, and Jay, *The Federalist Papers*, 225.
66. *Ibid.*, 224.
67. *Ibid.*, 523.
68. *Ibid.*
69. *Ibid.*
70. *Ibid.*, 523–24.
71. *Ibid.*, 524.
72. *Ibid.*
73. *Ibid.*
74. *Ibid.*, 524–25.
75. U.S. Constitution, Amendment I.
76. U.S. Constitution, Amendment II.
77. U.S. Constitution, Amendment IV.
78. James Madison, "Speech Introducing Bill of Rights," Jun 8, 1789, in *The Bill of Rights: Original Meaning and Current Understanding*, Vol. 1 (Eugene W. Hickok, Jr. ed., University Press of Virginia, 1999), 438.
79. U.S. Constitution, Amendment IX.
80. U.S. Constitution, Amendment X.
81. Herman Vandenburg Ames, *The Proposed Amendments to the Constitution of the United States*, Vol. 2 (Washington: Government Printing Office, 1897), 185.
82. Akhil Reed Amar, *The Bill of Rights as a Constitution*, 100 Yale L.J. 1131, 1153 (1991).
83. *Ibid.*
84. U.S. Constitution, Amendment I.
85. Amar, *The Bill of Rights as a Constitution*, 100 Yale L.J. 1131, 1152.
86. James Wilson, *The Works of the Honorable James Wilson*, Vol. 2 (Bird Wilson, ed., Philadelphia: Lorenzo Press, 1804), 454.
87. Hamilton, Madison, and Jay, *The Federalist Papers*, 3.

CHAPTER 3 – ON AMERICAN MORES

1. James Madison, "Letter to Littleton Dennis Teackle," Mar. 29, 1826, in *Letters and Other Writings of James Madison*, Vol. 3 (Philadelphia: J.B. Lippencott & Co., 1865) 523.
2. James Madison, "Letter to W.T. Barry," Aug. 4, 1822, in *Our Sacred Honor* (William J. Bennett, ed., Simon & Schuster, 1997) 258.
3. John Adams, *The Political Writings of John Adams* (George A. Peek, Jr., ed., Hackett Publishing Co., 2003), 103.
4. Benjamin Franklin, "Proposals Relating to the Education of Youth in Pennsylvania," 1749, in *Selections from the Writings of Benjamin Franklin* (U. Waldo Cutler, ed., New York: Thomas Y. Crowell & Co., 1905), 53.
5. Thomas Jefferson, "Letter to Hugh L. White," 1810, in *The Jefferson Cyclopedia* (John P. Foley, ed., Funk & Wagnalls, 1900), 275.
6. James Wilson, "Of the Study of the Law in the United States," 1790, in *The Quotable Founding Fathers* (Buckner F. Milton, Jr., ed., New England Publishing Associates, 2004), 163.
7. James Madison, "Memorial and Remonstrance," 1785, in *Encyclopedia of Religion in American Politics* (Jeffrey D. Schultz, John G. West, and Iain Maclean, ed., The Oryx Press, 1999), 280.
8. Thomas Jefferson, "Rights of British America," 1774, in *The Jefferson Cyclopedia*, 500.
9. Thomas Jefferson, "Notes on Virginia," 1782, in *The Jefferson Cyclopedia*, 500.
10. Benjamin Franklin, "Motion for Prayers in the Constitutional Convention," 1787, in *A Political and Civil History of the United States of America*, Vol. 2 (Timothy Pitkin, ed., New Haven: Hezekiah Howe and Durrie & Peck, 1828), 246.
11. Thomas Paine, "A Discourse to the Society of Theophilanthropists at Paris," in *The Theological Works of Thomas Paine* (London: R. Carlile, 1824), 194.
12. *Ibid.*, 196.
13. *Ibid.*, 199.
14. *Ibid.*, 194.
15. *Ibid.*, 196.
16. *Ibid.*, 197.
17. John Locke, *Two Treatises of Government* (Peter Laslett ed., Cambridge University Press, 2008) (1698), 309.
18. *Ibid.*, 305.
19. *Ibid.*
20. *Ibid.*, 309.
21. John Adams, "Letter to Abigail Adams," Oct. 29, 1775, in *Letters of John Adams, Addressed to his Wife*, Vol. 1 (Charles Francis Adams, ed., Boston: Charles C. Little and James Brown, 1841), 73.
22. Thomas Jefferson, "Letter to Colonel Charles Yancy," Jan. 6, 1816, in *The Quotable Founding Fathers* (Buckner F. Milton, Jr., ed., New England Publishing Associates, 2004), 104.
23. Noah Webster, "On the Education of Youth in America, 1788, in *The Quotable Founding Fathers*, 70.
24. *Ibid.*
25. George Washington, "Letter to the Commissioners of the Federal District," Jan. 28, 1795, in *The Writings of George Washington*, Vol. 11 (Jared Sparks, ed., Boston: Russell, Shattuck, and Williams, 1836), 14.
26. St. George Tucker, *William Blackstone's Commentaries with Notes*, Vol. 1 (Philadelphia: William Young Birch and Abraham Small, 1803), xvii.
27. Alexis de Tocqueville, *Democracy in America* (The Library of America, 2004) (1835), 351–52.
28. *Ibid.*, 331.
29. *Ibid.*, 270.
30. *Ibid.*, 68.
31. *Ibid.*, 315–16.
32. *Ibid.*, 350–51.
33. *Ibid.*, 352.
34. *Ibid.*
35. Virginia Declaration of Rights, 1776.
36. Richard Henry Lee, "Letter to Colonel Mortin Pickett," Mar. 5, 1786, in *The Letters of Richard Henry Lee*, Vol. 2 (James Curtis Ballagh, ed., New York: The MacMillan Company, 1914), 411.

37. Samuel Adams, in William V. Wells, *The Life and Public Services of Samuel Adams*, Vol. 1 (Boston: Little, Brown, and Company, 1865), 22.

38. *Ibid.*

39. James Madison, "Speech to Virginia Ratifying Convention" (Elliot's *Debates*, 3.537), in Alexander Hamilton, James Madison, and John Jay, *The Federalist Papers* (Bantam Classic 2003) (1787–88), xxiii.

40. Benjamin Franklin, "Letter to Samuel Johnson," Aug. 23, 1750, in *The Works of Benjamin Franklin*, Vol. 7 (Jared Sparks, ed., London: Benjamin Franklin Stevens, 1882), 48.

41. Noah Webster, "On the Education of Youth in America," 1788, in *The Quotable Founding Fathers*, 320.

42. George Washington, "Letter to George Steptoe Washington," December 5, 1790, in *Our Country's Founders* (William J. Bennett, ed., Aladdin Paperbacks, 1998), 142.

43. George Washington, "First Inaugural Address," Apr. 30, 1789.

44. John Adams, "Letter to Mercy Warren," 1776, in *Warren-Adams Letters*, Vol. 1 (Massachusetts Historical Society, 1917), 222.

45. Samuel Adams, "Letter to James Warren," 1775, in *The Quotable Founding Fathers*, 143.

46. Benjamin Franklin, "Letter to Messrs. The Abbes Chalut and Arnaud," Apr. 17, 1787, in *The Writings of Benjamin Franklin*, Vol. 10 (Jared Sparks, ed., Boston: Tappan, Whittemore and Mason, 1840), 297.

47. John Witherspoon, "The Dominion of Providence Over the Passions of Men," May 17, 1776, in *The Selected Writings of John Witherspoon* (Thomas Miller, ed., Southern Illinois University, 1990), 144.

48. Thomas Jefferson, *Notes on the State of Virginia* (London: Burlington-House, 1837), 275.

49. Hamilton, Madison, and Jay, *The Federalist Papers*, 342.

50. Samuel Adams, "Letter to James Warren," Feb. 12, 1779.

51. George Washington, "Letter to Marquis de Lafayette," Feb. 7, 1788, in *The Writings of George Washington*, Vol. 9 (Jared Sparks, ed., Boston: Russell, Odiorne, and Metcalf, and Hilliard, Gray, and Co., 1835), 318.

52. Benjamin Rush, "On the Mode of Education Proper in a Republic," 1798, in *Our Sacred Honor* (William J. Bennett, ed., Simon & Schuster, 1997), 412.

53. Gouveneur Morris, "Notes on the Form of a Constitution for France," in *The Life of Gouverneur Morris*, Vol. 3 (Jared Sparks, ed., Boston: Gray and Bowen, 1832), 483.

54. St. George Tucker, *William Blackstone's Commentaries with Notes*, Vol. 1, 42.

55. Benjamin Franklin, "Letter to Thomas Paine," in Jared Sparks, *The Works of Benjamin Franklin*, Vol. 10 (Jared Sparks, ed., Boston: Tappan, 1844), 282.

56. *Ibid.*

57. *Ibid.*

58. John Adams, "Letter to Zabdiel Adams," Jun. 21, 1776, in *The Works of John Adams*, Vol. 9 (Charles Francis Adams, ed., Boston: Little, Brown, 1854), 401.

59. George Washington, "Farewell Address," 1796.

60. Samuel Adams, *Boston Gazette*, Oct. 5, 1772, in *The Writings of Samuel Adams*, Vol. 2 (The Echo Library, 2006), 1999.

61. Gouverneur Morris, "An Inaugural Discourse Delivered Before the New York Historical Society," Sep. 4, 1816, in *Collections of the New York Historical Society for the Year 1821* (New York: E. Bliss and E. White, 1821), 32, 34.

62. Robert Winthrop, "Either by the Bible or the Bayonet," May 28, 1849, in *Addresses and Speeches on Various Occasions* (Boston: Little, Brown & Co., 1852), 172.

63. James McHenry, "Address to the people of Maryland," in Bernard C. Steiner, *One Hundred and Ten Years of Bible Society Work in Maryland* (Maryland Bible Society, 1921), 14.

64. John Adams, "Diary entry dated Aug. 14, 1796," in *The Works of John Adams*, Vol. 3 (Charles Francis Adams, ed., Boston: Charles C. Little and James Brown, 1851), 423.

65. James Wilson, "Of the General Principles of Law and Obligation," in *The Works of the Honourable James Wilson*, Vol. 1 (Bird Wilson, ed., Philadelphia: Bronson and Chauncey, 1804), 106.

66. John Jay, "Message from the Governor," Nov. 4, 1800, in *Messages from the Governors*, Vol. 2 (J.B. Lyon Company, State Printers, 1909), 467.

67. Abraham Baldwin, "Franklin College Charter," in Charles C. Jones, *Biographical Sketches of the Delegates from Georgia to the Continental Congress* (Boston: Houghton, Mifflin, and Company, 1891), 6–7.

68. Charles Carroll, "Letter to James McHenry," Nov. 4, 1800, in Bernard C. Steiner, *The Life and Correspondence of James McHenry* (Cleveland: The Burrows Brothers, 1907), 475.

69. Jedidiah Morse, "A Sermon Exhibiting the Present Dangers and Consequent Duties of the Citizens of the United States of America," Apr. 25, 1799, in Jedidiah Mores, *The Day of the National Fast* (Massachusetts: Printed by Samuel Etheridge, 1799), 9.

70. Fisher Ames, "Eulogy on Washington," Feb. 8, 1800, *Works of Fisher Ames* (Boston:T. B. Watt & Co., 1809), 127.

71. Henry Laurens, "Letter to Oliver Hart and Elharon Winchester," Mar. 30, 1776, *The Papers of Henry Laurens*, Vol. 11 (George C. Rogers Jr. and David R. Chestnutt, eds., Columbia: University of South Carolina Press, 1988), 200.

72. John Hancock, "Inaugural Address as Governor of Massachusetts," 1780, in Abram English Brown, *John Hancock, His Book* (Boston: Lee and Shepard, 1898), 269.

73. John Adams, "Letter to the Officers of the First Brigade of the Third Division of the Militia of Massachusetts," Oct. 11, 1798, *The Works of John Adams, Second President of the United States*, Vol. 9 (Charles Francis Adams, ed., Boston: Little, Brown, and Co. 1854), 229.

74. Maryland Constitution, Part I, Article III (amended by Article XI).

75. Delaware Constitution, Article I § 1.

76. New Hampshire Constitution, Articles V and VI (amended 1968).

77. Connecticut Constitution, Article I § 1.

78. Vermont Constitution, Chapter I, Article III.

79. Virginia Constitution, Article I § 16.

80. New Jersey Constitution, Article XIX.

81. South Carolina Constitution, Article XXXVIII (reconstituted 1895).

82. Maryland Constitution, Article XXXIII (reconstituted 1864).

83. Maryland Constitution, Article XXXV (reconstituted 1864).

84. North Carolina Constitution, Article XXII (reconstituted 1868).

85. Richard Dobbs Spaight, Jul. 30, 1788 in *The Debates in the Several State Conventions on the Adoption of the Federal Constitution*, Vol. 4 (J. Elliot, ed., Washington, 1836), 208.

86. James Madison, "Statement at the Virginia Ratifying Convention," in Alonzo Trevier Jones, *The Rights of the People* (Oakland: Pacific Press Publishing Co., 1895), 112.

87. U.S. Constitution, Amendment I.

88. Thomas Jefferson, "Letter to Danbury Baptist Association," Jan. 1, 1802, http://www.usconstitution.net/jeffwall.html.

89. Thomas Jefferson, "Letter to Samuel Miller," 1808, in *The Jefferson Cyclopedia*, 742.

90. Thomas Jefferson, "Letter to Thomas Cooper," 1822, in *Jefferson Himself* (Bernard Mayo, ed., University Press of Virginia, 1970), 323.

91. Tocqueville, *Democracy in America*, 340.

92. *Ibid.*

93. *Ibid.*, 343.

94. *Ibid.*

95. *Ibid.*, 343–44.

96. *Ibid.*, 345.

97. *Ibid.*, 47.

98. *Ibid.*, 61.

99. *Ibid.*, 336.

100. *Ibid.*, 338.

101. *Ibid.*, 456.

102. *Ibid.*, 338.

103. *Ibid.*, 49.

104. *Ibid.*

105. *Ibid.*, 338.

106. *Ibid.*

107. *Ibid.*

108. *Ibid.*, 338 n. 3.

109. *Ibid.*, 338.

110. *Ibid.*, 338–39.
111. *Ibid.*, 338.
112. *Ibid.*
113. *Ibid.*, 341 n.4.
114. *Ibid.*, 349.
115. *Ibid.*, 351.
116. *Ibid.*, 502.
117. *Ibid.*, 504.
118. *Ibid.*
119. *Ibid.*, 508.
120. *Ibid.*, 335.
121. *Ibid.*, 334.
122. *Ibid.*, 332.
123. *Ibid.*, 332–33.
124. *Ibid.*, 333.
125. *Ibid.*
126. *Ibid.*, 335.
127. *Ibid.*, 641.
128. *Ibid.*, 639.
129. *Ibid.*, 639–40.
130. Hamilton, Madison, and Jay, *The Federalist Papers*, 316.
131. Tocqueville, *Democracy in America*, 640.
132. *Ibid.*, 502.
133. *Ibid.*, 502–03.
134. *Ibid.*, 503.
135. *Ibid.*
136. *Ibid.*
137. *Ibid.*, 336.
138. *Ibid.*, 356.

CHAPTER 4 – ON POPULAR CONSTITUTIONALISM

1. U.S. Constitution, Preamble (emphasis added).
2. Alexander Hamilton, James Madison, and John Jay, *The Federalist Papers* (Bantam Classic 2003) (1787–88), 215.
3. Thomas Jefferson, "Letter to Wilson Nicholas," 1803, in *The Jefferson Cyclopedia* (John P. Foley, ed., Funk & Wagnalls, 1900), 190.
4. St. George Tucker, *William Blackstone's Commentaries with Notes*, Vol. 1 (Philadelphia: William Young Birch and Abraham Small, 1803), 61 (emphasis in original).
5. James Wilson, "Of the Study of Law in the United States," in *The Works of the Honorable James Wilson*, Vol. 1 (Bird Wilson, ed., Philadelphia: Lorenzo Press, 1804), 14.
6. Thomas Jefferson, "Letter to Albert Gallatin," 1808, in *The Real Thomas Jefferson* (Andrew M. Allison, ed.), 511.
7. Thomas Jefferson, "Reply to Address," Mar. 1801, in *The Jefferson Cyclopedia*, 193 (emphasis added).
8. Thomas Jefferson, "Letter to William Johnson," 1823, in *The Jefferson Cyclopedia*, 844.
9. James Madison, "Letter to Henry Lee," Jun. 15, 1824, in *Advice to my country* (David M. Battern, ed., University Press of Virginia, 1997), 34–35.
10. St. George Tucker, *William Blackstone's Commentaries with Notes*, Vol. 1, Appendix, 154.
11. *Ibid.*
12. Thomas Jefferson, "Letter to Wilson Nicholas," 1803, in *The Jefferson Cyclopedia*, 190.
13. National Mut. Ins. Co. v. Tidewater Transfer Co., 337 U.S. 582, 646 (1949) (dissenting opinion).
14. Poe v. Ullman, 367 U.S. 497, 542 (1961) (dissenting opinion).
15. U.S. Constitution, Article V.
16. George Washington, "Farewell Address," 1796.
17. Hamilton, Madison, and Jay, *The Federalist Papers*, 472–73.
18. *Ibid.*, 473 n.1.
19. *Ibid.*, 493–94.

20. *Ibid.*, 494.
21. Thomas Jefferson, "Letter to Charles Hammond," 1821, in *Proceedings of the . . . annual meeting*, Vol. 23 (John B. Minor, ed., Richmond Press, 1910), 243.
22. Thomas Jefferson, "Letter to A. Coray," in *The Jefferson Cyclopedia*, 449.
23. U.S. Constitution, Preamble.
24. Thomas Jefferson, "Letter to William Charles Jarvis," Sep. 28, 1820, in *The Writings of Thomas Jefferson*, Vol. 10 (Paul Leicester Ford, ed., 1898), 161.
25. Hamilton, Madison, and Jay, *The Federalist Papers*, 187.
26. *Ibid.*, 276.
27. An Act for the Punishment of Certain Crimes against the United States; ch. 74, 1 Stat. 596 (Jul. 14, 1798).
28. U.S. Constitution, Amendment I.
29. Thomas Jefferson, "The Anas," in *The Writings of Thomas Jefferson*, Vol. 1 (Paul Leicester Ford, ed., New York: G.P. Putnams's Sons, 1892), 165–66.
30. Bruce Miroff, "Alexander Hamilton: The Aristocrat as Visionary," *International Political Science Review*, Vol. 9, No. 1 (Jan. 1988), 43–49.
31. *Ibid.*, 47.
32. Nathanael Emmons, "Obedience to Civil Magistrates," Apr. 25, 1799, in *The Works of Nathanael Emmons*, Vol. 2 (Jacob Ide, ed., Boston: Crocker & Brewster, 1842), 135.
33. Nathaniel Emmons, "A Discourse Delivered on the National Fast," 1799, in *American Political Writing during the Founding Era*, Vol. 2 (Charles S. Hyneman and Donald S. Lutz, eds., 1983), 1027.
34. *Ibid.*
35. Emmons, "Obedience to Civil Magistrates," in *The Works of Nathanael Emmons*, Vol. 2, 135.
36. William Cocke, in *Annals of Congress*, Vol. 2 (Jan. 1802), 75.
37. John Randolph, in *Annals of Congress*, Vol. 2 (Jan. 1802), 661.
38. James Madison, "Letter to Mr. ___," 1834, in *Letters and Other Writings of James Madison*, Vol. 4 (Philadelphia: J. B. Lippencott & Co., 1865), 349–50.
39. James Madison, "Speech to the House of Representatives on the Removal Power of the President," in *The Papers of James Madison*, Vol. 12 (Robert A. Rutland et al., eds., 1975), 238.
40. James Madison, "Report on the Alien and Sedition Acts," Jan. 7, 1802, in *James Madison, Writings* (Jack Rakove, ed., Library of America, 1999), 613–14.
41. John Bacon, in *Annals of Congress*, Vol. 2 (Jan. 1802), 983.
42. Thomas Jefferson, "Letter to Abigail Adams," 1804, in *The Writings of Thomas Jefferson*, Vol. 8 (Paul Leicester Ford ed., 1897), 310.
43. Thomas Jefferson, "Letter to William Charles Jarvis," Sep. 28, 1820, in *The Writings of Thomas Jefferson*, Vol. 10 (Paul Leicester Ford, ed., 1898), 161.
44. *Ibid.*, 160.
45. *Ibid.*, 161.
46. The Kentucky Resolution of Nov. 16, 1798.
47. The Virginia Resolution of Dec. 24, 1798.
48. *Ibid.*
49. Thomas Jefferson, "Letter to Spencer Roane," in *The Jefferson Cyclopedia*, 741.
50. Nathanial Macon, in *Annals of Congress*, Vol. 2 (Jan. 1802), 717.
51. "Report on the Alien and Sedition Acts," in *James Madison: Writings*, (Jack Rakove, ed., Library of America, 1999), 614.
52. The Judiciary Act of 1801, 2. Stat. 89, Feb. 13, 1801.
53. *Ibid.*
54. James M. O'Fallon, *Marbury*, 44 Stan L. Rev. 219, 241–42 (1992).
55. *Ibid.*, 242.
56. *Ibid.*
57. Larry D. Kramer, *The People Themselves* (Oxford University Press, 2004), 124.
58. *Ibid.*
59. Marbury v. Madison, 5 U.S. 137, 168, 173 (1803).
60. Kramer, *The People Themselves*, 127.
61. Marbury v. Madison, 5 U.S. 137, 180 (emphasis added).
62. *Ibid.*, 177.

63. Thomas Jefferson, "Letter to William C. Jarvis," Sep. 20, 1820, in *The Writings of Thomas Jefferson*, Vol. 15 (Andrew A. Lipscomb and Albert Bergh, eds., 1904), 277–78.
64. *Ibid.*
65. *Ibid.*
66. Thomas Jefferson, "Letter to Spencer Roane," Sep. 6, 1819, in *The Writings of Thomas Jefferson*, Vol. 15, 213.
67. G. Edward White, *The Marshall Court and Cultural Change, 1815–1835* (abr. Ed. 1988), 119.
68. Thomas Jefferson, "Letter to George Hay," Jun. 2, 1807, in *The Writings of Thomas Jefferson*, Vol. 9 (Paul Leicester Ford, ed., G. P. Putnam's Sons, 1898), 53–54.
69. Alexis de Tocqueville, *Democracy in America* (The Library of America, 2004) (1835), 307.
70. *Ibid.*, 308.
71. Hamilton, Madison, and Jay, *The Federalist Papers*, 307.
72. *Ibid.*, 316.
73. U.S. Constitution, Article I, § 8.
74. Thomas Jefferson, "Opinion Against the Constitutionality of the National Bank," Feb. 5, 1791, in *Writings of Thomas Jefferson*, Vol. 3 (H.A. Washington, ed., New York: Riker, Thorne, & Co., 1854), 556.
75. The Kentucky Resolution of Nov. 16, 1798.
76. Hamilton, Madison, and Jay, *The Federalist Papers*, 187.
77. *Ibid.*, 186 (emphasis in original).
78. *Ibid.*
79. *Ibid.*
80. Thomas Jefferson, "Letter to William Johnson," Oct. 27, 1822, in *The Jefferson Cyclopedia*, 675.
81. Kramer, *The People Themselves*, 194.
82. Martin Van Buren, "Observations in the Senate on Mr. Foote's Amendment," Feb. 12, 1828, in *The Life and Political Opinions of Martin Van Buren* (William M. Holland, ed., Hartford, Belknap & Hamersley 1836), 281–82.
83. Richard E. Ellis, *The Union at Risk* (New York: Oxford Univ. Press, 1987), 13–14.
84. *Ibid.*, 17–18.
85. *Ibid.*, 19.
86. *Ibid.*, 13–14.
87. Daniel Feller, "King Andrew and the Bank," *Humanities*, Vol. 29, No. 1 (Jan./Feb. 2008).
88. *Ibid.*
89. Andrew Jackson, "State of the Union Address," Dec. 8, 1829.
90. Feller, "King Andrew and the Bank."
91. McCulloch v. Maryland, 17 U.S. 316, 401 (1819).
92. *Ibid.*, 421.
93. *Ibid.*, 413–14 (emphasis added).
94. Hamilton, Madison, and Jay, *The Federalist Papers*, 187.
95. James Madison, *The Virginia Report of 1800*.
96. Spencer Roane, "Hampden," in *John Marshall's Defense of McCulloch v. Maryland* (Gerald Gunther, ed., Stanford: Stanford Univ. Press, 1969) 110.
97. Feller, "King Andrew and the Bank."
98. *Ibid.*
99. *Ibid.*
100. Andrew Jackson, "Veto Message," Jul. 10, 1832.
101. *Ibid.*
102. *Ibid.*
103. McCulloch v. Maryland, 17 U.S. 316, 423.
104. Jackson, "Veto Message," (emphasis added).
105. *Ibid.*
106. Martin Van Buren, *Inquiry into the Origins and Course of Political Parties in the United States* (Hurd and Houghton, New York, 1867), 329.
107. *Ibid.*, 329–30.
108. *Ibid.*, 330.
109. *Ibid.*, 336.
110. *Ibid.*, 348.
111. *Ibid.*, 332 (quoting *The Federalist*, No. 48).

112. *Ibid.*, 332 (quoting *The Federalist*, No. 49).
113. *Ibid.*, 333 (quoting *The Federalist*, Nos. 78 and 81).
114. *Ibid.*, 333.
115. *Ibid.*, 336.
116. *Ibid.*
117. *Ibid.*
118. *Ibid.*, 335.
119. *Ibid.*, 351.
120. Jackson, "Veto Message."
121. *Summary Of The Proceedings Of A Convention Of Republican Delegates* (Albany: Packard and Van Benthuysen, 1832).
122. Feller, "King Andrew and the Bank."
123. *Congressional Record*, 106th Cong., 1st Sess. S1665 (Feb. 12, 1999).
124. Feller, "King Andrew and the Bank."
125. Francis Fisher Browne, *The Every-Day Life of Abraham Lincoln* (University of Nebraska Press 1995) (1887), 262.
126. Republican Platform of 1856.
127. Declaration of Independence.
128. Stephen A. Douglas, "Lincoln-Douglas Debates," in *Lincoln, Speeches and Writings 1832-1858* (Literary Classics of the United States, Inc., 1989), 399.
129. Benjamin Franklin, "Letter to the Rev. Dean Woodward," Apr. 10, 1773, in *The Works of Benjamin Franklin*, Vol. 8 (Jared Sparks, ed., Boston: Tappan, Whittemore, and Mason, 1839), 42.
130. George Washington, "Letter to Robert Morris," Apr. 12, 1786, in *George Washington: A Collection* (W.B. Allen, ed., Indianapolis: Liberty Fund, 1988), 319.
131. Thomas Jefferson, "Legal Argument," 1770, in *The Jefferson Cyclopedia*, 693 (emphasis added).
132. Luther Martin, "The Genuine Information Delivered to the Legislature of the State of Maryland Relative to the Proceedings of the General Convention Held at Philadelphia," in *Secret Proceedings and Debates of the Convention* (Cincinnati: Alston Mygatt, 1838), 64.
133. Benjamin Rush, 1794, in La Roy Sutherland, The Testimony of God Against Slavery, 2d ed. (Boston: Isaac Knapp,1836), 153.
134. Henry Laurens, "Letter to John Laurens," Aug. 14, 1776, in *Materials for History Printed From Original Manuscripts, the Correspondence of Henry Laurens of South Carolina* (Frank Moore, ed., New York: Zenger Club, 1861), 20.
135. George Mason, "Speech at the Constitutional Convention," Aug.21, 1787, in Kate Mason Rowland, *The Life of George Mason*, Vol. 2 (New York: G. P. Putnam's Sons, 1892), 160.
136. David Brion Davis, *Inhuman Bondage: The Rise and Fall of Slavery in the New World* (Oxford University Press, 2006), 124.
137. John Jay, "Letter to the English Anti-Slavery Society," Jun. 1788, in *The Correspondence and Public Papers of John Jay*, Vol. 3 (Henry P. Johnston, ed., New York: G. P. Putnam's Sons, 1891), 342.
138. Benjamin Franklin, "Letter to the Rev. Dean Woodward," Apr. 10, 1773, in *The Works of Benjamin Franklin*, Vol. 8, 42.
139. Thomas Jefferson, *The Writings of Thomas Jefferson*, Vol. 1 (Paul Leicester Ford, ed., New York: G. P. Putnam's Sons, 1892), 34.
140. *Ibid.*
141. George Mason, "Statement at the Virginia Ratifying Convention," Jun. 17, 1788, in George Bancroft, *History of the United States of America*, Vol. 6 (New York: D. Appleton and Co., 1884), 431.
142. Douglas Harper, "Slavery in the North," http://www.slavenorth.com/.
143. Colonel Tal. P. Shaffner, *The War in America* (London: Hamilton, Adams, and Co. 1862), 259.
144. Thomas Jefferson, "Letter to David Barrow," May 1, 1815, in *The Works of Thomas Jefferson*, Vol. 11 (Paul Leicester Ford, ed., New York and London: G. P. Putnam's Sons, 1905), 470–71.
145. Northwest Ordinance, Jul. 13, 1787.
146. U.S. Constitution, Article I, § 9.
147. U.S. Constitution, Article I, § 2.

148. James Madison, "Debate in the Virginia Convention," Jun. 17, 1788, in *The Records of the Federal Convention of 1787*, Vol. 3 (Max Farrand, ed., New Haven: Yale University Press, 1911), 324–25.

149. James Wilson, "Debate in the Pennsylvania Convention," Dec. 3, 1787, in *The Records of the Federal Convention of 1787*, Vol. 3, 161.

150. John Quincy Adams, *An Oration on the Sixty-First Anniversary of the Declaration of Independence* (1837), 50 (quoting *Jefferson's Writings*, Vol. 1, p. 40) (emphasis in original).

151. *The Collected Works of Abraham Lincoln*, Vol. 3 (The Abraham Lincoln Association, 1953), 18 (emphasis in original).

152. *Ibid.* (emphasis in original).

153. Republican Platform of 1856.

154. Harry v. Decker, 1 Miss. 36 (Miss. 1818); Rankin v. Lydia, 2 A. K. Marsh 467 (Ky. 1820); Wilson v. Melvin, 4 Mo. 592 (Mo. 1837).

155. Dred Scott v. Sandford, 60 U.S. 390, 404–05 (1857).

156. *Ibid.*, 404.

157. U.S. Constitution, Article 1, § 9.

158. Dred Scott v. Sandford, 60 U.S. 390, 450.

159. *Ibid.*, 452.

160. *Ibid.*, 410.

161. U.S. Constitution, Article IV, § 3.

162. *Political Debates between Abraham Lincoln and Stephen Douglas* (The Burrows Brothers Company, 1894), 11 (emphasis in original).

163. "Lincoln-Douglas Debates," in *The Writings of Abraham Lincoln*, Vol. 3 (Arthur Brooks Lapsley, ed., New York: G. P. Putnam's Sons, 1923), 33.

164. *Political Debates between Abraham Lincoln and Stephen Douglas*, 233.

165. *Ibid.*

166. *Ibid.*, 101 (emphasis in original).

167. *Ibid.* (emphasis in original).

168. *Ibid.*

169. Democratic Party Platform of 1860.

170. Abraham Lincoln, "Letter to H.L. Pierce and others," Apr. 6. 1859, in *Complete Works of Abraham Lincoln*, Vol. 5 (John G. Nicolay and John Hay, eds., The Lamb Publishing Company, New York, 1894), 125.

171. Abraham Lincoln, "Letter to H.L. Pierce and others," in *Complete Works of Abraham Lincoln*, Vol. 5, 126–27.

172. *Ibid.*, 126.

173. *Ibid.*, 127.

174. Republican Platform of 1860.

175. Abraham Lincoln, "First Inaugural Address," Mar. 4, 1861.

176. *Ibid.*

177. *Ibid.*

178. *Ibid.* (*quoting* U.S. Constitution, Article IV, § 2).

179. Robert Morgan, "The 'Great Emancipator' and the Issue of Race," *The Journal of Historical Review*, Sep.-Oct., 1993 (Vol. 13, No. 5), 4–25.

180. Abraham Lincoln, "Letter to Albert Hodges," Apr. 4, 1864, in Browne, *The Every-Day Life of Abraham Lincoln*, 551–52.

181. Lincoln, "First Inaugural Address."

182. *Ibid.*

183. Kramer, *The People Themselves*, 212.

184. *Ibid.*

185. Abraham Lincoln, "Gettysburg Address," Nov. 19, 1863, in Browne, *The Every-Day Life of Abraham Lincoln*, 604.

186. *Ibid.*

187. U.S. Constitution, Amendment XIV, § 1.

188. Declaration of Independence.

189. *Congressional Globe*, 38th Cong., 1st Sess. 1202 (1864).

190. John Jay, "Letter to Salmon P. Chase," Jan. 5, 1867, in *Diary and Correspondence of Salmon P. Chase*, Vol. 2 (Washington: Government Printing Office, 1903), 518.

191. J. H. Martindale, "Letter to John Sherman," May 12, 1866, in *Sherman Papers*.
192. Richard M. Valelly, *The Two Reconstructions: The Struggle for Black Enfranchisement* (University of Chicago Press, 2004), 29.
193. Reconstruction Acts, 39 Cong. Ch. 153, 14 Stat. 428 (Mar. 2, 1867); 40 Cong. Ch. 6, 15 Stat. 2 (Mar. 23, 1867); 40 Cong. Ch. 30, 15 Stat. 14 (Jul. 19, 1867); 40 Cong. Ch. 25, 15 Stat. 41 (Mar. 11, 1868). Tennessee was excluded from the Reconstruction Acts because it had already ratified the Fourteenth Amendment and was readmitted to the Union.
194. Reconstruction Acts, 39 Cong. Ch. 153, 14 Stat. 428 (Mar. 2, 1867).
195. *Ibid.*
196. *Ibid.*
197. *Ibid.*
198. William E. Nelson, *The Fourteenth Amendment* (Harvard University Press, 1988), 61.
199. Thaddeus Stevens, "Some Remarks on Reconstruction," Feb. 14, 1866, in *Stevens Papers* (emphasis in original).
200. Thaddeus Stevens, "Speech in Support of the Fourteenth Amendment," in Michael Kent Curtis, *No State Shall Abridge* (Duke University Press 1986), 86.
201. *Congressional Globe*, 39th Cong., 1st Sess., 2961 (Jun. 5, 1866).
202. *Congressional Globe*, 39th Cong., 1st Sess., 421 (1866).
203. Nelson, *The Fourteenth Amendment*, 143.
204. *Ibid.*, 8.
205. *The Selected Papers of Thaddeus Stevens*, Vol. 2 (Beverly Wilson Palmer & Holly Byers Ochoa, eds., University of Pittsburgh Press, 1998), 158.
206. *Congressional Globe*, 39th Cong., 1st Sess. 134 app. (1866).
207. "Civil Rights Bill," Charlestown *Virginia Free Press*, Apr. 19, 1866, p. 2, col. 1.
208. R. M. Patton, "Governor's Message," *Mobile Daily Advertiser and Register*, Nov. 13, 1866, p. 2, col. 8.
209. *Congressional Globe*, 39th Cong., 1st Sess. 1271 (1866).
210. "The Evils of Centralization," New York *Evening Post*, Dec. 6, 1865, p. 2, col. 1.
211. William Horatio Barnes, *History of the Thirty-ninth Congress of the United States* (New York: Harper & Brothers, 1868), 447–48.
212. *Congressional Globe*, 39th Cong., 1st Sess. 2542 (1866).
213. *Congressional Globe*, 39th Cong., 1st Sess. 1088 (1866).
214. *Congressional Globe*, 39th Cong., 2d Sess. 40 (1866).
215. *The Pending Canvass! Speech of the Hon. Thaddeus Stevens, delivered at Bedford, Pa., on Tuesday Evening, September 4, 1866* (Lancaster, Pa., 1866), 11.
216. Nelson, *The Fourteenth Amendment*, 115.
217. *Congressional Globe*, 39th Cong., 1st Sess. 1760-61 (1866).
218. "Civil Rights Bill," *The Right Way*, April 21, 1866, p. 1, col. 4–5.
219. *Ibid.*
220. Nelson, *The Fourteenth Amendment*, 110–11.
221. Hamilton, Madison, and Jay, *The Federalist Papers*, 284.
222. *Ibid.*, 162–63.
223. *Ibid.*, 180.
224. *Ibid.*, 163.
225. *Congressional Globe*, 39th Cong., 1st Sess. 1065 (1866).
226. *Ibid.*
227. *Ibid.*
228. Nelson, *The Fourteenth Amendment*, 112.
229. U.S. Constitution, Amendment XIV, § 1; The Slaughterhouse Cases, 83 U.S. 36 (1873).
230. Charles Rice, "The Bill of Rights and the Doctrine of Incorporation," in *The Bill of Rights: Original Meaning and Current Understanding* (Eugene W. Hickok, Jr. ed., University Press of Virginia 1999), 15.
231. U.S. Constitution, Amendment XIV, § 1.
232. *Ibid.*
233. The Slaughterhouse Cases, 83 U.S. 36, 114–15 (Bradley, dissenting).
234. *Ibid.*, 114 (Bradley, dissenting).
235. *Ibid.*, 116 (Bradley, dissenting).
236. *Ibid.*, 76 (quoting Corfield v. Coryell, 4 Wash. C.C. 371 (C.C.E.D.Pa. 1823)).

237. *Ibid.*
238. *Ibid.*, 77.
239. *Ibid.*, 78.
240. *Ibid.*
241. U.S. Constitution, Amendment XIV, § 5.
242. The Civil Rights Act of 1866, 14 Stat. 27, Apr. 9, 1866.
243. *Ibid.*
244. Thomas Jefferson, "Letter to Spencer Roane," Sep. 6, 1819, in *The Writings of Thomas Jefferson*, Vol. 15 (Andrew A. Lipscomb and Albert Bergh, eds., 1904), 213.
245. U.S. Constitution, Amendment XIV, § 1.
246. Alexander Hamilton, "Remarks on an Act for Regulating Elections," Feb. 6, 1787, in *The Works of Alexander Hamilton*, Vol. 8 (Henry Cabot Lodge, ed., New York: G. P. Putnam's Sons, 1904), 28.
247. Munn v. Illinois, 94 U.S. 113 (1877).
248. *Ibid.*
249. Allgeyer v. Louisiana, 165 U.S. 578, 589 (1897).
250. Lochner v. New York, 198 U.S. 45 (1905).
251. *Ibid.*, 56.
252. *Ibid.*, 57.
253. U.S. Constitution, Amendment V.
254. Theodore Roosevelt, *An Autobiography* (New York: Charles Scribner's Sons, 1920), 357.
255. 1912 Platform of the Progressive Party, Aug. 7, 1912.
256. Theodore Roosevelt, "A Charter for Democracy," Feb. 12, 1912, Ohio State Constitutional Convention, Columbus, OH.
257. *Ibid.*
258. *Ibid.*
259. *Ibid.*
260. "The Presidency: The Roosevelt Week," *Time*, Jul. 11, 1932.
261. Franklin D. Roosevelt, "Address on Constitution Day," Sep. 17, 1937.
262. *Ibid.* (emphasis added).
263. *Ibid.*
264. West Coast Hotel v. Parrish, 300 U.S. 379, 391 (1937).
265. *Ibid.*
266. United States v. Carolene Products, 304 U.S. 144, 152 (1938).
267. *Ibid.*, 152 n4.
268. U.S. Constitution, Amendment XIV, § 1.
269. Civil Rights Act of 1875, 18 Stat. 336 (1875).
270. Civil Rights Cases, 109 U.S. 3 (1883).
271. Plessy v. Ferguson, 163 U.S. 537 (1896).
272. Korematsu v. United States, 323 U.S. 214 (1944).
273. *Ibid.*, 216.
274. *Ibid.*
275. Neal Katyal, "Confession of Error: The Solicitor General's Mistakes During the Japanese-American Internment Cases," May 20, 2011.
276. *Ibid.*
277. Korematsu v. United States, 323 U.S. 214, 243 (Jackson, dissenting).
278. *Ibid.*, 246 (Jackson, dissenting).
279. *Ibid.*, 242 (Murphy, dissenting).
280. Barron v. Baltimore, 32 U.S. (7 Pet.) 243, 250 (1833).
281. United States v. Cruikshank, 92 U.S. 542, 551 (1875).
282. *Ibid.*, 552.
283. *Ibid.*, 554–55.
284. U.S. Constitution, Amendment I.
285. Gitlow v. New York, 268 U.S. 652, 666 (1925).
286. Near v. Minnesota, 283 U.S. 697, 707 (1931).
287. Everson v. Board of Education, 330 U.S. 1, 15 (1947).
288. *Ibid.*, 15–16.

289. Mapp v. Ohio, 367 U.S. 643 (1961) (incorporating the protection against unreasonable search and seizure); Ker v. California, 374 U.S. 23 (1963) (incorporating the standards for judging whether a search or seizure undertaken without a warrant was unreasonable); Aguilar v. Texas, 378 U.S. 108 (1964) (incorporating warrant requirements).
290. Malloy v. Hogan, 378 U.S. 1 (1964) (incorporating the privilege against self-incrimination); Benton v. Maryland, 395 U.S. 784 (1969) (incorporating the protection against double jeopardy).
291. Gideon v. Wainwright, 372 U.S. 335 (1963) (incorporating the right to assistance of counsel); Pointer v. Texas, 380 U.S. 400 (1965) (incorporating the right to confront adverse witnesses); Washington v. Texas, 388 U.S. 14 (1967) (incorporating the right to compulsory process to obtain witness testimony); Klopfer v. North Carolina, 386 U.S. 213 (1967) (incorporating the right to a speedy trial); Duncan v. Louisiana, 391 U.S. 145 (1968) (incorporating the right to trial by an impartial jury).
292. Robinson v. California, 370 U.S. 660 (1962).
293. Griswold v. Connecticut, 381 U.S. 479 (1965).
294. *Ibid.*, 484 (citation removed).
295. *Ibid.*, 482.
296. *Ibid.*, 484.
297. *Ibid.*, 485 (internal quotations removed).
298. *Ibid.*, 484.
299. *Ibid.*, 484 (1965 (citing U.S. Constitution, Amendment IX).
300. U.S. Constitution, Amendment X.
301. Roe v. Wade, 410 U.S. 113 (1973).
302. *Ibid.*, 153.
303. *Ibid.*, 155.
304. *Ibid.*, 159.
305. *Ibid.*, 162.
306. *Ibid.*
307. *Ibid.*, 163.
308. *Ibid.*
309. *Ibid.*
310. *Ibid.*, 163–64.
311. *Ibid.*, 164.
312. Planned Parenthood of Southeastern Pa. v. Casey, 505 U.S. 833, 846 (1992).
313. *Ibid.*
314. *Ibid.*
315. *Ibid.*, 878.
316. *Ibid.*
317. *Ibid.*, 893–94.
318. *Ibid.*, 849.
319. *Ibid.*, 857.
320. *Ibid.*, 877.
321. *Ibid.*, 851.
322. Lawrence v. Texas, 539 U.S. 558 (2003).
323. *Ibid.*, 562.
324. *Ibid.*, 565.
325. *Ibid.*, 573–74.
326. *Ibid.*, 578.
327. Bowers v. Hardwick, 478 U.S. 186, 196 (1986).
328. *Ibid.*
329. Lawrence v. Texas, 539 U.S. 558, 578.
330. *Ibid.*, 599 (Scalia, dissenting).
331. *Ibid.* (Scalia, dissenting).
332. Griswold v. Connecticut, 381 U.S. 479, 482.
333. McDonald v. Chicago, 561 U.S. ___ , 130 S.Ct. 3020 (2010).
334. Cooper v. Aaron, 358 U.S. 1 (1958).
335. *Ibid.*, 17–18 (1958) (citation omitted) (emphasis added).
336. James M. O'Fallon, *Marbury*, 44 Stan L. Rev. 219, 242 (1992).
337. Baker v. Carr, 369 U.S. 186, 211 (1962) (emphasis added).

338. United States v. Nixon, 418 U.S. 683, 705 (1974).
339. Goldwater v. Carter, 444 U.S. 996, 1001 (1979).
340. *Ibid.*
341. Thompson v. Oklahoma 487 U.S. 815, 833 n.40 (1988) (citation omitted).
342. Miller v. Johnson, 515 U.S. 900, 922-23 (1995) (citations omitted).
343. United States v. Morrison, 529 U.S. 598, 616 n.7 (2000) (citations omitted).
344. Tocqueville, *Democracy in America*, 307.
345. *Ibid.*
346. *Ibid.*, 308.
347. Franklin D. Roosevelt, "Address on Constitution Day," Sep. 17, 1937.
348. J. M. Balkin, "Populism and Progressivism as Constitutional Categories," 104 *Yale L.J.* 1935, 1951 (1995).
349. Roberto Mangbeira Unger, *What Should Legal Analysis Become?* (1996), 72.
350. *Ibid.*, 73.
351. James Madison, "Who are the Best Keepers of the People's Liberties?" *The National Gazette*, Dec. 20, 1792.
352. Van Buren, *Inquiry into the Origin and Course of Political Parties in the United States*, 352.
353. Colorado v. Connelly, 474 U.S. 1050, 1053 (1986) (emphasis added, quotations omitted) (quoting Florida v. Meyers, 446 U.S. 380, 387 (Stevens, dissenting)).
354. Boumediene v. Bush, 553 U.S. 723 (2008).
355. *Ibid.*, 808–42 (Scalia, dissenting) (characterizing the Court's opinion as a "bait-and-switch" for its abrupt departure from prior case law).
356. *Ibid.*, 765–66.
357. *Ibid.*, 765.
358. *Ibid.*, 842 (Scalia, dissenting).
359. *Ibid.*, 843 (Scalia, dissenting).
360. "Ruling may delay war crimes trials," *Chicago Tribune*, Jun. 13, 2008.
361. *Originalism: A Quarter-Century of Debate* (Stevent G. Calabresi, ed., Regnery Publishing Inc., 2007), 343.
362. Anthony Lewis, "Law or Power?" *New York Times*, Oct. 27, 1986, A23.
363. Edwin Meese III, "The Tulane Speech: What I Meant," *Washington Post*, Nov. 13, 1986, A21.
364. Kramer, *The People Themselves*, 227–28
365. Patrick Leahy, "Speech to the Senate on the Supreme Court," Feb. 28, 2001, http://www.c-spanvideo.org/videoLibrary/clip.php?appid=596375494.
366. *Ibid.*
367. Thomas Jefferson, "Letter to Abigail Adams," 1804, in *The Writings of Thomas Jefferson*, Vol. 8 (Paul Leicester Ford ed., 1897), 310.
368. James Madison, "Speech to the House of Representatives on the Removal Power of the President," in *The Papers of James Madison*, Vol. 12 (Robert A. Rutland et al., eds., 1975), 238.
369. *Ibid.*
370. Andrew Jackson, "Veto Message," Jul. 10, 1832.
371. Van Buren, *Inquiry into the Origin and Course of Political Parties in the United States*, 351–52.
372. Abraham Lincoln, "First Inaugural Address," Mar. 4, 1861.
373. Theodore Roosevelt, "A Charter for Democracy," Feb. 12, 1912, Ohio State Constitutional Convention, Columbus, OH.
374. *Ibid.*
375. Franklin D. Roosevelt, "Address on Constitution Day," Sep. 17, 1937 (emphasis added).
376. *Ibid.*

CHAPTER 5 – ON ECONOMIC LIBERTY

1. Roy C. Smith, *Adam Smith and the Origins of American Enterprise* (St. Martin's Press 2002), xiii.
2. Robert L. Heilbroner, *The Worldly Philosophers* (Simon & Schuster, 1995), 50; Lorraine Smith Pangle, *The Political Philosophy of Benjamin Franklin* (The Johns Hopkins University Press 2007), 30.
3. Thomas Jefferson, *Writings* (The Library of America, 1984), 1176.
4. Adam Smith, *The Wealth of Nations* (New York: Modern Library, 1937), 14.

5. Heilbroner, *The Worldly Philosophers*, 70.
6. Joseph A. Schumpeter, *Capitalism, Socialism, and Democracy* (New York: Harper, 1975, 82–85).
7. Heilbroner, *The Worldly Philosophers*, 57.
8. Thomas Paine, "Rights of Man," in *Common Sense, Rights of Man, and Other Essential Writings of Thomas Paine* (Signet Classics 2003) (1776), 273.
9. James Madison, "Letter to Thomas Cooper," Mar. 23, 1824, in *Letters and Other Writings of James Madison*, Vol. 3 (Philadelphia: J. B. Lippencott & Co., 1865), 428.
10. Thomas Jefferson, "Letter to John Adams," 1785, in *The Jefferson Cyclopedia* (John P. Foley, ed., Funk & Wagnalls, 1900), 882.
11. Alexander Hamilton, James Madison, and John Jay, *The Federalist Papers* (Bantam Classic 2003) (1787-88), 63.
12. *Ibid.*, 35.
13. U.S. Constitution, Article I, § 8.
14. James Madison, "Letter to Thomas Cooper," Mar. 22, 1824, in *Letters and Other Writings of James Madison*, Vol. 3, 428.
15. *Ibid.*, 429.
16. *Ibid.*, 430.
17. Alexander Hamilton, "Report on Manufactures," Dec. 5, 1791.
18. Madison, "Letter to Thomas Cooper," Mar. 22, 1824, in *Letters and Other Writings of James Madison*, Vol. 3, 429.
19. *Ibid.*
20. *Ibid.*, 428.
21. *Ibid.*, 430.
22. Hamilton, Madison, and Jay, *The Federalist Papers*, 381.
23. Paine, "Rights of Man," in *Common Sense, Rights of Man, and Other Essential Writings of Thomas Paine*, 273.
24. Hamilton, Madison, and Jay, *The Federalist Papers*, 202.
25. George Washington, "Farewell Address," 1796.
26. Thomas Jefferson, "First Inaugural Address," Mar. 4, 1801.
27. United States v. Lopez, 514 U.S. 549, 553 (1995).
28. Hammer v. Dagenhart, 247 U.S. 251 (1918).
29. *Ibid.*, 273.
30. *Ibid.*, 272.
31. *Ibid.*, 274.
32. A. L. A. Schechter Poultry Corp. v. United States, 295 U.S. 495 (1935).
33. *Ibid.*, 524.
34. Franklin D. Roosevelt, "Message to Congress Recommending Enactment of the National Industrial Recovery Act," May 17, 1933.
35. *Ibid.*
36. *Ibid.*
37. Franklin D. Roosevelt, "Statement on Signing the National Industrial Recovery Act," Jun. 16, 1933.
38. A. L. A. Schechter Poultry Corp. v. United States, 295 U.S. 495, 499.
39. *Ibid.*, 554.
40. *Ibid.*, 528–29.
41. *Ibid.*, 549.
42. Guffey Bituminous Coal Conservation Act (49 Stat. 991), August 30, 1935.
43. Carter v. Carter Coal Co., 298 U.S. 238, 280–81 (1936).
44. *Ibid.*, 309–10.
45. *Ibid.*, 303.
46. *Ibid.*, 293.
47. *Ibid.*, 293–94.
48. *Ibid.*, 294.
49. *Ibid.*
50. *Ibid.*, 295 (citation omitted).
51. *Ibid.*, 295–96.
52. NLRB v. Jones & Laughlin Steel Corp., 301 U.S. 1, 37 (1937).
53. *Ibid.*

54. United States v. Darby, 312 U.S. 100 (1941).
55. *Ibid.*, 113.
56. *Ibid.*
57. *Ibid.*
58. *Ibid.*, 114 (citing Gibbons v. Ogden, 22 U.S. 1, 197 (1824)).
59. *Ibid.*, 123–24.
60. *Ibid.*, 124 (emphasis added).
61. *Ibid.*
62. Wickard v. Filburn, 317 U.S. 111 (1942).
63. Franklin D. Roosevelt, "Statement on Signing the Agricultural Adjustment Act of 1938," Feb. 16, 1938.
64. United States v. Butler, 297 U.S. 1 (1936).
65. *Ibid.*, 68.
66. *Ibid.*, 78.
67. Wickard v. Filburn, 317 U.S. 111, 120.
68. *Ibid.*, 125.
69. *Ibid.*, 114.
70. *Ibid.*, 127–28.
71. *Ibid.*, 128.
72. *Ibid.*
73. *Ibid.*, 129.
74. Franklin D. Roosevelt, "Address Accepting the Presidential Nomination at the Democratic National Convention in Chicago," Jul. 2, 1932.
75. *Ibid.*
76. Franklin D. Roosevelt, "Annual Message to Congress," Jan. 4, 1935.
77. Franklin D. Roosevelt, "First Inaugural Address," Mar. 4, 1933.
78. Franklin D. Roosevelt, "Annual Message to Congress," Jan. 3, 1936.
79. *Ibid.*
80. Franklin D. Roosevelt, "Annual Message to Congress," Jan. 4, 1935.
81. Franklin D. Roosevelt, "Address Accepting the Presidential Nomination at the Democratic National Convention in Chicago," Jul. 2, 1932.
82. *Ibid.*
83. *Ibid.*
84. Franklin D. Roosevelt, "Acceptance Speech for the Renomination for the Presidency," Philadelphia, Jun. 27, 1936.
85. Franklin D. Roosevelt, "Address Accepting the Presidential Nomination at the Democratic National Convention in Chicago," Jul. 2, 1932.
86. Franklin D. Roosevelt, "Address to the Democratic National Convention in Chicago," Jul. 20, 1944.
87. John Franklin Fort, "Message to the Legislature of New Jersey," Feb. 7, 1910, in Journal of the Sixty-Sixth Senate of the State of New Jersey (Trenton: MacCrellish & Quigley, 1910), 110.
88. Paine, "Common Sense," in *Common Sense, Rights of Man, and Other Essential Writings of Thomas Paine*, 5
89. Paine, "Rights of Man," in *Common Sense, Rights of Man, and Other Essential Writings of Thomas Paine*, 293.
90. Norris Brown, "Shall the Income Tax Amendment Be Ratified?" *The Editorial Review*, Apr. 1910.
91. *Ibid.*
92. Internal Revenue Service, "Personal Exemptions and Individual Tax Rates, 1913-2002," http://www.irs.gov/pub/irs-soi/02inpetr.pdf.
93. *Ibid.*
94. *Ibid.*
95. "100 Years of U.S. Consumer Spending," *Bureau of Labor and Statistics*, http://www.bls.gov/opub/uscs/1918-19.pdf.
96. Internal Revenue Service, "Personal Exemptions and Individual Tax Rates, 1913-2002."
97. *Ibid.*
98. U.S. Constitution, Amendment IV.
99. Hamilton, Madison, and Jay, *The Federalist Papers*, 121.

100. Thomas Jefferson, "First Inaugural Address," Mar. 4, 1801.
101. Thomas Jefferson, "Letter to Joseph Milligan," Apr. 6, 1816, in *The Jefferson Cyclopedia*, 852.
102. Hamilton, Madison, and Jay, *The Federalist Papers*, 122.
103. Loan Association v. Topeka, 87 U.S. 655, 662 (1874).
104. Franklin D. Roosevelt, "Address Accepting the Presidential Nomination at the Democratic National Convention in Chicago," Jul. 2, 1932.
105. Veronique de Rugy, "High Taxes and High Budget Deficits," *Tax & Budget Bulletin*, Cato Institute, No. 14, Mar. 2003.
106. Internal Revenue Service, "Personal Exemptions and Individual Tax Rates, 1913-2002."
107. Railroad Retirement Bd. v. Alton Railroad Co., 295 U.S. 330 (1935).
108. *Ibid.*, 344–45.
109. *Ibid.*, 374.
110. Arthur M. Schlesinger, Jr., *The Coming of the New Deal* (First Mariner Books 1986) 308-09.
111. Helvering v. Davis, 301 U.S. 619, 635 (1937).
112. James Madison, "On the Memorial of the Relief Committee of Baltimore," Jan. 10, 1794, in *The Debates in the Several State Conventions on the Adoption of the Federal Constitution*, Vol. 4 (Jonathan Elliot, ed., Washington, 1836), 431.
113. Samuel Adams, "Letter to Deberdt," in William Vincent Wells, *The Life and Public Service of Samuel Adams*, Vol. 1 (Boston: Little, Brown, and Company, 1865), 154.
114. Steward Machine Co. v. Davis, 301 U.S. 548 (1937).
115. U.S. Constitution, Article I, § 8.
116. Steward Machine Co. v. Davis, 301 U.S. 548, 586–87.
117. A. L. A. Schechter Poultry Corp. v. United States, 295 U.S. 495, 528–29 (1935).
118. Carter v. Carter Coal Co., 298 U.S. 238, 292 (1936) (citation omitted).
119. Thomas Jefferson, "National Bank Opinion," Feb. 1791, in *The Jefferson Cyclopedia*, 69.
120. James Madison, *Annals of Congress*, 3d Congress, 1st Session, 170.
121. James Madison, "Letter to Edmund Pendleton," Jan. 21, 1792, in George W. Nilsson, "There Is No 'General Welfare Power' in the Constitution of the United States," *American Bar Association Journal*, Vol. 47, No. 1, 46.
122. John Locke, *Two Treatises of Government* (Peter Laslett ed., Cambridge University Press, 2008) (1698), 350–51.
123. John Adams, *The Political Writings of John Adams* (George A. Peek, Jr., ed. Hackett Publishing Company 2003), 148.
124. *Ibid.*, 193.
125. Samuel Adams and Benjamin Franklin, "The Report of the Committee of Correspondence to the Boston Town Meeting," Nov. 20, 1772.
126. James Madison, "Property," Mar. 27, 1792, in *Letters and Other Writings of James Madison*, Vol. 4 (Philadelphia: J. B. Lippencott & Co., 1865), 478–79.
127. James Madison, "Speech to the Virginia Constitutional Convention of 1829," in *Classics of American Political and Constitutional Thought*, Vol. 1 (Scott J. Hammond, et al., eds., Hackett Publishing Company, 2007), 757.
128. Charles de Montesquieu, *The Spirit of the Laws* (Franz Neumann ed., Hafner Press, 1949) (1748), 208.
129. Benjamin Franklin, "On the Price of Corn and the Management of the Poor," *The London Chronicle*, Nov. 29, 1766.
130. Benjamin Franklin, "Letter to Mr. Small," Nov. 5, 1789, in *Memoirs of Benjamin Franklin*, Vol. 1 (Philadelphia: McCarty & Davis, 1834), 618.
131. Benjamin Franklin, "On the Price of Corn and the Management of the Poor," *The London Chronicle*, Nov. 29, 1766.
132. James Wilson, "On the History of Property," in *The Works of the Honourable James Wilson*, L.L.D., Vol. 3 (Philadelphia: Lorenzo, 1804), 195.
133. Vanhorne's Lessee v. Dorrance, 2 U.S. 304, 310 (1795).
134. Loan Association v. Topeka, 87 U.S. 655, 664 (1874).
135. George Sutherland, "Principle or Expedient," in *Proceedings and committee reports - New York Bar Association*, January 1921 (The Argus Company, Printers, Albany 1921), 278.
136. Franklin D. Roosevelt, "Address as Governor of New York," Mar. 3, 1930.
137. Franklin D. Roosevelt, "Acceptance Speech for the Renomination for the Presidency," Philadelphia, Jun. 27, 1936.

138. Franklin D. Roosevelt, "Annual Message to Congress," Jan. 3, 1936.
139. Franklin D. Roosevelt, "Acceptance Speech for the Renomination for the Presidency," Philadelphia, Jun. 27, 1936.
140. Franklin D. Roosevelt, "State of the Union Message to Congress," Jan. 11, 1944.
141. Russell Kirk and James McClelland, *The Political Principles of Robert A. Taft* (Transaction Publishers, New Brunswick, NJ 2010), 45–46.
142. David Boaz, "Hitler, Mussolini, Roosevelt," *Reason*, Oct. 2007.
143. Karl Marx and Frederick Engels, "The Communist Manifesto," Feb. 1848.
144. Franklin D. Roosevelt, "Address Accepting the Presidential Nomination at the Democratic National Convention in Chicago," Jul. 2, 1932.
145. Marx and Engels, "The Communist Manifesto."
146. Franklin D. Roosevelt, "Acceptance Speech for the Renomination for the Presidency," Philadelphia, Jun. 27, 1936.
147. *Ibid.*
148. Marx and Engels, "The Communist Manifesto."
149. *Ibid.*
150. *Ibid.*
151. *Ibid.*
152. *Ibid.*
153. Franklin D. Roosevelt, "Radio Address to the Democratic National Convention Accepting the Nomination," Jul. 19, 1940.
154. *Ibid.*
155. Franklin D. Roosevelt, "First Inaugural Address," Mar. 4, 1933.
156. Franklin D. Roosevelt, "Annual Message to Congress," Jan. 3, 1934.
157. Benito Mussolini, "Review of: Looking Forward," in Wolfgang Schivelbusch, *Three New Deals* (New York: Picador, 2006), 23.
158. Franklin D. Roosevelt, "Annual Message to Congress," Jan. 3, 1936.
159. *Ibid.*
160. *Ibid.*
161. Herbert Hoover, "Radio Address," Oct. 24, 1940, in *Addresses upon the American road; 1940-1941* (C. Scribner's Sons, 1941), 238.
162. Franklin D. Roosevelt, "State of the Union Message to Congress," Jan. 11, 1944.
163. *Ibid.* (emphasis added).
164. Cass Sunstein, *The Second Bill of Rights: FDR's Unfinished Revolution and Why We Need It More Than Ever* (Basic Books 2004), 5.
165. *Ibid.*, 108.
166. *Ibid.*
167. Barack Obama, 2001 Interview on the Civil Rights Movement, http://themoderatevoice.com/23805/obamas-redistribution-of-wealth-quote-in-context/.
168. *Ibid.*
169. *Ibid.*
170. Hayley Tsukayama and Liz Lucas, "Thousands cheer Obama at rally for change," *Missourian*, Oct. 30, 2008.
171. Sunstein, *The Second Bill of Rights*, 1.
172. Gonzales v. Raich, 545 U.S. 1 (2005).
173. *Ibid.*, 18.
174. *Ibid.*, 67 (Thomas J., dissenting).
175. *Ibid.*, 69 (Thomas J., dissenting) (*citing* The Federalist, No. 45).
176. United States v. Morrison, 529 U.S. 598, 627 (2000) (Thomas, concurring).
177. *Ibid.*
178. Patient Protection and Affordable Care Act of 2010, Pub. L. No. 111-148.
179. Nat'l Fed'n of Indep. Bus. (NFIB) v. Sebelius, 567 U.S. ___ (2012).
180. *Ibid.*, slip op. at 20, 24, 26.
181. *Ibid.* (Scalia, Kennedy, Thomas, and Alito, dissenting), slip op. at 3.
182. Jan Crawford, "Roberts switched views to uphold health care law," *CBS News*, Jul. 1, 2012.
183. NFIB v. Sebelius, 567 U.S. ___ (Thomas, dissenting) (internal citations removed), slip op. at 1–2.
184. *Ibid.*, slip op. at 41.
185. *Ibid.*, 44.

186. "Obama on whether individual mandate is a tax: 'It is absolutely not,'" *FoxNews.com*, Jun. 28, 2012.
187. *Ibid.*
188. *Ibid.*
189. NFIB v. Sebelius, 567 U.S. ___ (Scalia, Kennedy, Thomas, and Alito, dissenting), slip op. at 18.
190. U.S. Constitution, Article I, § 7.
191. NFIB v. Sebelius, 567 U.S. ___, slip op. at 33.
192. *Ibid.* (Scalia, Kennedy, Thomas, and Alito, dissenting), slip op. at 24–25.
193. *Ibid.* (Scalia, Kennedy, Thomas, and Alito, dissenting) (internal citations removed), slip op. at 27–28.
194. NFIB v. Sebelius, 567 U.S. ___, slip op. at 40.
195. U.S. Constitution, Article I, § 8.
196. U.S. Constitution, Article I, § 9.
197. NFIB v. Sebelius, 567 U.S. ___, slip op. at 41.
198. *Ibid.*, 42.
199. Benjamin Franklin, "Letter to Mr. Le Roy," Nov. 13, 1789, in *Memoirs of Benjamin Franklin*, Vol. 1 (Philadelphia: McCarty & Davis, 1834), 619.
200. NFIB v. Sebelius, 567 U.S. ___, slip op. at 42.
201. *Ibid.*
202. Hamilton, Madison, and Jay, *The Federalist Papers*, 477, 476.
203. NFIB v. Sebelius, 567 U.S. ___, slip op. at 6.
204. Milton Friedman, *Capitalism and Freedom* (The University of Chicago Press 1962), 38.
205. David Kupelian, "Bernanke: Federal Reserve *caused* Great Depression," *WorldNetDaily*, Mar. 19, 2008.
206. Harold L. Cole and Lee E. Ohanian, "How Government Prolonged the Depression," *The Wall Street Journal*, Feb. 2, 2009.
207. Meg Sullivan, "FDR's policies prolonged Depression by 7 years, UCLA economists calculate," *UCLA Newsroom*, Aug. 2004.
208. Cole and Ohanian, "How Government Prolonged the Depression," *The Wall Street Journal*.
209. Sullivan, "FDR's policies prolonged Depression by 7 years, UCLA economists calculate," *UCLA Newsroom*.
210. John B. Taylor, "How Government Created the Financial Crisis," *The Wall Street Journal*, Feb. 9, 2009.
211. *Ibid.*
212. Stan Liebowitz, "The Real Scandal: How Feds Invited the Mortgage Mess," *The New York Post*, Feb. 5, 2008.
213. Peter J. Wallison, "The True Origins of This Financial Crisis," *The American Spectator*, Feb. 2009.
214. *Ibid.*
215. *Ibid.*
216. Liebowitz, "The Real Scandal: How Feds Invited the Mortgage Mess," *The New York Post*.
217. David Jackson, "Obama: 'Toughest financial reforms since the Great Depression,'" *USA Today*, Jun. 25, 2010.
218. John W. Schoen, "Obama moves to close deal on financial reform," *MSNBC*, Apr. 22, 2010.
219. James Madison, "Speech to the Virginia Ratifying Convention," Jun. 1788, in *American Eloquence: A Collection of Speeches and Addresses*, (Frank Moore, ed., New York, D. Appleton and Company, 1857), 127.
220. Declaration of Independence.
221. Paine, "Common Sense," in *Common Sense, Rights of Man, and Other Essential Writings of Thomas Paine*, 3.
222. Paine, "Rights of Man," in *Common Sense, Rights of Man, and Other Essential Writings of Thomas Paine*, 307.
223. *Ibid.*
224. James Madison, "A Memorial and Remonstrance," 1785, in *The Gospel Advocate and Impartial Investigator*, Vol. 7 (O. A. Browson, ed., Doubleday & Allen, 1829), 62.
225. James Madison, "Detached Memoranda," circa 1817-32, in Forrest Church, *So Help Me God* (2007), 355.
226. Neil Boortz and John Linder, *Fair Tax: The Truth* (2008), xxiv.

227. Office of Management and Budget, "Report to Congress on the Costs and Benefits of Federal Regulations," Sep. 30, 1997.
228. Nicole V. Crain and W. Mark Crain, "The Regulation Tax Keeps Growing," *The Wall Street Journal*, Sep. 27, 2010.
229. Derived from U.S. government spending and economic data at http://www.usgovernmentspending.com/.
230. James Madison, "Letter to Thomas Cooper," Mar. 23, 1824, in *Letters and Other Writings of James Madison*, Vol. 3 (Philadelphia: J. B. Lippencott & Co., 1865), 428.
231. Hamilton, Madison, and Jay, *The Federalist Papers*, 65.
232. *Ibid.*, 63.
233. Thomas Jefferson, "Letter to John Adams," 1785, in *The Jefferson Cyclopedia*, 882.
234. Thomas Jefferson, "First Inaugural Address," 1801.
235. George Washington, "Farewell Address," 1796.
236. John Locke, *Two Treatises of Government*, 350–51.
237. James Madison, "Speech to the Virginia Constitutional Convention of 1829," in *Classics of American Political and Constitutional Thought*, Vol. 1 (Scott J. Hammond, et al., eds., Hackett Publishing Company, 2007), 757.
238. James Madison, "Property," Mar. 27, 1792, in *Letters and Other Writings of James Madison*, Vol. 4 (Philadelphia: J. B. Lippencott & Co., 1865), 478–79.
239. John Adams, *The Political Writings of John Adams* (George A. Peek, Jr., ed. Hackett Publishing Company 2003), 193.
240. *Ibid.*, 148.

CHAPTER 6 – ON TYRANNY

1. *The Records of the Federal Convention of 1787*, Vol. 3 (Max Farrand, ed., 1911, reprinted 1934), Appendix A, 85.
2. John Locke, *Two Treatises of Government* (Peter Laslett ed., Cambridge University Press, 2008) (1698), 398–99.
3. *Ibid.*, 399.
4. *Ibid.*, 400.
5. *Ibid.*
6. Thomas Paine, "Rights of Man," in *Common Sense, Rights of Man, and Other Essential Writings of Thomas Paine* (Signet Classics 2003) (1792), 304.
7. Thomas Jefferson, "Diffusion of Knowledge Bill," in *The Jefferson Cyclopedia* (John P. Foley, ed., Funk & Wagnalls, 1900), 389.
8. Thomas Jefferson, "Letter to Edward Carrington," 1788, in *The Jefferson Cyclopedia*, 500.
9. Benjamin Franklin, *The Life and Writings of Benjamin Franklin*, Vol. 1 (Philadelphia: McCarty & Davis: 1834), 182.
10. *Ibid.*
11. James Monroe, "Speech in the Virginia Ratifying Convention," in *Debates and Other Proceedings of the Convention of Virginia*, 2d edition (David Robertson, ed., Richmond: Enquirer Press, 1805), 154.
12. *Ibid.*
13. Alexander Hamilton, James Madison, and John Jay, *The Federalist Papers* (Bantam Classic 2003) (1787–88), 77.
14. Joseph Story, *Commentaries on the Constitution*, Vol. 1 (Boston: Hilliard, Gray, and Company, 1833), 489.
15. Hamilton, Madison, and Jay, *The Federalist Papers*, 181 (emphasis in original).
16. Alexander Hamilton, "Speech to the New York Ratifying Convention," 1788, in *The Works of Alexander Hamilton*, Vol. 2 (John C. Hamilton, ed., New York: John F. Trow, 1850), 449.
17. Thomas Jefferson, "Letter to Judge William Johnson," 1823, in *The Jefferson Cyclopedia*, 844–45.
18. Thomas Jefferson, "Letter to Gideon Granger," Aug. 1800, in *The Jefferson Cyclopedia*, 132.
19. Thomas Jefferson, "Letter to Charles Hammond," 1821, in *The Jefferson Cyclopedia*, 131.
20. Thomas Jefferson, "Letter to Joseph C. Cabell," 1816, in *The Jefferson Cyclopedia*, 131.
21. Thomas Jefferson, "The Kentucky Resolution of 1798," in *The Works of Thomas Jefferson*, Vol. 8 (Paul Leicester Ford, G. P. Putnam's Sons, New York and London, 1904), 475.

22. Alexis de Tocqueville, *Democracy in America* (The Library of America, 2004) (1835), 184.
23. *Ibid.*, 301.
24. *Ibid.*, 184.
25. *Ibid.*, 102.
26. *Ibid.*, 182–83.
27. *Ibid.*, 102.
28. *Ibid.*, 105.
29. *Ibid.*
30. *Ibid.*, 301.
31. *Ibid.*, 109.
32. *Ibid.*, 796.
33. *Ibid.*, 787.
34. *Ibid.*, 60.
35. *Ibid.*
36. *Ibid.*, 834.
37. *Ibid.*, 60.
38. *Ibid.*, 584.
39. *Ibid.*, 60.
40. *Ibid.*
41. *Ibid.*
42. *Ibid.*, 584.
43. *Ibid.*
44. *Ibid.*, 795.
45. *Ibid.*
46. *Ibid.*, 109.
47. *Ibid.*, 794 n.1.
48. *Ibid.*, 802.
49. *Ibid.*, 254.
50. *Ibid.*, 795–96.
51. *Ibid.*, 294.
52. *Ibid.*, 108.
53. *Ibid.*, 590.
54. *Ibid.*
55. *Ibid.*
56. *Ibid.*, 337.
57. *Ibid.*, 302.
58. *Ibid.*, 818–19.
59. *Ibid.*, 819.
60. *Ibid.*
61. *Ibid.*, 820–21.
62. *Ibid.*, 821.
63. *Ibid.*, 80.
64. Patient Protection and Affordable Care Act of 2010, Pub. L. No. 111-148.
65. "Implementation Timeline," *The Henry J. Kaiser Family Foundation*, http://healthreform.kff.org/timeline.aspx.
66. Peter Barry Chowka, "Rep. Dingell: It's taken a long time to 'control the people,'" *American Thinker*, Mar. 24, 2010 (emphasis added).
67. John Conyers, comments at the National Press Club, Jul. 27, 2009, available at http://www.americanthinker.com/blog/2009/07/conyers_why_bother_to_read_bil.html.
68. Mort Kondracke, "Obama Unfairly Targets Insurance as Enemy of Reform," *Roll Call*, Jul. 30, 2009.
69. Glenn Thrush, Nancy Pelosi: "Insurers are 'immoral' villains," *Politico*, Jul. 31, 2009.
70. Joan Walsh, "Too much tea party racism," *Salon.com*, Mar. 20, 2010.
71. Jim Geraghty, "Rep. John Dingle: Health Care Opponents Remind Me of the Klan & White Supremacists," *National Review Online*, Aug. 11, 2009.
72. "Congressman Defends His 'Constitution' Comments on Health Care Law," *Foxnews.com*, Apr. 3, 2010.

73. Matt Cover, "Sebelius: Congress 'Carefully Weighed Its Authority' on Obamacare—Even Though Members Couldn't Say Where Constitution Authorized It," Mar. 12, 2012, *cnsnews.com*.
74. *Ibid.*
75. *Ibid.*
76. *Ibid.*
77. U.S. Constitution, Article I, § 8.
78. Matt Cover, "Hoyer Says Constitution's 'General Welfare' Clause Empowers Congress to Order Americans to Buy Health Insurance," Oct. 21, 2009, *cnsnews.com*.
79. Tocqueville, *Democracy in America*, 337.
80. Matt Cover, "Hoyer Says Constitution's 'General Welfare' Clause Empowers Congress to Order Americans to Buy Health Insurance," Oct. 21, 2009, *cnsnews.com*.
81. NFIB v. Sebelius, 567 U.S. ___ (2012), slip op. at 5.
82. Hamilton, Madison, and Jay, *The Federalist Papers*, 251–52.
83. *Ibid.*, 251.
84. James Madison, *Annals of Congress*, 3d Congress, 1st Session, 170.
85. James Madison, "Letter to Edmund Pendleton," Jan. 21, 1792, in George W. Nilsson, "There Is No 'General Welfare Power' in the Constitution of the United States," *American Bar Association Journal*, Vol. 47, No. 1, 46.
86. Thomas Jefferson, "National Bank Opinion," Feb. 1791, in *The Jefferson Cyclopedia*, 69.
87. Hamilton, Madison, and Jay, *The Federalist Papers*, 303.
88. James Wilson, "Of Man, as a Member of Society," in *The Works of James Wilson*, Vol. 1 (James DeWitt Andrews, ed., Chicago: Callaghan and Company, 1896), 275.
89. Abraham Lincoln, "Lincoln's Reply at Alton," in *Political Debates between Abraham Lincoln and Stephen Douglas* (Columbus: Follett, Foster, and Company, 1860), 225 (emphasis in original).
90. *Ibid.*
91. Hamilton, Madison, and Jay, *The Federalist Papers*, 339.
92. *Ibid.*, 55.
93. Fisher Ames, "The Dangers of American Liberty," 1805, in *Works of Fisher Ames* (Boston: T.B. Wait & Co., 1809), 384.
94. U.S. Constitution, Article IV, § 4.
95. Fisher Ames, "The Dangers of American Liberty," 1805, in *Works of Fisher Ames*, 384.
96. Hamilton, Madison, and Jay, *The Federalist Papers*, 51.
97. *Ibid.*, 55–56.
98. James Madison, "Speech in the Virginia State Convention of 1829–30," Dec. 2, 1829, in *Letters and Other Writings of James Madison*, Vol. 4 (Philadelphia: J.B. Lippincott & Co., 1865), 51.
99. James Madison, "Vices of the Political System of the United States," *National Gazette*, April 1787.
100. *Ibid.*
101. Hamilton, Madison, and Jay, *The Federalist Papers*, 5.
102. Joseph Story, *Commentaries on the Constitution of the United States*, Vol. 2 (Thomas M. Cooley, ed., Boston: Little, Brown, and Co., 1873), 631.
103. Charles de Montesquieu, *The Spirit of the Laws* (Franz Neumann ed., Hafner Press, 1949) (1748), 110.
104. *Ibid.*, 109–10.
105. *Ibid.*, 110.
106. *Ibid.*
107. Paine, "Rights of Man," in *Common Sense, Rights of Man, and Other Essential Writings*, 314.
108. *Ibid.*
109. Thomas Jefferson, "Letter to Thomas Cooper," 1802, in *The Jefferson Cyclopedia*, 459.
110. Thomas Jefferson, "Letter to William Ludlow," 1824, in *The Jefferson Cyclopedia*, 459.
111. "A-Z Index of U.S. Government Departments and Agencies," Jan. 17, 2012, http://www.usa.gov/directory/federal/index.shtml.
112. Tom Coburn, "2011 Wastebook: A Guide to Some of the Most Wasteful and Low Priority Government Spending of 2011," http://www.coburn.senate.gov/.
113. Derived from U.S. government spending and economic data at http://www.usgovernmentspending.com/.

114. Statement of the Comptroller General of the United States, Feb. 26, 2010, http://www.gao.gov/financial/fy2009/09frusg.pdf.

115. "The Debt to the Penny and Who Holds It," http://www.treasurydirect.gov/.

116. *Ibid.*

117. Matt Welch, "Obama Takes Off the Gloves," Dec. 8, 2011, *Reason Magazine*; "The Debt to the Penny and Who Holds It," http://www.treasurydirect.gov/.

118. US Federal Debt as a Percent of GDP, http://www.usgovernmentspending.com/; Stephen Dinan, "Debt now equals total U.S. economy," *The Washington Times*, Feb. 14, 2011.

119. Historical Debt Outstanding – Annual 1791–1849, http://www.savingsbonds.gov/; Data Sets, GDP-US, http://www.measuringworth.com/.

120. Benjamin Franklin, *Memoirs of Benjamin Franklin*, Vol. 2 (Philadelphia: McCarty & Davis, 1834), 479.

121. Thomas Jefferson, "Letter to Samuel Kerchival," 1816, in *The Jefferson Cyclopedia*, 235.

122. Thomas Jefferson, "Letter to Governor Plumer," 1816, in *The Jefferson Cyclopedia*, 272.

123. Paine, "Common Sense," in *Common Sense, Rights of Man, and Other Essential Writings*, 27.

124. George Washington, "Fifth Annual Address to Congress," Dec. 3, 1793, in *A Compilation of the Messages and Papers of the Presidents*, Vol. 1 (James D. Richardson, ed., Government Printing Office 1896), 142.

125. George Washington, "Farewell Address," 1796.

126. Thomas Jefferson, "Letter to J. W. Eppes," Sep. 1813, in *The Jefferson Cyclopedia*, 226.

127. Thomas Jefferson, "Letter to John Taylor," 1816, in *The Jefferson Cyclopedia*, 369.

128. James Madison, "Speech to Congress," Feb. 11, 1790, in *The Writings of James Madison: 1789–1790*, Vol. 5 (Gaillard Hunt, ed., G.P. Putnam's Sons, 1904), 446.

129. James Madison, "Speech on Public Credit in the House of Representatives," Apr. 22, 1790, in *The Debates and Proceedings in the Congress of the United States*, Vol. 2 (Joseph Gales, ed., Washington: Gales and Seaton, 1834), 1595–96.

130. US Federal Debt as a Percent of GDP, http://www.usgovernmentspending.com/.

131. *Ibid.*

132. *Ibid.*

133. Franklin D. Roosevelt, 1932 Campaign Speech, in Michael J. Sandel, *Democracy's Discontent* (Harvard University Press 1996), 259.

134. *Ibid.*

135. Derived from U.S. government spending and economic data at http://www.usgovernmentspending.com/.

136. *Ibid.*

137. *Ibid.*

138. *Ibid.*

139. *Ibid.*; Brian Doherty, "monetary Apocolypsageddon Update: U.S. Debt to GDP Ratio Over 100 and Rising," Feb. 24, 2012, *reason.com*.

140. Derived from U.S. government spending and economic data at http://www.usgovernmentspending.com/.

141. *Ibid.*

142. *Ibid.*

143. *Ibid.*

144. Statement of the Comptroller General of the United States, Feb. 26, 2010, http://www.gao.gov/financial/fy2009/09frusg.pdf.

145. Army Sgt. 1st Class Tyrone C. Marshall Jr., "Debt is Biggest Threat to National Security, Chairman Says," *American Forces Press Service*, Sep. 22, 2011.

146. CNN Wire Staff, "Obama defends budget priorities," *CNN Politics*, Feb. 14, 2011.

147. The Budget for the Fiscal Year 2012, Summary Tables, Table S-3, 174; Matt Cover, "Obama Budget Doubles National Debt to $26.3 Trillion in 10 years," *cnsnews.com*, Feb. 14, 2011.

148. Fred Lucas, "Treasury Secretary: Obama's Budget Leads to 'Unsustainable Obligations,'" *cnsnews.com*, Feb. 17, 2011.

149. Andrew Stiles, "An Economy Built to Crash: Geithner Admits Obama Budget 'Unsustainable' for Second Year in Row," *The Washington Free Beacon*, Feb. 16, 2012.

150. Tocqueville, *Democracy in America*, 640.

151. *Ibid.*, 639.

152. *The Records of the Federal Convention of 1787*, Vol. 3 (Max Farrand, ed., 1911, reprinted 1934), Appendix A, 85.
153. Hamilton, Madison, and Jay, *The Federalist Papers*, 55.
154. John Adams, "Letter to Abigail Adams," July 7, 1775 in *The Letters of John and Abigail Adams* (Penguin Books 2004), 74.

CHAPTER 7 – ON REVOLUTION

1. Mercy Warren, *History of the Rise, Progress, and Termination of the American Revolution*, Vol. 3 (Boston: Manning and Loring, 1805), 413–14 (emphasis in original).
2. John Locke, *Two Treatises of Government* (Peter Laslett ed., Cambridge University Press, 2008) (1698), 412–13.
3. *Ibid.*, 367.
4. *Ibid.*
5. Virginia Declaration of Rights, 1776.
6. Declaration of Independence.
7. Thomas Paine, "Common Sense," in *Common Sense, Rights of Man, and Other Essential Writings of Thomas Paine* (Signet Classics 2003) (1792), 51.
8. Benjamin Franklin, Notes, Feb. 1775, in *Memoirs of the Life and Writings of Benjamin Franklin*, Vol. 1 (London: A. J. Valpy, 1818), 270.
9. Patrick Henry, "Speech to the Virginia Convention," Mar. 23, 1775, in Moses Coit Tyler, *Patrick Henry* (Boston and New York: Houghton, Mifflin & Co., 1898), 147.
10. Samuel Adams, "Address to the People of Pennsylvania," Jan. 1776, in William Vincent Wells, *The Life and Public Services of Samuel Adams*, Vol. 2 (Boston: Little, Brown, and Company, 1865), 362.
11. Thomas Paine, "The Crisis, Number I," in *Common Sense, Rights of Man, and Other Essential Writings*, 75.
12. *Ibid.*, 76 (emphasis in original).
13. Thomas Jefferson, "Notes on Virginia," 1782, in *The Jefferson Cyclopedia* (John P. Foley, ed., Funk & Wagnalls, 1900), 210.
14. Locke, *Two Treatises of Government*, 411.
15. *Ibid.*, 416–17.
16. *Ibid.*
17. Constitution of Pennsylvania, Sep. 28, 1776.
18. Constitution of New York, Apr. 20, 1777.
19. Leonard W. Levy, *Seasoned Judgments: The American Constitution, Rights, and History* (1995), 307.
20. Constitution of the Commonwealth of Massachusetts, Part the First, Article VII.
21. Articles of Confederation, Article III.
22. Locke, *Two Treatises of Government*, 418 (emphasis in original).
23. U.S. Constitution, Preamble.
24. Alexander Hamilton, James Madison, and John Jay, *The Federalist Papers* (Bantam Classic 2003) (1787–88), 187.
25. Thomas Jefferson, "Letter to William Charles Jarvis," Sep. 28, 1820, in *The Writings of Thomas Jefferson*, Vol. 10 (Paul Leicester Ford, ed., 1898), 161.
26. Thomas Paine, "Rights of Man," in *Common Sense, Rights of Man, and Other Essential Writings of Thomas Paine* (Signet Classics 2003) (1792), 262.
27. *Ibid.*, 346.
28. Thomas Jefferson, "Letter to Spencer Roane," in *The Jefferson Cyclopedia*, 741.
29. Andrew Jackson, *First Annual Message*, Dec. 8, 1829.
30. Richard E. Ellis, *The Union at Risk* (New York: Oxford Univ. Press, 1987), 13–14.
31. Abraham Lincoln, "Letter to H.L. Pierce and others," Apr. 6. 1859, in *Complete Works of Abraham Lincoln*, Vol. 5 (John G. Nicolay and John Hay, eds., New York: The Lamb Publishing Company, 1894), 126–27.
32. *Political Debates between Abraham Lincoln and Stephen Douglas* (The Burrows Brothers Company, 1894), 101.
33. Abraham Lincoln, "Speech at Cincinnati," Sep. 17, 1859, in *The Wisdom of Abraham Lincoln* (Marion Mills Miller, ed., New York: A. Wessels Co., 1908), 88.

34. Charles de Montesquieu, *The Spirit of the Laws* (Franz Neumann ed., Hafner Press, 1949) (1748), 117.
35. George Washington, "Circular Letter addressed to the Governors," Jun. 8, 1783, in *The Life of George Washington*, Vol. 2 (John Marshall, ed., Philadelphia: James Crissy, and Thomas, Cowperthwait and Co., 1843), 81–82.

EPILOGUE

1. Thomas Jefferson, "Letter to Henry Lee," 1825, in *The Jefferson Cyclopedia* (John P. Foley, ed., Funk & Wagnalls, 1900), 243.
2. Thomas Paine, "Rights of Man," in *Common Sense, Rights of Man, and Other Essential Writings of Thomas Paine* (Signet Classics 2003) (1792), 275.
3. Francis Fisher Brown, *The Every-Day Life of Abraham Lincoln* (University of Nebraska Press, 1995) (1887), 144–46; *Life and Works of Abraham Lincoln*, Vol. 2 (Marion Mills Miller, ed., New York: The Current Literature Publishing Co., 1907), 14–20.

INDEX

CPSIA information can be obtained at www.ICGtesting.com
Printed in the USA
BVOW011542101212

307795BV00001B/5/P